Persona4
*Vol.3: Shuji SOGABE /ATLUS

ENGLISH EDITION
Translation: M. KIRIE HAYASHI
Lettering: MARSHALL DILLON

UDON STAFF
Chief of Operations: ERIK KO
Director of Publishing: MATT MOYLAN
Senior Editor: ASH PAULSEN
VP of Sales: JOHN SHABLESKI
Senior Producer: LONG VO
Marketing Manager: JENNY MYUNG
Production Manager: JANICE LEUNG
Japanese Liaison: STEVEN CUMMINGS

PERSONA 4 Volume 3
©ATLUS ©SEGA All Rights Reserved.
©Shuji SOGABE 2010
Edited by ASCII MEDIA WORKS
First published in 2010 by KADOKAWA CORPORATION, Tokyo.
English translation rights arranged with KADOKAWA CORPORATION, Tokyo.

English language version published by UDON Entertainment Inc.
118 Tower Hill Road, C1, PO Box 20008
Richmond Hill, Ontario, L4K 0K0 CANADA

www.UDONentertainment.com

First Printing: June 2016
ISBN-13: 1927925797
ISBN-10: 978-1927925799

Printed in the United States

◇! WHOOPS ◇!

This is the back of the boo[k]

You're looking at the last page of the book, not the first one.

PERSONA 4 is a comic series originally published in Japan. Japanese c[omics] (known as "manga") are traditionally read from right to left, the revers[e of] most English comics.

In this English edition, the Japanese format has been left intact. Check [out the] example below to see how to read the word balloons in the proper orde[r].

Now head to the front of the book and enjoy PERSONA 4!

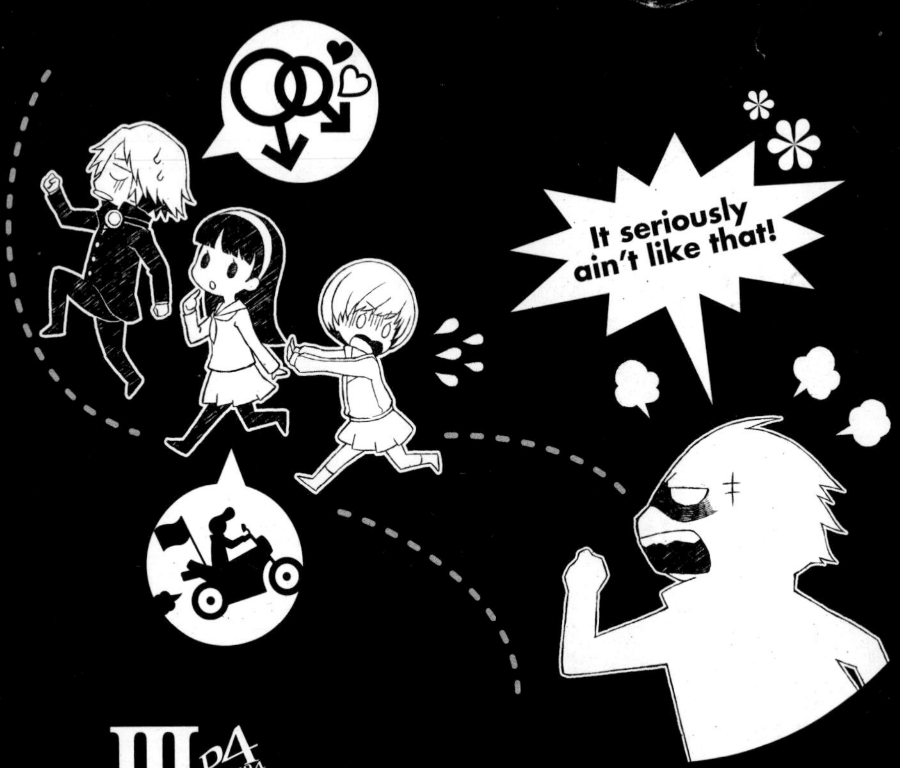
It seriously ain't like that!

III Persona4

#Vol.3: Shuji SOGABE / ATLUS

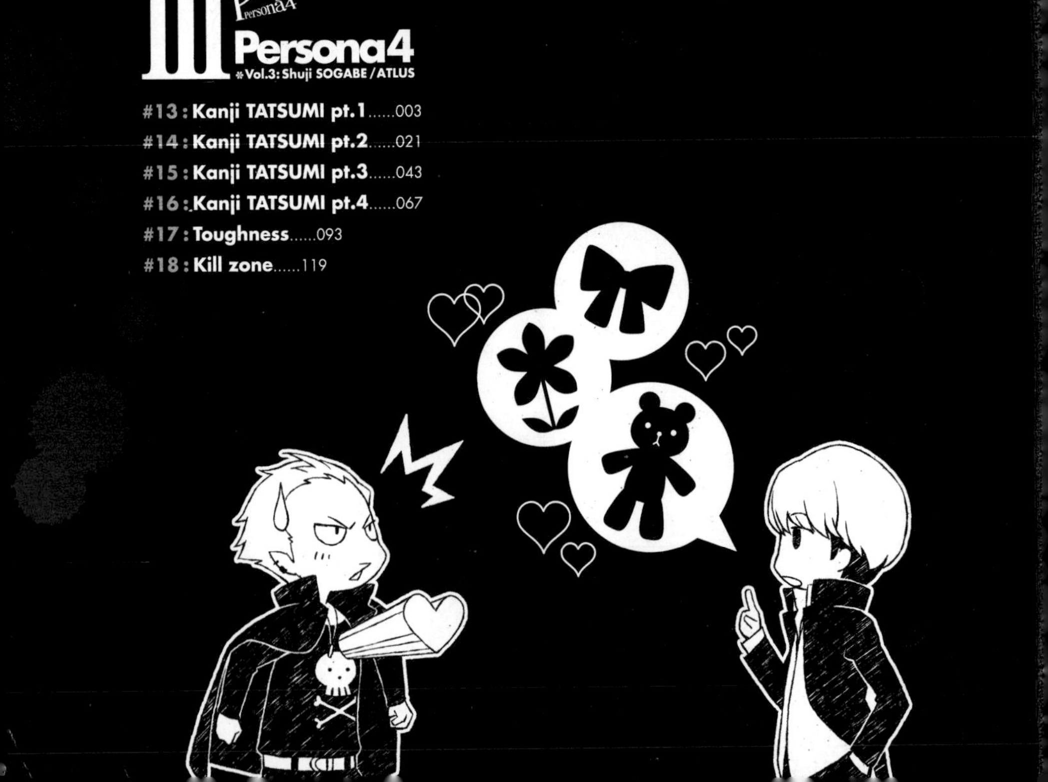

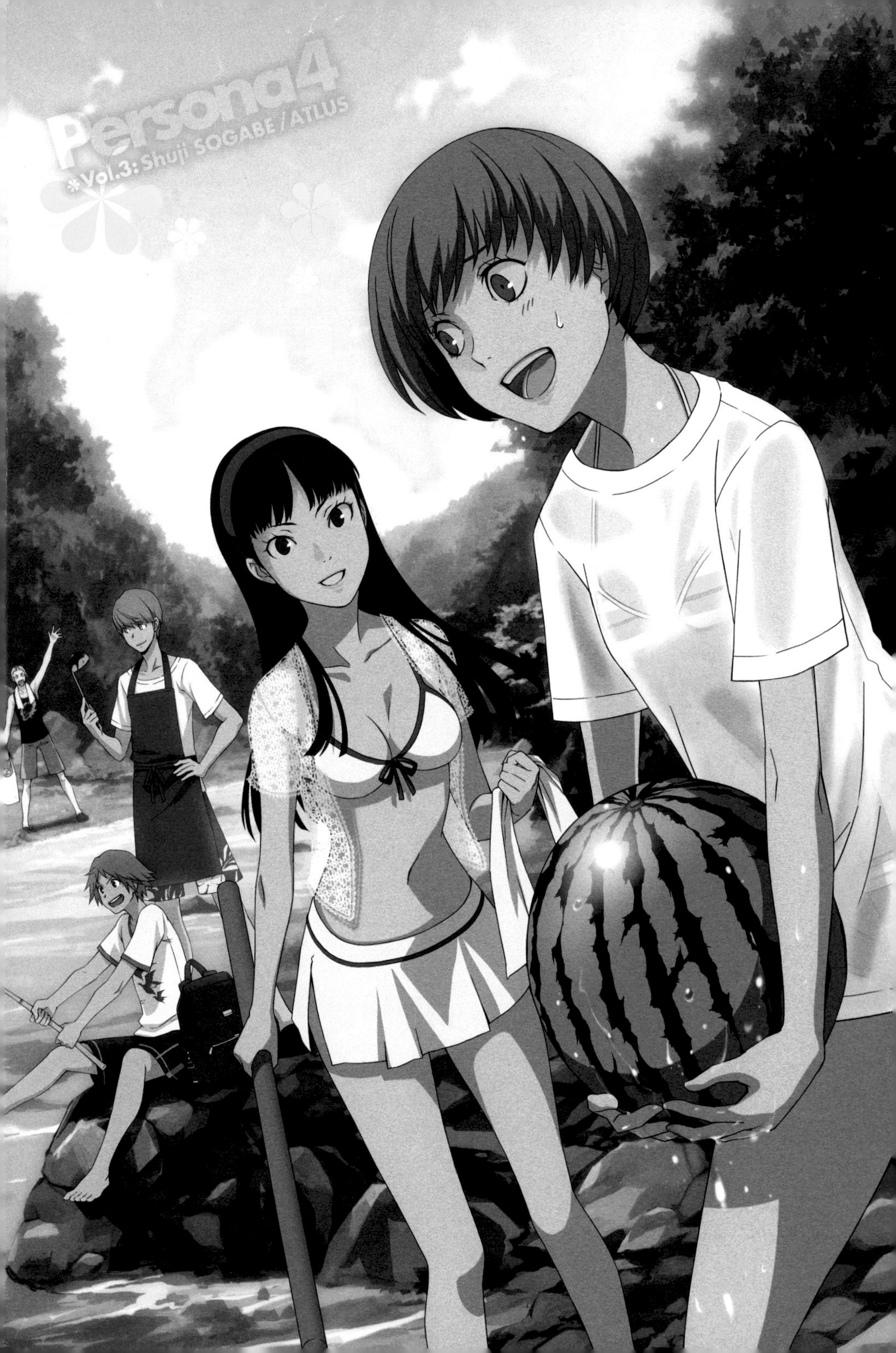
Persona4
Vol.3: Shuji SOGABE / ATLUS

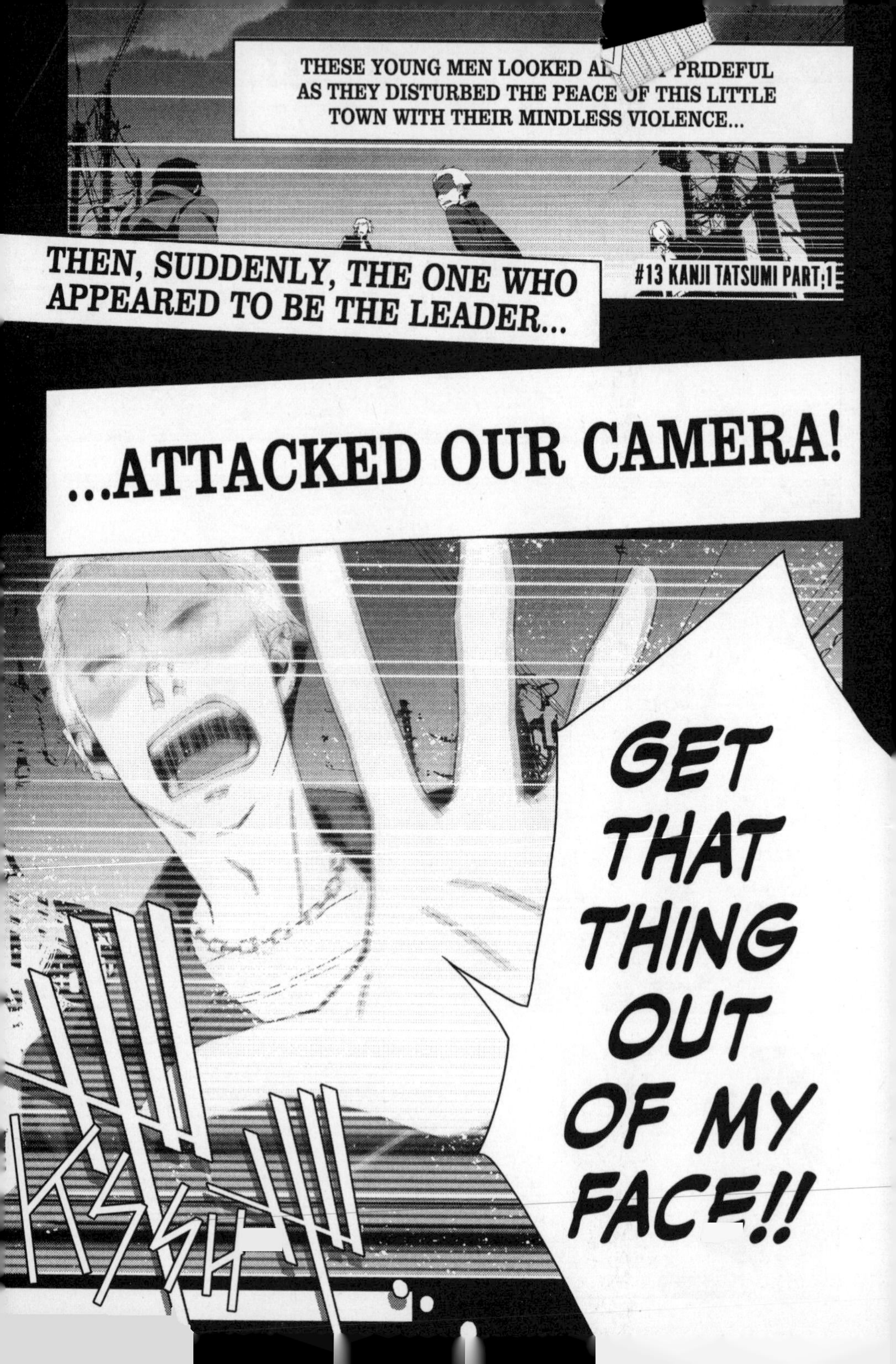
THESE YOUNG MEN LOOKED AL PRIDEFUL AS THEY DISTURBED THE PEACE OF THIS LITTLE TOWN WITH THEIR MINDLESS VIOLENCE...
#13 KANJI TATSUMI PART 1
THEN, SUDDENLY, THE ONE WHO APPEARED TO BE THE LEADER...
...ATTACKED OUR CAMERA!
GET THAT THING OUT OF MY FACE!!
KSSH!!!

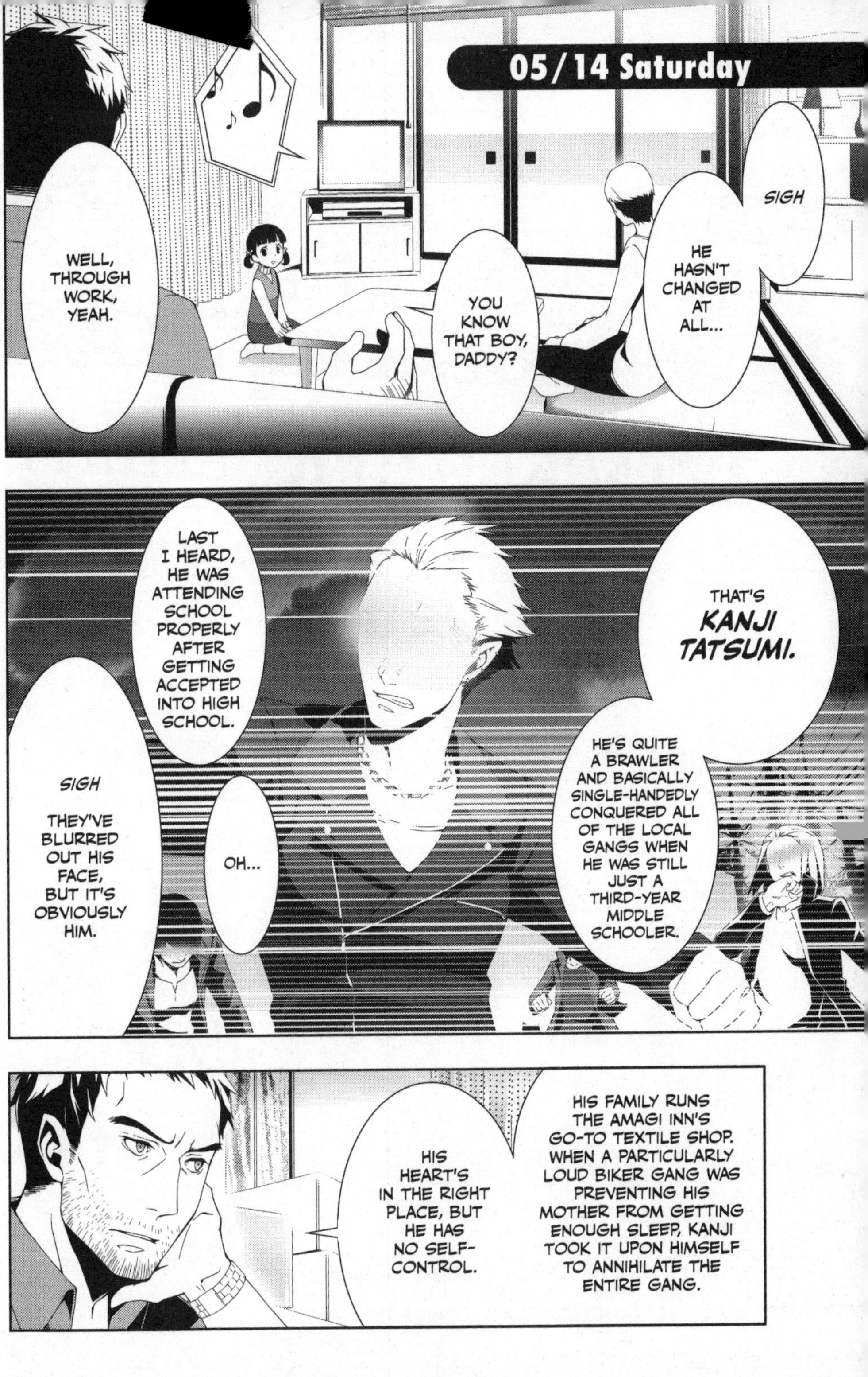
05/14 Saturday
SIGH
HE HASN'T CHANGED AT ALL...
YOU KNOW THAT BOY, DADDY?
WELL, THROUGH WORK, YEAH.
THAT'S KANJI TATSUMI.
HE'S QUITE A BRAWLER AND BASICALLY SINGLE-HANDEDLY CONQUERED ALL OF THE LOCAL GANGS WHEN HE WAS STILL JUST A THIRD-YEAR MIDDLE SCHOOLER.
LAST I HEARD, HE WAS ATTENDING SCHOOL PROPERLY AFTER GETTING ACCEPTED INTO HIGH SCHOOL.
OH...
SIGH
THEY'VE BLURRED OUT HIS FACE, BUT IT'S OBVIOUSLY HIM.
HIS FAMILY RUNS THE AMAGI INN'S GO-TO TEXTILE SHOP. WHEN A PARTICULARLY LOUD BIKER GANG WAS PREVENTING HIS MOTHER FROM GETTING ENOUGH SLEEP, KANJI TOOK IT UPON HIMSELF TO ANNIHILATE THE ENTIRE GANG.
HIS HEART'S IN THE RIGHT PLACE, BUT HE HAS NO SELF-CONTROL.

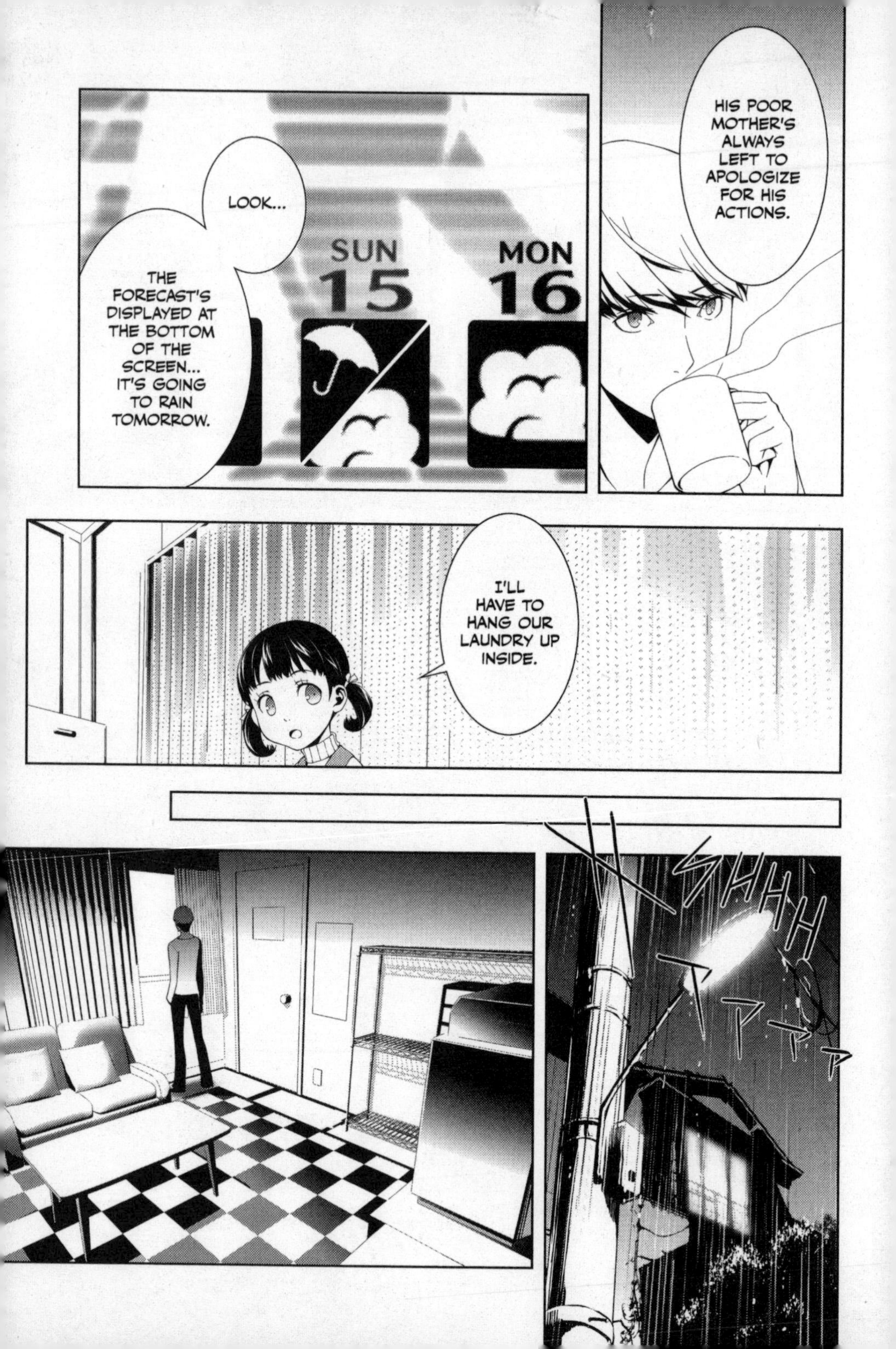
HIS POOR MOTHER'S ALWAYS LEFT TO APOLOGIZE FOR HIS ACTIONS.
LOOK...
THE FORECAST'S DISPLAYED AT THE BOTTOM OF THE SCREEN... IT'S GOING TO RAIN TOMORROW.
SUN 15
MON 16
I'LL HAVE TO HANG OUR LAUNDRY UP INSIDE.
SHHHH

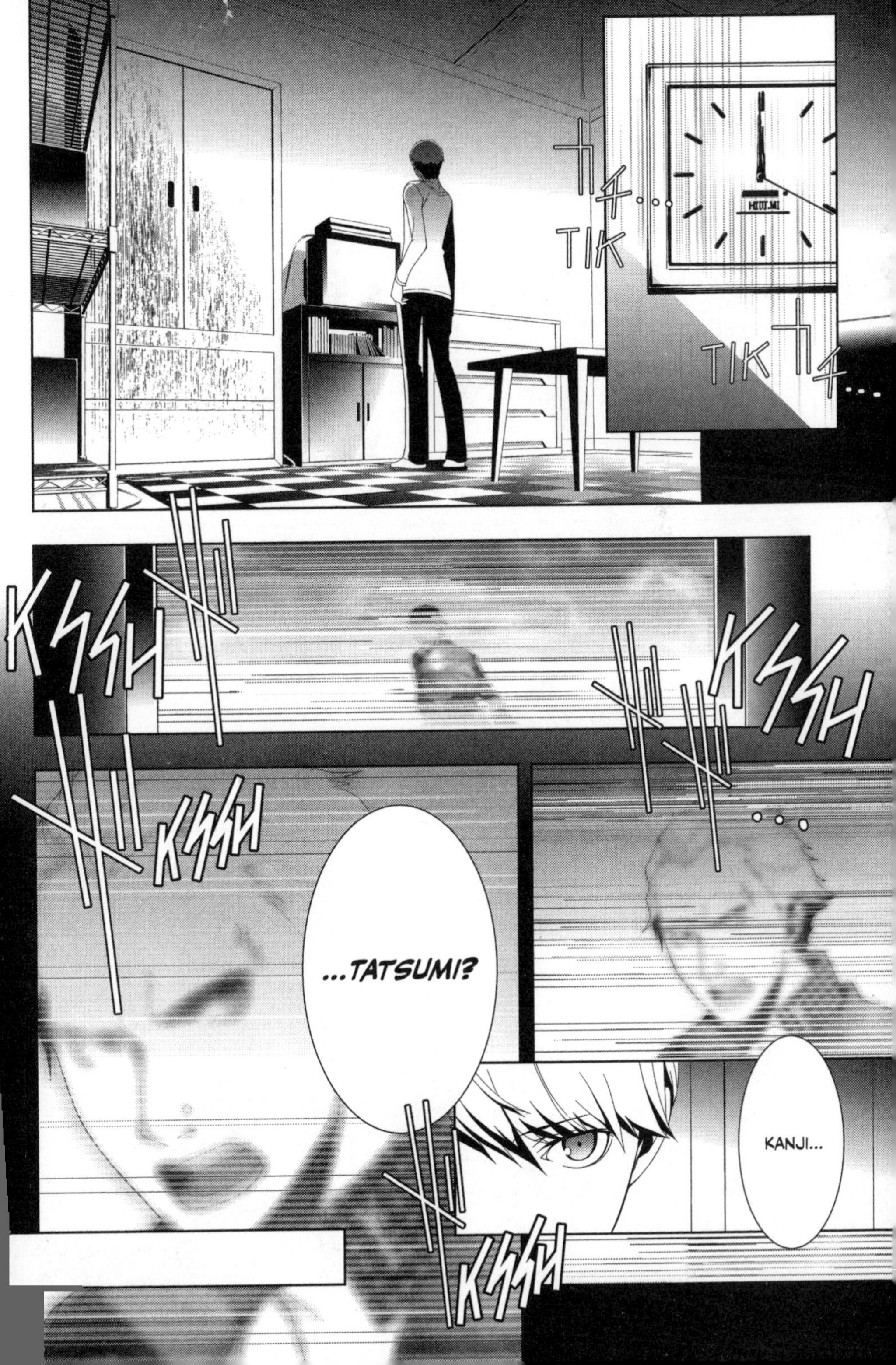

カチ...
TIK
TIK
カチ...
KSSH
KSSH
...
KSSH
...TATSUMI?
KANJI...
KSSH

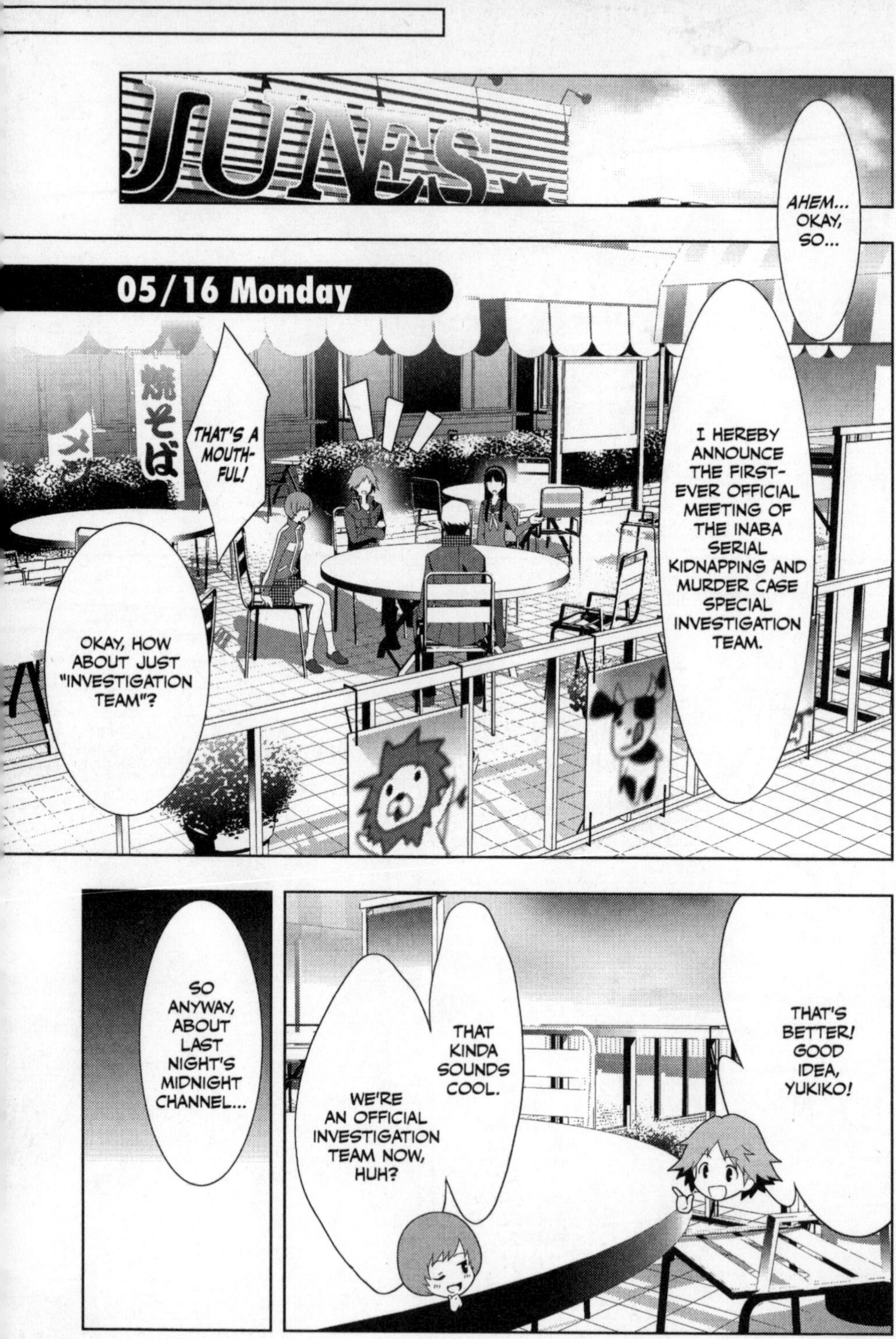
JUNES
AHEM... OKAY, SO...
05/16 Monday
I HEREBY ANNOUNCE THE FIRST-EVER OFFICIAL MEETING OF THE INABA SERIAL KIDNAPPING AND MURDER CASE SPECIAL INVESTIGATION TEAM.
焼そば
THAT'S A MOUTH-FUL!
OKAY, HOW ABOUT JUST "INVESTIGATION TEAM"?
THAT'S BETTER! GOOD IDEA, YUKIKO!
THAT KINDA SOUNDS COOL.
WE'RE AN OFFICIAL INVESTIGATION TEAM NOW, HUH?
SO ANYWAY, ABOUT LAST NIGHT'S MIDNIGHT CHANNEL...

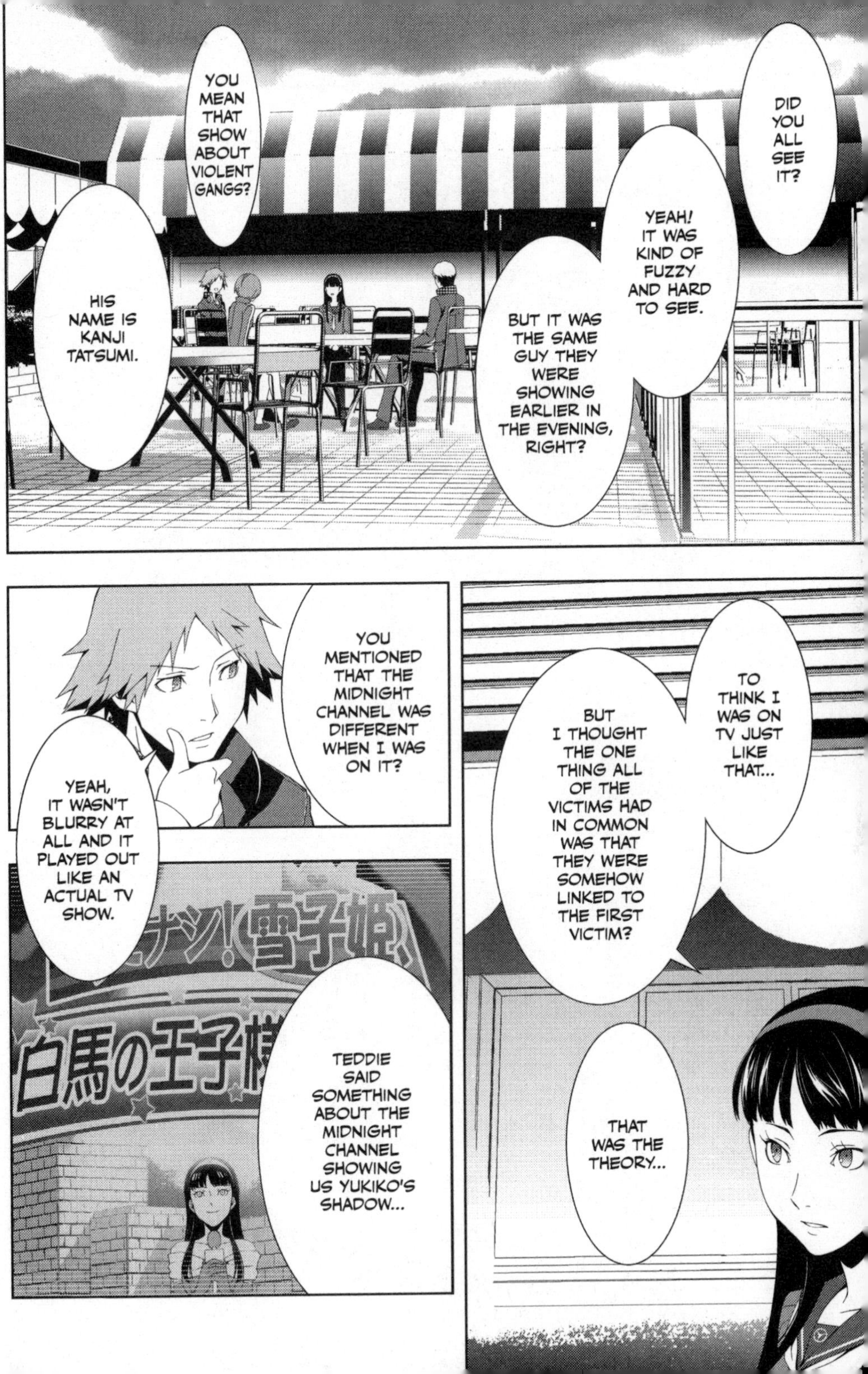
DID YOU ALL SEE IT?
YEAH! IT WAS KIND OF FUZZY AND HARD TO SEE.
BUT IT WAS THE SAME GUY THEY WERE SHOWING EARLIER IN THE EVENING, RIGHT?
YOU MEAN THAT SHOW ABOUT VIOLENT GANGS?
HIS NAME IS KANJI TATSUMI.
TO THINK I WAS ON TV JUST LIKE THAT...
BUT I THOUGHT THE ONE THING ALL OF THE VICTIMS HAD IN COMMON WAS THAT THEY WERE SOMEHOW LINKED TO THE FIRST VICTIM?
THAT WAS THE THEORY...
YOU MENTIONED THAT THE MIDNIGHT CHANNEL WAS DIFFERENT WHEN I WAS ON IT?
YEAH, IT WASN'T BLURRY AT ALL AND IT PLAYED OUT LIKE AN ACTUAL TV SHOW.
TEDDIE SAID SOMETHING ABOUT THE MIDNIGHT CHANNEL SHOWING US YUKIKO'S SHADOW...

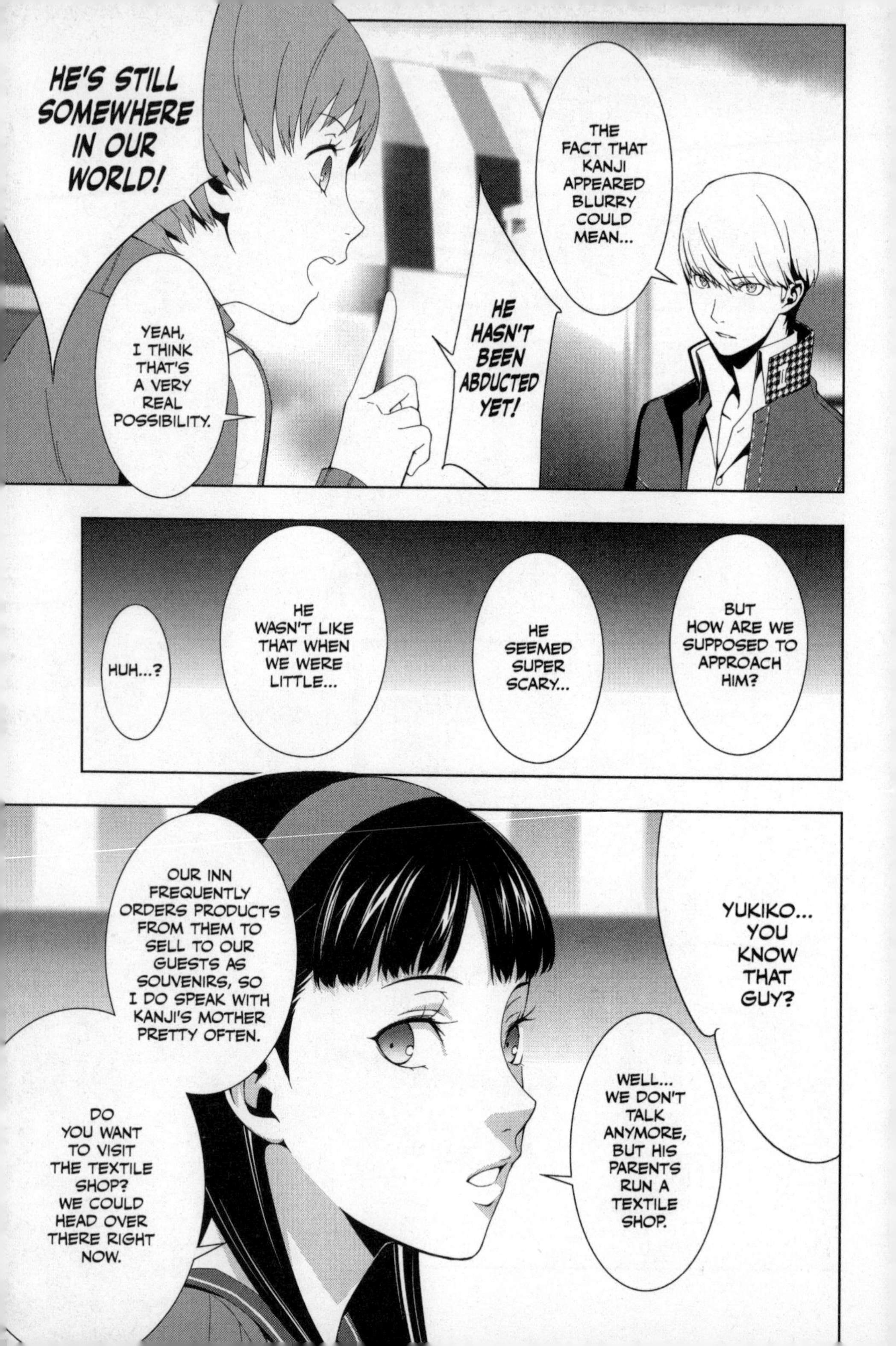
THE FACT THAT KANJI APPEARED BLURRY COULD MEAN...
HE HASN'T BEEN ABDUCTED YET!
HE'S STILL SOMEWHERE IN OUR WORLD!
YEAH, I THINK THAT'S A VERY REAL POSSIBILITY.
BUT HOW ARE WE SUPPOSED TO APPROACH HIM?
HE SEEMED SUPER SCARY...
HE WASN'T LIKE THAT WHEN WE WERE LITTLE...
HUH...?
YUKIKO... YOU KNOW THAT GUY?
WELL... WE DON'T TALK ANYMORE, BUT HIS PARENTS RUN A TEXTILE SHOP.
OUR INN FREQUENTLY ORDERS PRODUCTS FROM THEM TO SELL TO OUR GUESTS AS SOUVENIRS, SO I DO SPEAK WITH KANJI'S MOTHER PRETTY OFTEN.
DO YOU WANT TO VISIT THE TEXTILE SHOP? WE COULD HEAD OVER THERE RIGHT NOW.

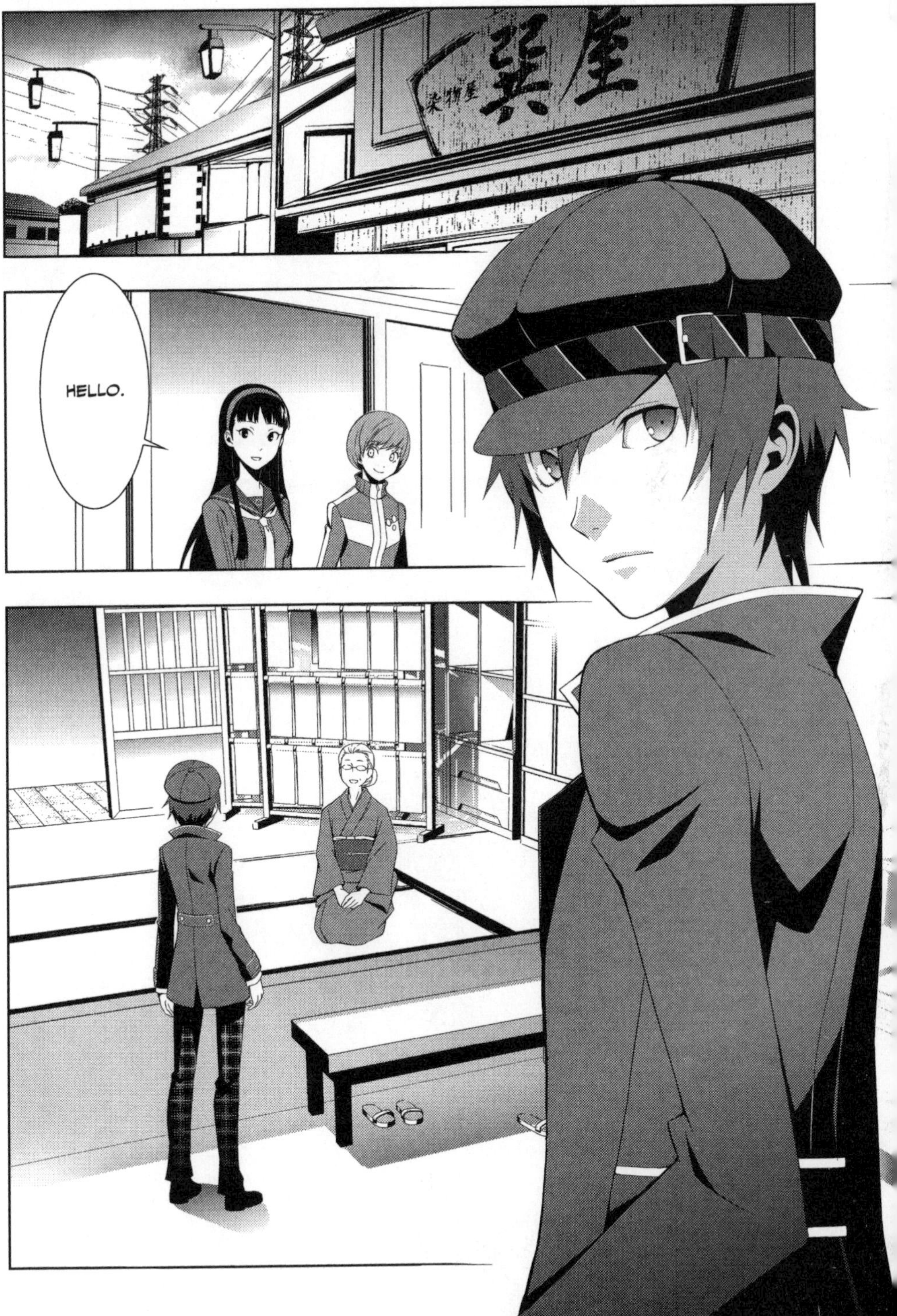
巽屋
染物屋
HELLO.

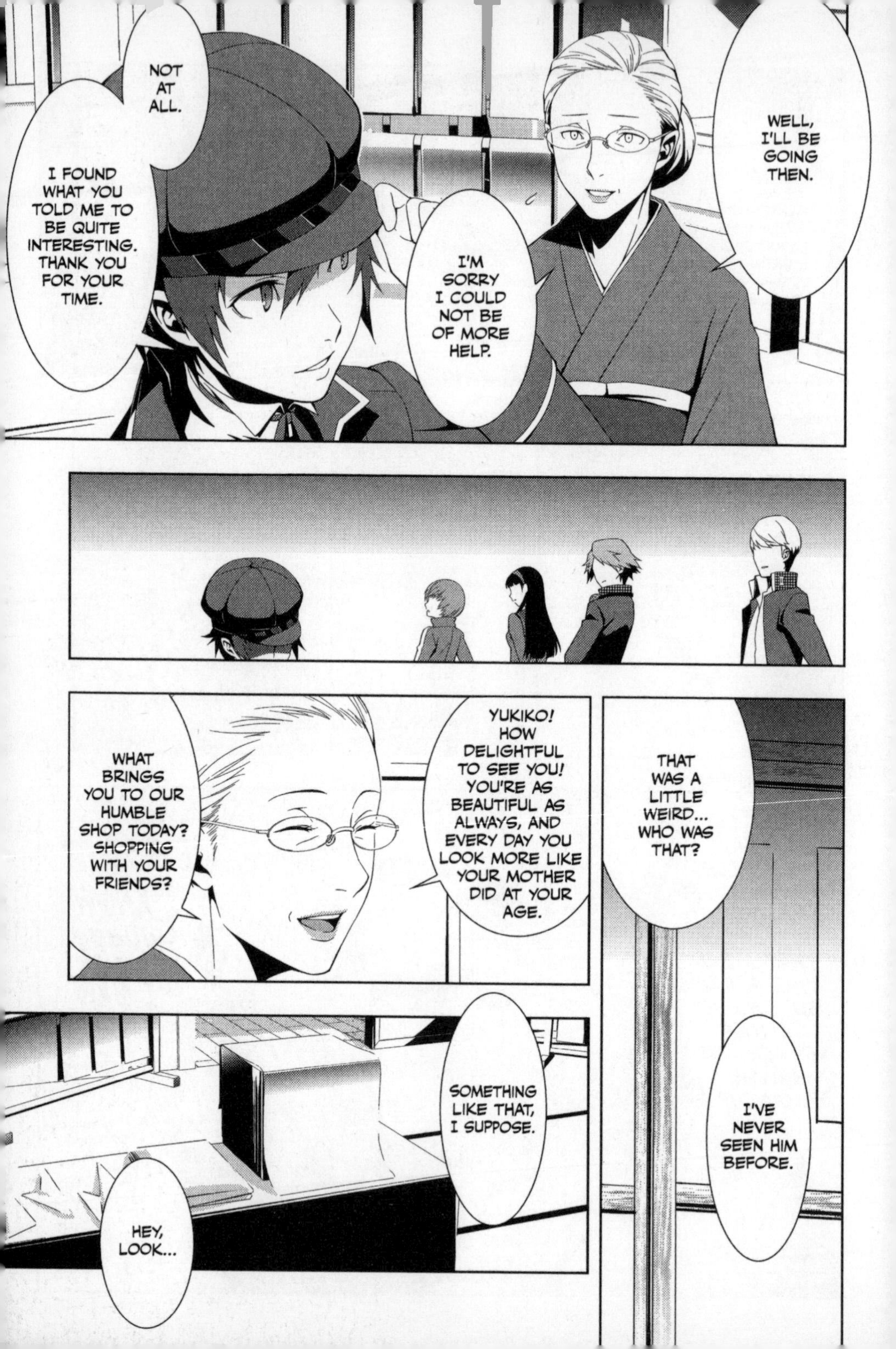
WELL, I'LL BE GOING THEN.
I'M SORRY I COULD NOT BE OF MORE HELP.
NOT AT ALL.
I FOUND WHAT YOU TOLD ME TO BE QUITE INTERESTING. THANK YOU FOR YOUR TIME.
THAT WAS A LITTLE WEIRD... WHO WAS THAT?
I'VE NEVER SEEN HIM BEFORE.
YUKIKO! HOW DELIGHTFUL TO SEE YOU! YOU'RE AS BEAUTIFUL AS ALWAYS, AND EVERY DAY YOU LOOK MORE LIKE YOUR MOTHER DID AT YOUR AGE.
WHAT BRINGS YOU TO OUR HUMBLE SHOP TODAY? SHOPPING WITH YOUR FRIENDS?
SOMETHING LIKE THAT, I SUPPOSE.
HEY, LOOK...

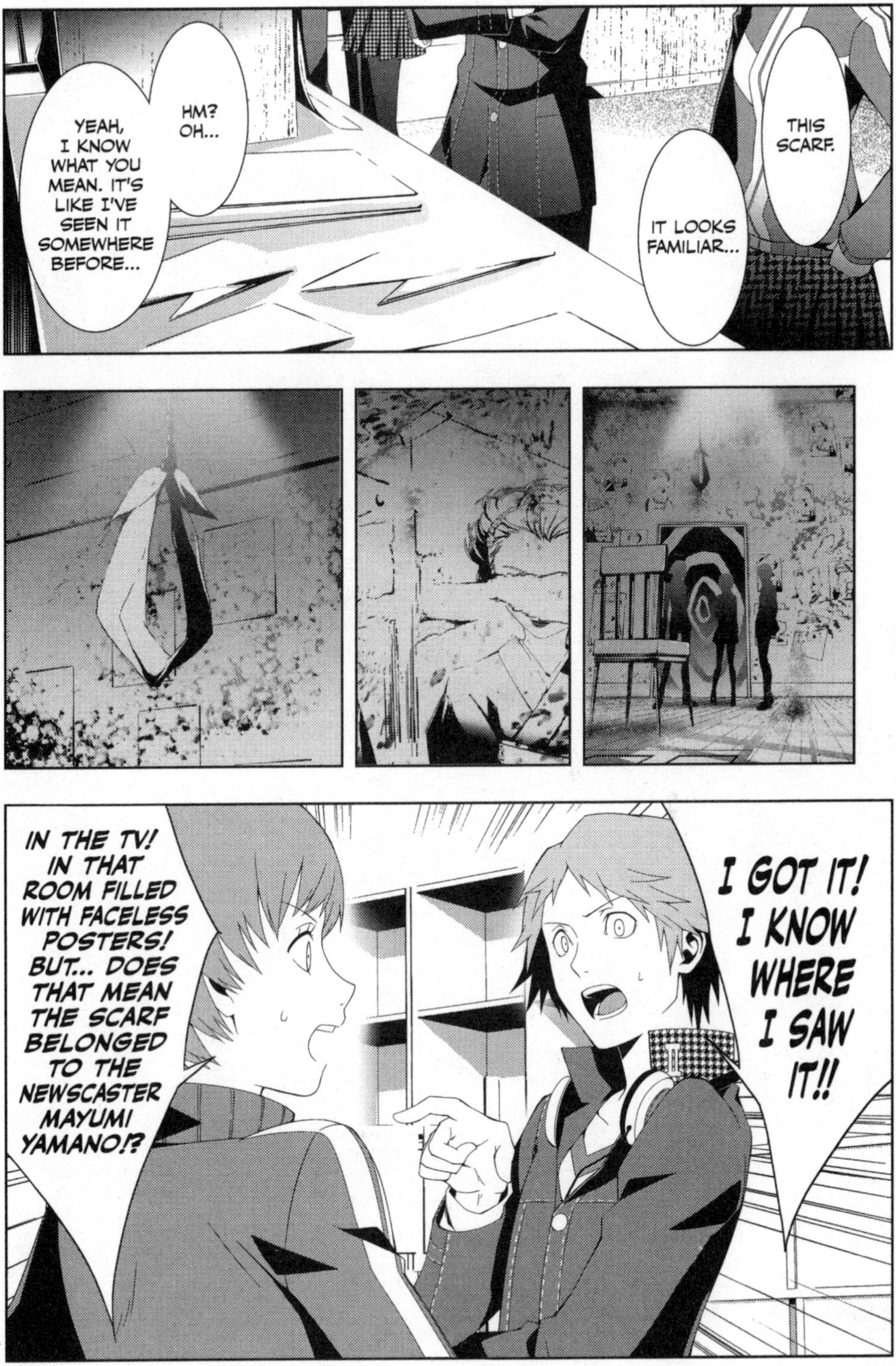
THIS SCARF.
IT LOOKS FAMILIAR...
HM? OH...
YEAH, I KNOW WHAT YOU MEAN. IT'S LIKE I'VE SEEN IT SOMEWHERE BEFORE...
I GOT IT! I KNOW WHERE I SAW IT!!
IN THE TV! IN THAT ROOM FILLED WITH FACELESS POSTERS! BUT... DOES THAT MEAN THE SCARF BELONGED TO THE NEWSCASTER MAYUMI YAMANO!?

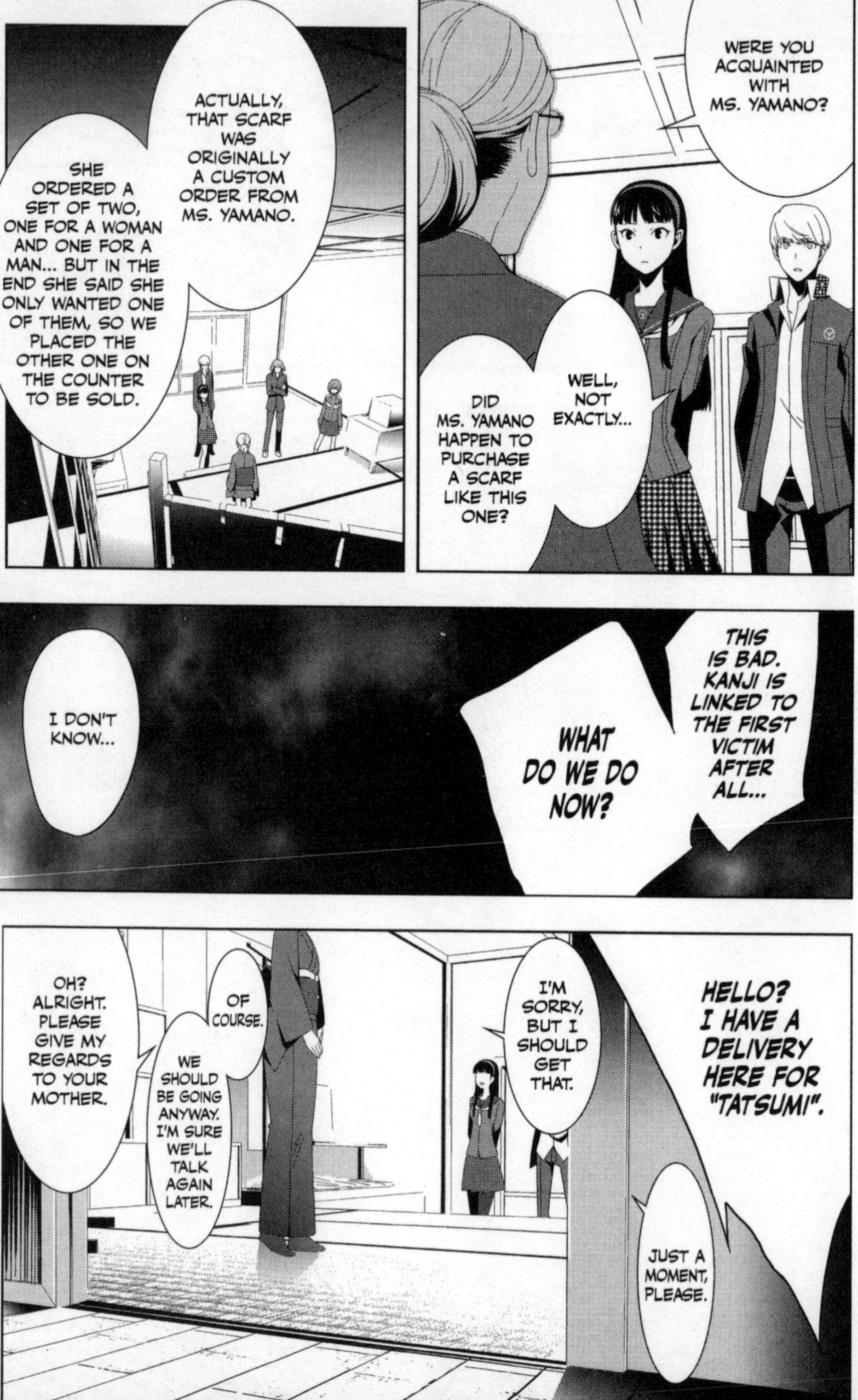
WERE YOU ACQUAINTED WITH MS. YAMANO?
WELL, NOT EXACTLY...
DID MS. YAMANO HAPPEN TO PURCHASE A SCARF LIKE THIS ONE?
ACTUALLY, THAT SCARF WAS ORIGINALLY A CUSTOM ORDER FROM MS. YAMANO.
SHE ORDERED A SET OF TWO, ONE FOR A WOMAN AND ONE FOR A MAN... BUT IN THE END SHE SAID SHE ONLY WANTED ONE OF THEM, SO WE PLACED THE OTHER ONE ON THE COUNTER TO BE SOLD.
THIS IS BAD. KANJI IS LINKED TO THE FIRST VICTIM AFTER ALL...
WHAT DO WE DO NOW?
I DON'T KNOW...
HELLO? I HAVE A DELIVERY HERE FOR "TATSUMI".
JUST A MOMENT, PLEASE.
I'M SORRY, BUT I SHOULD GET THAT.
OF COURSE.
WE SHOULD BE GOING ANYWAY. I'M SURE WE'LL TALK AGAIN LATER.
OH? ALRIGHT. PLEASE GIVE MY REGARDS TO YOUR MOTHER.

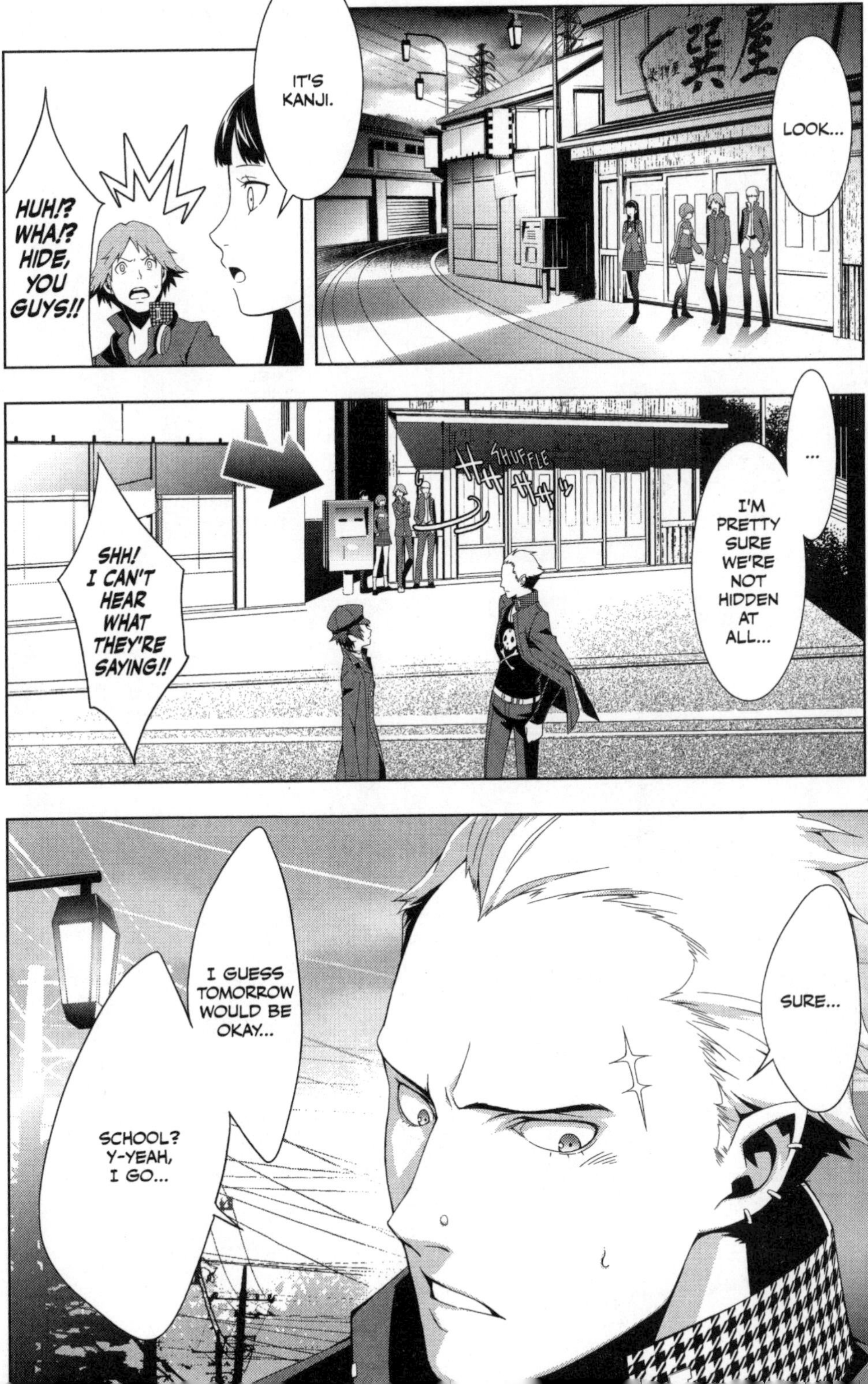
LOOK...
IT'S KANJI.
HUH!? WHA!? HIDE, YOU GUYS!!
...
I'M PRETTY SURE WE'RE NOT HIDDEN AT ALL...
SHUFFLE
SHH! I CAN'T HEAR WHAT THEY'RE SAYING!!
SURE...
I GUESS TOMORROW WOULD BE OKAY...
SCHOOL? Y-YEAH, I GO...

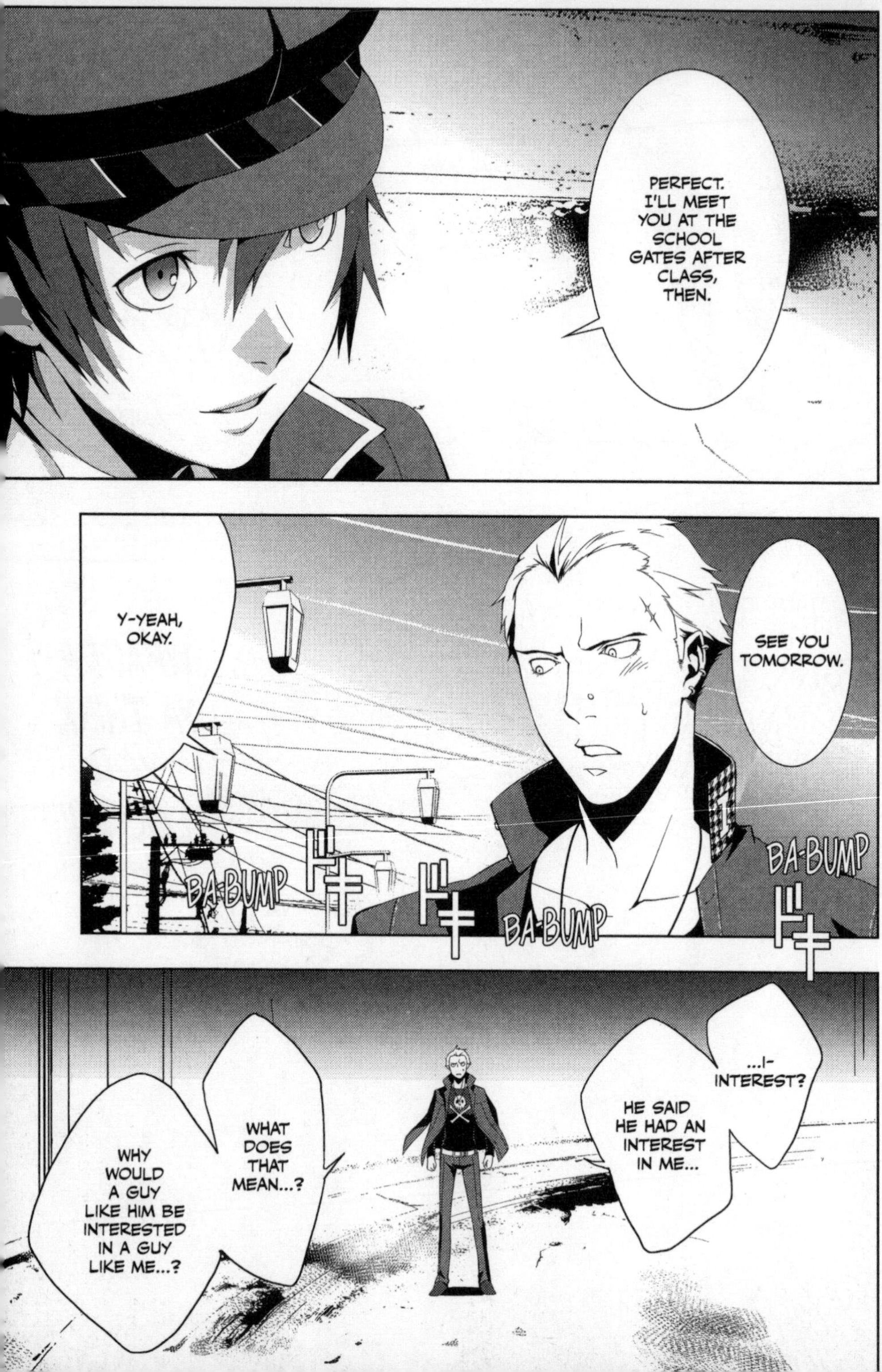
PERFECT. I'LL MEET YOU AT THE SCHOOL GATES AFTER CLASS, THEN.
SEE YOU TOMORROW.
Y-YEAH, OKAY.
BA-BUMP
ドキ
BA-BUMP
ドキ
BA-BUMP
ドキ
...I- INTEREST?
HE SAID HE HAD AN INTEREST IN ME...
WHAT DOES THAT MEAN...?
WHY WOULD A GUY LIKE HIM BE INTERESTED IN A GUY LIKE ME...?

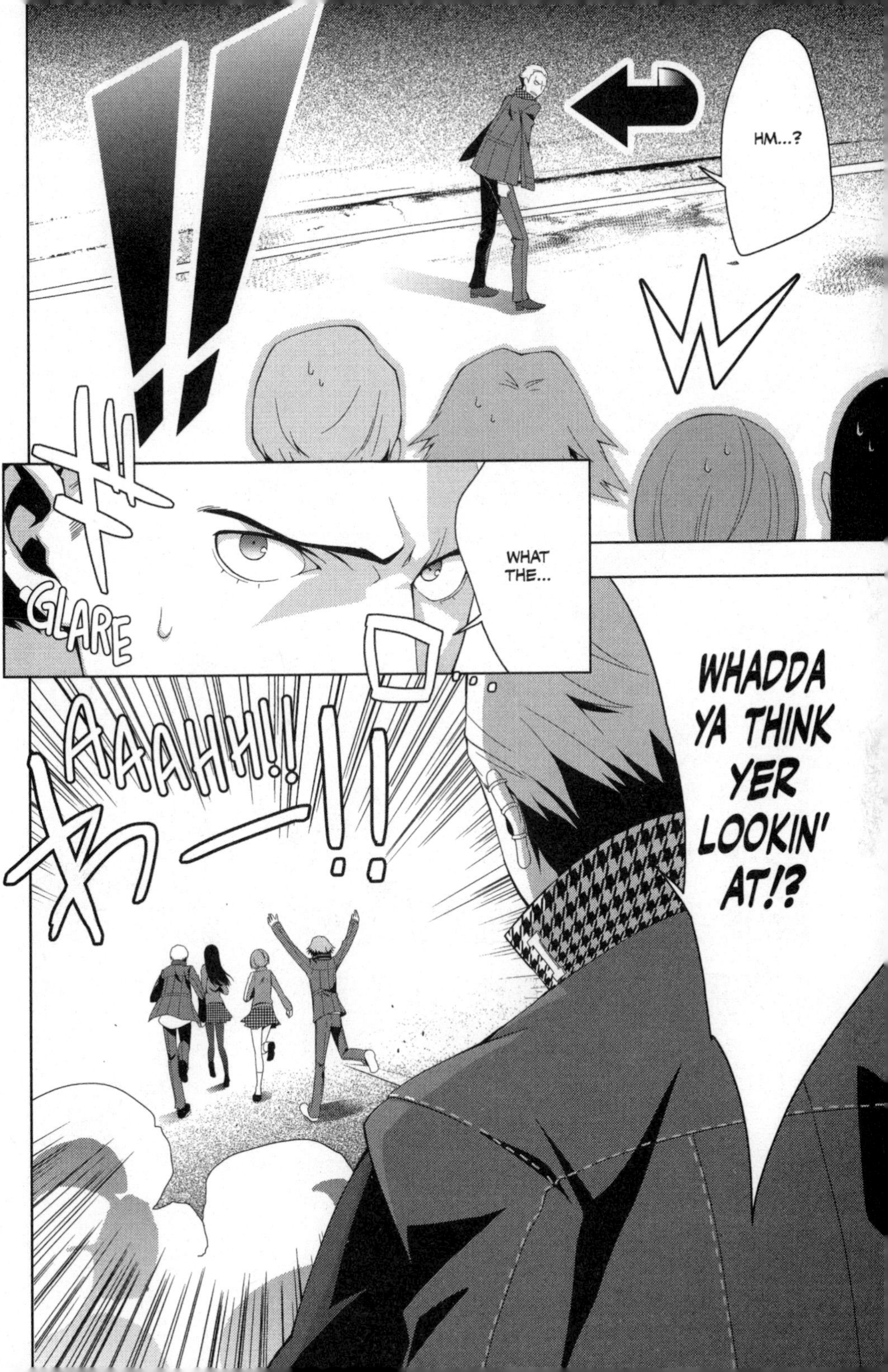
HM...?
!!
WHAT THE...
GLARE
WHADDA YA THINK YER LOOKIN' AT!?
AAAHH!!
あー!!

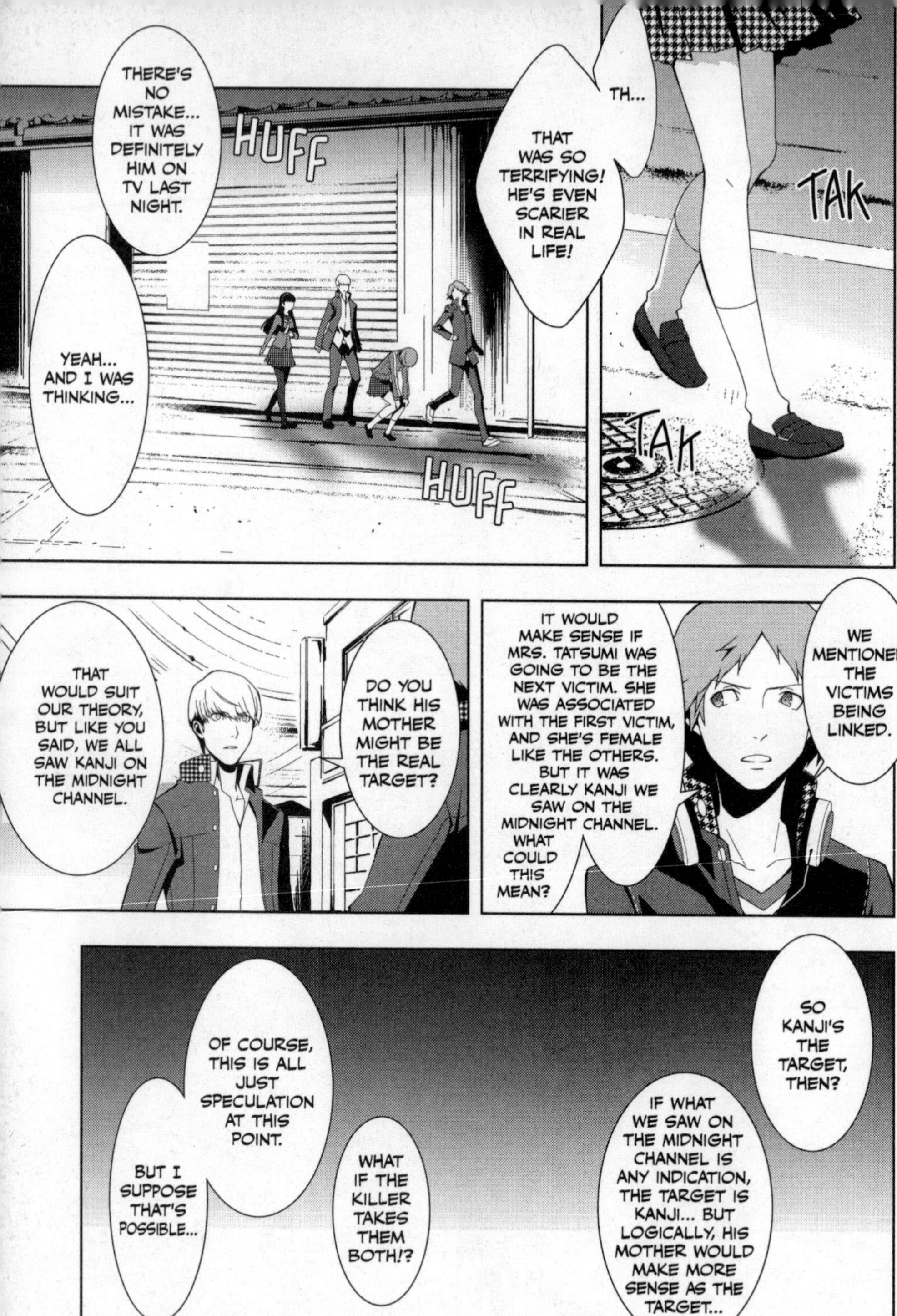
TH...
THAT WAS SO TERRIFYING! HE'S EVEN SCARIER IN REAL LIFE!
TAK
TAK
THERE'S NO MISTAKE... IT WAS DEFINITELY HIM ON TV LAST NIGHT.
HUFF
YEAH... AND I WAS THINKING...
HUFF
WE MENTIONED THE VICTIMS BEING LINKED.
IT WOULD MAKE SENSE IF MRS. TATSUMI WAS GOING TO BE THE NEXT VICTIM. SHE WAS ASSOCIATED WITH THE FIRST VICTIM, AND SHE'S FEMALE LIKE THE OTHERS. BUT IT WAS CLEARLY KANJI WE SAW ON THE MIDNIGHT CHANNEL. WHAT COULD THIS MEAN?
DO YOU THINK HIS MOTHER MIGHT BE THE REAL TARGET?
THAT WOULD SUIT OUR THEORY, BUT LIKE YOU SAID, WE ALL SAW KANJI ON THE MIDNIGHT CHANNEL.
SO KANJI'S THE TARGET, THEN?
IF WHAT WE SAW ON THE MIDNIGHT CHANNEL IS ANY INDICATION, THE TARGET IS KANJI... BUT LOGICALLY, HIS MOTHER WOULD MAKE MORE SENSE AS THE TARGET...
OF COURSE, THIS IS ALL JUST SPECULATION AT THIS POINT.
WHAT IF THE KILLER TAKES THEM BOTH!?
BUT I SUPPOSE THAT'S POSSIBLE...

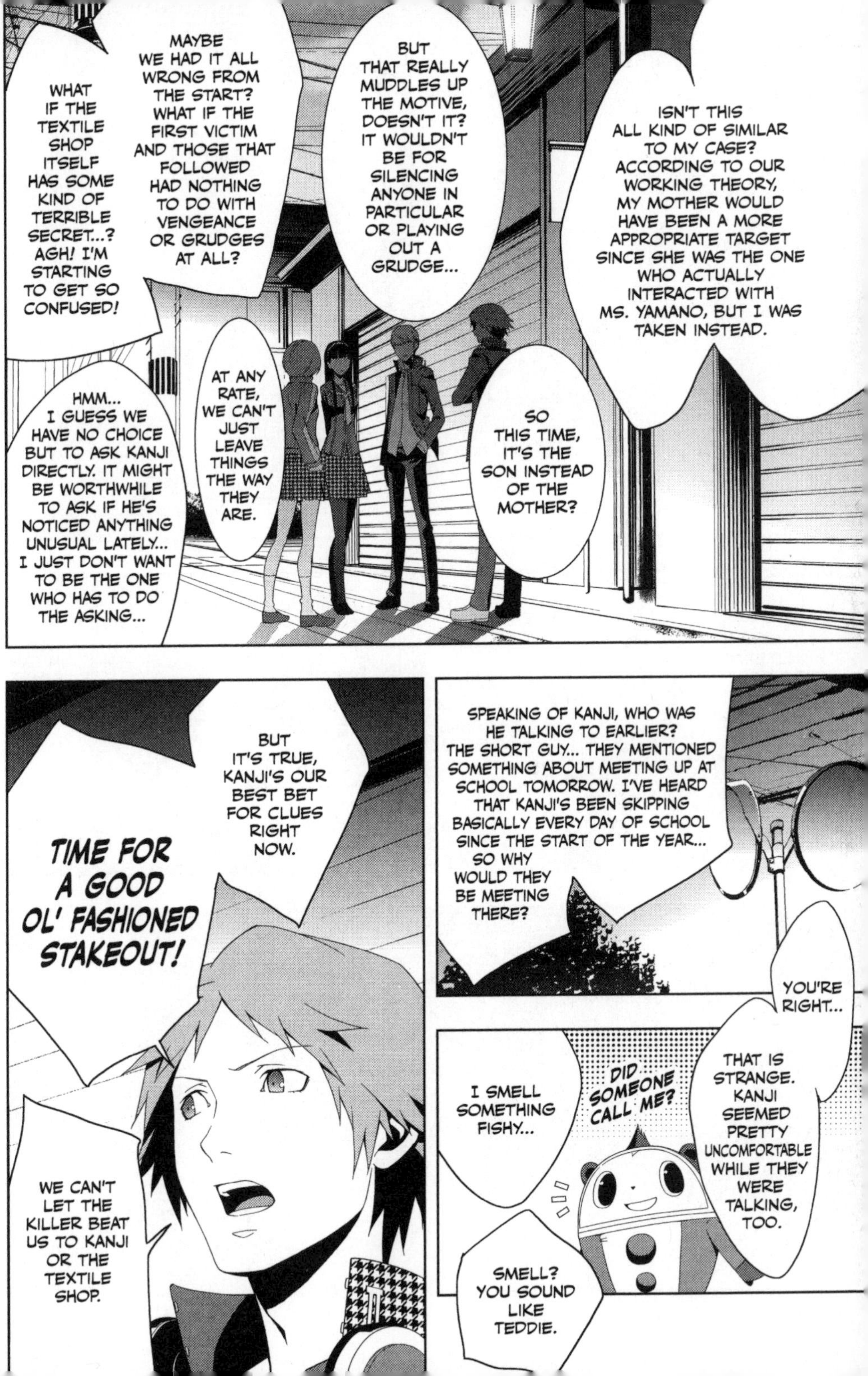
ISN'T THIS ALL KIND OF SIMILAR TO MY CASE? ACCORDING TO OUR WORKING THEORY, MY MOTHER WOULD HAVE BEEN A MORE APPROPRIATE TARGET SINCE SHE WAS THE ONE WHO ACTUALLY INTERACTED WITH MS. YAMANO, BUT I WAS TAKEN INSTEAD.
BUT THAT REALLY MUDDLES UP THE MOTIVE, DOESN'T IT? IT WOULDN'T BE FOR SILENCING ANYONE IN PARTICULAR OR PLAYING OUT A GRUDGE...
MAYBE WE HAD IT ALL WRONG FROM THE START? WHAT IF THE FIRST VICTIM AND THOSE THAT FOLLOWED HAD NOTHING TO DO WITH VENGEANCE OR GRUDGES AT ALL?
WHAT IF THE TEXTILE SHOP ITSELF HAS SOME KIND OF TERRIBLE SECRET...? AGH! I'M STARTING TO GET SO CONFUSED!
SO THIS TIME, IT'S THE SON INSTEAD OF THE MOTHER?
AT ANY RATE, WE CAN'T JUST LEAVE THINGS THE WAY THEY ARE.
HMM... I GUESS WE HAVE NO CHOICE BUT TO ASK KANJI DIRECTLY. IT MIGHT BE WORTHWHILE TO ASK IF HE'S NOTICED ANYTHING UNUSUAL LATELY... I JUST DON'T WANT TO BE THE ONE WHO HAS TO DO THE ASKING...
SPEAKING OF KANJI, WHO WAS HE TALKING TO EARLIER? THE SHORT GUY... THEY MENTIONED SOMETHING ABOUT MEETING UP AT SCHOOL TOMORROW. I'VE HEARD THAT KANJI'S BEEN SKIPPING BASICALLY EVERY DAY OF SCHOOL SINCE THE START OF THE YEAR... SO WHY WOULD THEY BE MEETING THERE?
YOU'RE RIGHT...
THAT IS STRANGE. KANJI SEEMED PRETTY UNCOMFORTABLE WHILE THEY WERE TALKING, TOO.
DID SOMEONE CALL ME?
I SMELL SOMETHING FISHY...
SMELL? YOU SOUND LIKE TEDDIE.
BUT IT'S TRUE, KANJI'S OUR BEST BET FOR CLUES RIGHT NOW.
TIME FOR A GOOD OL' FASHIONED STAKEOUT!
WE CAN'T LET THE KILLER BEAT US TO KANJI OR THE TEXTILE SHOP.

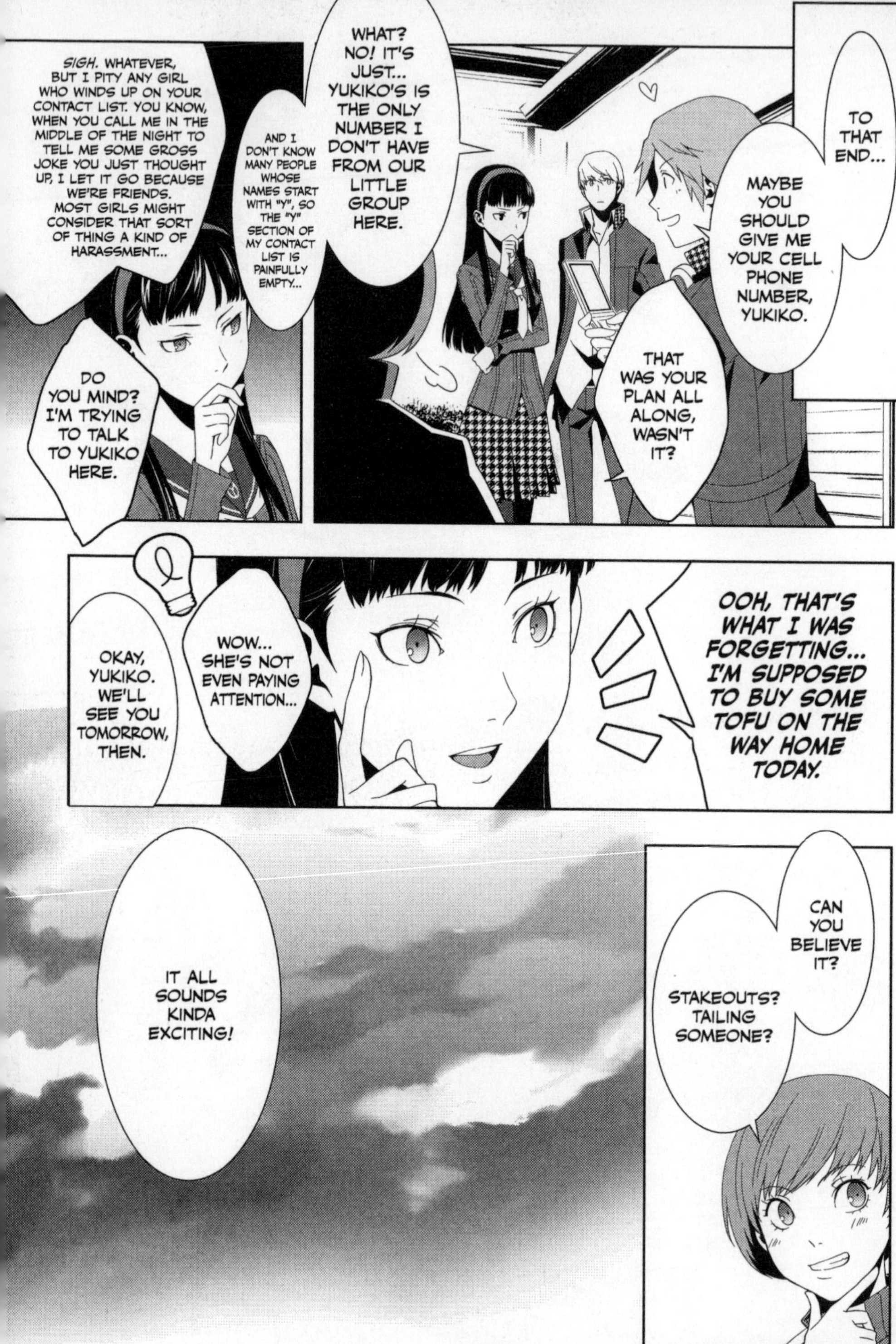
TO THAT END...
MAYBE YOU SHOULD GIVE ME YOUR CELL PHONE NUMBER, YUKIKO.
THAT WAS YOUR PLAN ALL ALONG, WASN'T IT?
WHAT? NO! IT'S JUST... YUKIKO'S IS THE ONLY NUMBER I DON'T HAVE FROM OUR LITTLE GROUP HERE.
AND I DON'T KNOW MANY PEOPLE WHOSE NAMES START WITH "Y", SO THE "Y" SECTION OF MY CONTACT LIST IS PAINFULLY EMPTY...
SIGH. WHATEVER, BUT I PITY ANY GIRL WHO WINDS UP ON YOUR CONTACT LIST. YOU KNOW, WHEN YOU CALL ME IN THE MIDDLE OF THE NIGHT TO TELL ME SOME GROSS JOKE YOU JUST THOUGHT UP, I LET IT GO BECAUSE WE'RE FRIENDS. MOST GIRLS MIGHT CONSIDER THAT SORT OF THING A KIND OF HARASSMENT...
DO YOU MIND? I'M TRYING TO TALK TO YUKIKO HERE.
OOH, THAT'S WHAT I WAS FORGETTING... I'M SUPPOSED TO BUY SOME TOFU ON THE WAY HOME TODAY.
WOW... SHE'S NOT EVEN PAYING ATTENTION...
OKAY, YUKIKO. WE'LL SEE YOU TOMORROW, THEN.
CAN YOU BELIEVE IT?
STAKEOUTS? TAILING SOMEONE?
IT ALL SOUNDS KINDA EXCITING!

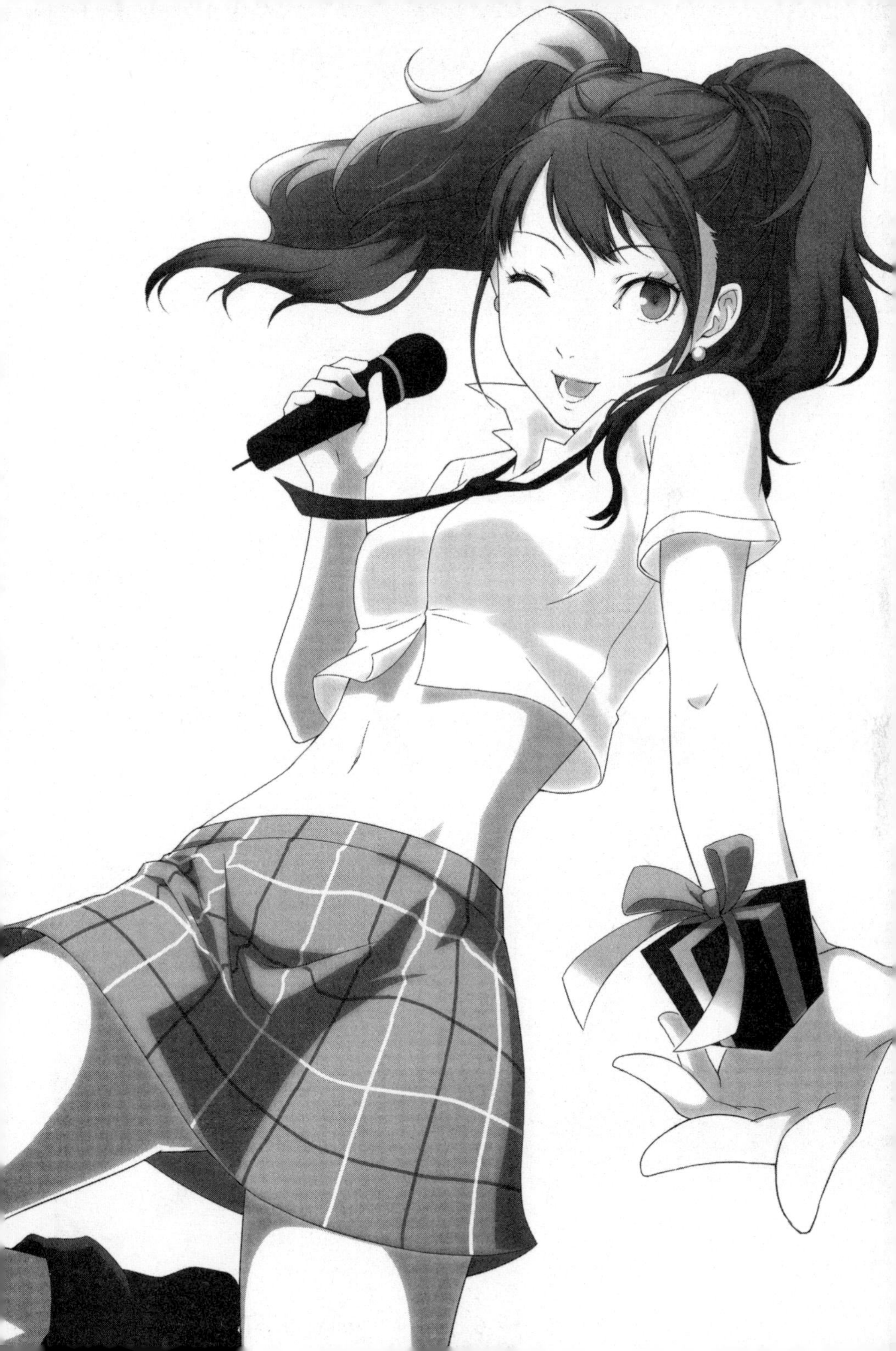

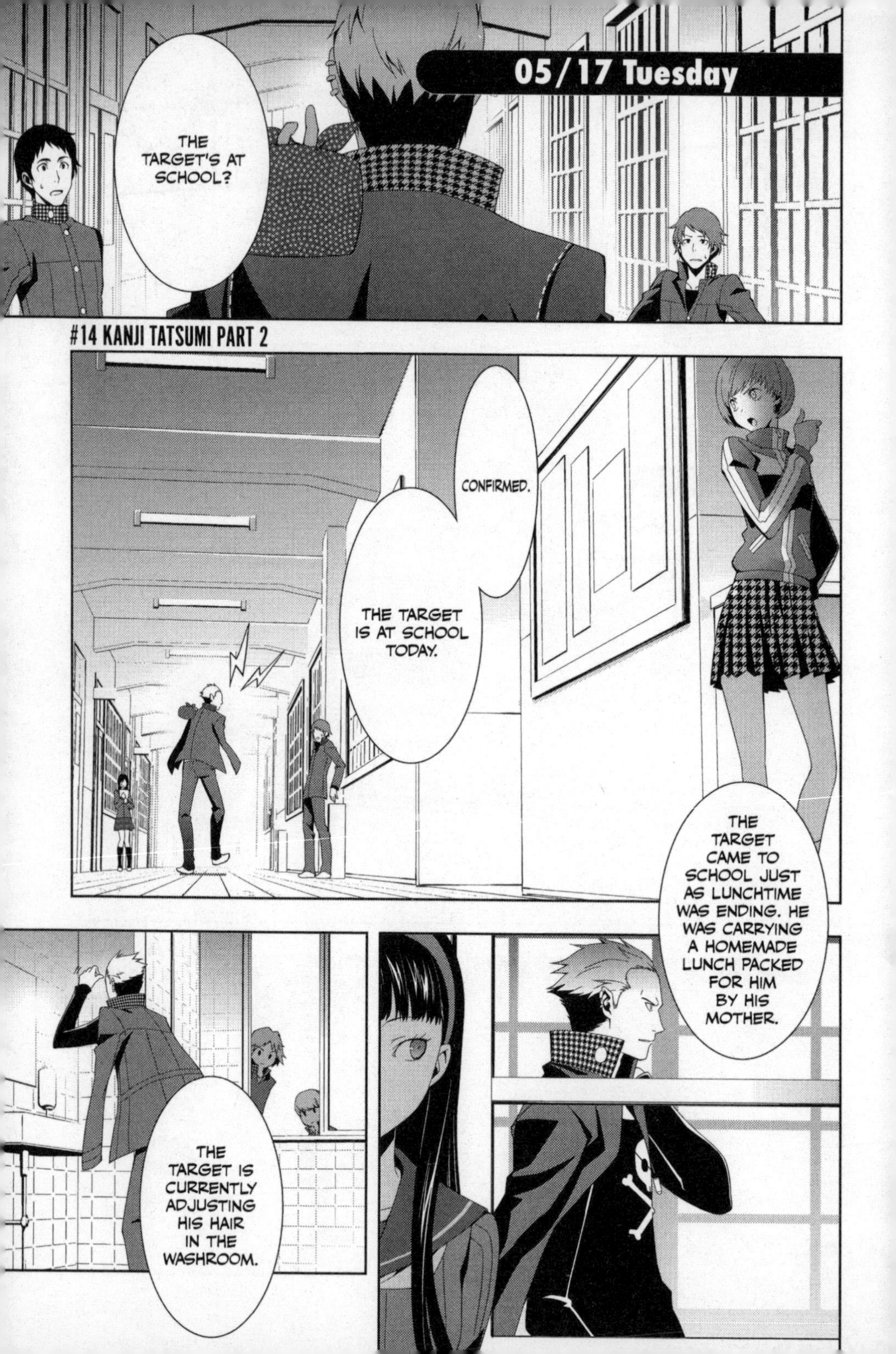
05/17 Tuesday
THE TARGET'S AT SCHOOL?
#14 KANJI TATSUMI PART 2
CONFIRMED.
THE TARGET IS AT SCHOOL TODAY.
THE TARGET CAME TO SCHOOL JUST AS LUNCHTIME WAS ENDING. HE WAS CARRYING A HOMEMADE LUNCH PACKED FOR HIM BY HIS MOTHER.
THE TARGET IS CURRENTLY ADJUSTING HIS HAIR IN THE WASHROOM.

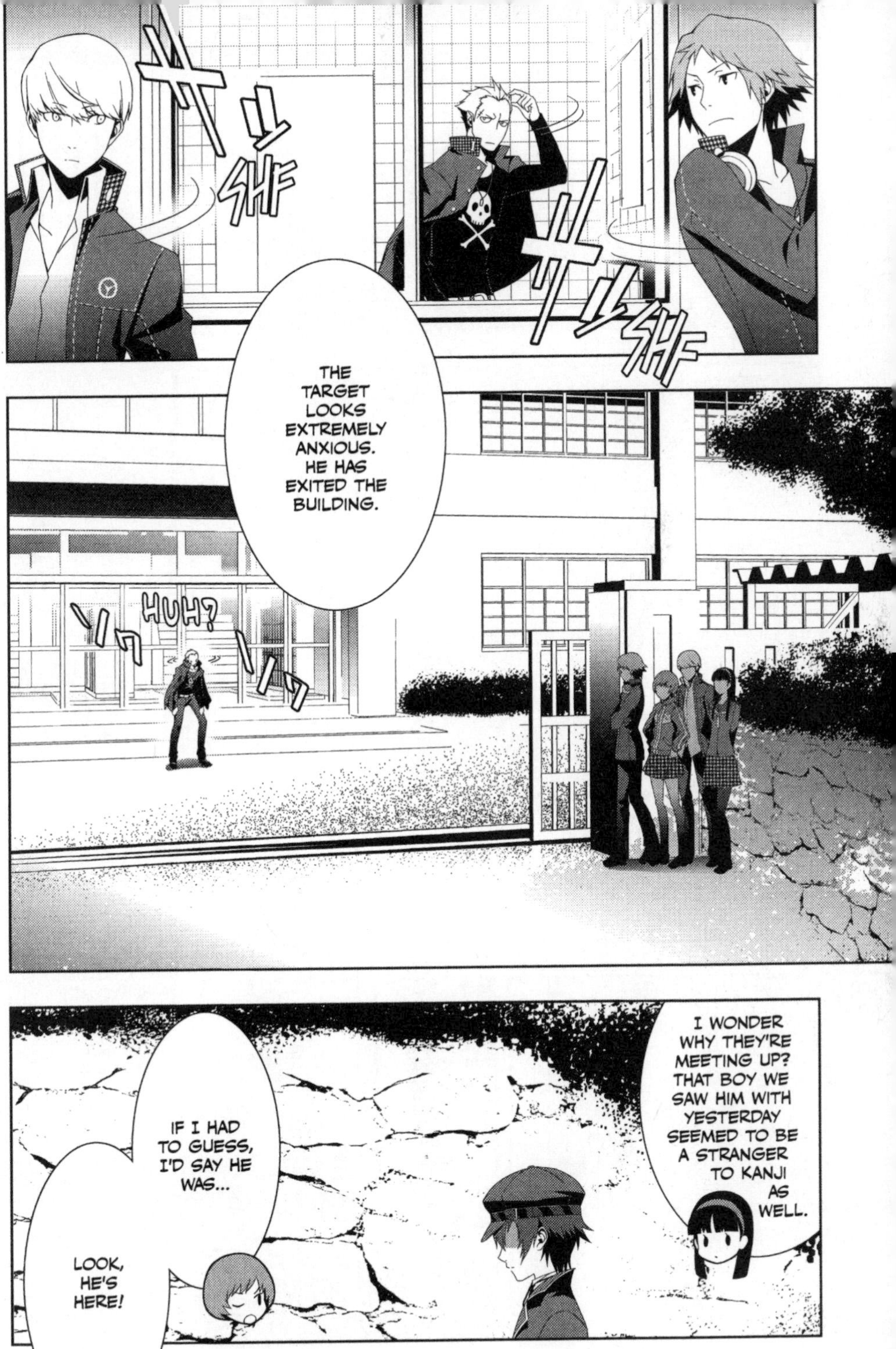
SHF
SHF
THE TARGET LOOKS EXTREMELY ANXIOUS. HE HAS EXITED THE BUILDING.
HUH?
I WONDER WHY THEY'RE MEETING UP? THAT BOY WE SAW HIM WITH YESTERDAY SEEMED TO BE A STRANGER TO KANJI AS WELL.
IF I HAD TO GUESS, I'D SAY HE WAS...
LOOK, HE'S HERE!

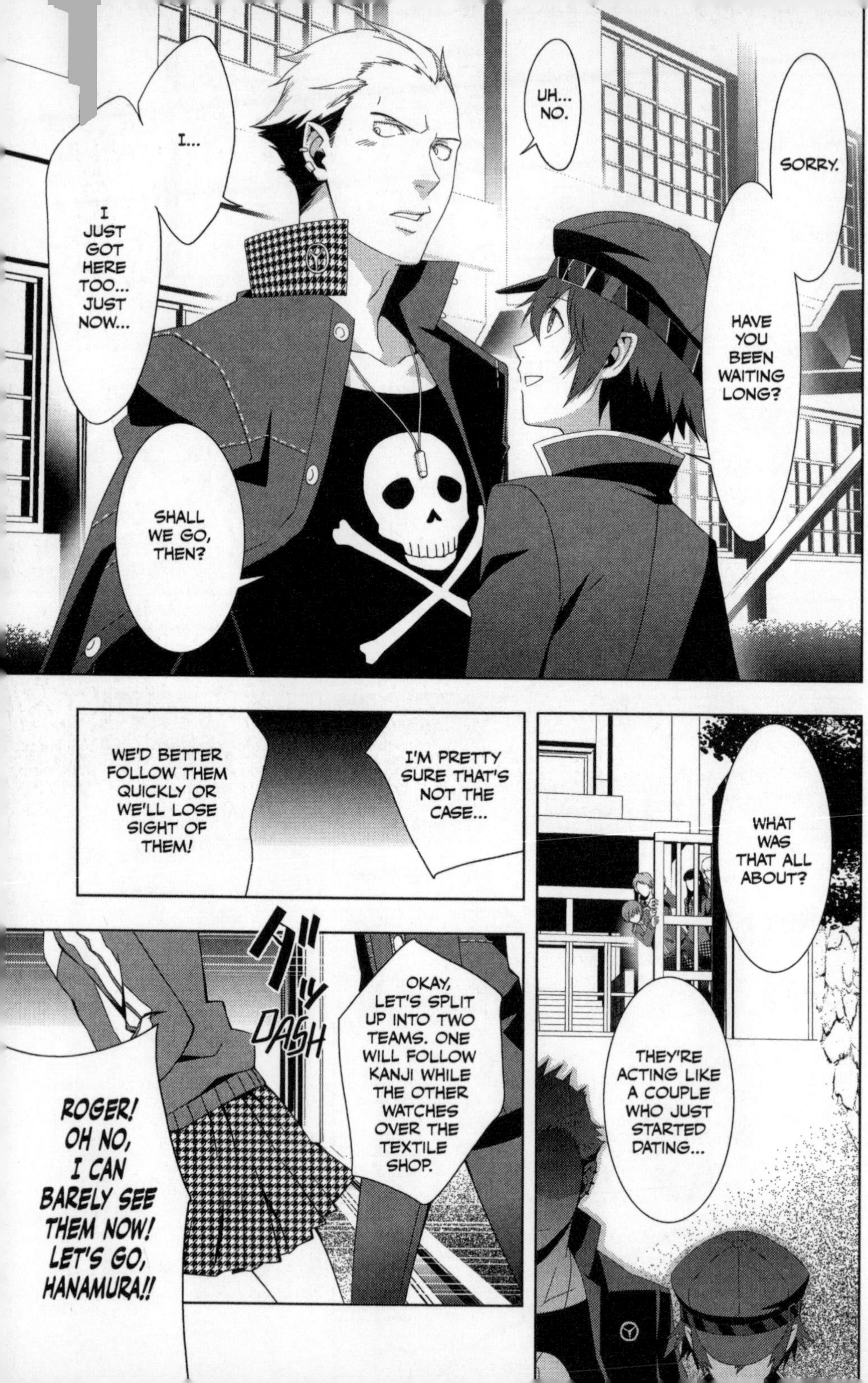
SORRY.
HAVE YOU BEEN WAITING LONG?
UH... NO.
I...
I JUST GOT HERE TOO... JUST NOW...
SHALL WE GO, THEN?
WHAT WAS THAT ALL ABOUT?
THEY'RE ACTING LIKE A COUPLE WHO JUST STARTED DATING...
I'M PRETTY SURE THAT'S NOT THE CASE...
WE'D BETTER FOLLOW THEM QUICKLY OR WE'LL LOSE SIGHT OF THEM!
OKAY, LET'S SPLIT UP INTO TWO TEAMS. ONE WILL FOLLOW KANJI WHILE THE OTHER WATCHES OVER THE TEXTILE SHOP.
DASH
ROGER! OH NO, I CAN BARELY SEE THEM NOW! LET'S GO, HANAMURA!!

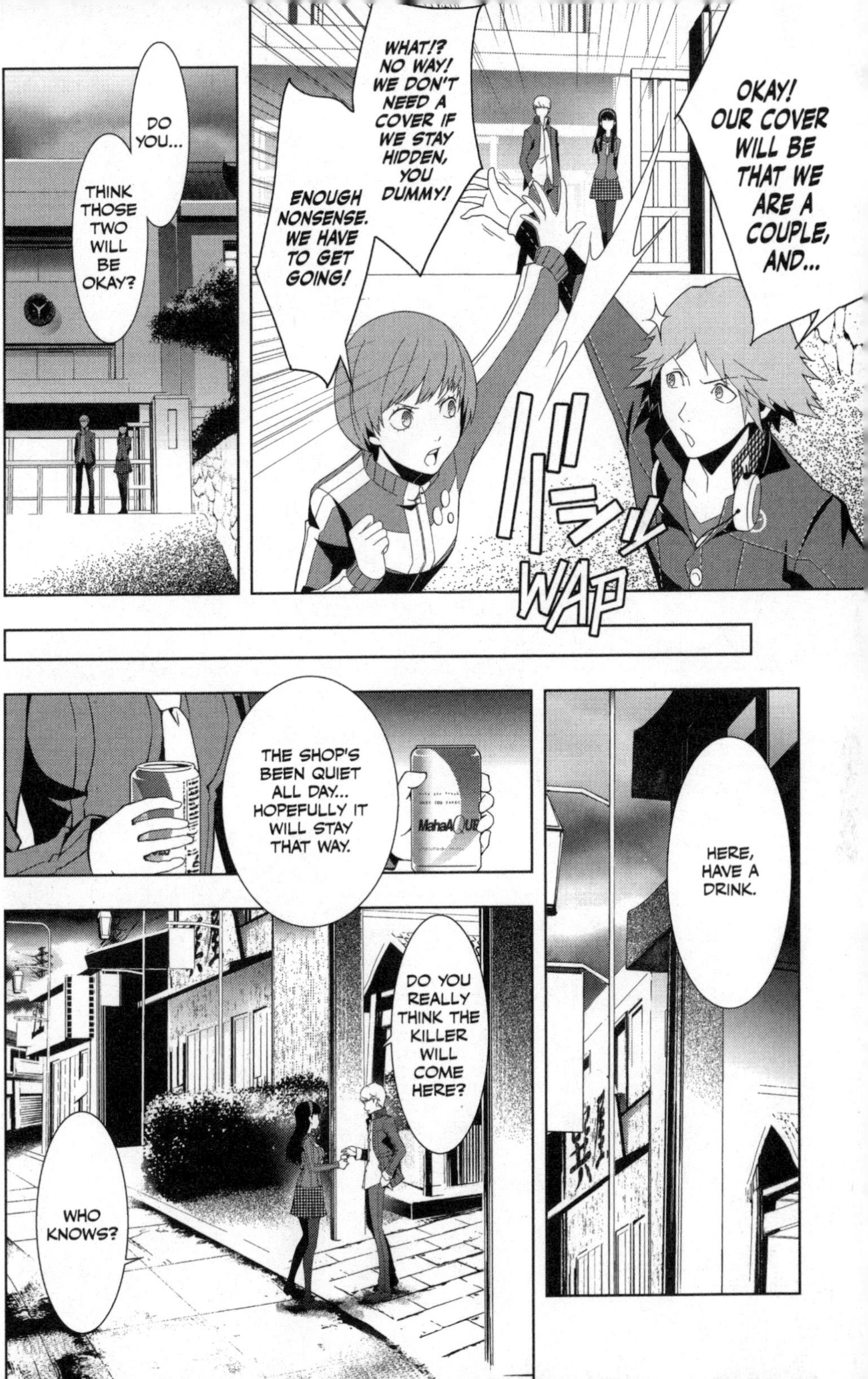
OKAY! OUR COVER WILL BE THAT WE ARE A COUPLE, AND...
WHAT!? NO WAY! WE DON'T NEED A COVER IF WE STAY HIDDEN, YOU DUMMY!
ENOUGH NONSENSE. WE HAVE TO GET GOING!
WAP
DO YOU...
THINK THOSE TWO WILL BE OKAY?
HERE, HAVE A DRINK.
THE SHOP'S BEEN QUIET ALL DAY... HOPEFULLY IT WILL STAY THAT WAY.
DO YOU REALLY THINK THE KILLER WILL COME HERE?
WHO KNOWS?

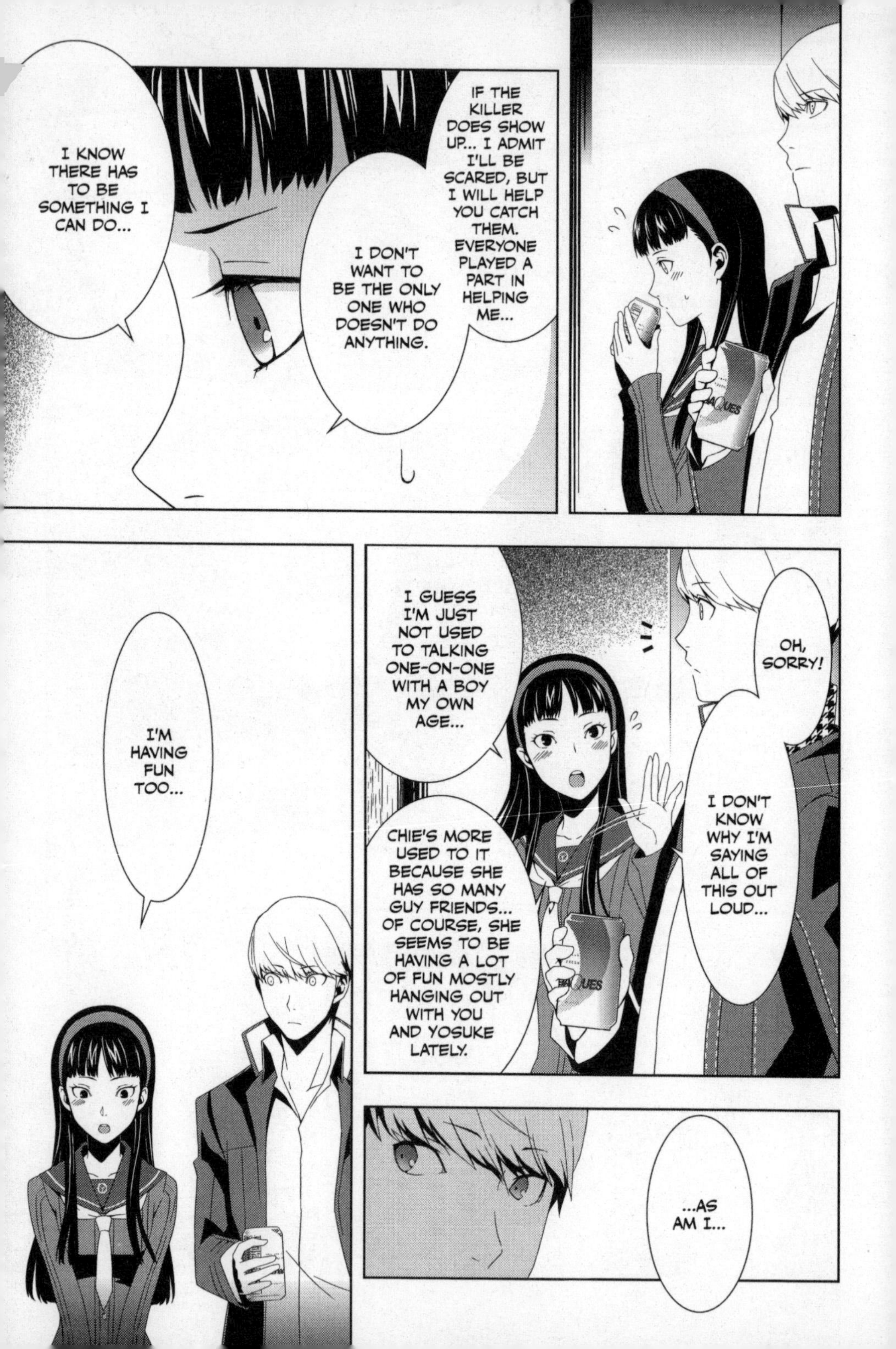
IF THE KILLER DOES SHOW UP... I ADMIT I'LL BE SCARED, BUT I WILL HELP YOU CATCH THEM. EVERYONE PLAYED A PART IN HELPING ME...
I DON'T WANT TO BE THE ONLY ONE WHO DOESN'T DO ANYTHING.
I KNOW THERE HAS TO BE SOMETHING I CAN DO...
OH, SORRY!
I DON'T KNOW WHY I'M SAYING ALL OF THIS OUT LOUD...
I GUESS I'M JUST NOT USED TO TALKING ONE-ON-ONE WITH A BOY MY OWN AGE...
CHIE'S MORE USED TO IT BECAUSE SHE HAS SO MANY GUY FRIENDS... OF COURSE, SHE SEEMS TO BE HAVING A LOT OF FUN MOSTLY HANGING OUT WITH YOU AND YOSUKE LATELY.
...AS AM I...
I'M HAVING FUN TOO...

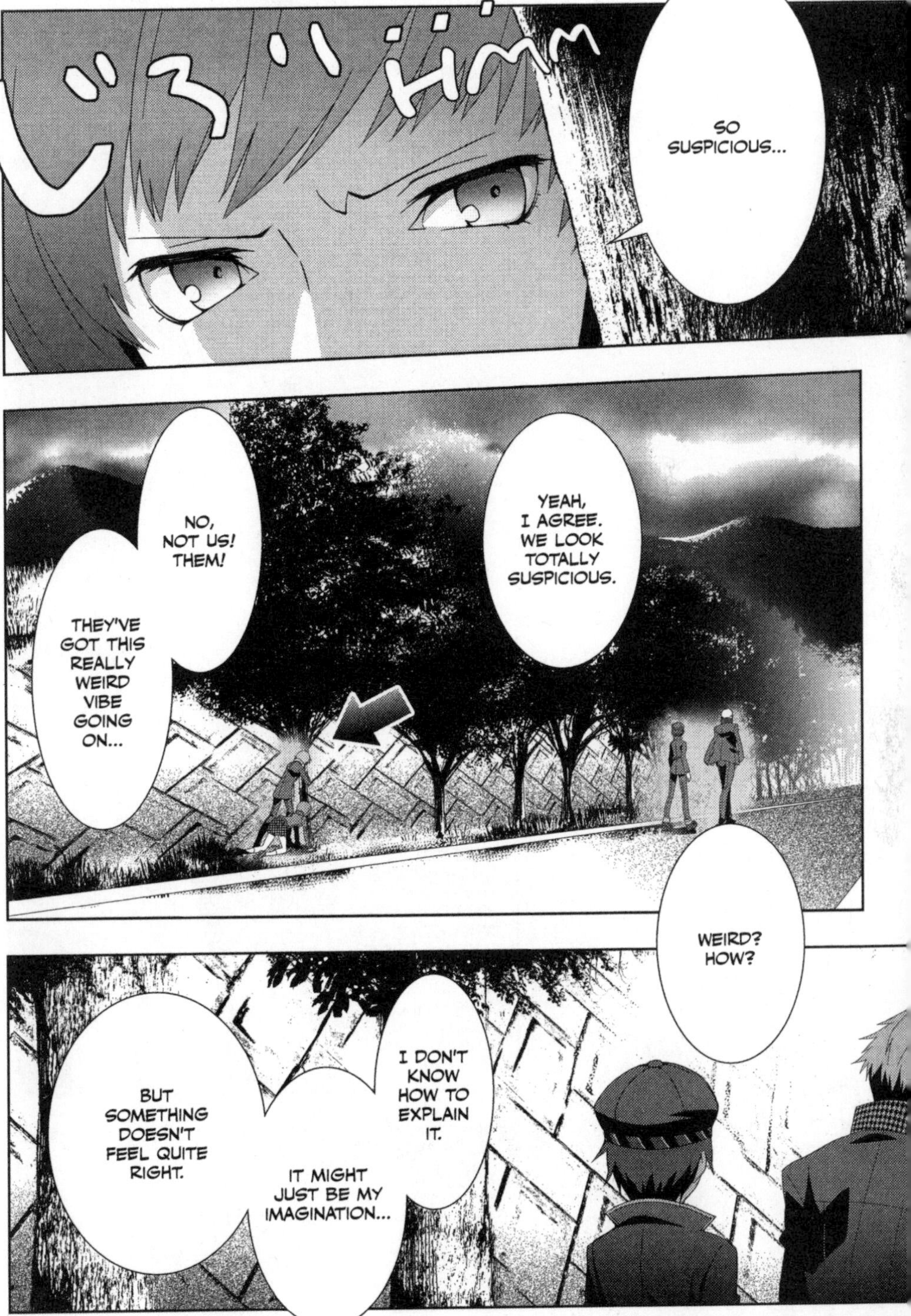
SO SUSPICIOUS...
じろっ
Hmm
YEAH, I AGREE. WE LOOK TOTALLY SUSPICIOUS.
NO, NOT US! THEM!
THEY'VE GOT THIS REALLY WEIRD VIBE GOING ON...
WEIRD? HOW?
I DON'T KNOW HOW TO EXPLAIN IT.
IT MIGHT JUST BE MY IMAGINATION...
BUT SOMETHING DOESN'T FEEL QUITE RIGHT.

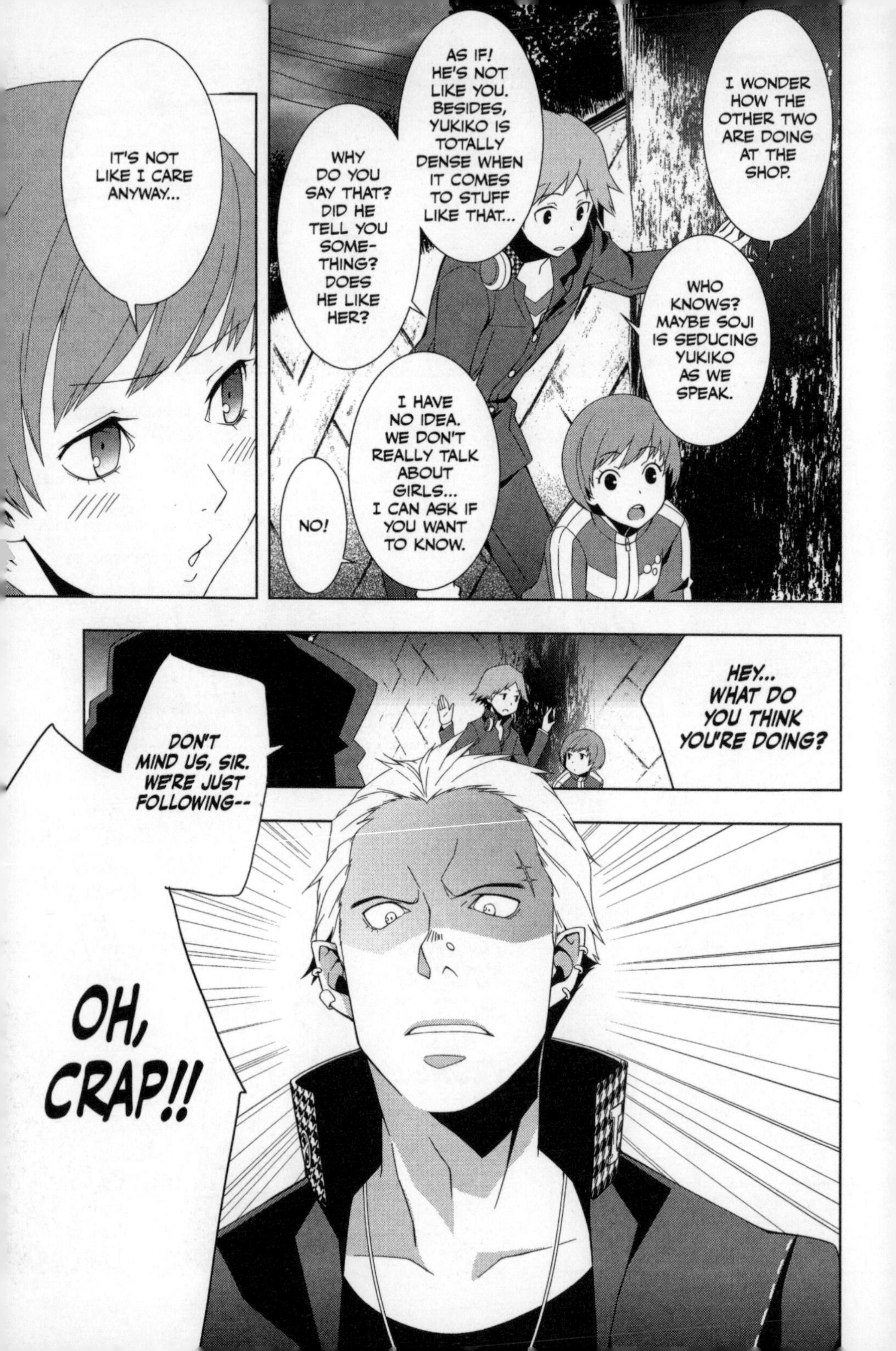
I WONDER HOW THE OTHER TWO ARE DOING AT THE SHOP.
WHO KNOWS? MAYBE SOJI IS SEDUCING YUKIKO AS WE SPEAK.
AS IF! HE'S NOT LIKE YOU. BESIDES, YUKIKO IS TOTALLY DENSE WHEN IT COMES TO STUFF LIKE THAT...
WHY DO YOU SAY THAT? DID HE TELL YOU SOME-THING? DOES HE LIKE HER?
I HAVE NO IDEA. WE DON'T REALLY TALK ABOUT GIRLS... I CAN ASK IF YOU WANT TO KNOW.
NO!
IT'S NOT LIKE I CARE ANYWAY...
HEY... WHAT DO YOU THINK YOU'RE DOING?
DON'T MIND US, SIR. WE'RE JUST FOLLOWING--
OH, CRAP!!

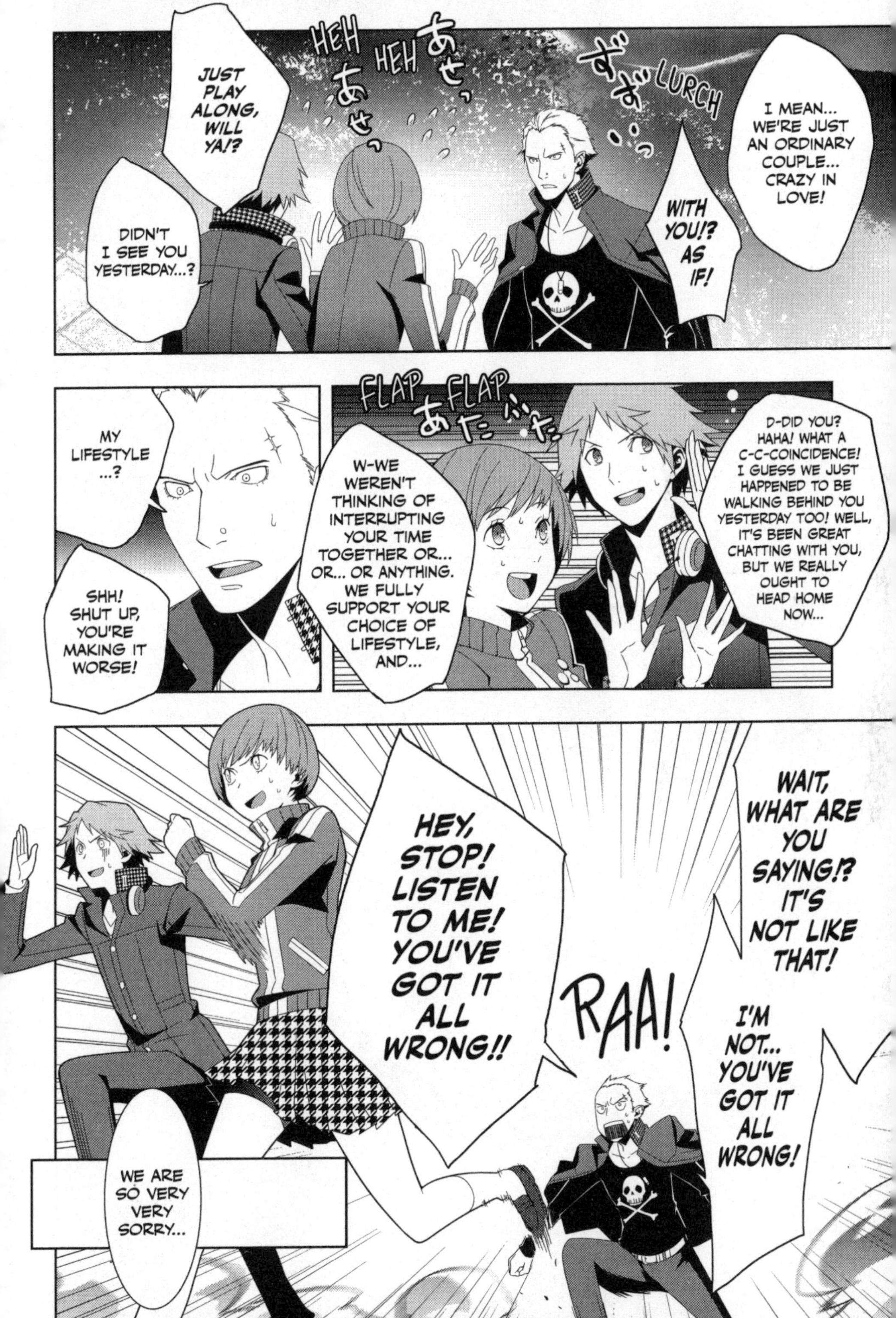
I MEAN... WE'RE JUST AN ORDINARY COUPLE... CRAZY IN LOVE!
WITH YOU!? AS IF!
ずずっ
LURCH
HEH HEH
あせあせっ
JUST PLAY ALONG, WILL YA!?
DIDN'T I SEE YOU YESTERDAY...?
D-DID YOU? HAHA! WHAT A C-C-COINCIDENCE! I GUESS WE JUST HAPPENED TO BE WALKING BEHIND YOU YESTERDAY TOO! WELL, IT'S BEEN GREAT CHATTING WITH YOU, BUT WE REALLY OUGHT TO HEAD HOME NOW...
FLAP FLAP
あたふた
W-WE WEREN'T THINKING OF INTERRUPTING YOUR TIME TOGETHER OR... OR... OR ANYTHING. WE FULLY SUPPORT YOUR CHOICE OF LIFESTYLE, AND...
MY LIFESTYLE ...?
SHH! SHUT UP, YOU'RE MAKING IT WORSE!
WAIT, WHAT ARE YOU SAYING!? IT'S NOT LIKE THAT!
I'M NOT... YOU'VE GOT IT ALL WRONG!
RAA!
HEY, STOP! LISTEN TO ME! YOU'VE GOT IT ALL WRONG!!
WE ARE SO VERY VERY SORRY...

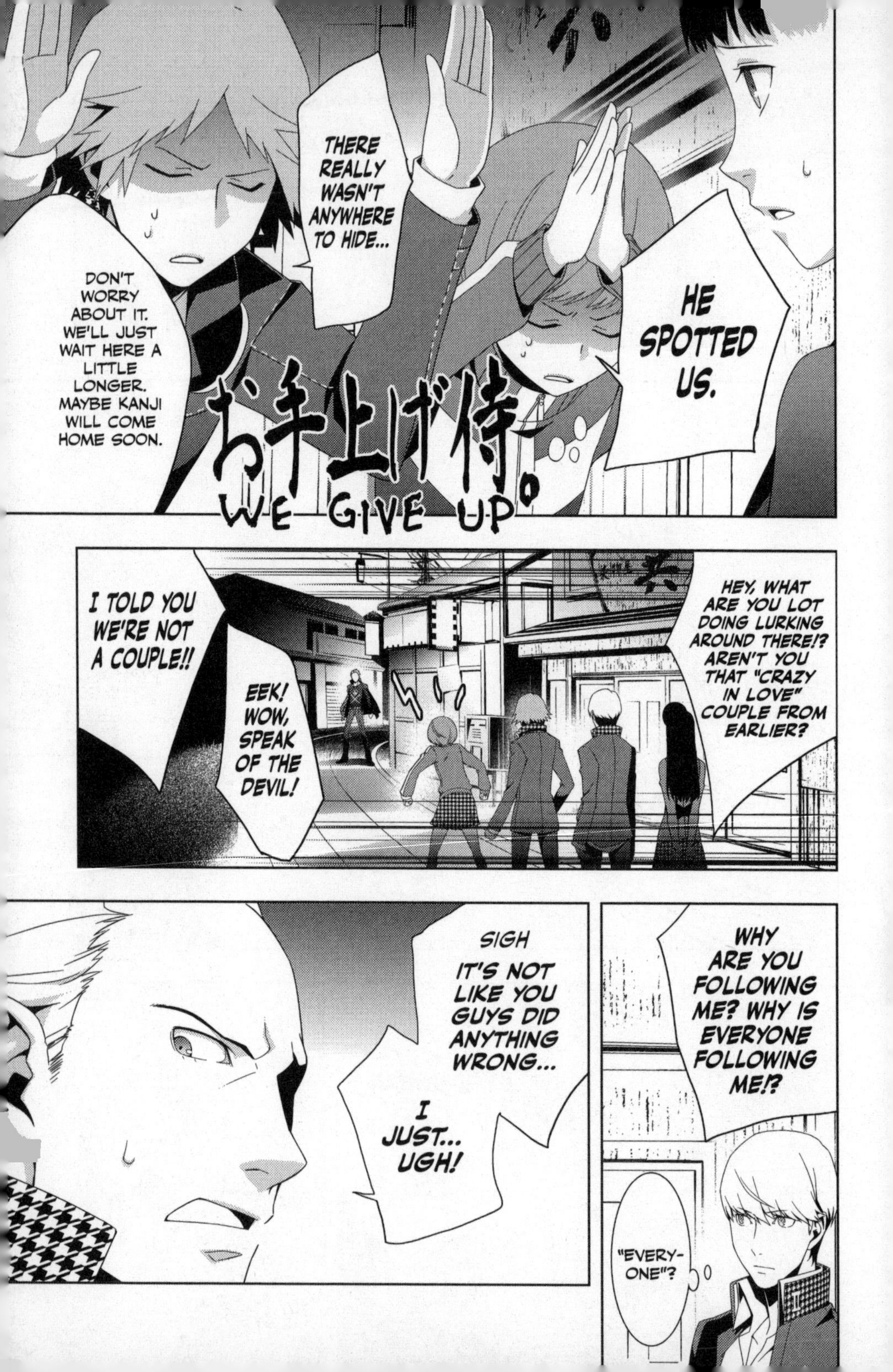
HE SPOTTED US.
THERE REALLY WASN'T ANYWHERE TO HIDE...
DON'T WORRY ABOUT IT. WE'LL JUST WAIT HERE A LITTLE LONGER. MAYBE KANJI WILL COME HOME SOON.
お手上げ侍。
WE GIVE UP
HEY, WHAT ARE YOU LOT DOING LURKING AROUND THERE!? AREN'T YOU THAT "CRAZY IN LOVE" COUPLE FROM EARLIER?
EEK! WOW, SPEAK OF THE DEVIL!
I TOLD YOU WE'RE NOT A COUPLE!!
WHY ARE YOU FOLLOWING ME? WHY IS EVERYONE FOLLOWING ME!?
"EVERY-ONE"?
SIGH
IT'S NOT LIKE YOU GUYS DID ANYTHING WRONG...
I JUST... UGH!

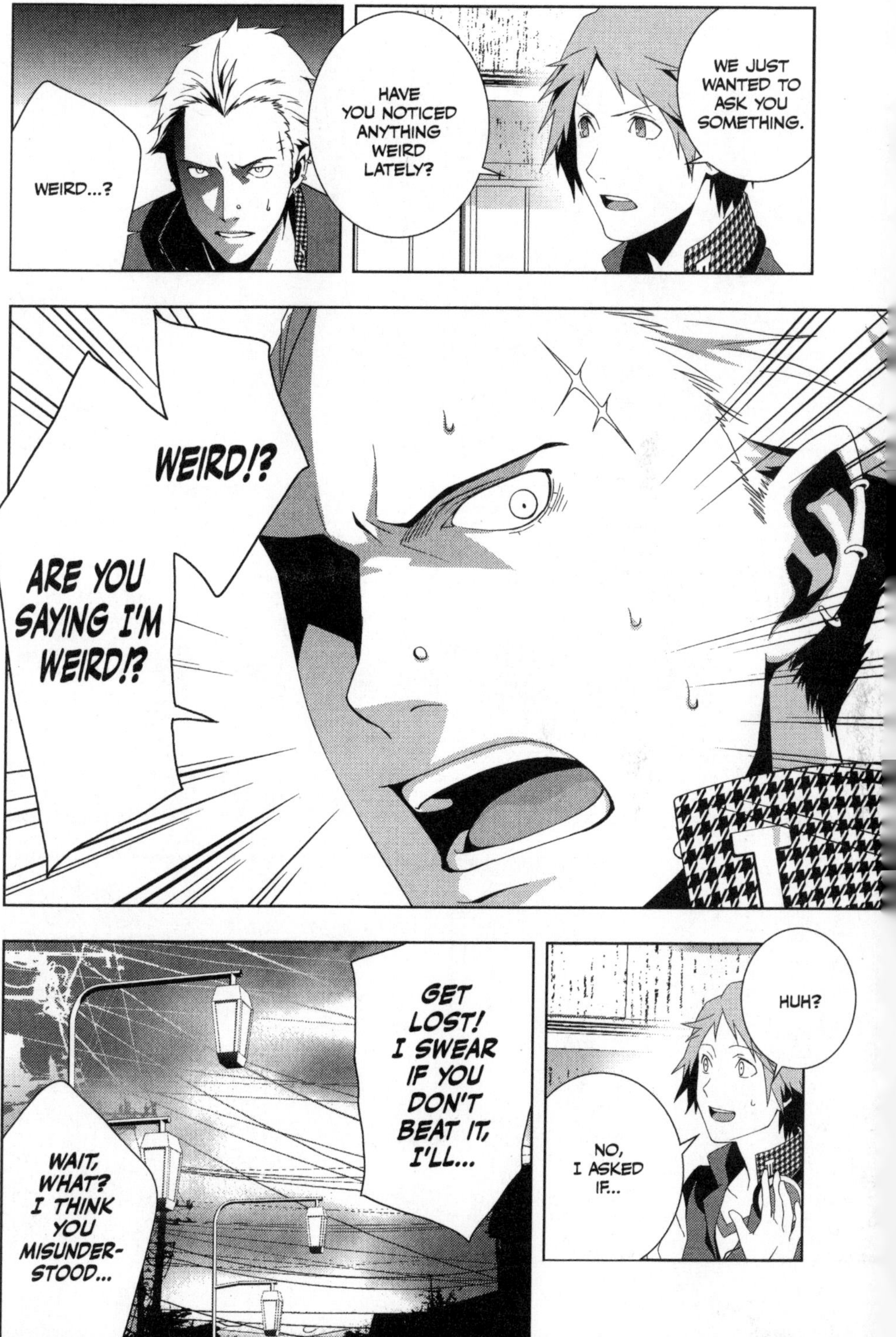
WE JUST WANTED TO ASK YOU SOMETHING.
HAVE YOU NOTICED ANYTHING WEIRD LATELY?
WEIRD...?
WEIRD!?
ARE YOU SAYING I'M WEIRD!?
HUH?
NO, I ASKED IF...
GET LOST! I SWEAR IF YOU DON'T BEAT IT, I'LL...
WAIT, WHAT? I THINK YOU MISUNDERSTOOD...

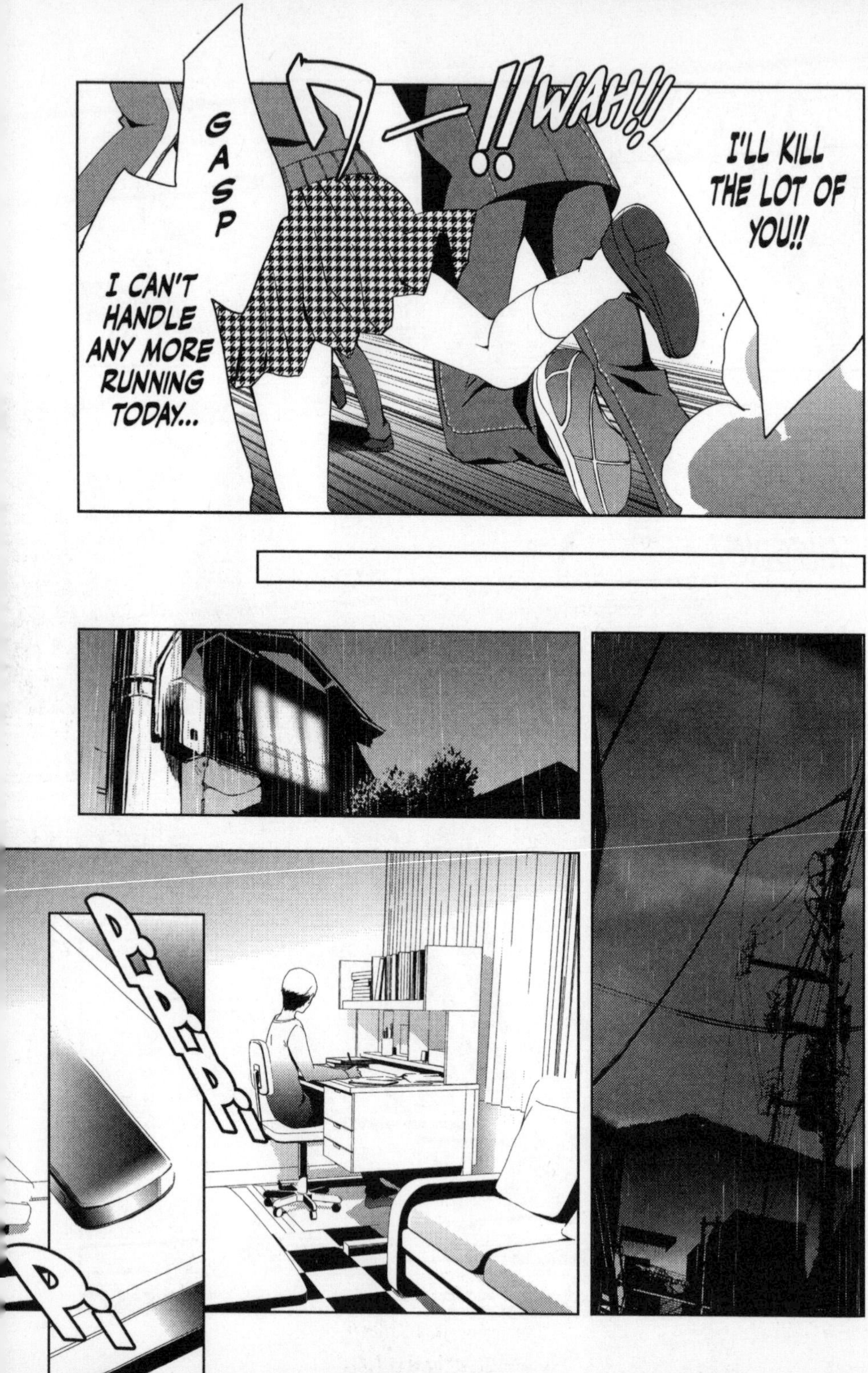
I'LL KILL THE LOT OF YOU!!
!!WAH!!
GASP
I CAN'T HANDLE ANY MORE RUNNING TODAY...
PIPIPI
PI

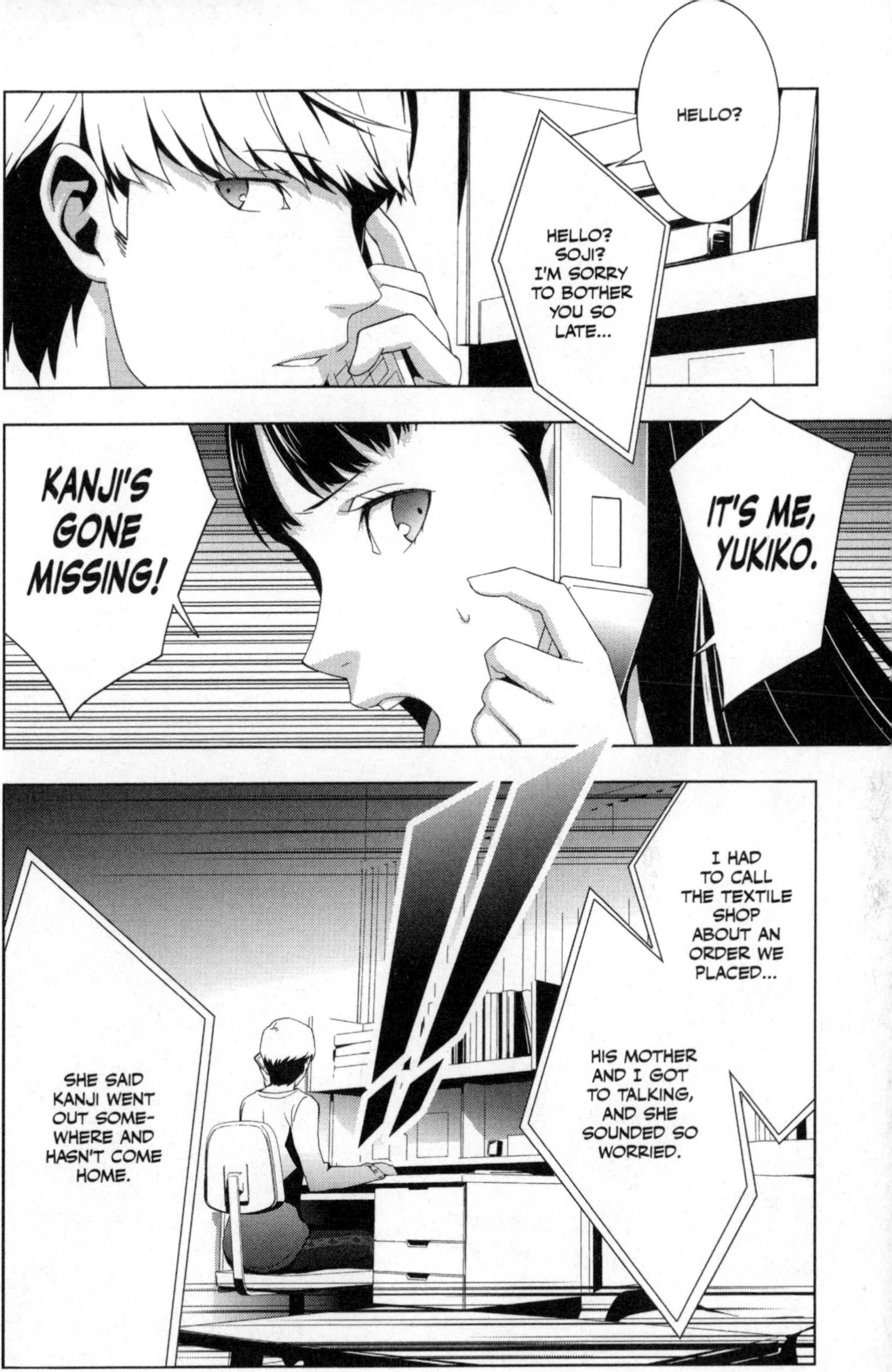
HELLO?
HELLO? SOJI? I'M SORRY TO BOTHER YOU SO LATE...
IT'S ME, YUKIKO.
KANJI'S GONE MISSING!
I HAD TO CALL THE TEXTILE SHOP ABOUT AN ORDER WE PLACED...
HIS MOTHER AND I GOT TO TALKING, AND SHE SOUNDED SO WORRIED.
SHE SAID KANJI WENT OUT SOME-WHERE AND HASN'T COME HOME.

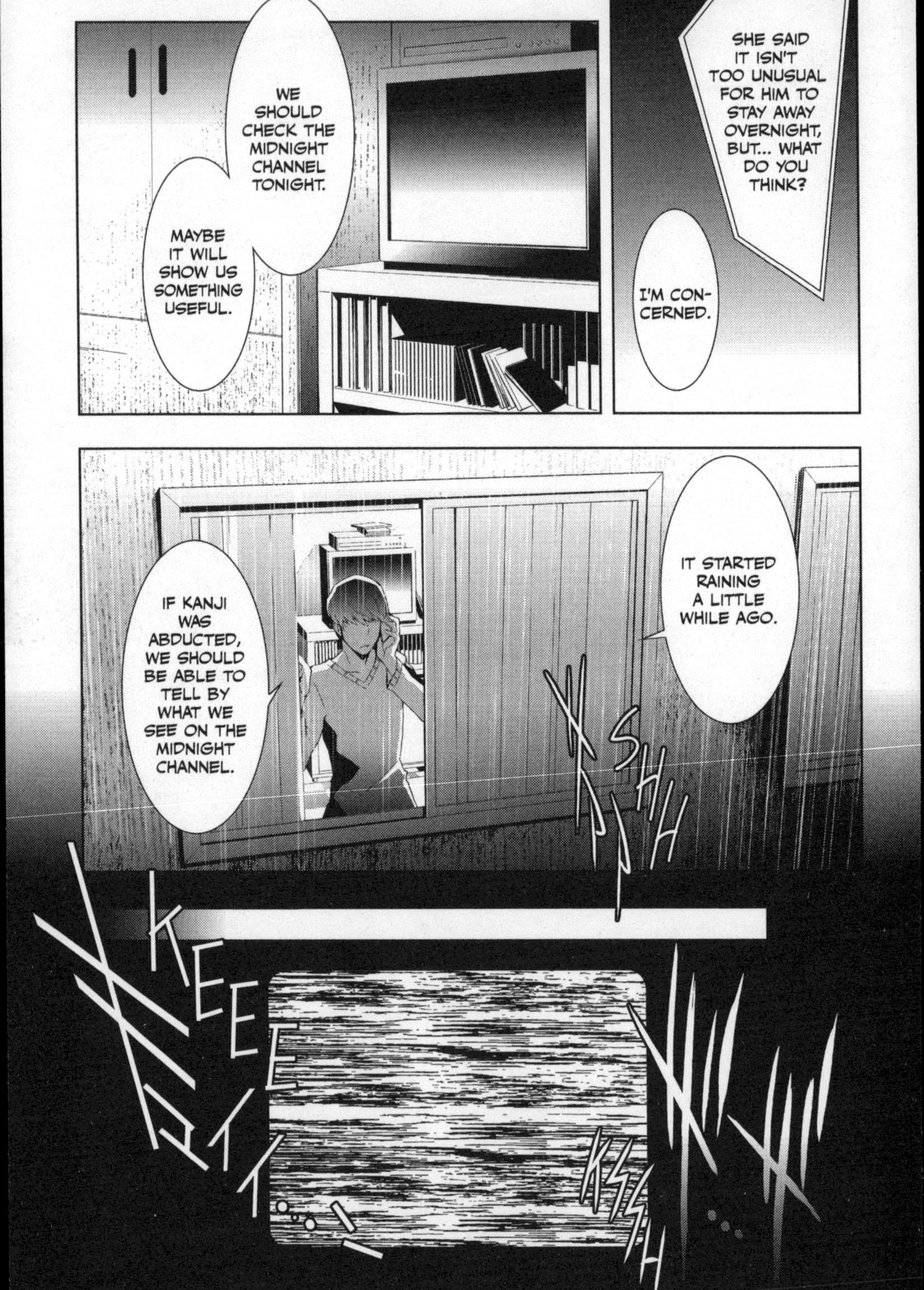
SHE SAID IT ISN'T TOO UNUSUAL FOR HIM TO STAY AWAY OVERNIGHT, BUT... WHAT DO YOU THINK?
I'M CON-CERNED.
WE SHOULD CHECK THE MIDNIGHT CHANNEL TONIGHT.
MAYBE IT WILL SHOW US SOMETHING USEFUL.
IT STARTED RAINING A LITTLE WHILE AGO.
IF KANJI WAS ABDUCTED, WE SHOULD BE ABLE TO TELL BY WHAT WE SEE ON THE MIDNIGHT CHANNEL.

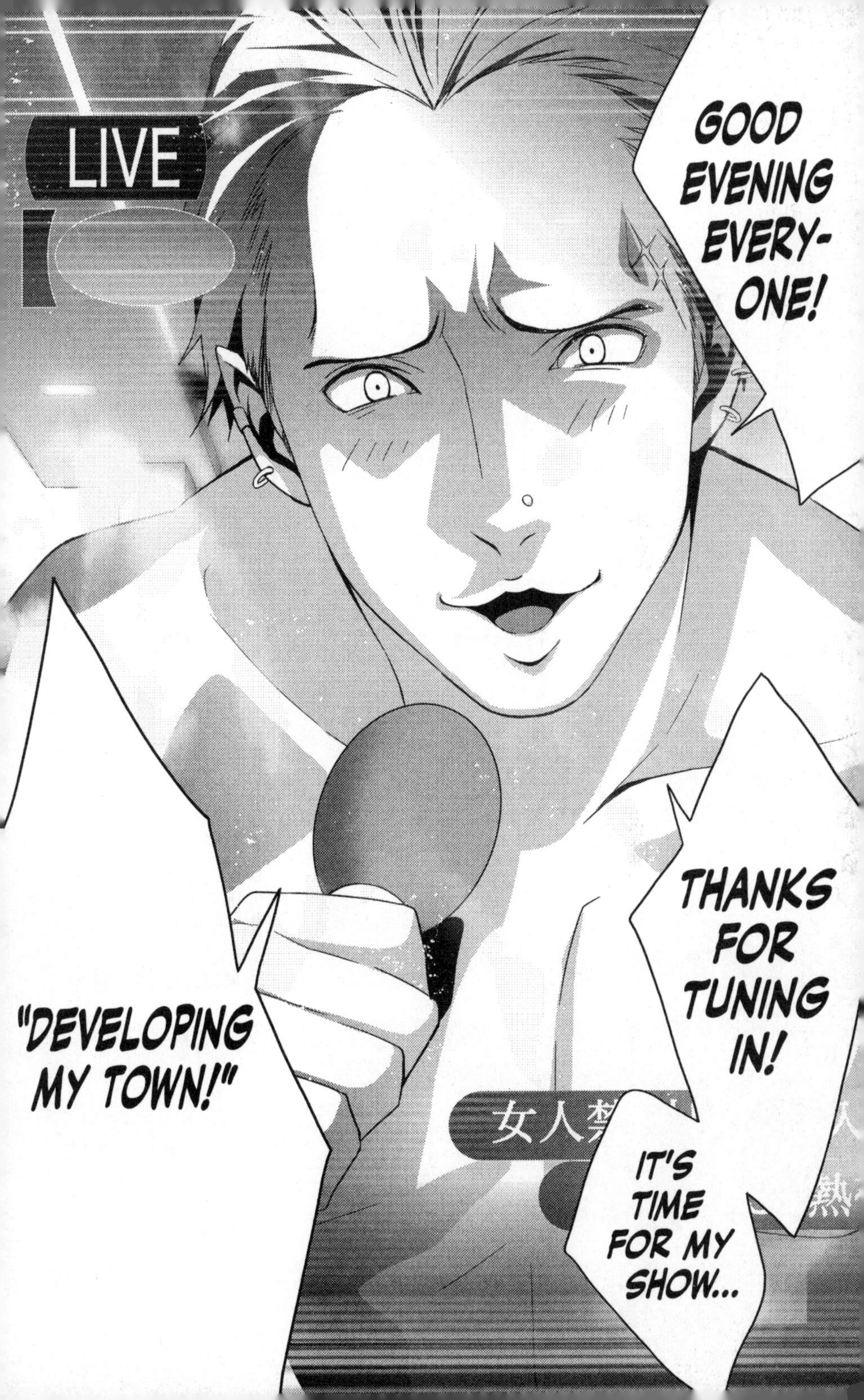
GOOD EVENING EVERY-ONE!
LIVE
THANKS FOR TUNING IN!
IT'S TIME FOR MY SHOW...
"DEVELOPING MY TOWN!"

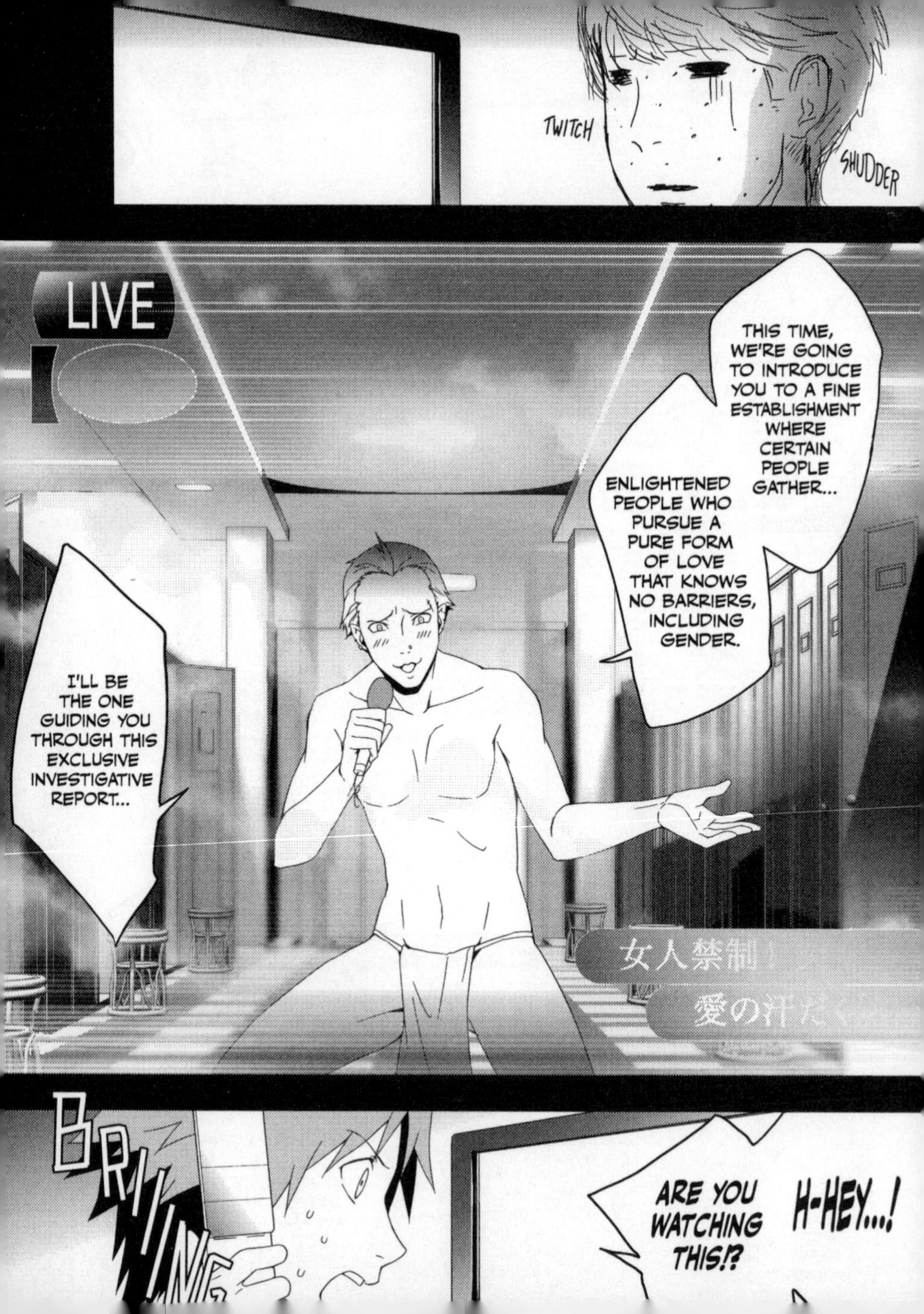
TWITCH
SHUDDER
LIVE
THIS TIME, WE'RE GOING TO INTRODUCE YOU TO A FINE ESTABLISHMENT WHERE CERTAIN PEOPLE GATHER...
ENLIGHTENED PEOPLE WHO PURSUE A PURE FORM OF LOVE THAT KNOWS NO BARRIERS, INCLUDING GENDER.
I'LL BE THE ONE GUIDING YOU THROUGH THIS EXCLUSIVE INVESTIGATIVE REPORT...
女人禁制
愛の汗だく
H-HEY...!
ARE YOU WATCHING THIS!?
BRIING

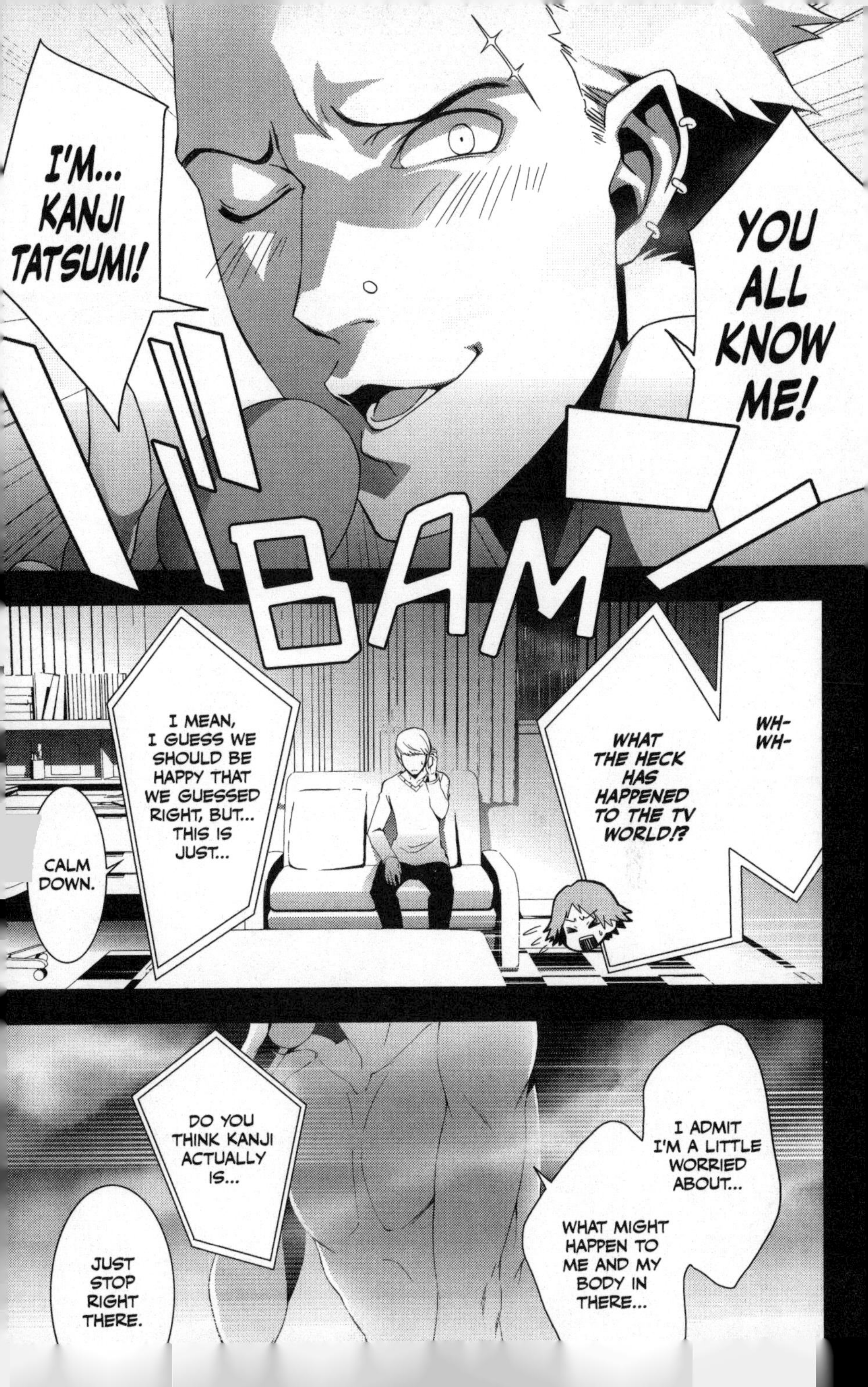
I'M... KANJI TATSUMI!
YOU ALL KNOW ME!
BAM
WH- WH-
WHAT THE HECK HAS HAPPENED TO THE TV WORLD!?
I MEAN, I GUESS WE SHOULD BE HAPPY THAT WE GUESSED RIGHT, BUT... THIS IS JUST...
CALM DOWN.
I ADMIT I'M A LITTLE WORRIED ABOUT...
WHAT MIGHT HAPPEN TO ME AND MY BODY IN THERE...
DO YOU THINK KANJI ACTUALLY IS...
JUST STOP RIGHT THERE.

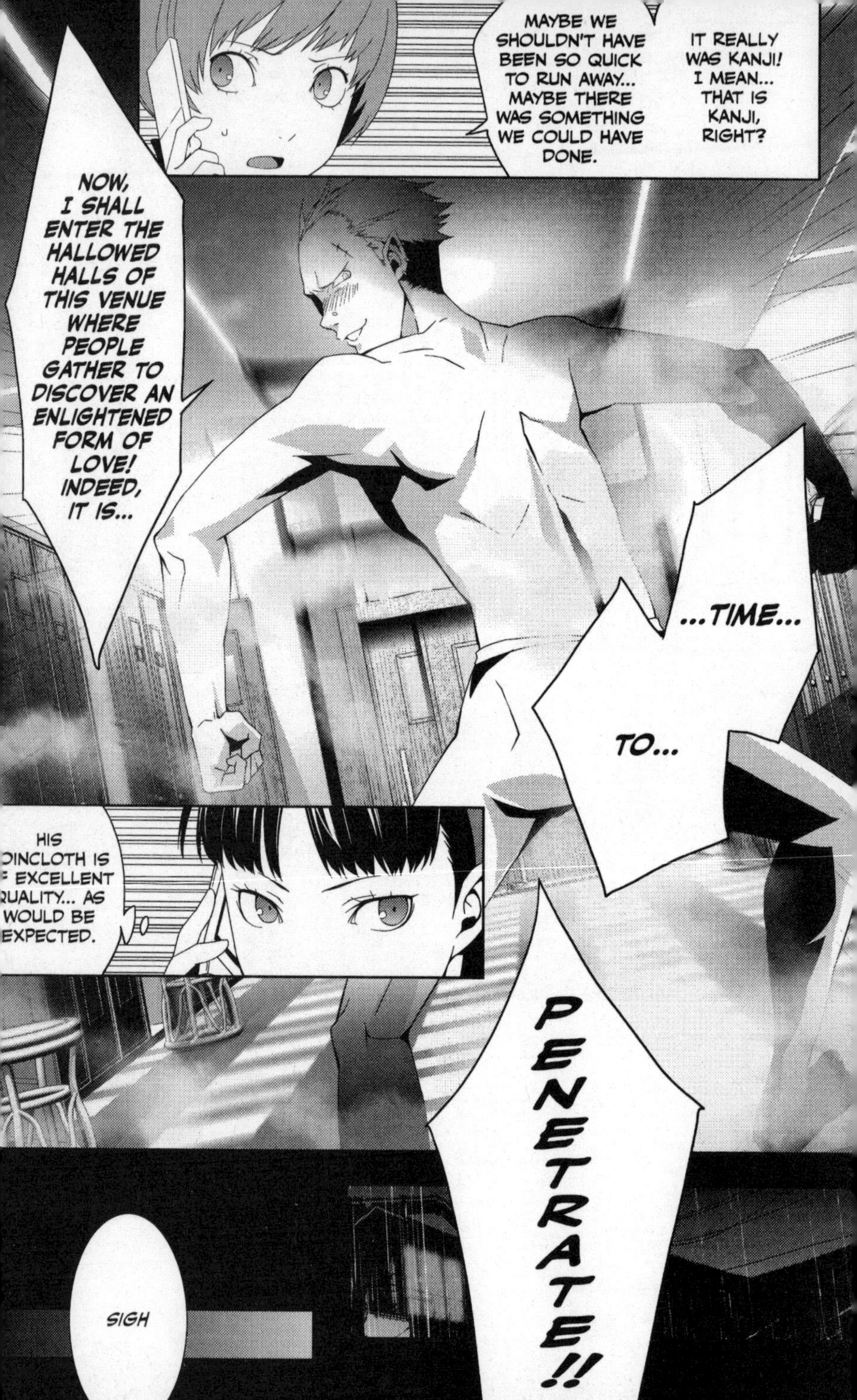
IT REALLY WAS KANJI! I MEAN... THAT IS KANJI, RIGHT?
MAYBE WE SHOULDN'T HAVE BEEN SO QUICK TO RUN AWAY... MAYBE THERE WAS SOMETHING WE COULD HAVE DONE.
NOW, I SHALL ENTER THE HALLOWED HALLS OF THIS VENUE WHERE PEOPLE GATHER TO DISCOVER AN ENLIGHTENED FORM OF LOVE! INDEED, IT IS...
...TIME...
TO...
PENETRATE!!
HIS OINCLOTH IS F EXCELLENT UALITY... AS WOULD BE EXPECTED.
SIGH

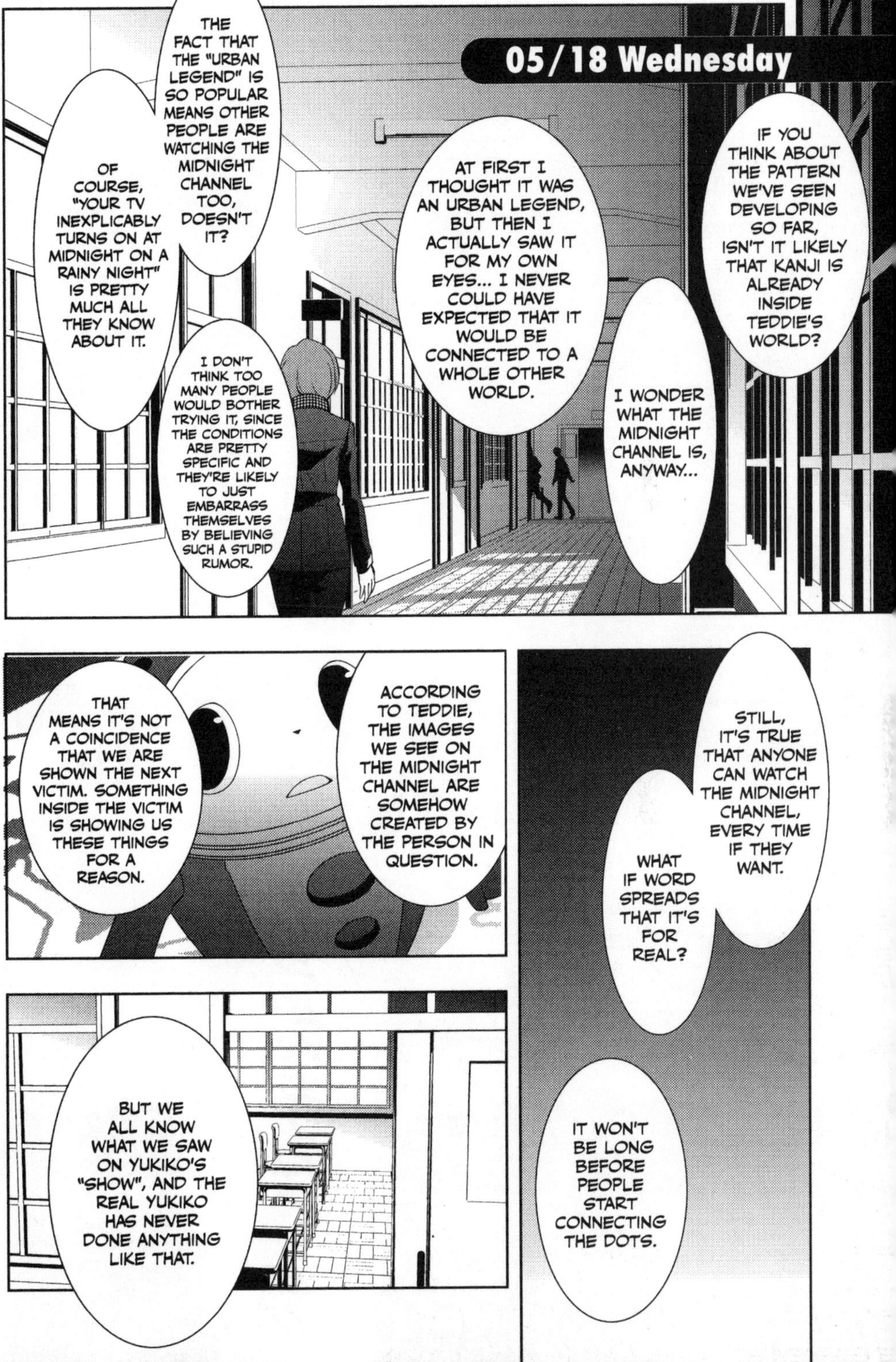
05/18 Wednesday
IF YOU THINK ABOUT THE PATTERN WE'VE SEEN DEVELOPING SO FAR, ISN'T IT LIKELY THAT KANJI IS ALREADY INSIDE TEDDIE'S WORLD?
I WONDER WHAT THE MIDNIGHT CHANNEL IS, ANYWAY...
AT FIRST I THOUGHT IT WAS AN URBAN LEGEND, BUT THEN I ACTUALLY SAW IT FOR MY OWN EYES... I NEVER COULD HAVE EXPECTED THAT IT WOULD BE CONNECTED TO A WHOLE OTHER WORLD.
THE FACT THAT THE "URBAN LEGEND" IS SO POPULAR MEANS OTHER PEOPLE ARE WATCHING THE MIDNIGHT CHANNEL TOO, DOESN'T IT?
OF COURSE, "YOUR TV INEXPLICABLY TURNS ON AT MIDNIGHT ON A RAINY NIGHT" IS PRETTY MUCH ALL THEY KNOW ABOUT IT.
I DON'T THINK TOO MANY PEOPLE WOULD BOTHER TRYING IT, SINCE THE CONDITIONS ARE PRETTY SPECIFIC AND THEY'RE LIKELY TO JUST EMBARRASS THEMSELVES BY BELIEVING SUCH A STUPID RUMOR.
STILL, IT'S TRUE THAT ANYONE CAN WATCH THE MIDNIGHT CHANNEL, EVERY TIME IF THEY WANT.
WHAT IF WORD SPREADS THAT IT'S FOR REAL?
IT WON'T BE LONG BEFORE PEOPLE START CONNECTING THE DOTS.
ACCORDING TO TEDDIE, THE IMAGES WE SEE ON THE MIDNIGHT CHANNEL ARE SOMEHOW CREATED BY THE PERSON IN QUESTION.
THAT MEANS IT'S NOT A COINCIDENCE THAT WE ARE SHOWN THE NEXT VICTIM. SOMETHING INSIDE THE VICTIM IS SHOWING US THESE THINGS FOR A REASON.
BUT WE ALL KNOW WHAT WE SAW ON YUKIKO'S "SHOW", AND THE REAL YUKIKO HAS NEVER DONE ANYTHING LIKE THAT.

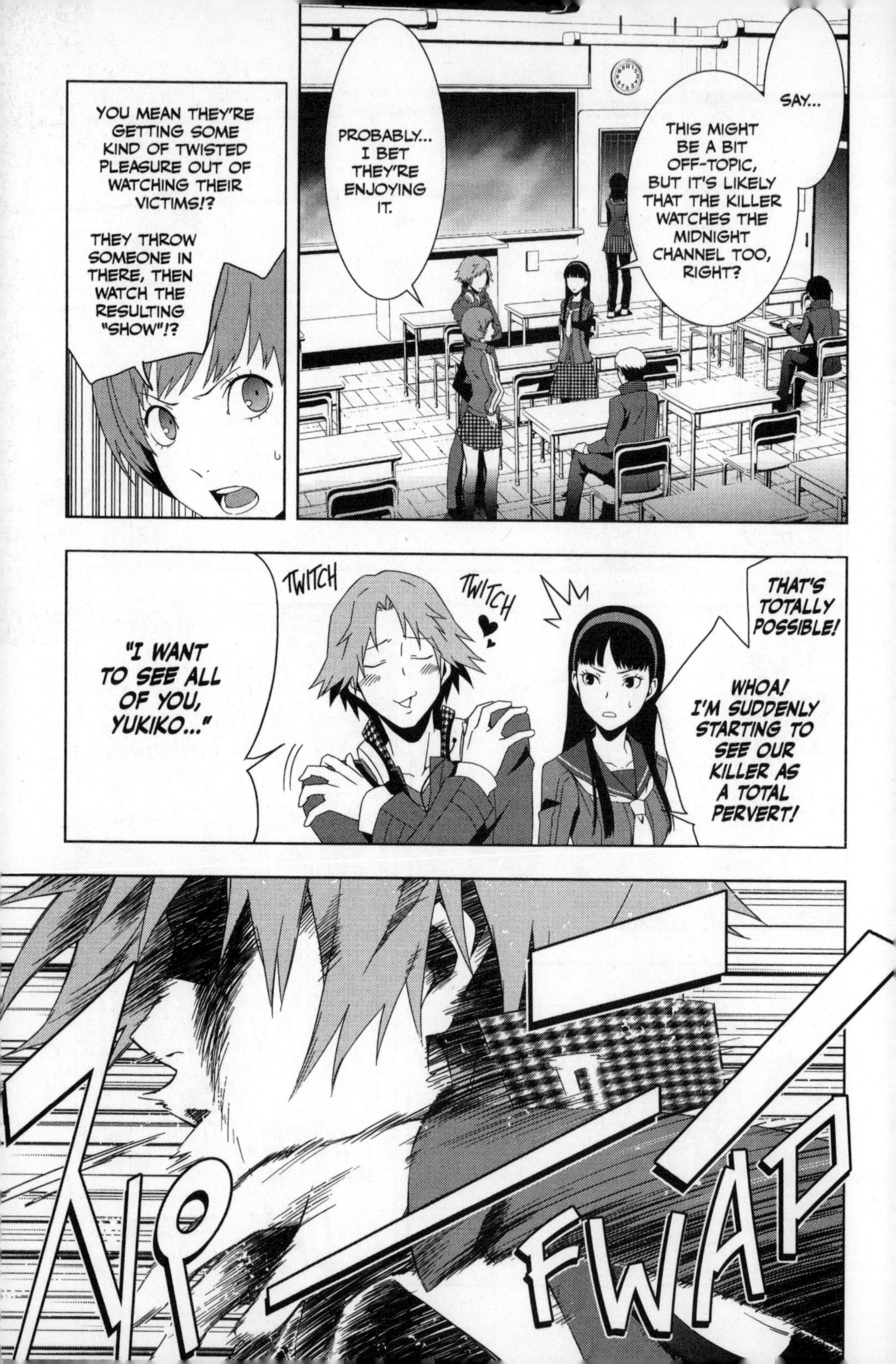
SAY...
THIS MIGHT BE A BIT OFF-TOPIC, BUT IT'S LIKELY THAT THE KILLER WATCHES THE MIDNIGHT CHANNEL TOO, RIGHT?
PROBABLY... I BET THEY'RE ENJOYING IT.
YOU MEAN THEY'RE GETTING SOME KIND OF TWISTED PLEASURE OUT OF WATCHING THEIR VICTIMS!?
THEY THROW SOMEONE IN THERE, THEN WATCH THE RESULTING "SHOW"!?
THAT'S TOTALLY POSSIBLE!
WHOA! I'M SUDDENLY STARTING TO SEE OUR KILLER AS A TOTAL PERVERT!
TWITCH
TWITCH
"I WANT TO SEE ALL OF YOU, YUKIKO..."
FWAP

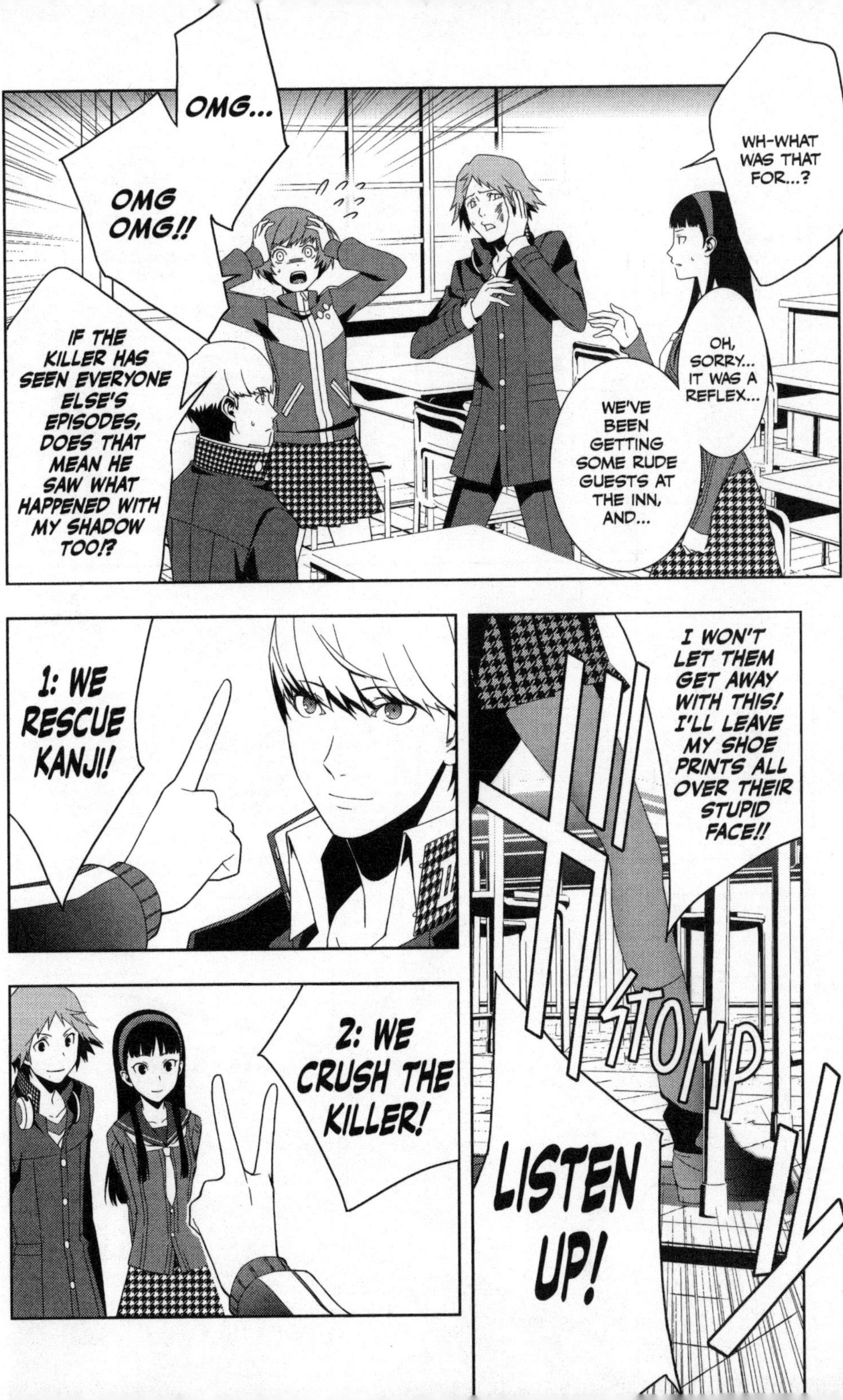
WH-WHAT WAS THAT FOR...?
OH, SORRY... IT WAS A REFLEX...
WE'VE BEEN GETTING SOME RUDE GUESTS AT THE INN, AND...
OMG...
OMG OMG!!
IF THE KILLER HAS SEEN EVERYONE ELSE'S EPISODES, DOES THAT MEAN HE SAW WHAT HAPPENED WITH MY SHADOW TOO!?
I WON'T LET THEM GET AWAY WITH THIS! I'LL LEAVE MY SHOE PRINTS ALL OVER THEIR STUPID FACE!!
STOMP
LISTEN UP!
1: WE RESCUE KANJI!
2: WE CRUSH THE KILLER!

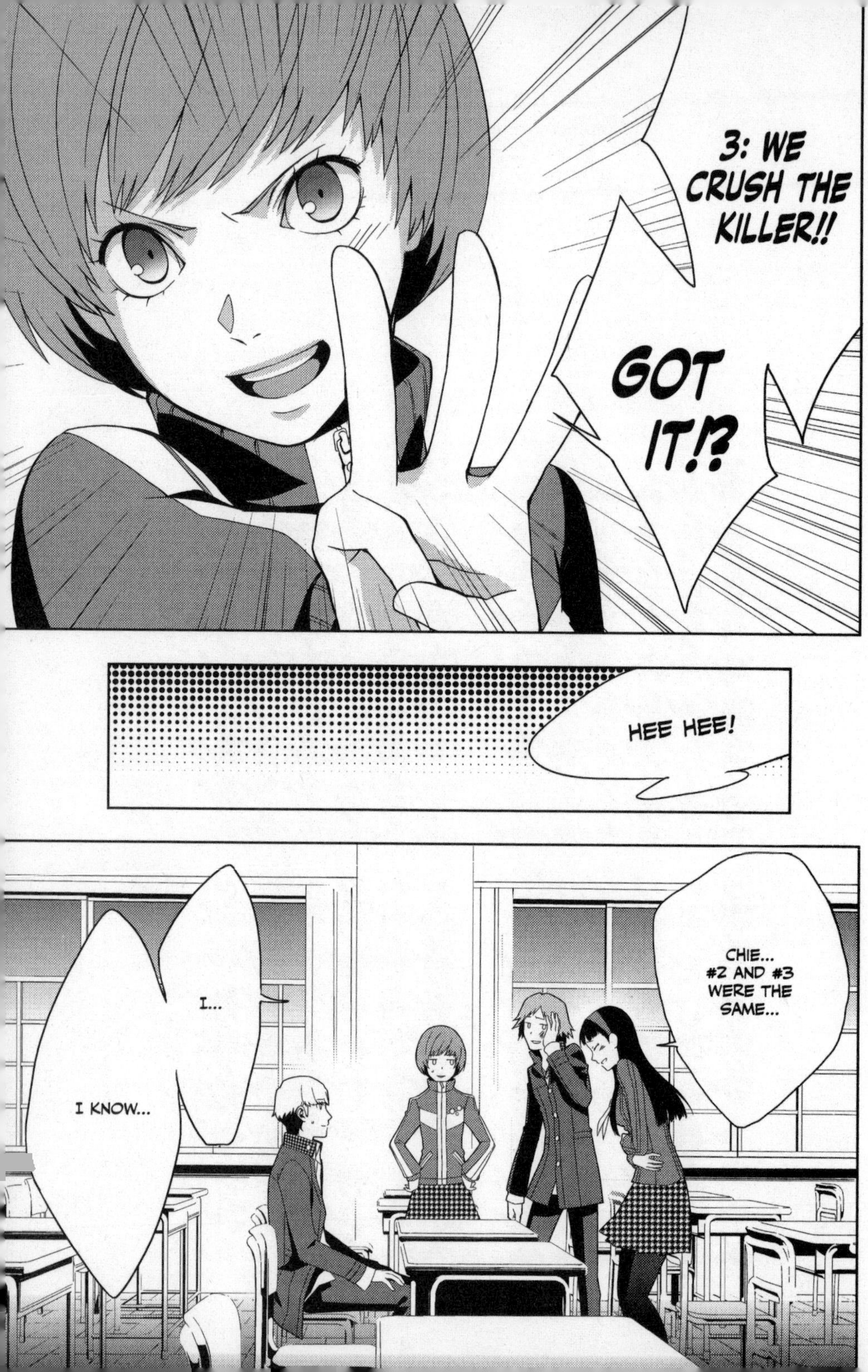
3: WE CRUSH THE KILLER!!
GOT IT!?
HEE HEE!
CHIE... #2 AND #3 WERE THE SAME...
I...
I KNOW...

Houndstooth pattern prototypes.
One of these was actually
used for the school uniforms.
Can you tell which one?

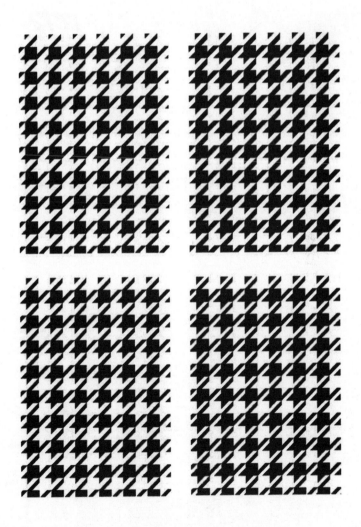

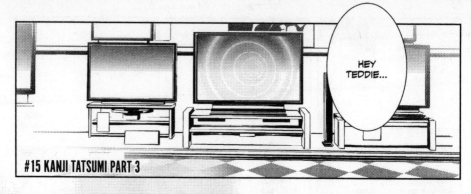

HEY TEDDIE...

#15 KANJI TATSUMI PART 3

05/18 Wednesday

SOMEONE NEW IS HERE, RIGHT?

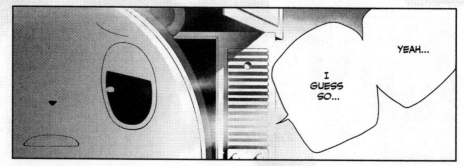

YEAH... I GUESS SO...

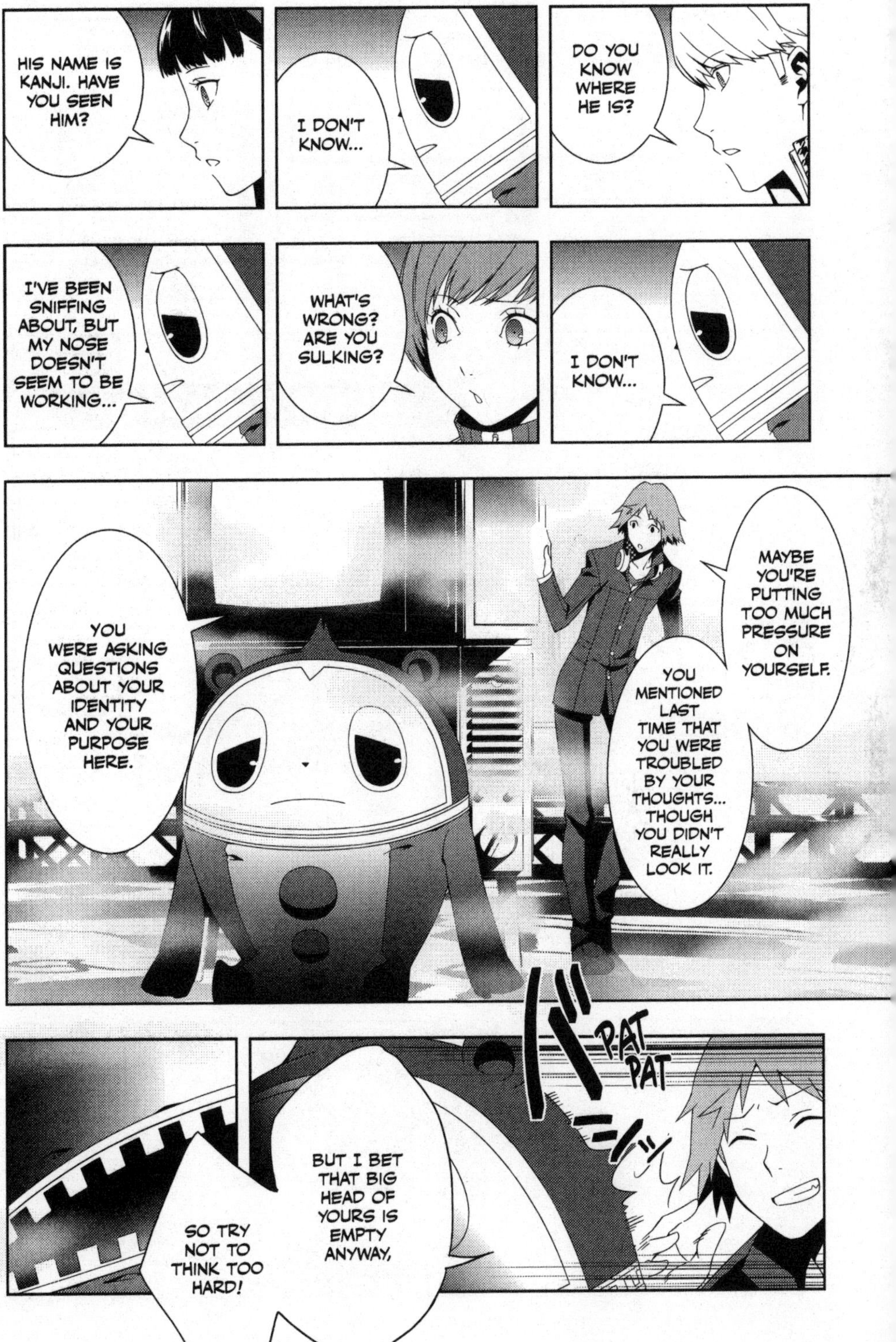
DO YOU KNOW WHERE HE IS?
I DON'T KNOW...
HIS NAME IS KANJI. HAVE YOU SEEN HIM?
I DON'T KNOW...
WHAT'S WRONG? ARE YOU SULKING?
I'VE BEEN SNIFFING ABOUT, BUT MY NOSE DOESN'T SEEM TO BE WORKING...
MAYBE YOU'RE PUTTING TOO MUCH PRESSURE ON YOURSELF.
YOU MENTIONED LAST TIME THAT YOU WERE TROUBLED BY YOUR THOUGHTS... THOUGH YOU DIDN'T REALLY LOOK IT.
YOU WERE ASKING QUESTIONS ABOUT YOUR IDENTITY AND YOUR PURPOSE HERE.
PAT PAT
BUT I BET THAT BIG HEAD OF YOURS IS EMPTY ANYWAY,
SO TRY NOT TO THINK TOO HARD!

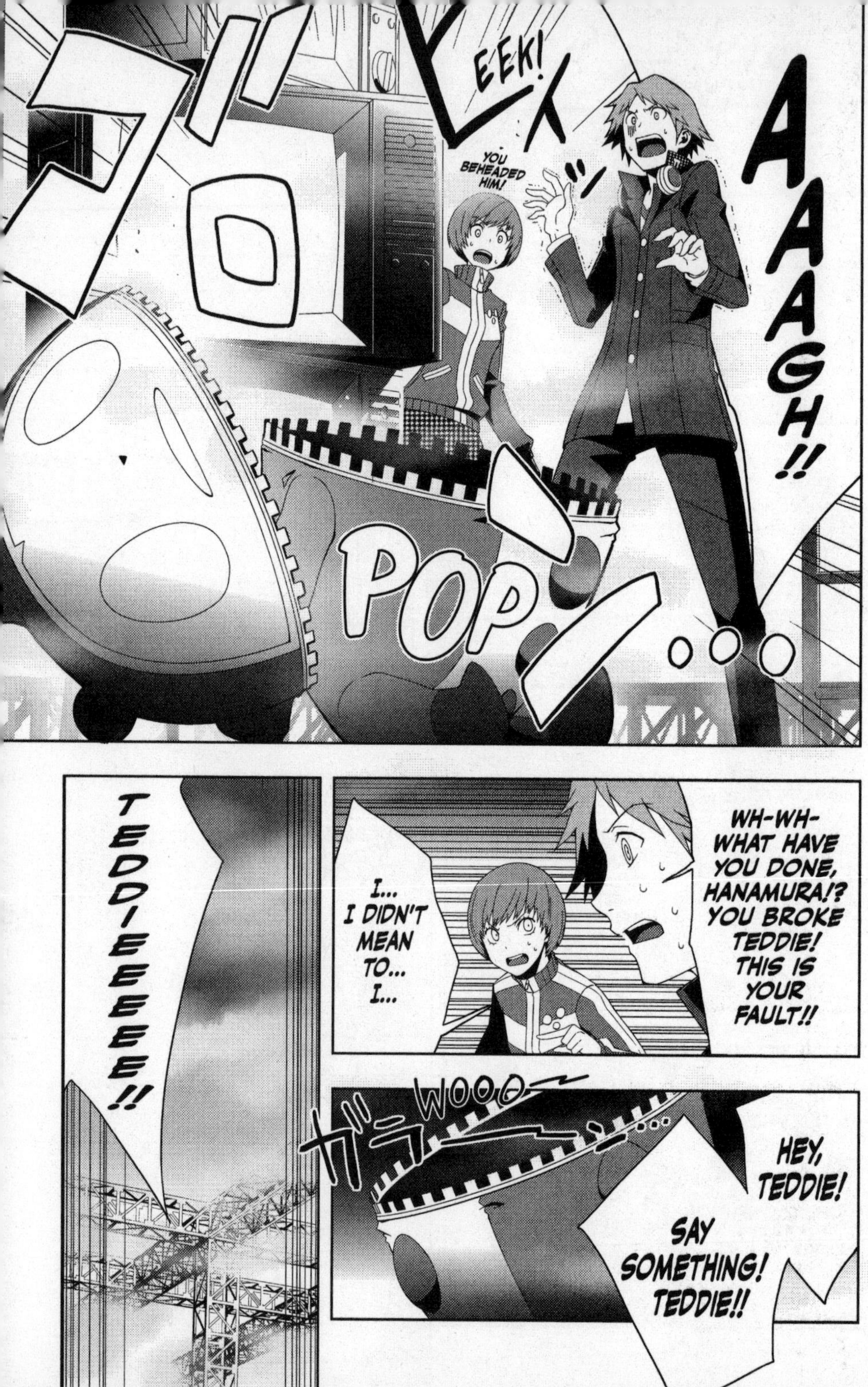
AAAGH!!
EEK!
YOU BEHEADED HIM!
POP
...
WH-WH-WHAT HAVE YOU DONE, HANAMURA!? YOU BROKE TEDDIE! THIS IS YOUR FAULT!!
I... I DIDN'T MEAN TO... I...
HEY, TEDDIE!
SAY SOMETHING! TEDDIE!!
WOOO—
TEDDIEEEEE!!

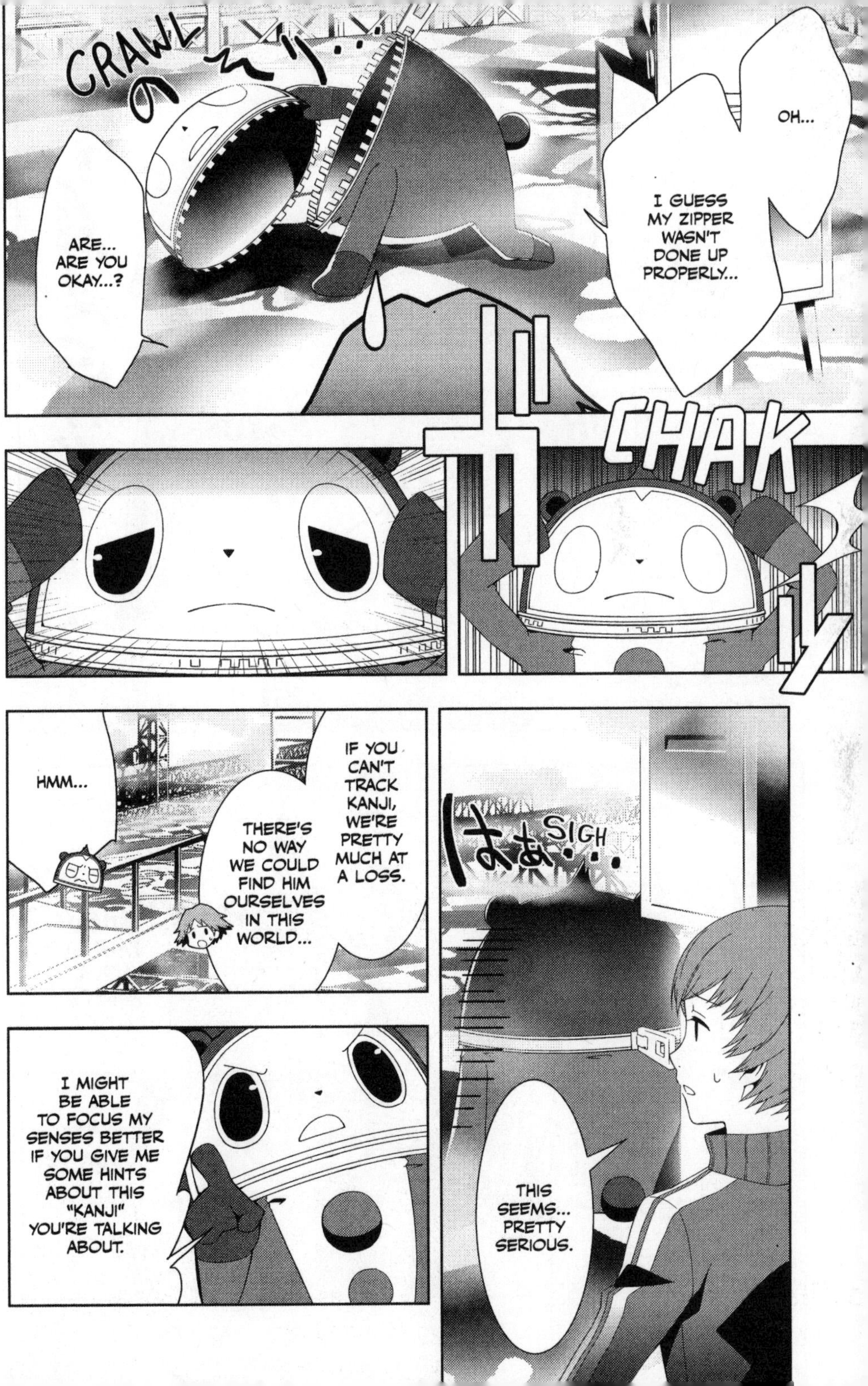
OH...
I GUESS MY ZIPPER WASN'T DONE UP PROPERLY...
CRAWL
ARE... ARE YOU OKAY...?
CHAK
SIGH
THIS SEEMS... PRETTY SERIOUS.
IF YOU CAN'T TRACK KANJI, WE'RE PRETTY MUCH AT A LOSS.
THERE'S NO WAY WE COULD FIND HIM OURSELVES IN THIS WORLD...
HMM...
I MIGHT BE ABLE TO FOCUS MY SENSES BETTER IF YOU GIVE ME SOME HINTS ABOUT THIS "KANJI" YOU'RE TALKING ABOUT.

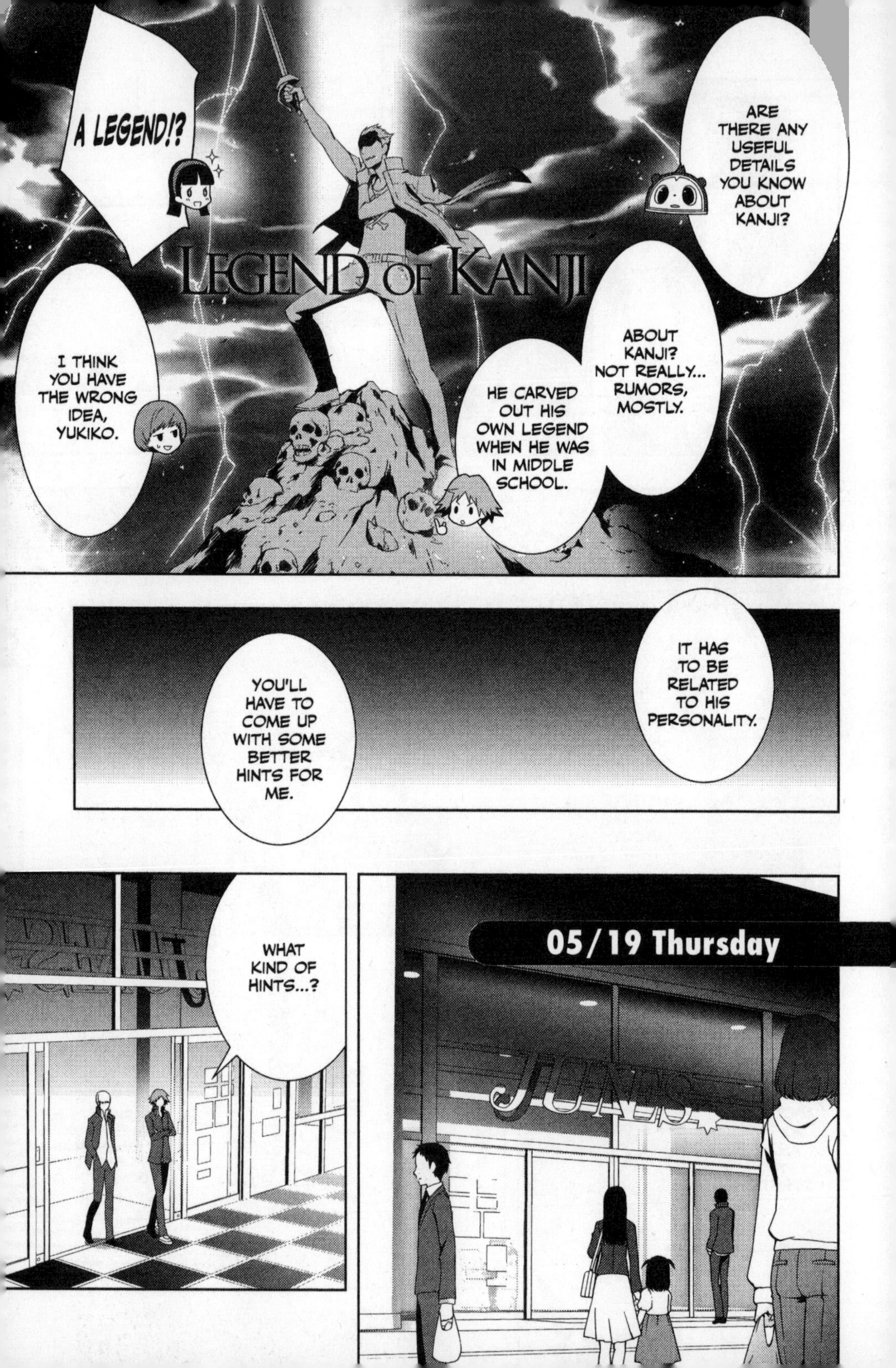
ARE THERE ANY USEFUL DETAILS YOU KNOW ABOUT KANJI?
ABOUT KANJI? NOT REALLY... RUMORS, MOSTLY.
HE CARVED OUT HIS OWN LEGEND WHEN HE WAS IN MIDDLE SCHOOL.
A LEGEND!?
LEGEND OF KANJI
I THINK YOU HAVE THE WRONG IDEA, YUKIKO.
IT HAS TO BE RELATED TO HIS PERSONALITY.
YOU'LL HAVE TO COME UP WITH SOME BETTER HINTS FOR ME.
05/19 Thursday
WHAT KIND OF HINTS...?

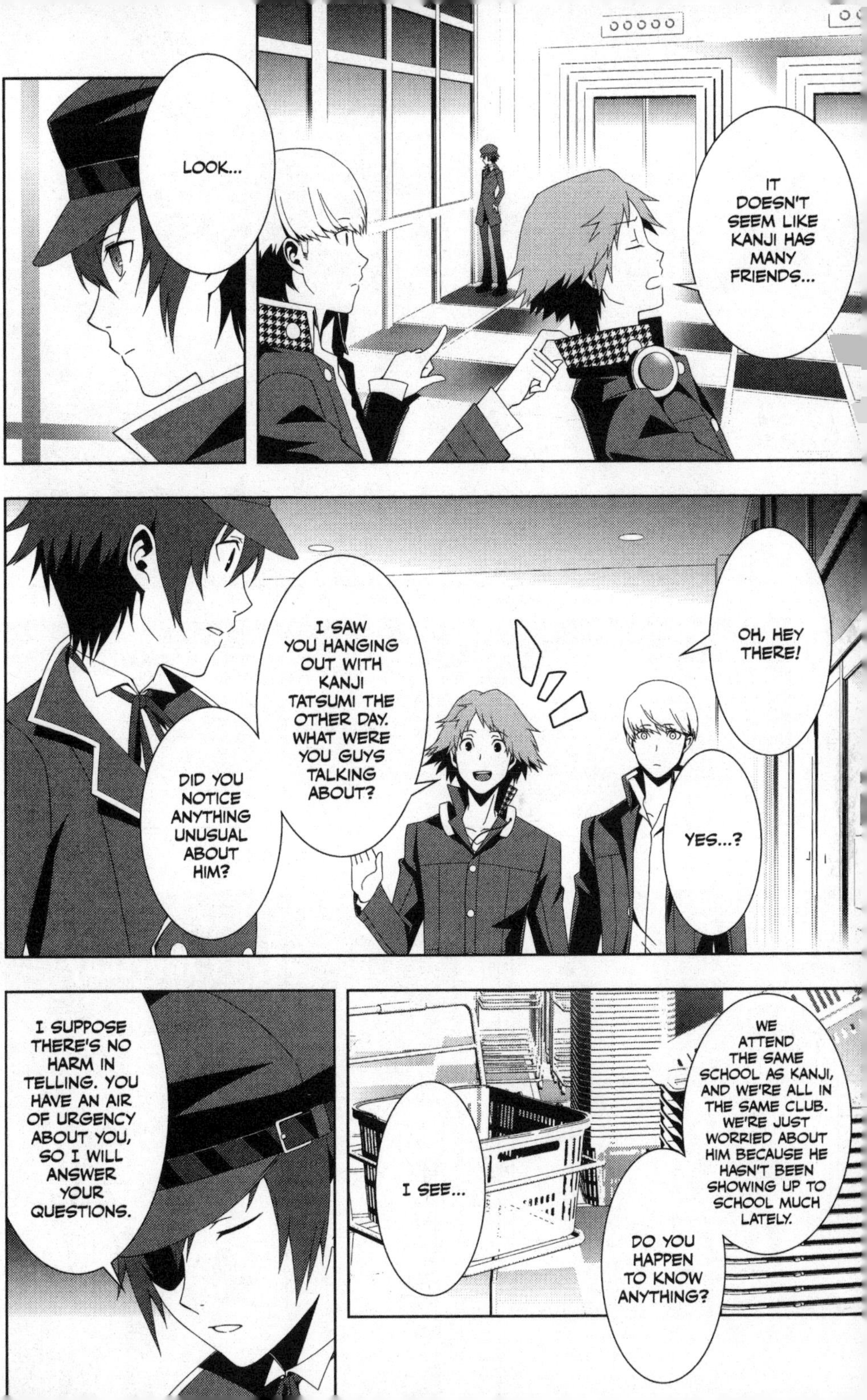
IT DOESN'T SEEM LIKE KANJI HAS MANY FRIENDS...
LOOK...
OH, HEY THERE!
YES...?
I SAW YOU HANGING OUT WITH KANJI TATSUMI THE OTHER DAY. WHAT WERE YOU GUYS TALKING ABOUT?
DID YOU NOTICE ANYTHING UNUSUAL ABOUT HIM?
WE ATTEND THE SAME SCHOOL AS KANJI, AND WE'RE ALL IN THE SAME CLUB. WE'RE JUST WORRIED ABOUT HIM BECAUSE HE HASN'T BEEN SHOWING UP TO SCHOOL MUCH LATELY.
DO YOU HAPPEN TO KNOW ANYTHING?
I SEE...
I SUPPOSE THERE'S NO HARM IN TELLING. YOU HAVE AN AIR OF URGENCY ABOUT YOU, SO I WILL ANSWER YOUR QUESTIONS.

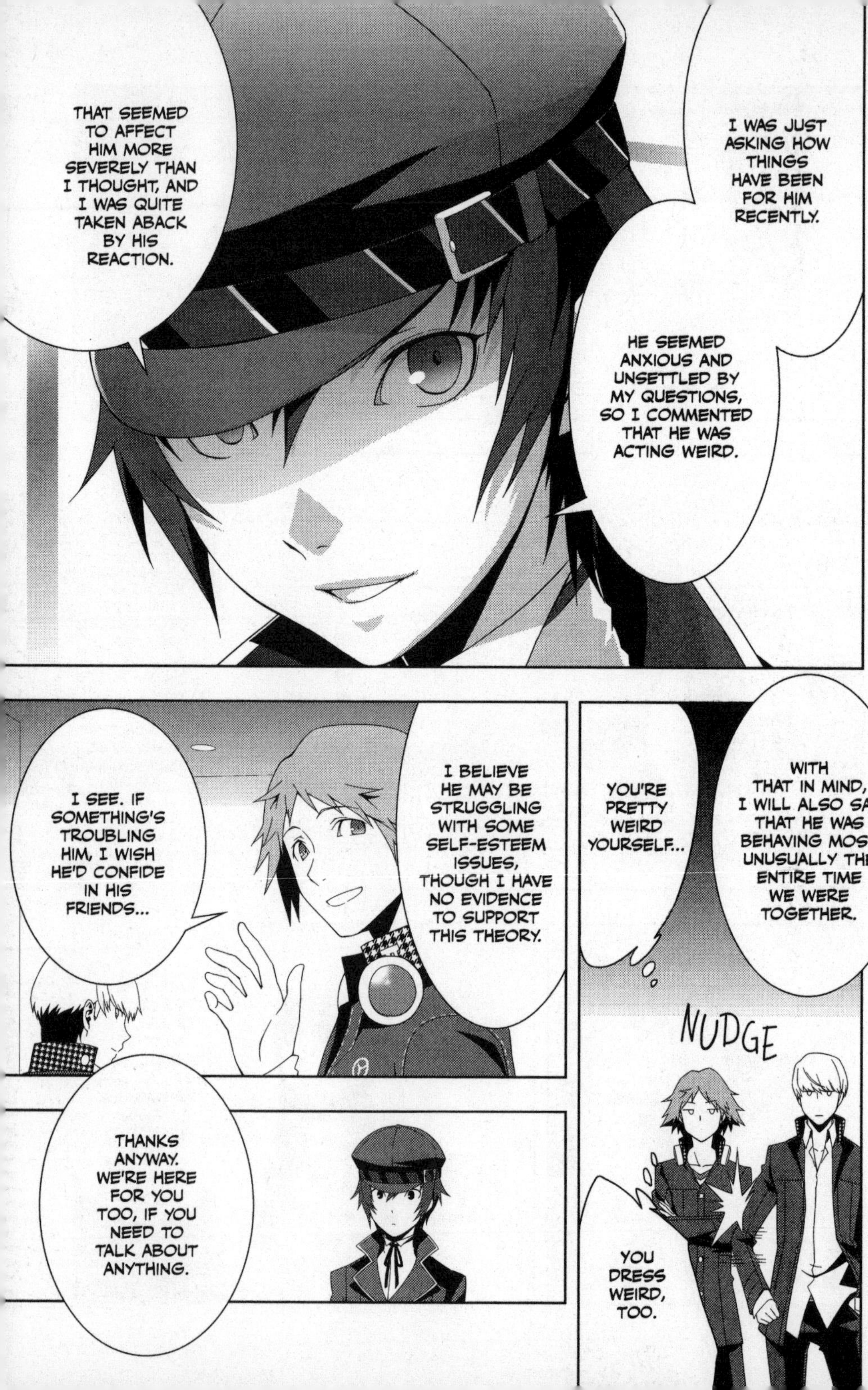
I WAS JUST ASKING HOW THINGS HAVE BEEN FOR HIM RECENTLY.
HE SEEMED ANXIOUS AND UNSETTLED BY MY QUESTIONS, SO I COMMENTED THAT HE WAS ACTING WEIRD.
THAT SEEMED TO AFFECT HIM MORE SEVERELY THAN I THOUGHT, AND I WAS QUITE TAKEN ABACK BY HIS REACTION.
WITH THAT IN MIND, I WILL ALSO SAY THAT HE WAS BEHAVING MOST UNUSUALLY THE ENTIRE TIME WE WERE TOGETHER.
YOU'RE PRETTY WEIRD YOURSELF...
NUDGE
YOU DRESS WEIRD, TOO.
I BELIEVE HE MAY BE STRUGGLING WITH SOME SELF-ESTEEM ISSUES, THOUGH I HAVE NO EVIDENCE TO SUPPORT THIS THEORY.
I SEE. IF SOMETHING'S TROUBLING HIM, I WISH HE'D CONFIDE IN HIS FRIENDS...
THANKS ANYWAY. WE'RE HERE FOR YOU TOO, IF YOU NEED TO TALK ABOUT ANYTHING.

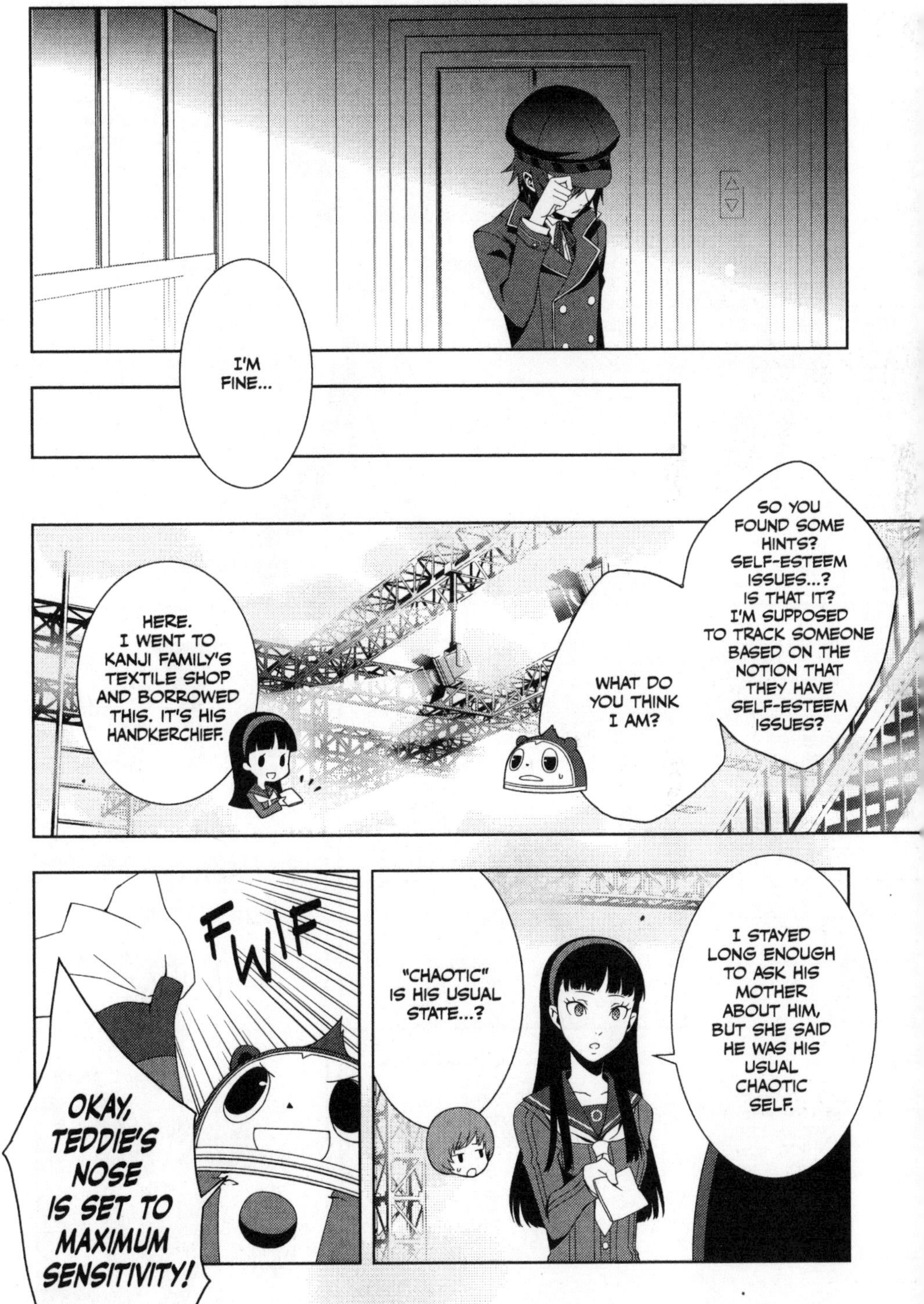
I'M FINE...
SO YOU FOUND SOME HINTS? SELF-ESTEEM ISSUES...? IS THAT IT? I'M SUPPOSED TO TRACK SOMEONE BASED ON THE NOTION THAT THEY HAVE SELF-ESTEEM ISSUES?
WHAT DO YOU THINK I AM?
HERE. I WENT TO KANJI FAMILY'S TEXTILE SHOP AND BORROWED THIS. IT'S HIS HANDKERCHIEF.
I STAYED LONG ENOUGH TO ASK HIS MOTHER ABOUT HIM, BUT SHE SAID HE WAS HIS USUAL CHAOTIC SELF.
"CHAOTIC" IS HIS USUAL STATE...?
FWIF
OKAY, TEDDIE'S NOSE IS SET TO MAXIMUM SENSITIVITY!

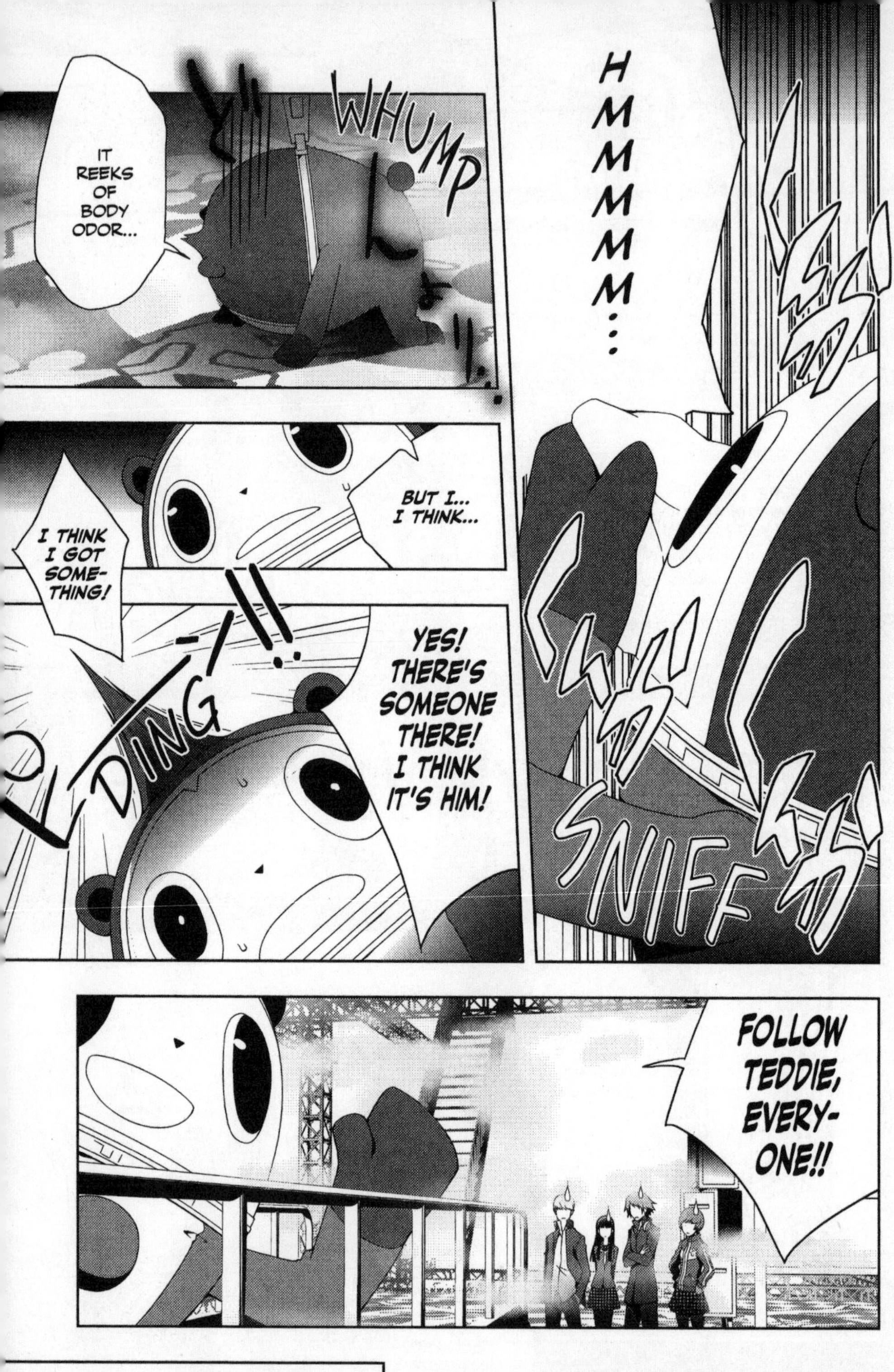
HMMMMM...
SNIFF
IT REEKS OF BODY ODOR...
WHUMP
BUT I... I THINK...
I THINK I GOT SOME-THING!
DING
YES! THERE'S SOMEONE THERE! I THINK IT'S HIM!
FOLLOW TEDDIE, EVERY-ONE!!

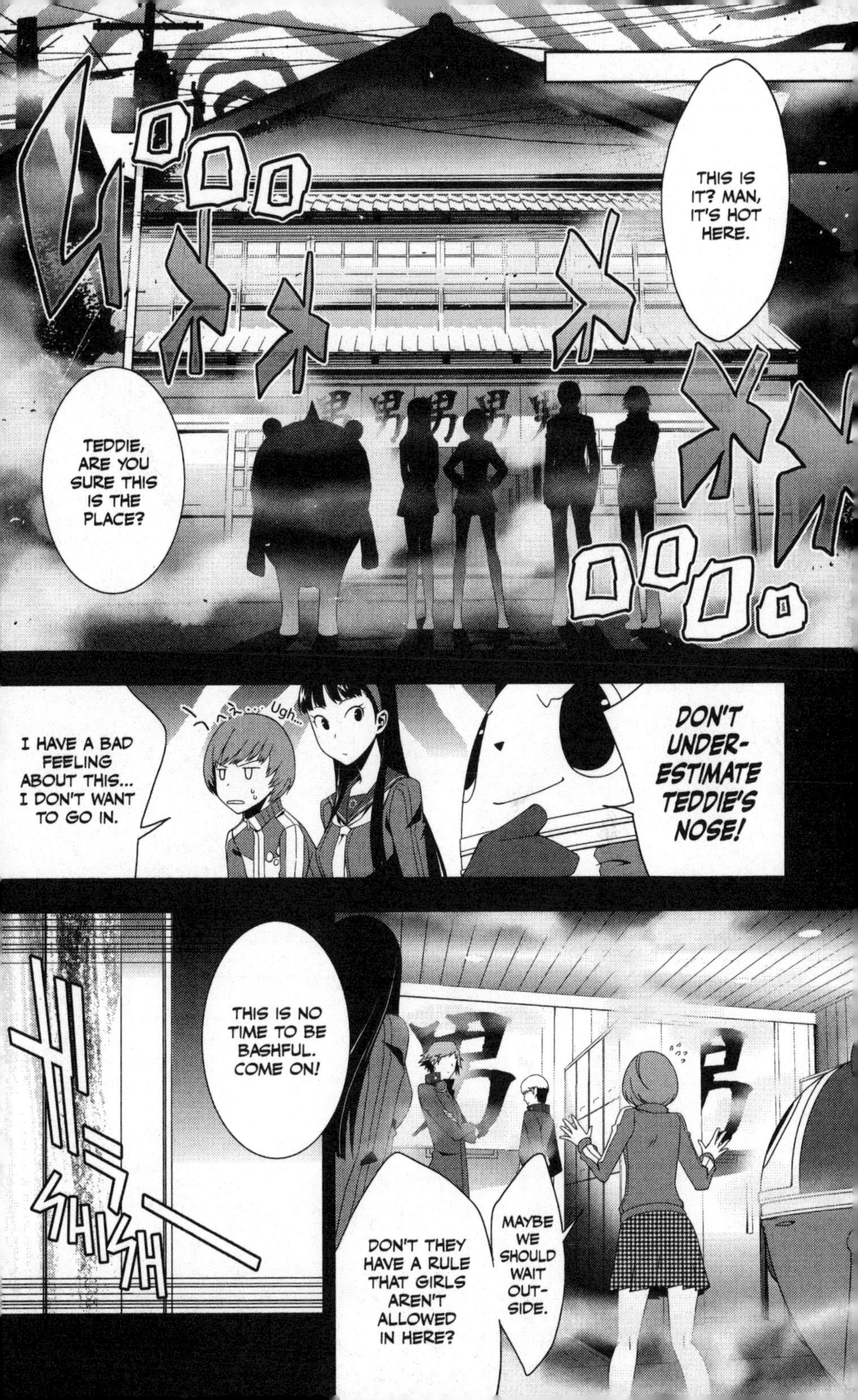
THIS IS IT? MAN, IT'S HOT HERE.
TEDDIE, ARE YOU SURE THIS IS THE PLACE?
DON'T UNDER-ESTIMATE TEDDIE'S NOSE!
Ugh...
I HAVE A BAD FEELING ABOUT THIS... I DON'T WANT TO GO IN.
THIS IS NO TIME TO BE BASHFUL. COME ON!
MAYBE WE SHOULD WAIT OUT-SIDE.
DON'T THEY HAVE A RULE THAT GIRLS AREN'T ALLOWED IN HERE?
SHISH

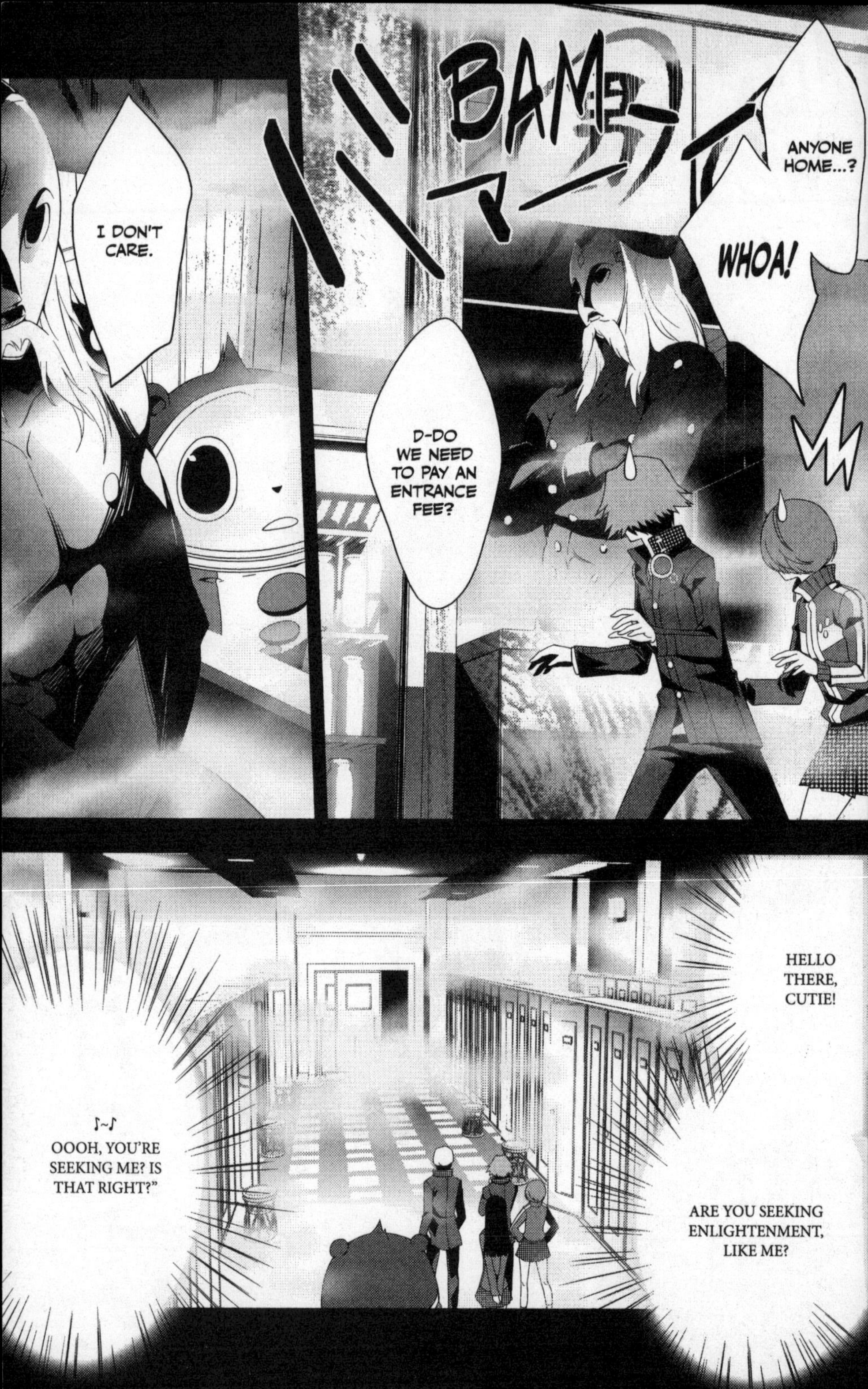
ANYONE HOME...?
BAM
WHOA!
D-DO WE NEED TO PAY AN ENTRANCE FEE?
I DON'T CARE.
HELLO THERE, CUTIE!
ARE YOU SEEKING ENLIGHTENMENT, LIKE ME?
♪~♪
OOOH, YOU'RE SEEKING ME? IS THAT RIGHT?"

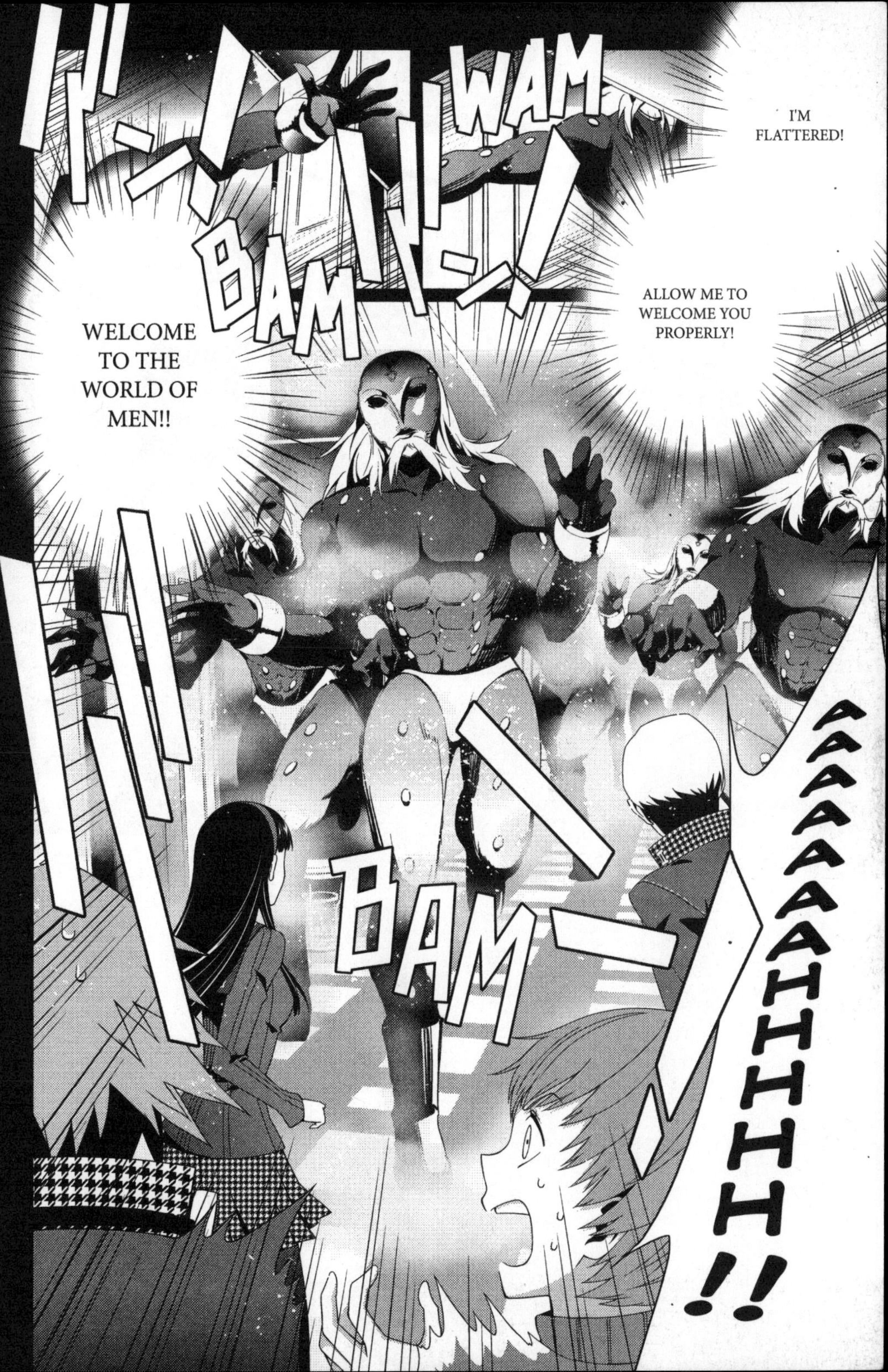
I'M FLATTERED!
WAM
ALLOW ME TO WELCOME YOU PROPERLY!
BAM
WELCOME TO THE WORLD OF MEN!!
AAAAAAAHHHHHH!!
BAM

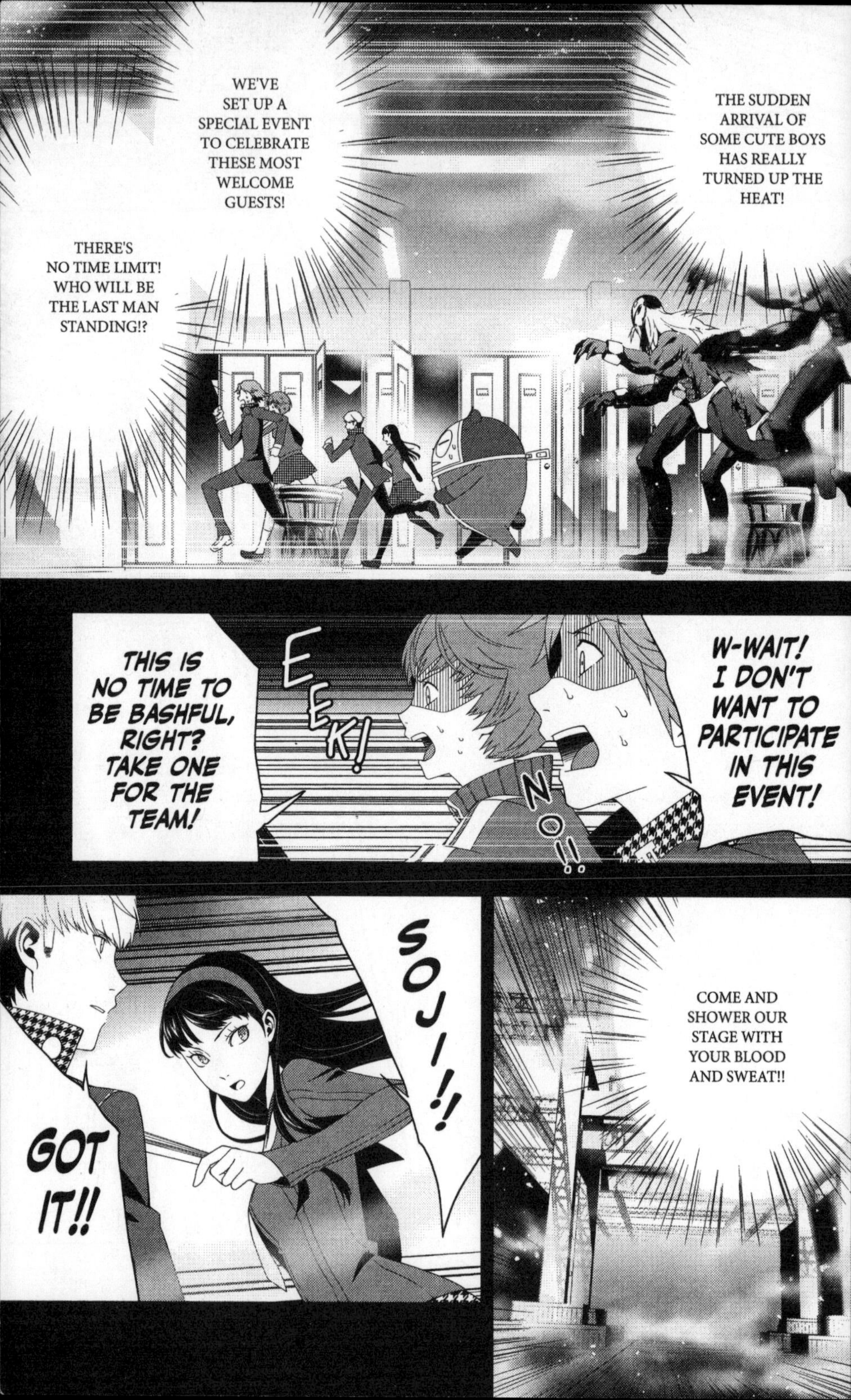
THE SUDDEN ARRIVAL OF SOME CUTE BOYS HAS REALLY TURNED UP THE HEAT!
WE'VE SET UP A SPECIAL EVENT TO CELEBRATE THESE MOST WELCOME GUESTS!
THERE'S NO TIME LIMIT! WHO WILL BE THE LAST MAN STANDING!?
W-WAIT! I DON'T WANT TO PARTICIPATE IN THIS EVENT!
NO!!
EEK!
THIS IS NO TIME TO BE BASHFUL, RIGHT? TAKE ONE FOR THE TEAM!
COME AND SHOWER OUR STAGE WITH YOUR BLOOD AND SWEAT!!
SOJI!!!
GOT IT!!

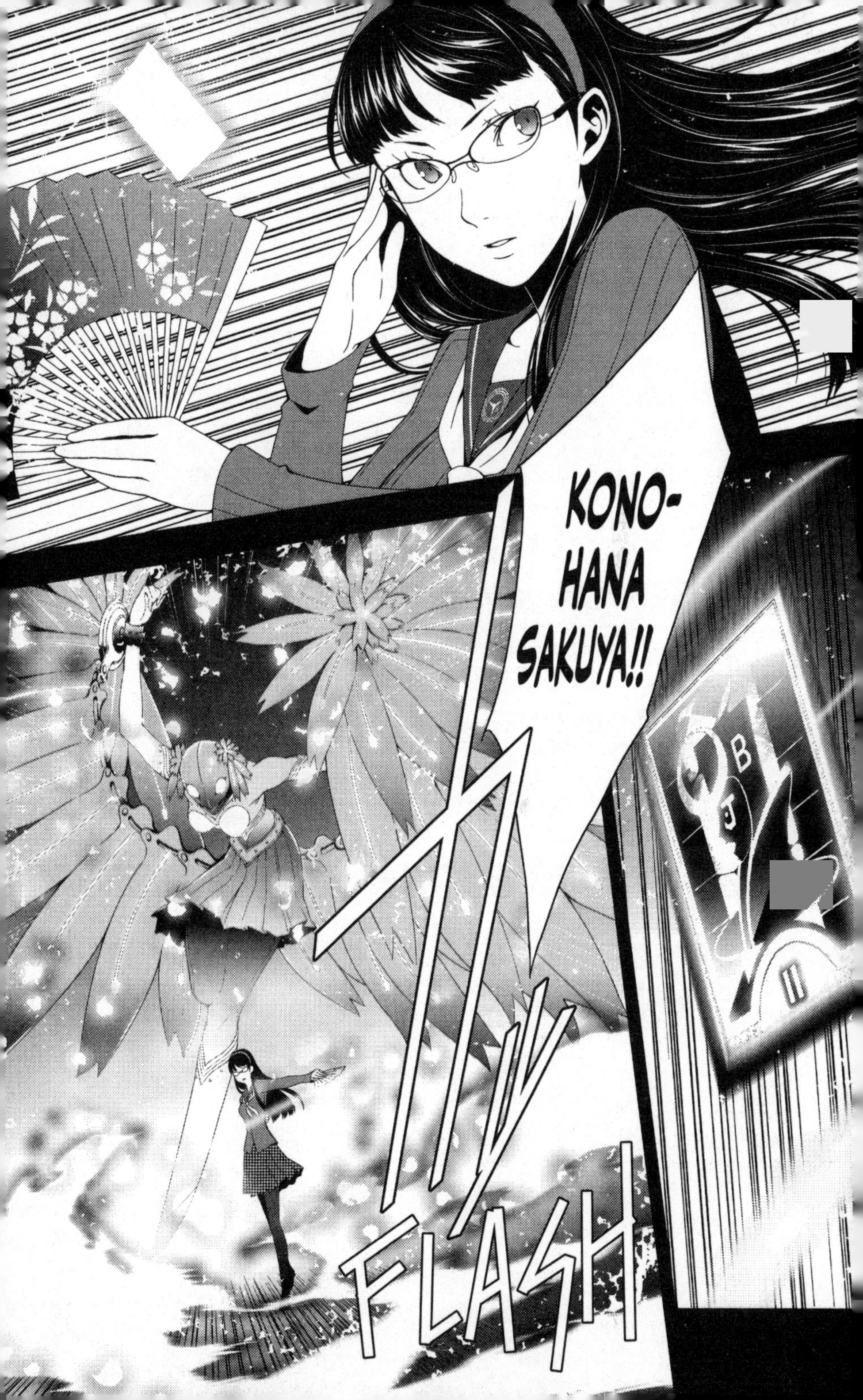
KONO-
HANA
SAKUYA!!
FLASH

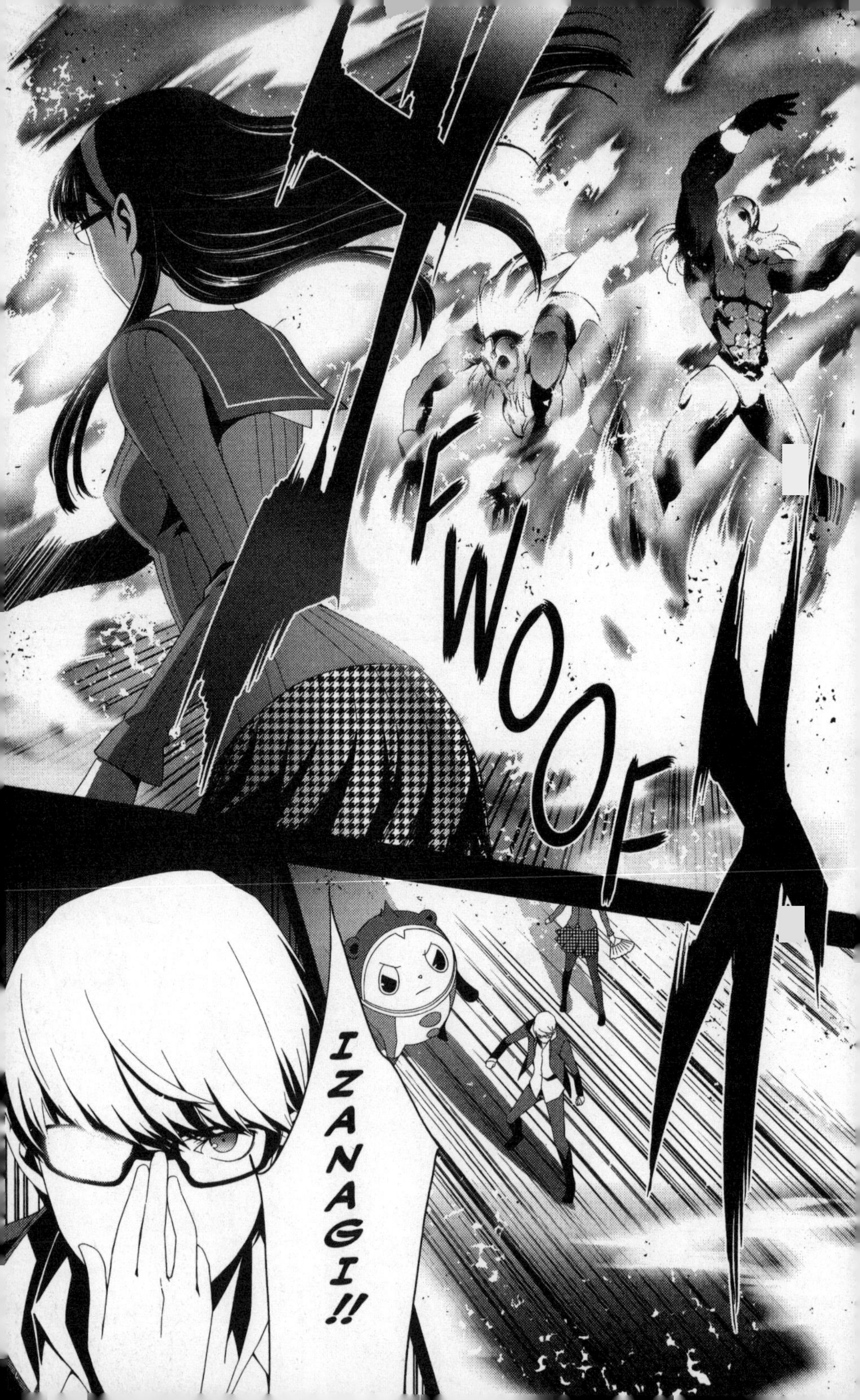
FWOOF
IZANAGI!!

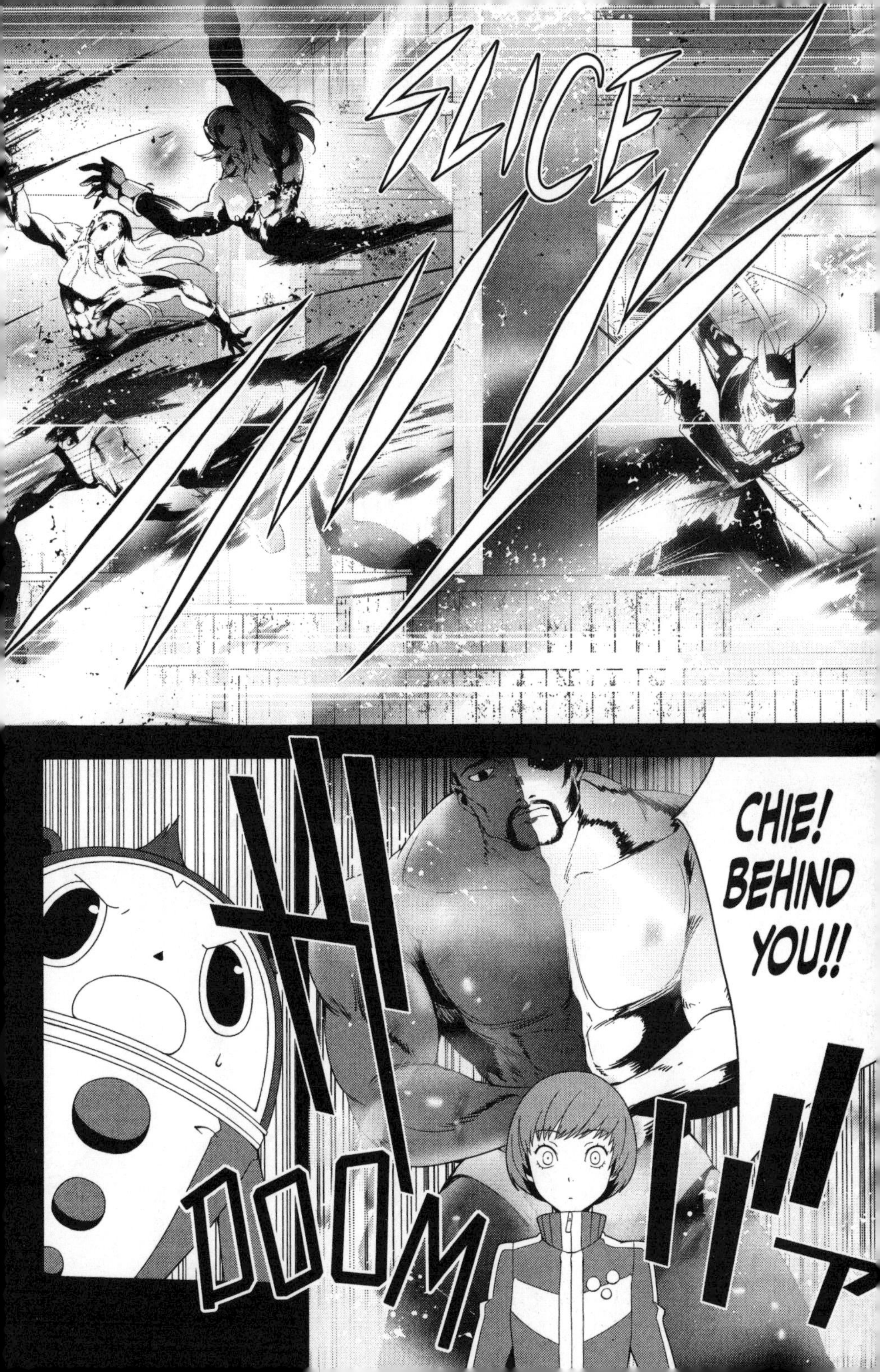
SLICE
CHIE! BEHIND YOU!!
DOOM

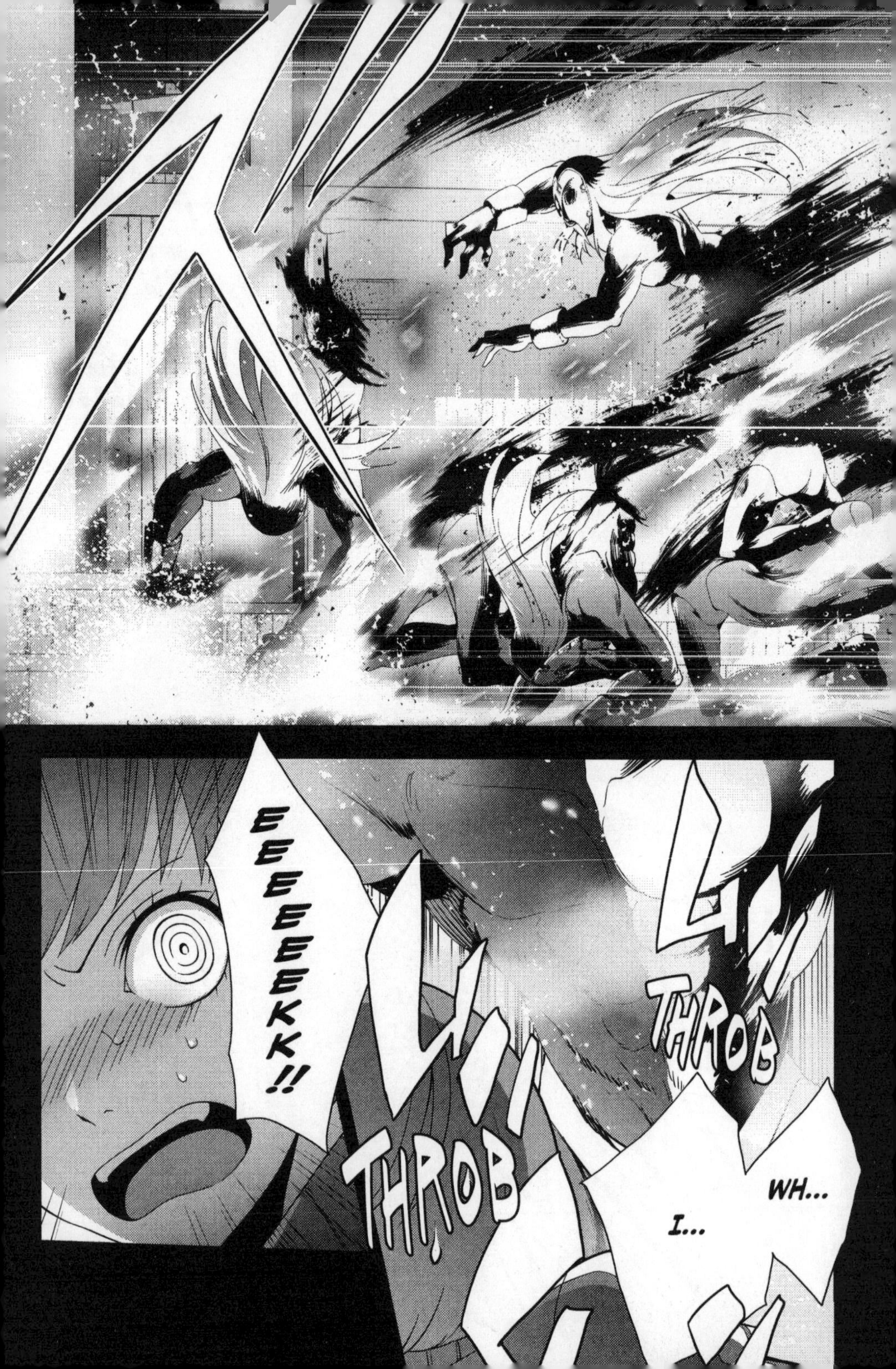
EEEEEEEKK!!
THROB
THROB
WH...
I...

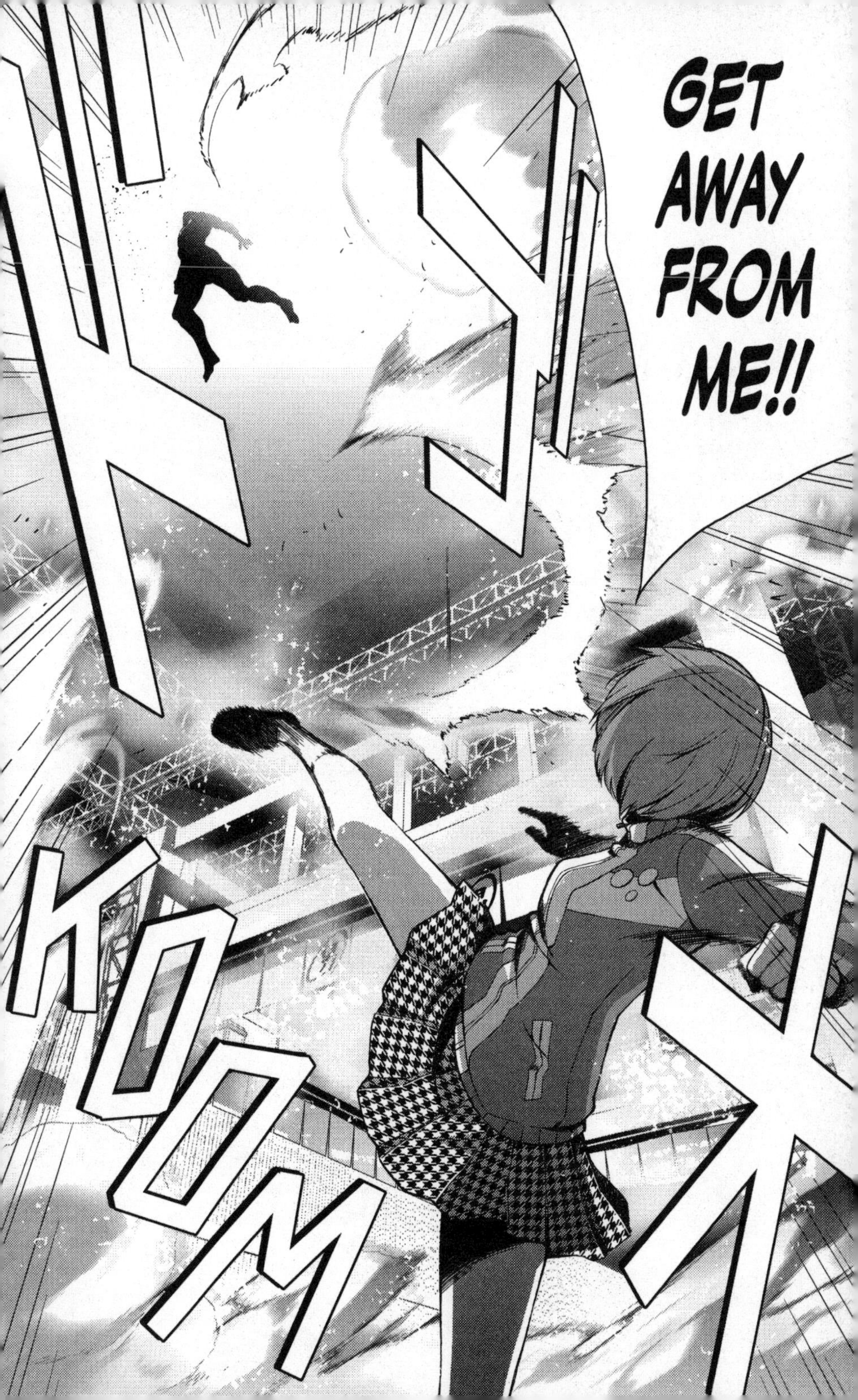
GET AWAY FROM ME!!
KOOM

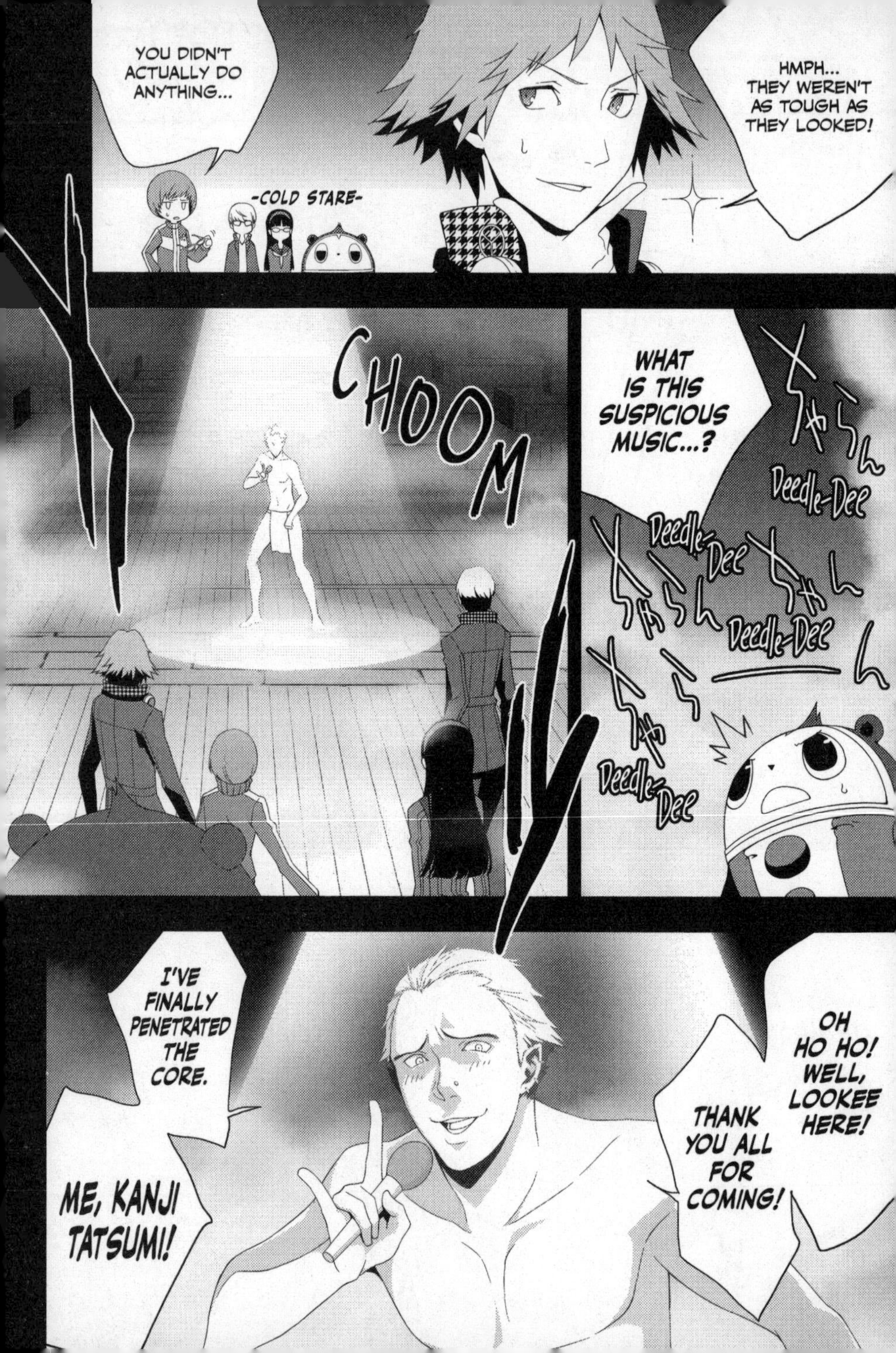
HMPH... THEY WEREN'T AS TOUGH AS THEY LOOKED!
YOU DIDN'T ACTUALLY DO ANYTHING...
-COLD STARE-
WHAT IS THIS SUSPICIOUS MUSIC...?
Deedle-Dee
Deedle-Dee
Deedle-Dee
Deedle-Dee
CHOOM
OH HO HO! WELL, LOOKEE HERE!
THANK YOU ALL FOR COMING!
I'VE FINALLY PENETRATED THE CORE.
ME, KANJI TATSUMI!

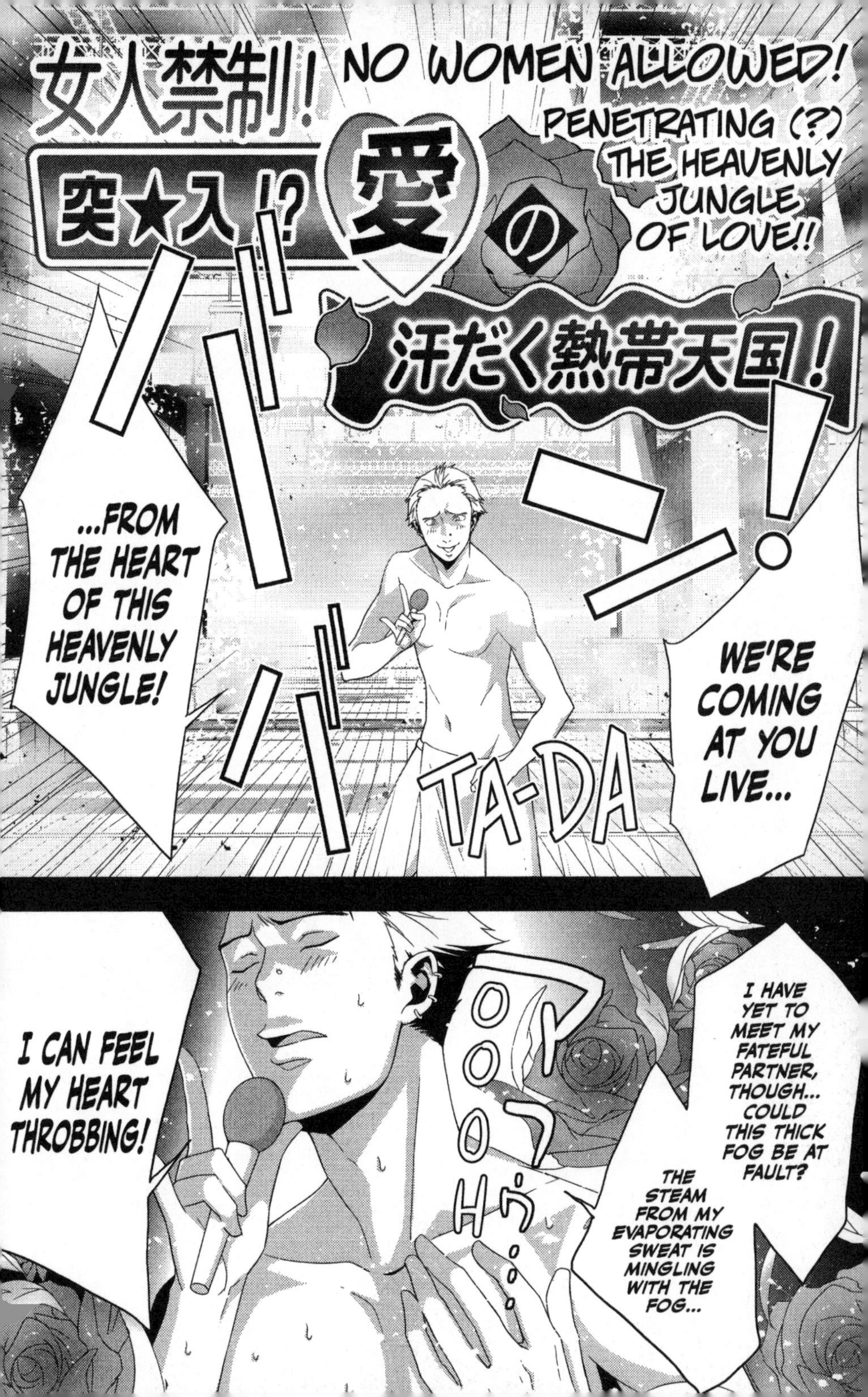
女人禁制!
突★入!? 愛の汗だく熱帯天国!
NO WOMEN ALLOWED!
PENETRATING (?) THE HEAVENLY JUNGLE OF LOVE!!
WE'RE COMING AT YOU LIVE...
...FROM THE HEART OF THIS HEAVENLY JUNGLE!
TA-DA
I HAVE YET TO MEET MY FATEFUL PARTNER, THOUGH... COULD THIS THICK FOG BE AT FAULT?
THE STEAM FROM MY EVAPORATING SWEAT IS MINGLING WITH THE FOG...
OOOOH
I CAN FEEL MY HEART THROBBING!

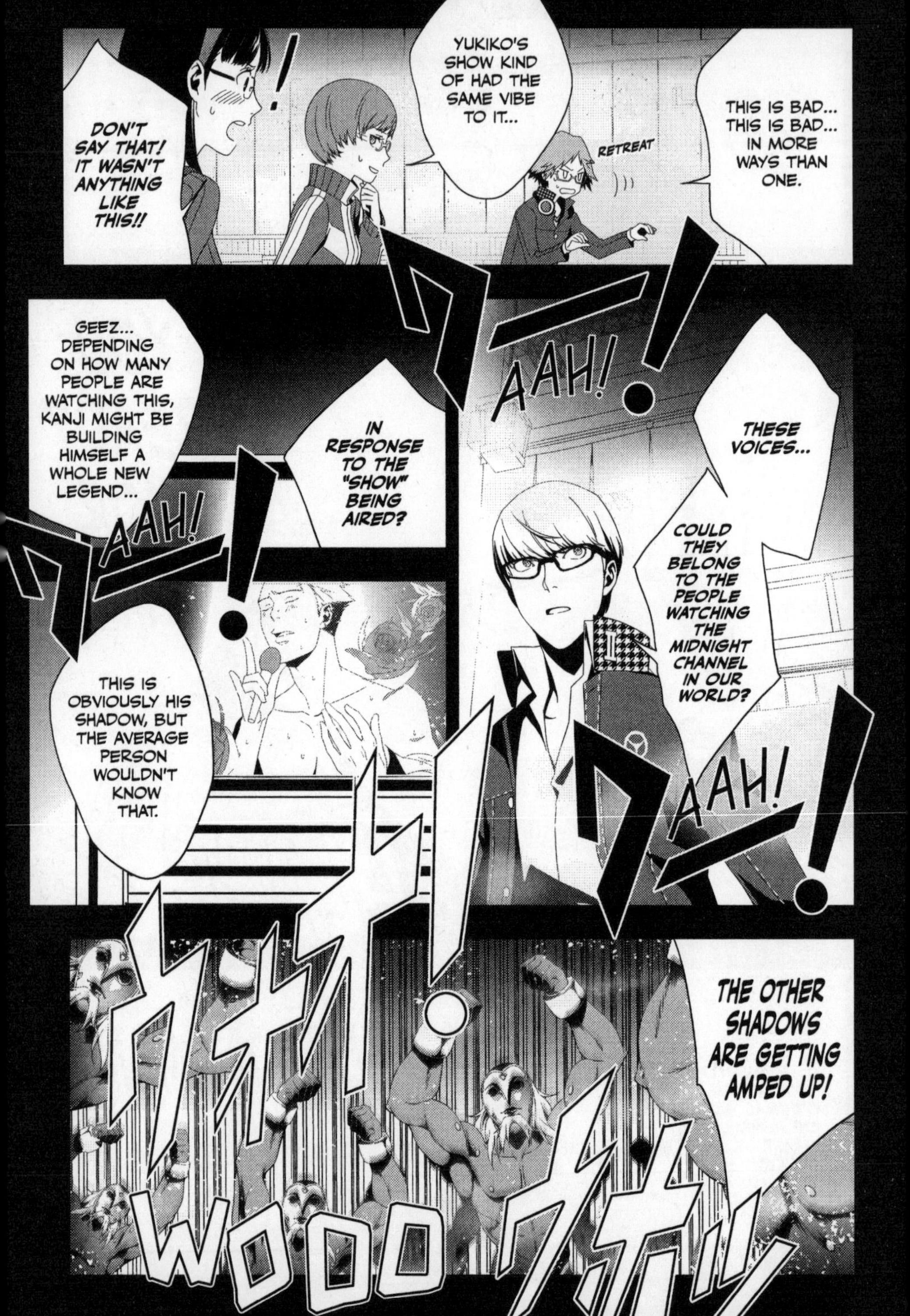
THIS IS BAD... THIS IS BAD... IN MORE WAYS THAN ONE.
RETREAT
YUKIKO'S SHOW KIND OF HAD THE SAME VIBE TO IT...
!
DON'T SAY THAT! IT WASN'T ANYTHING LIKE THIS!!
AAH!
THESE VOICES...
COULD THEY BELONG TO THE PEOPLE WATCHING THE MIDNIGHT CHANNEL IN OUR WORLD?
AAH!
IN RESPONSE TO THE "SHOW" BEING AIRED?
GEEZ... DEPENDING ON HOW MANY PEOPLE ARE WATCHING THIS, KANJI MIGHT BE BUILDING HIMSELF A WHOLE NEW LEGEND...
AAH!
THIS IS OBVIOUSLY HIS SHADOW, BUT THE AVERAGE PERSON WOULDN'T KNOW THAT.
THE OTHER SHADOWS ARE GETTING AMPED UP!
WOOO

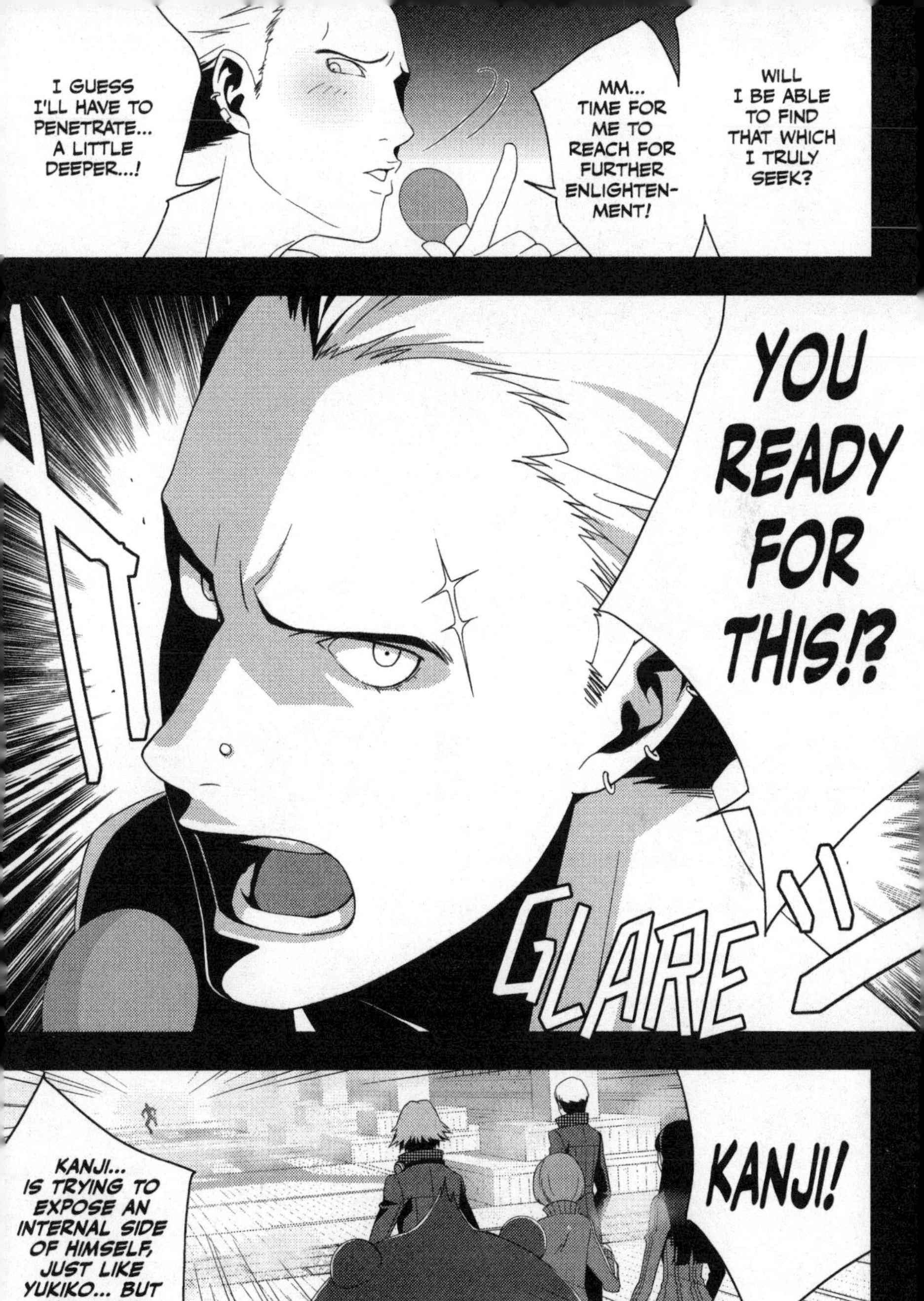
WILL I BE ABLE TO FIND THAT WHICH I TRULY SEEK?
MM... TIME FOR ME TO REACH FOR FURTHER ENLIGHTEN-MENT!
I GUESS I'LL HAVE TO PENETRATE... A LITTLE DEEPER...!
YOU READY FOR THIS!?
GLARE
KANJI!
KANJI... IS TRYING TO EXPOSE AN INTERNAL SIDE OF HIMSELF, JUST LIKE YUKIKO... BUT THIS MIGHT BE MORE DANGEROUS...

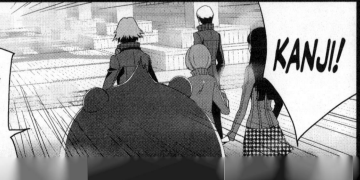

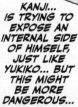

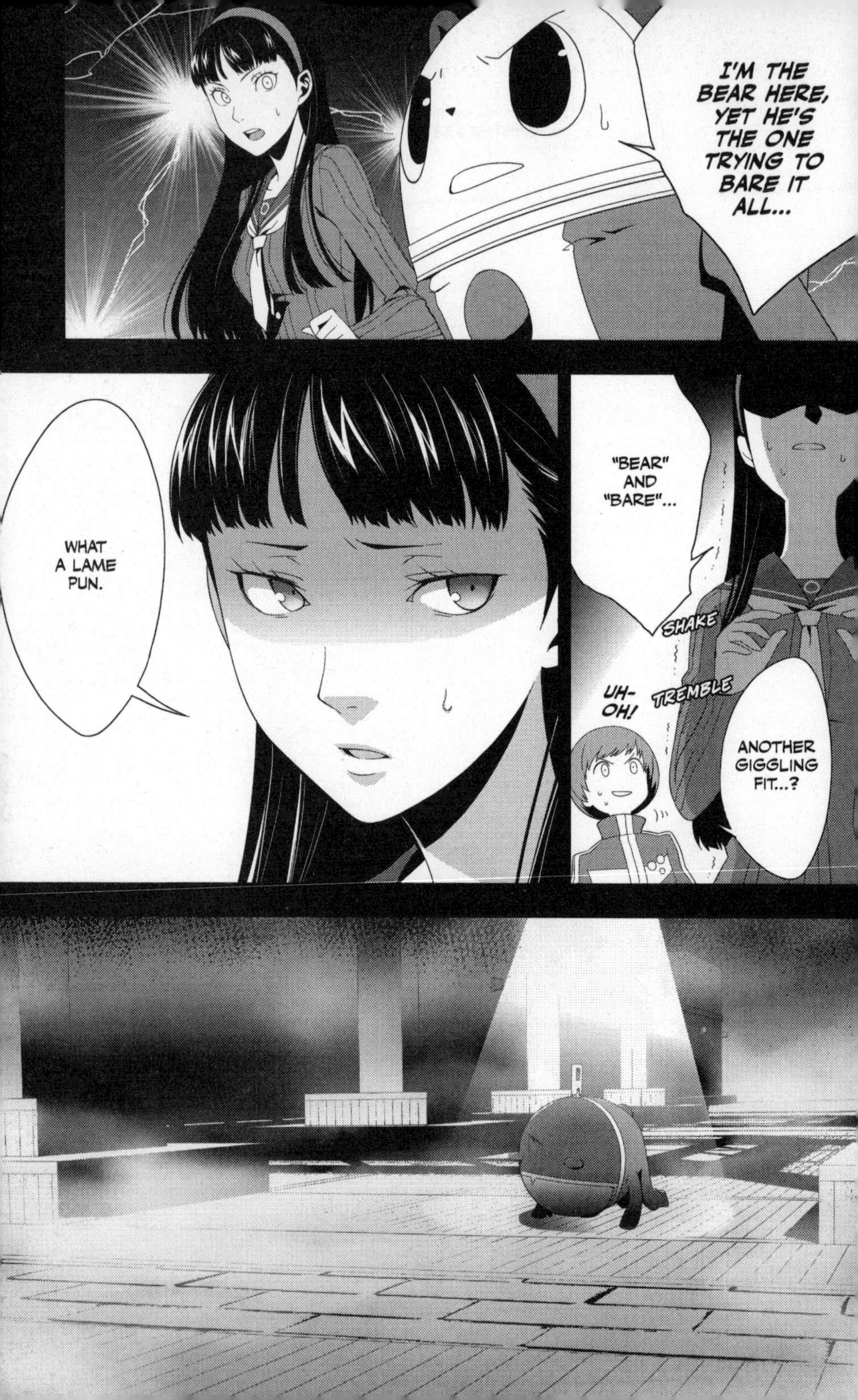
I'M THE BEAR HERE, YET HE'S THE ONE TRYING TO BARE IT ALL...
"BEAR" AND "BARE"...
SHAKE
TREMBLE
UH-OH!
ANOTHER GIGGLING FIT...?
WHAT A LAME PUN.

Design sketch

#16 KANJI TATSUMI PART 4

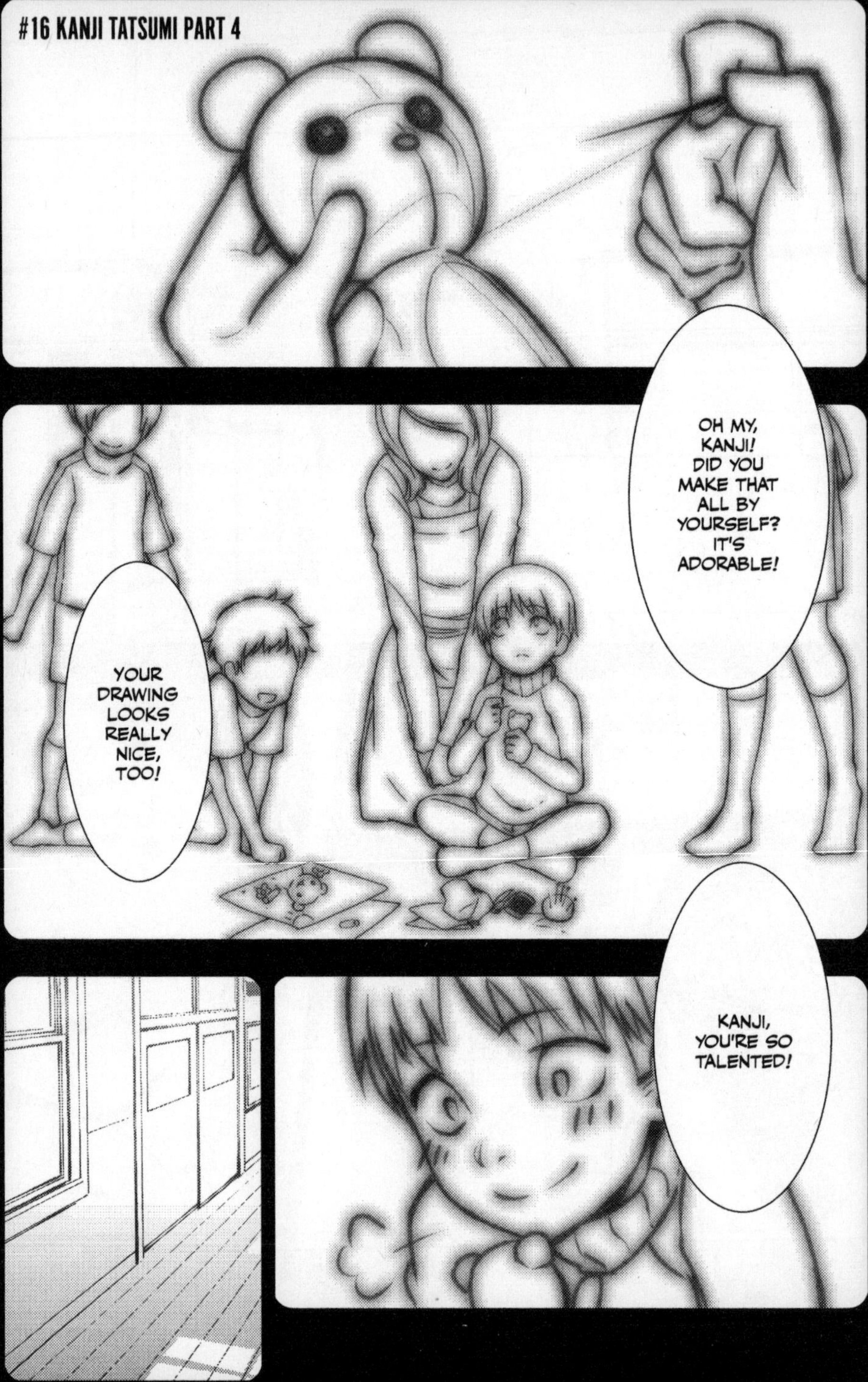
OH MY, KANJI! DID YOU MAKE THAT ALL BY YOURSELF? IT'S ADORABLE!
YOUR DRAWING LOOKS REALLY NICE, TOO!
KANJI, YOU'RE SO TALENTED!

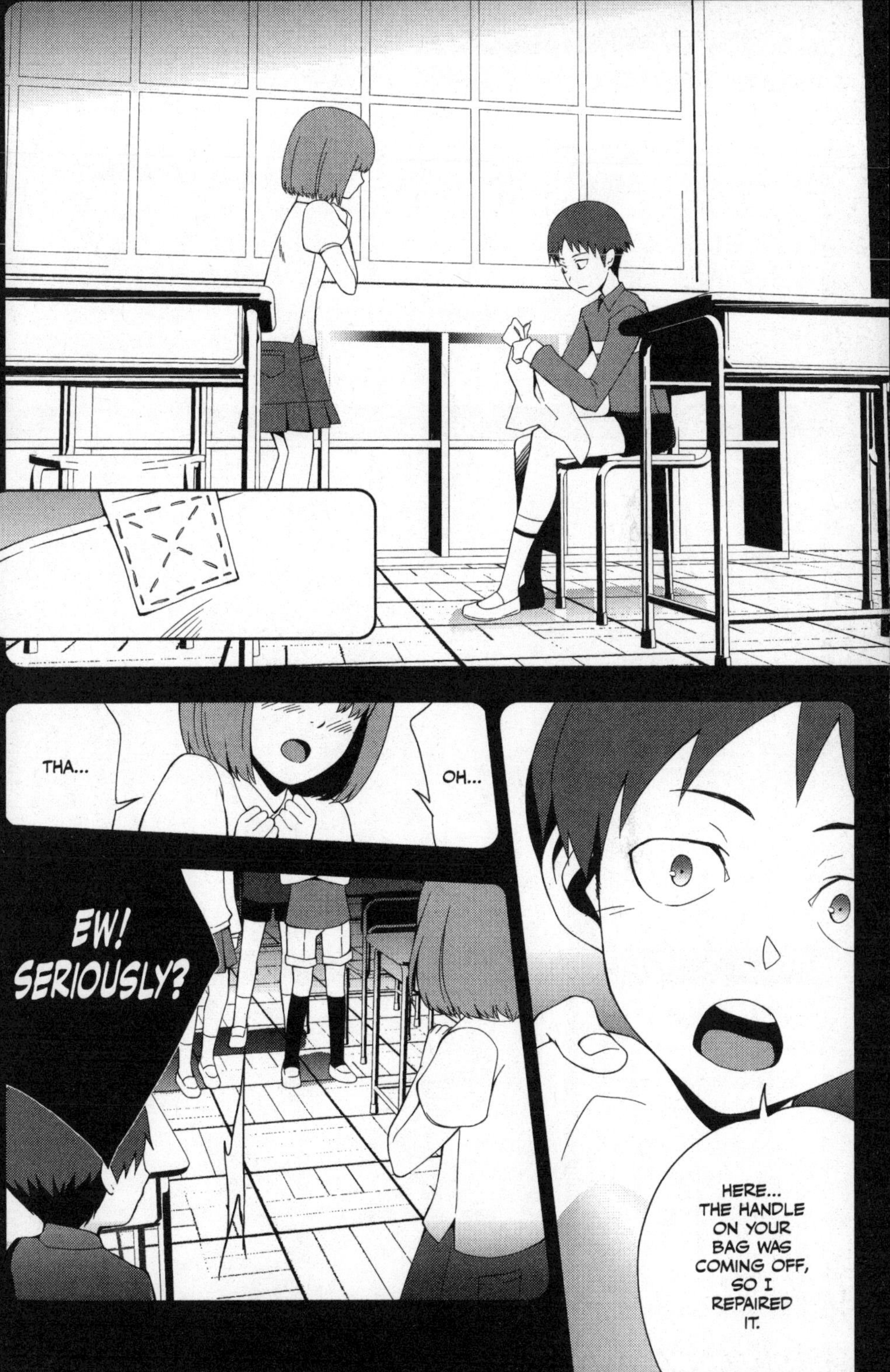
HERE... THE HANDLE ON YOUR BAG WAS COMING OFF, SO I REPAIRED IT.
OH...
THA...
EW! SERIOUSLY?

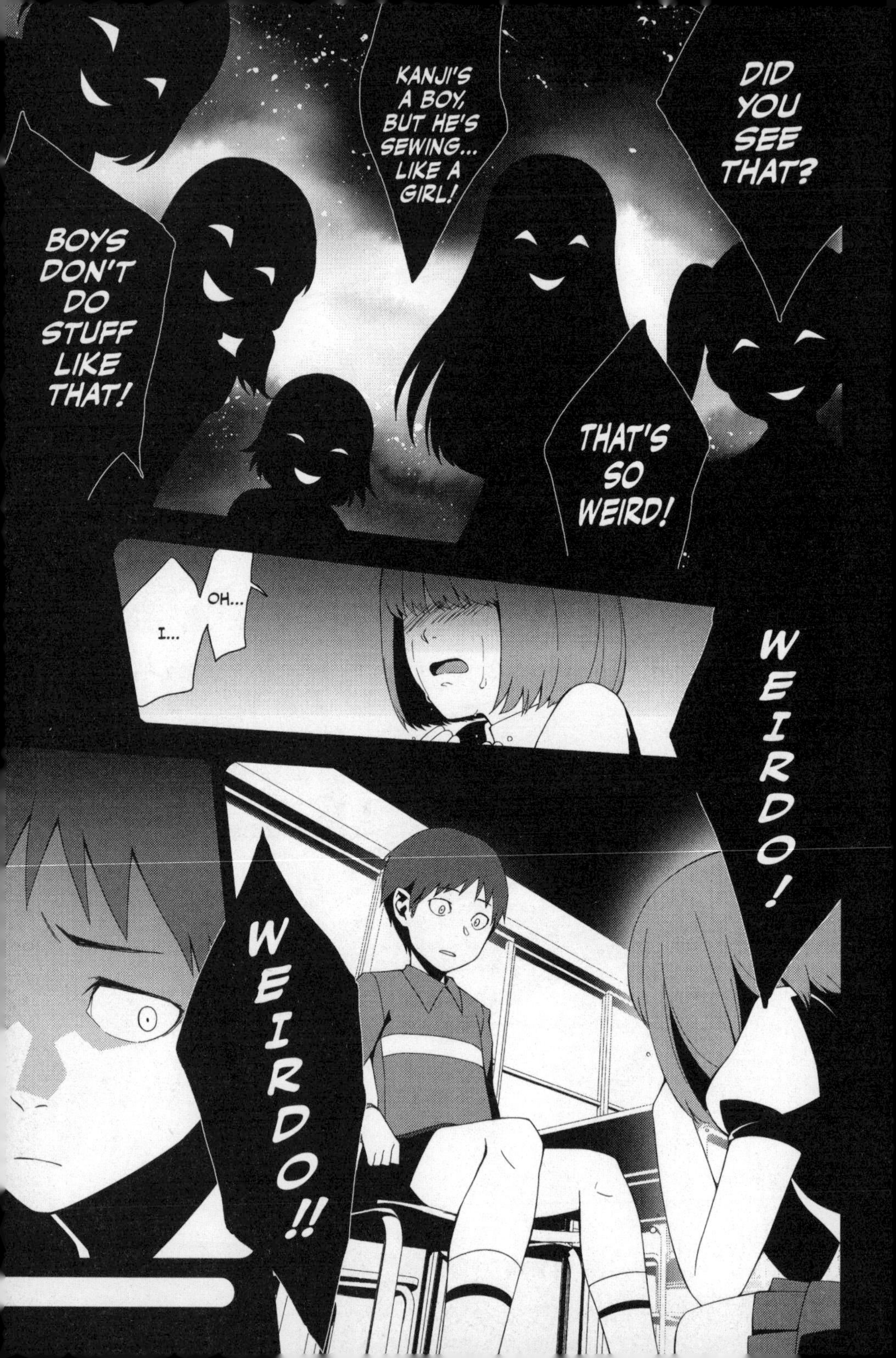
DID YOU SEE THAT?
KANJI'S A BOY, BUT HE'S SEWING... LIKE A GIRL!
BOYS DON'T DO STUFF LIKE THAT!
THAT'S SO WEIRD!
WEIRDO!
OH... I...
WEIRDO!!

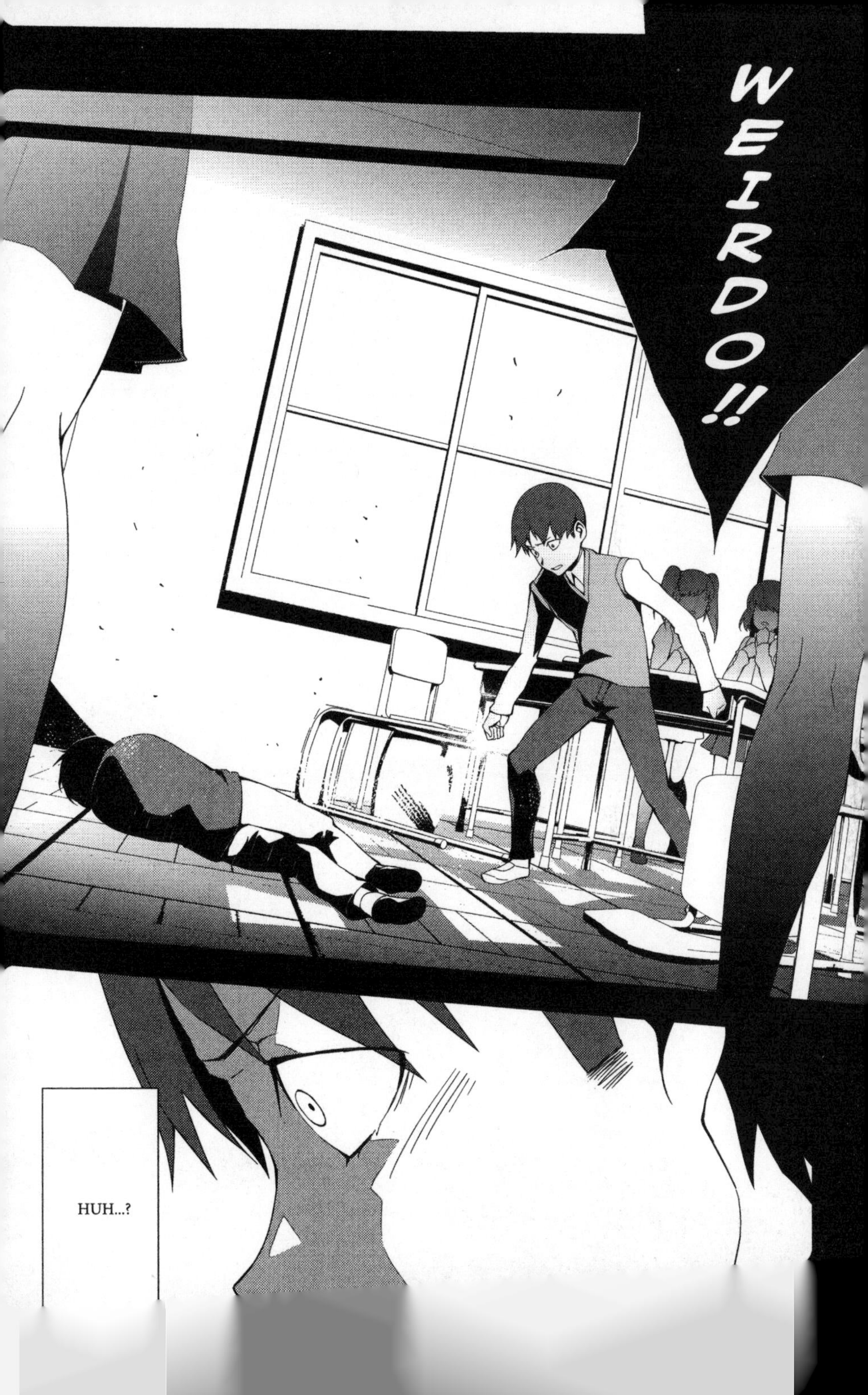
WEIRDO!!
HUH...?

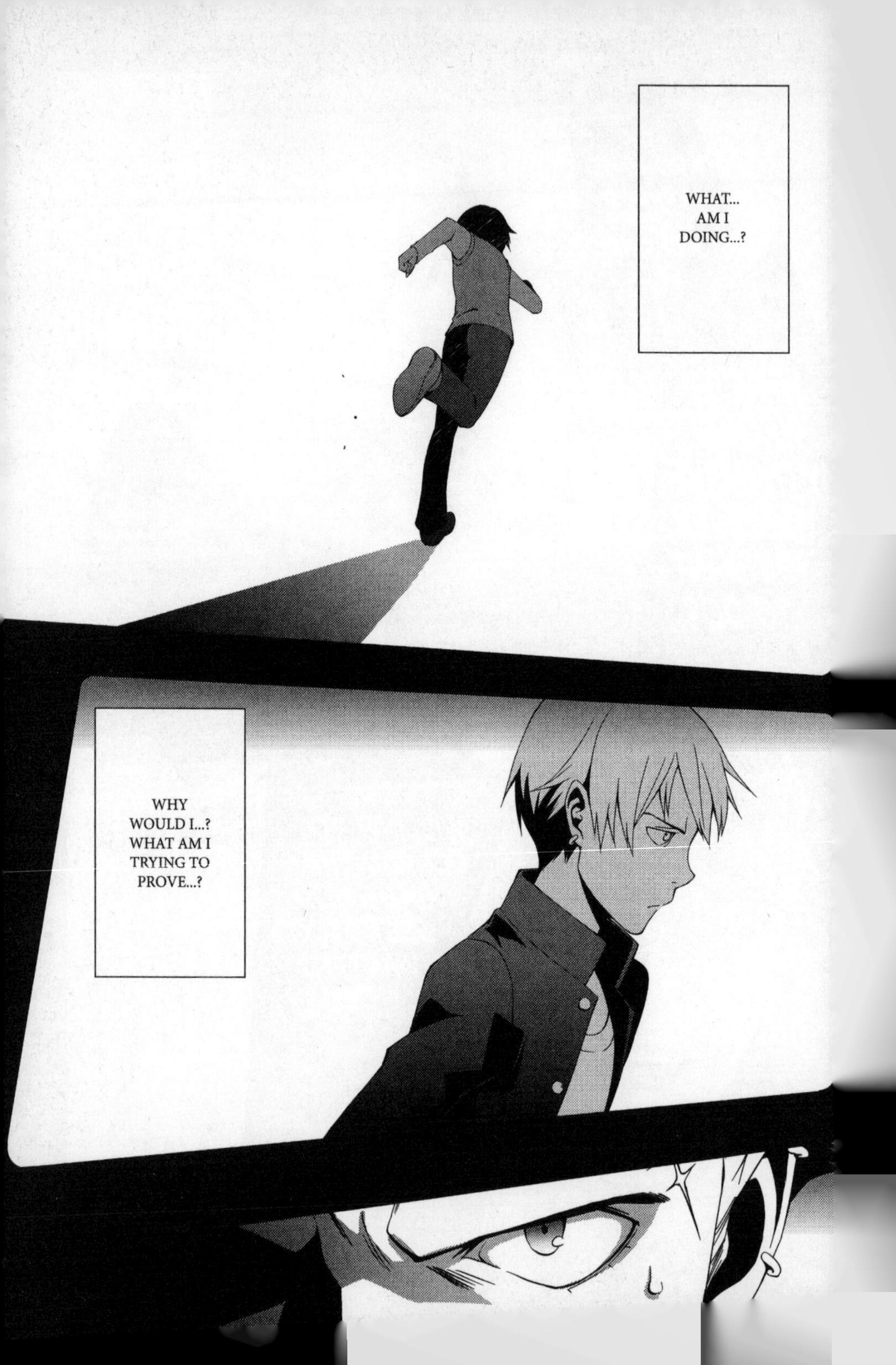
WHAT... AM I DOING...?
WHY WOULD I...? WHAT AM I TRYING TO PROVE...?

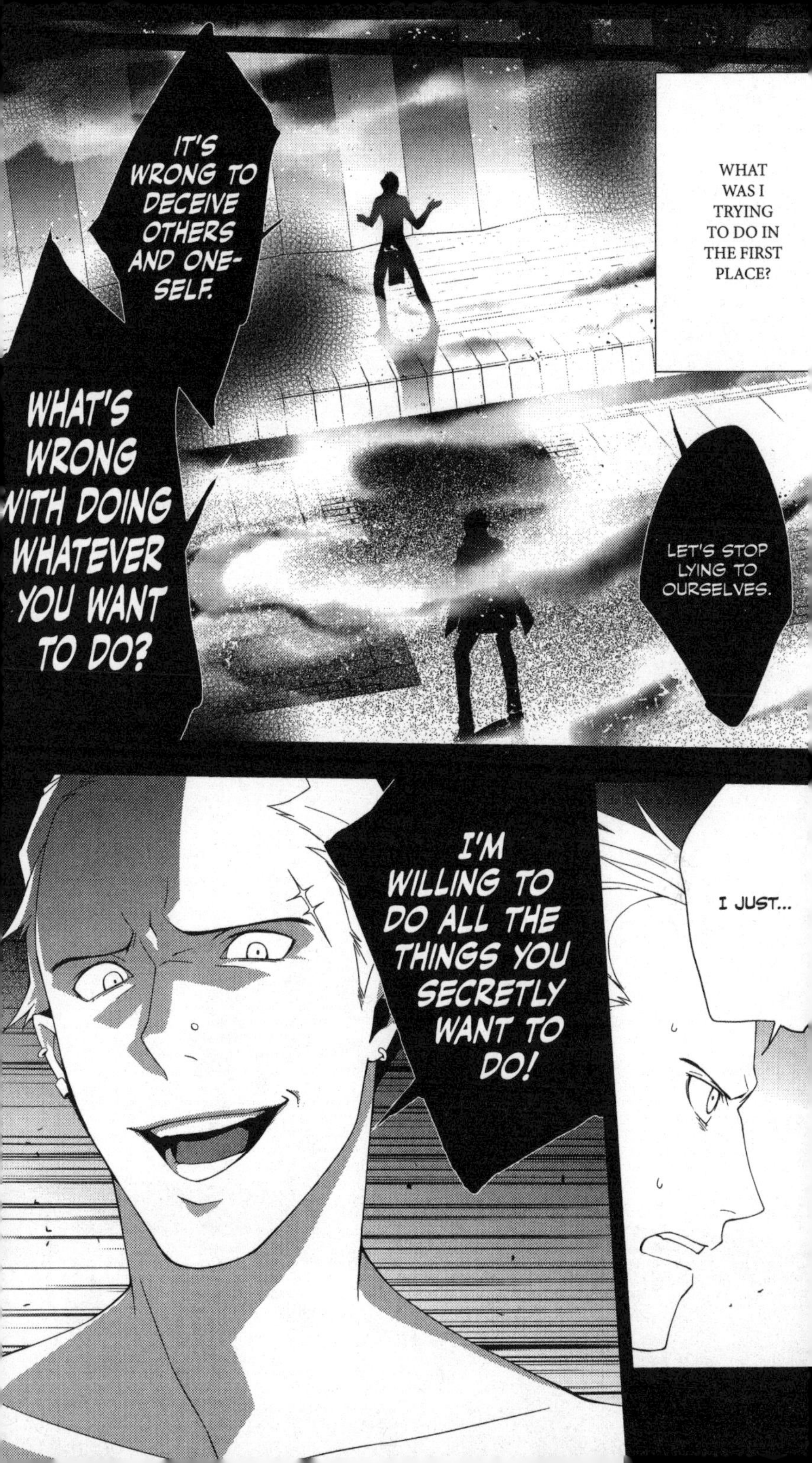
WHAT WAS I TRYING TO DO IN THE FIRST PLACE?
IT'S WRONG TO DECEIVE OTHERS AND ONE-SELF.
LET'S STOP LYING TO OURSELVES.
WHAT'S WRONG WITH DOING WHATEVER YOU WANT TO DO?
I JUST...
I'M WILLING TO DO ALL THE THINGS YOU SECRETLY WANT TO DO!

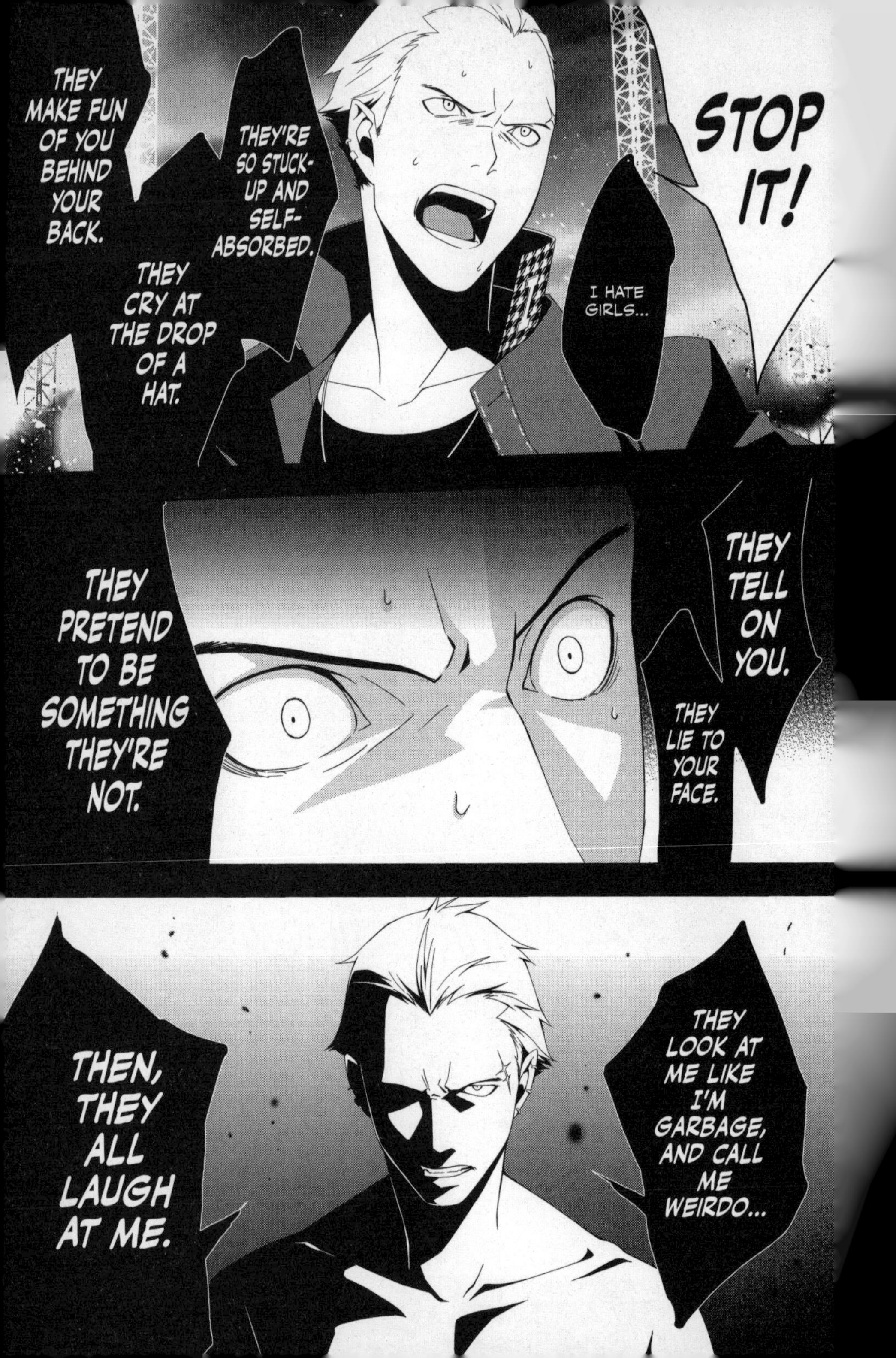
STOP IT!
I HATE GIRLS...
THEY'RE SO STUCK-UP AND SELF-ABSORBED.
THEY MAKE FUN OF YOU BEHIND YOUR BACK.
THEY CRY AT THE DROP OF A HAT.
THEY TELL ON YOU.
THEY LIE TO YOUR FACE.
THEY PRETEND TO BE SOMETHING THEY'RE NOT.
THEY LOOK AT ME LIKE I'M GARBAGE, AND CALL ME WEIRDO...
THEN, THEY ALL LAUGH AT ME.

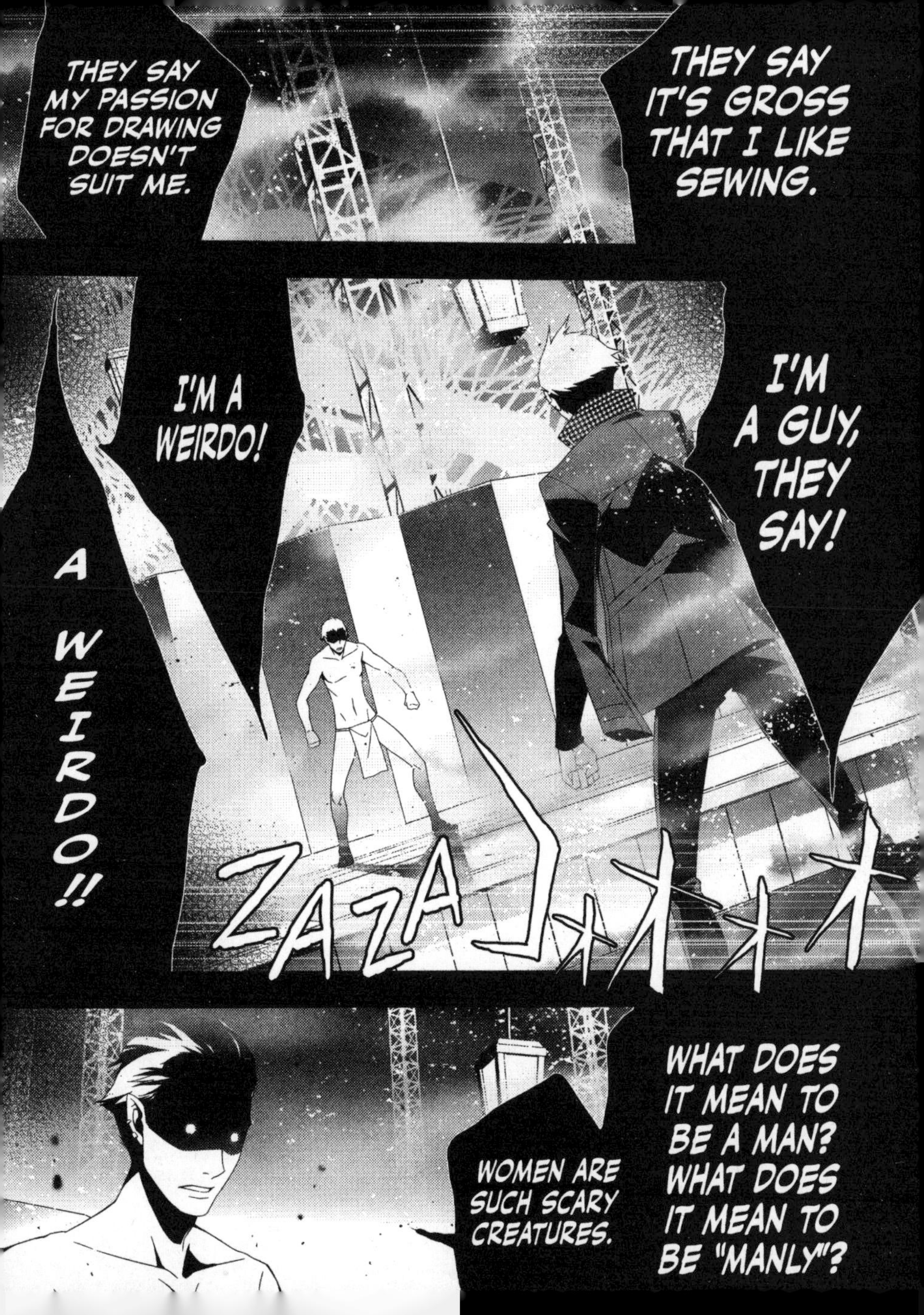
THEY SAY IT'S GROSS THAT I LIKE SEWING.
THEY SAY MY PASSION FOR DRAWING DOESN'T SUIT ME.
I'M A GUY, THEY SAY!
I'M A WEIRDO!
A WEIRDO!!
ZAZA
WHAT DOES IT MEAN TO BE A MAN? WHAT DOES IT MEAN TO BE "MANLY"?
WOMEN ARE SUCH SCARY CREATURES.

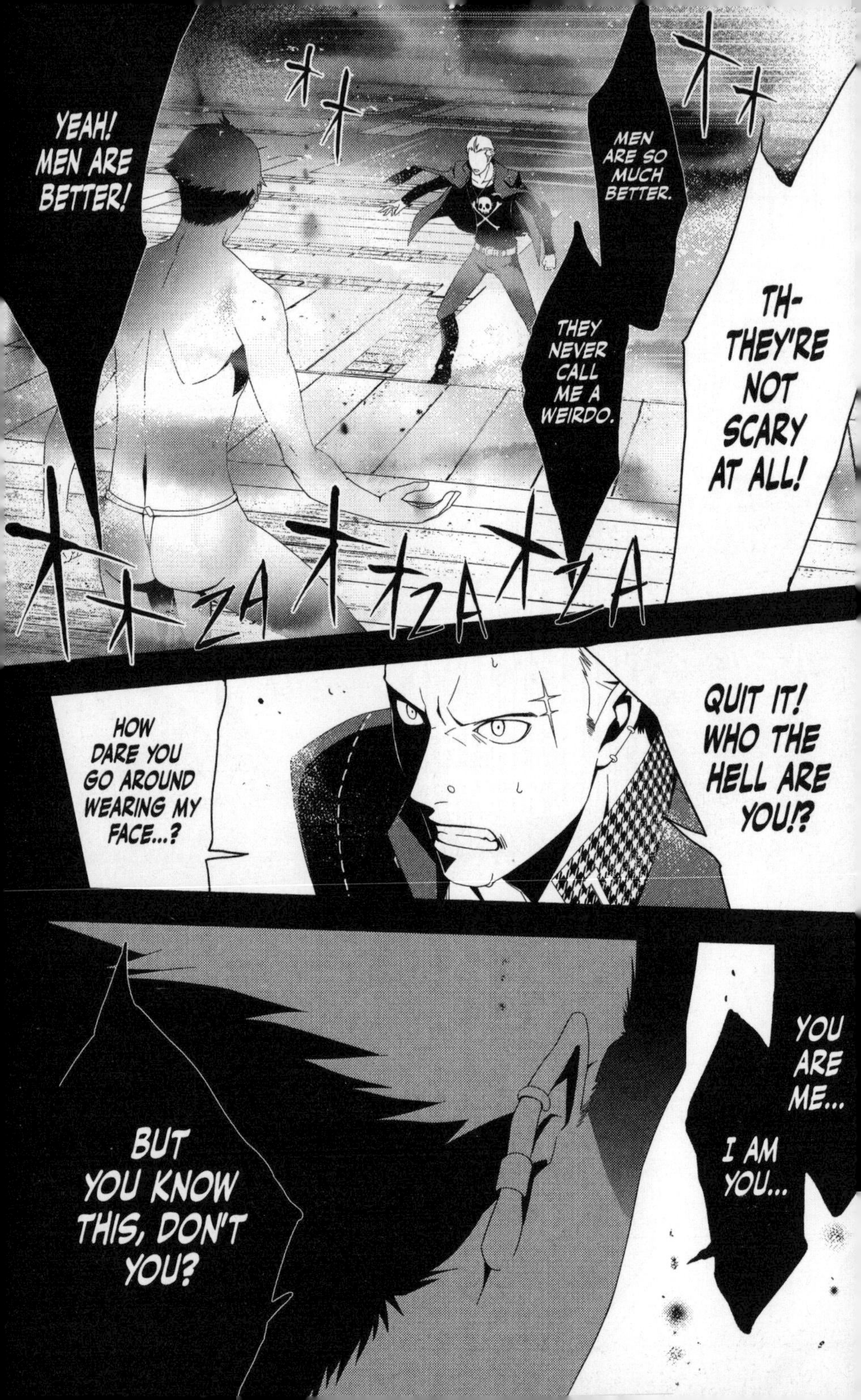
TH- THEY'RE NOT SCARY AT ALL!
MEN ARE SO MUCH BETTER.
THEY NEVER CALL ME A WEIRDO.
YEAH! MEN ARE BETTER!
ZA ZA ZA
QUIT IT! WHO THE HELL ARE YOU!?
HOW DARE YOU GO AROUND WEARING MY FACE...?
YOU ARE ME...
I AM YOU...
BUT YOU KNOW THIS, DON'T YOU?

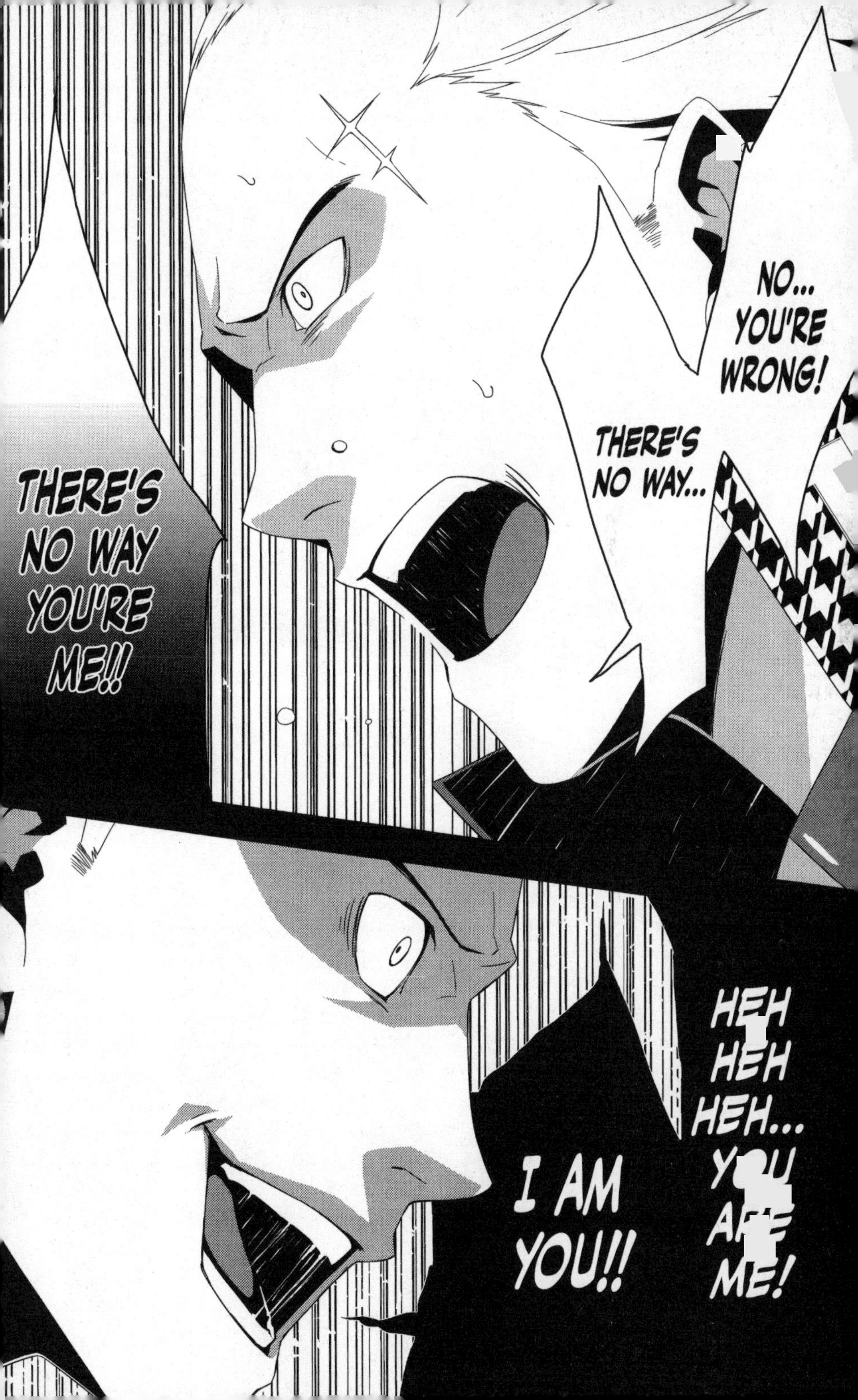
NO... YOU'RE WRONG!
THERE'S NO WAY...
THERE'S NO WAY YOU'RE ME!!
HEH HEH HEH... YOU ARE ME!
I AM YOU!!

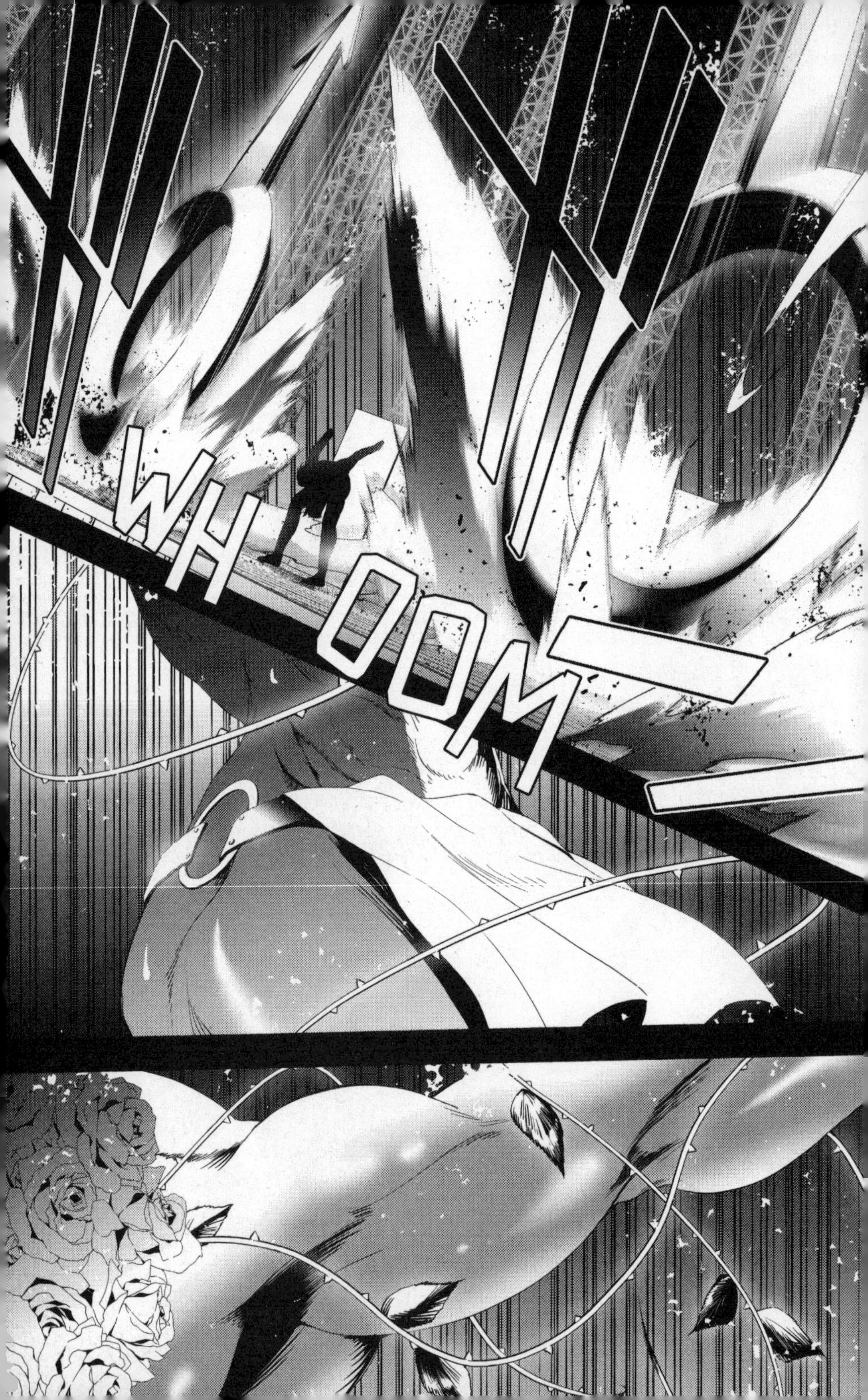
WHOOM

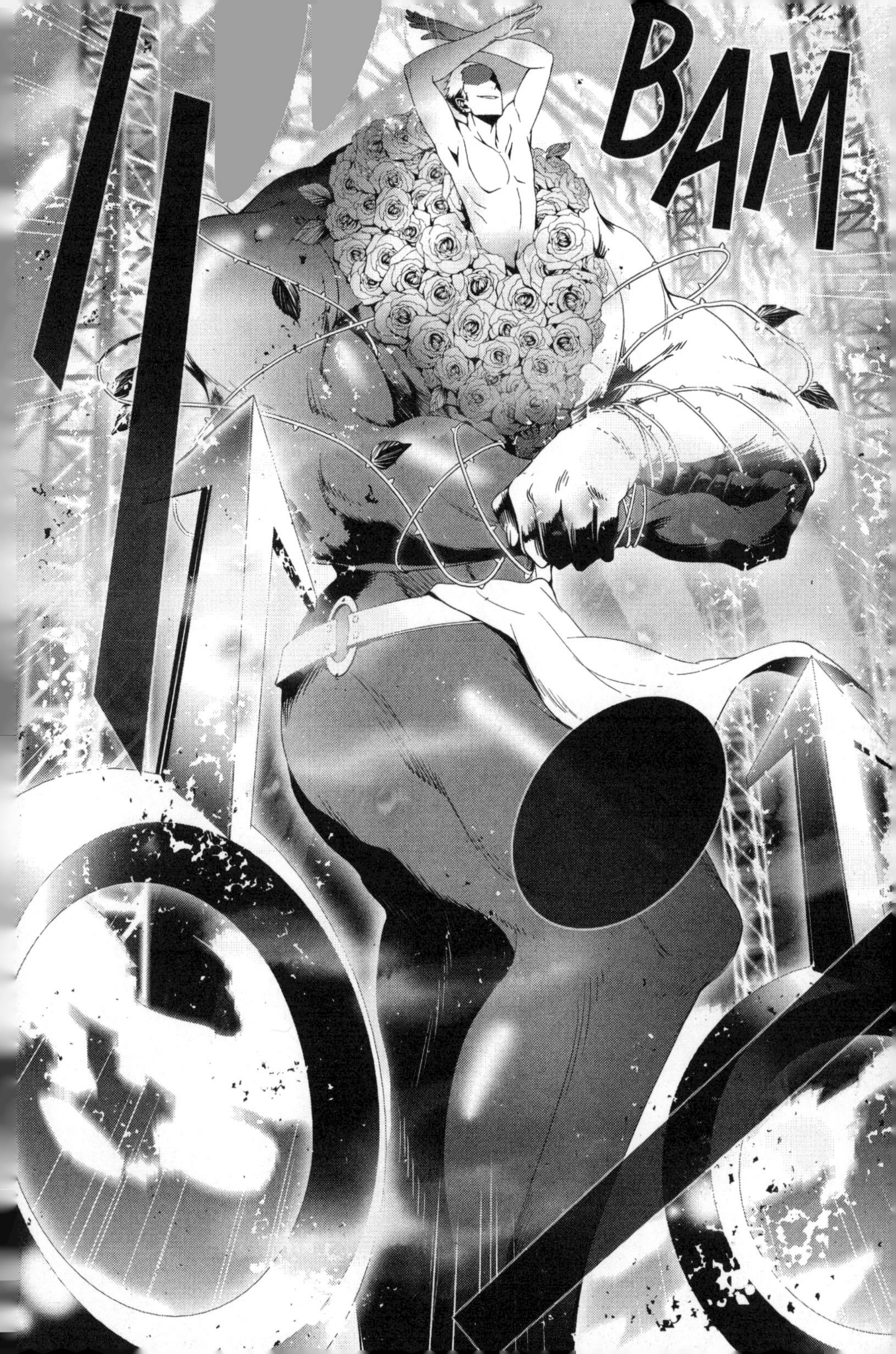
BAM

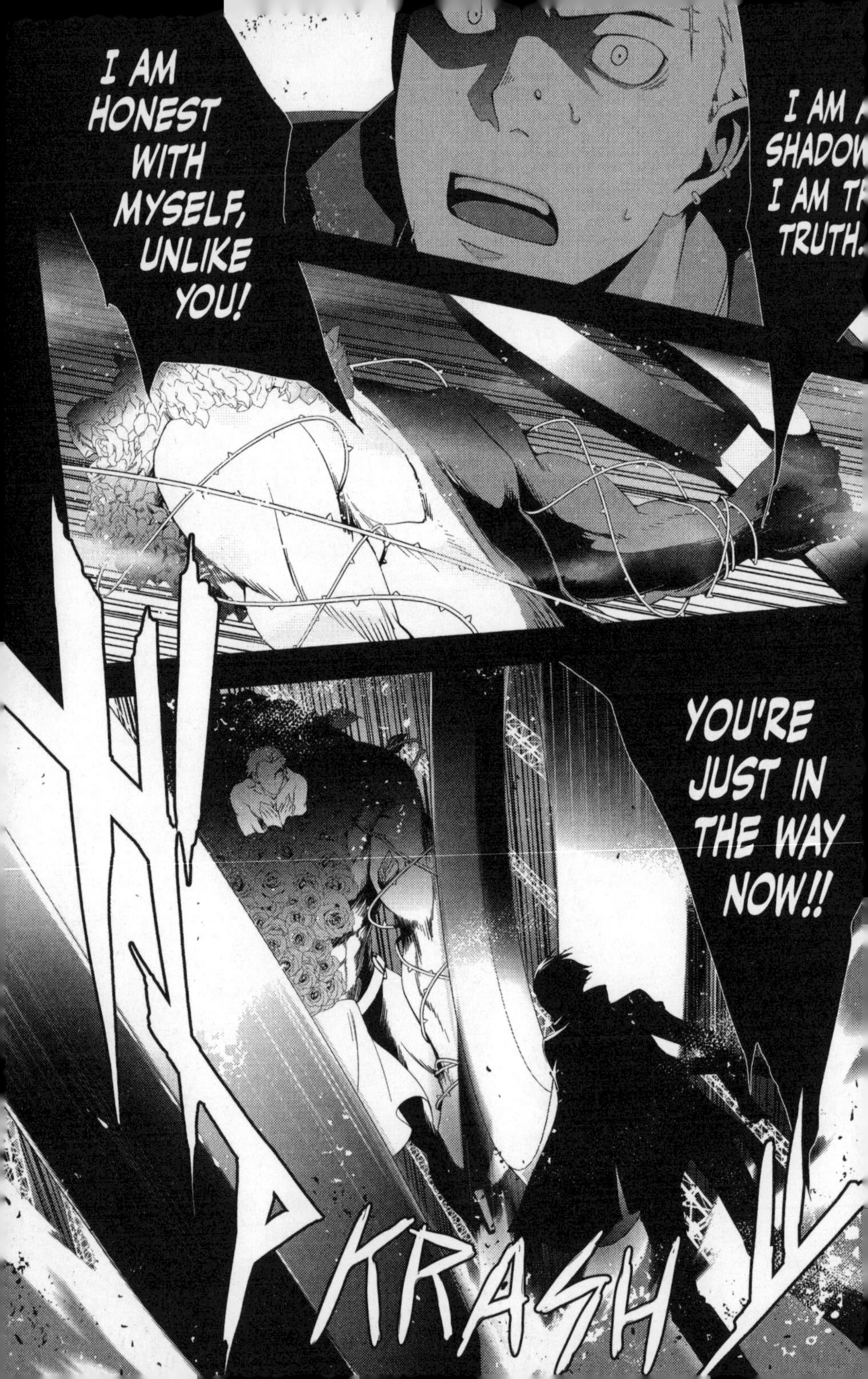
I AM SHADOW I AM TRUTH.
I AM HONEST WITH MYSELF, UNLIKE YOU!
YOU'RE JUST IN THE WAY NOW!!
KRASH

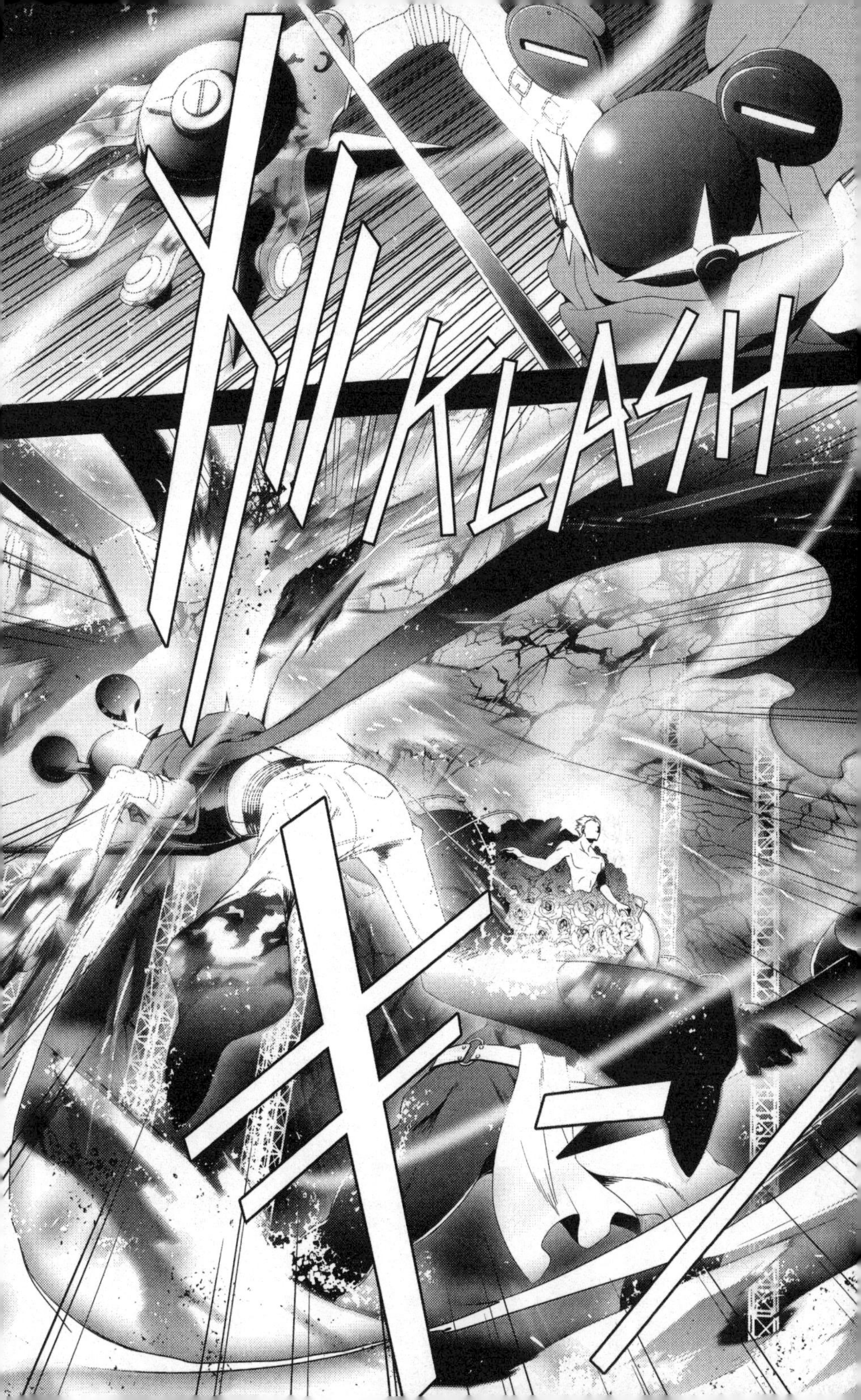
KLASH

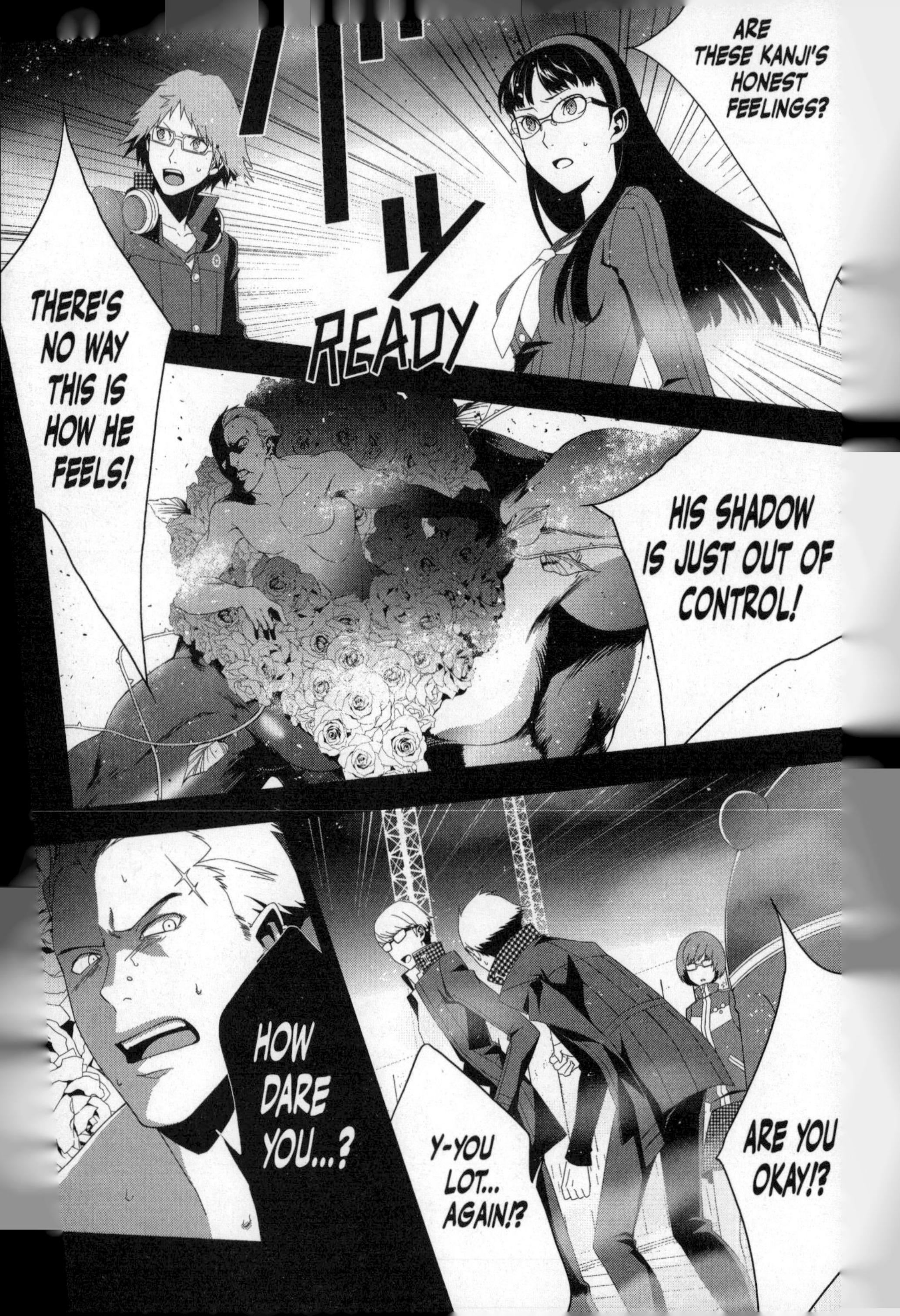
ARE THESE KANJI'S HONEST FEELINGS?
READY
THERE'S NO WAY THIS IS HOW HE FEELS!
HIS SHADOW IS JUST OUT OF CONTROL!
ARE YOU OKAY!?
Y-YOU LOT... AGAIN!?
HOW DARE YOU...?

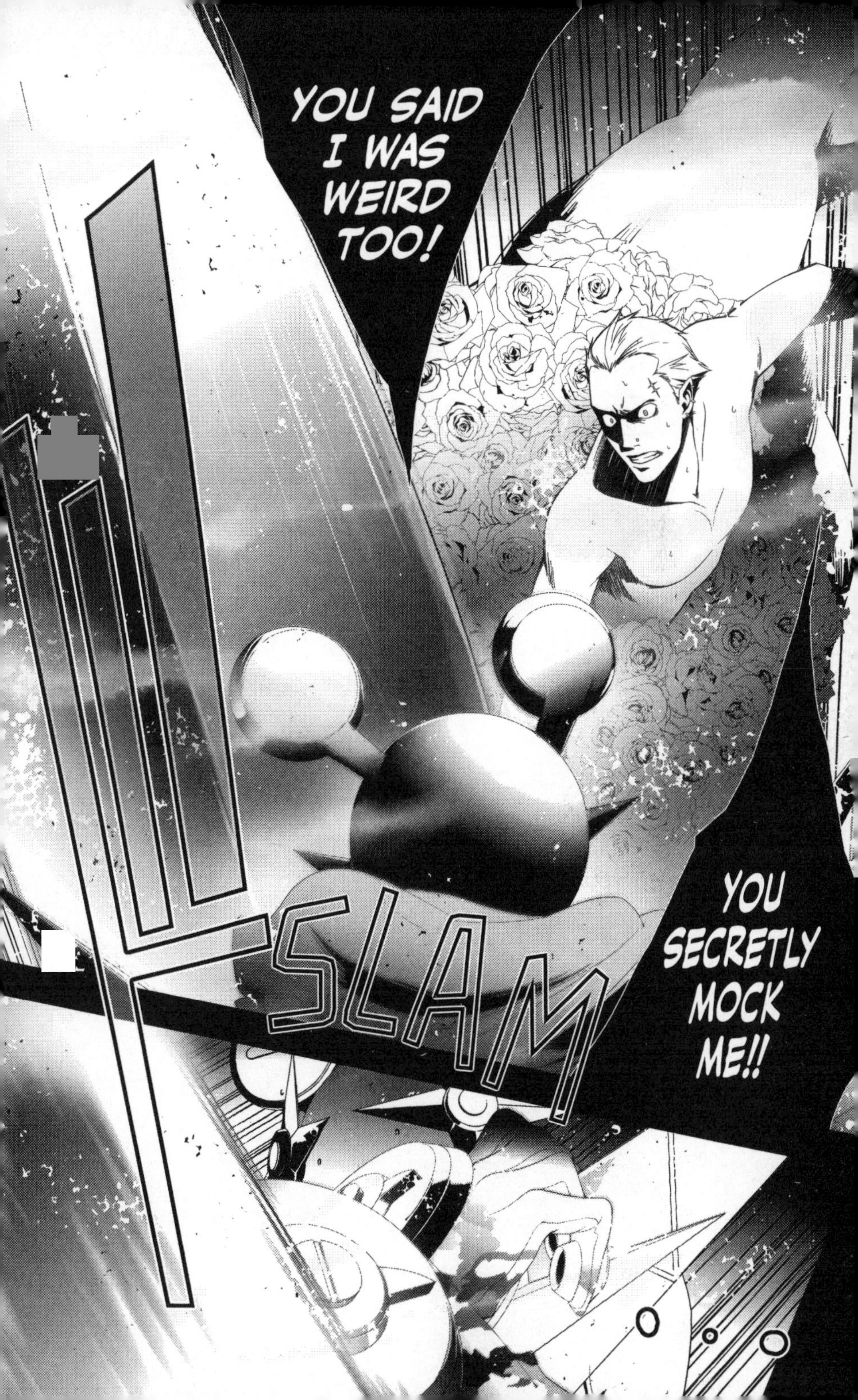
YOU SAID I WAS WEIRD TOO!
YOU SECRETLY MOCK ME!!
SLAM

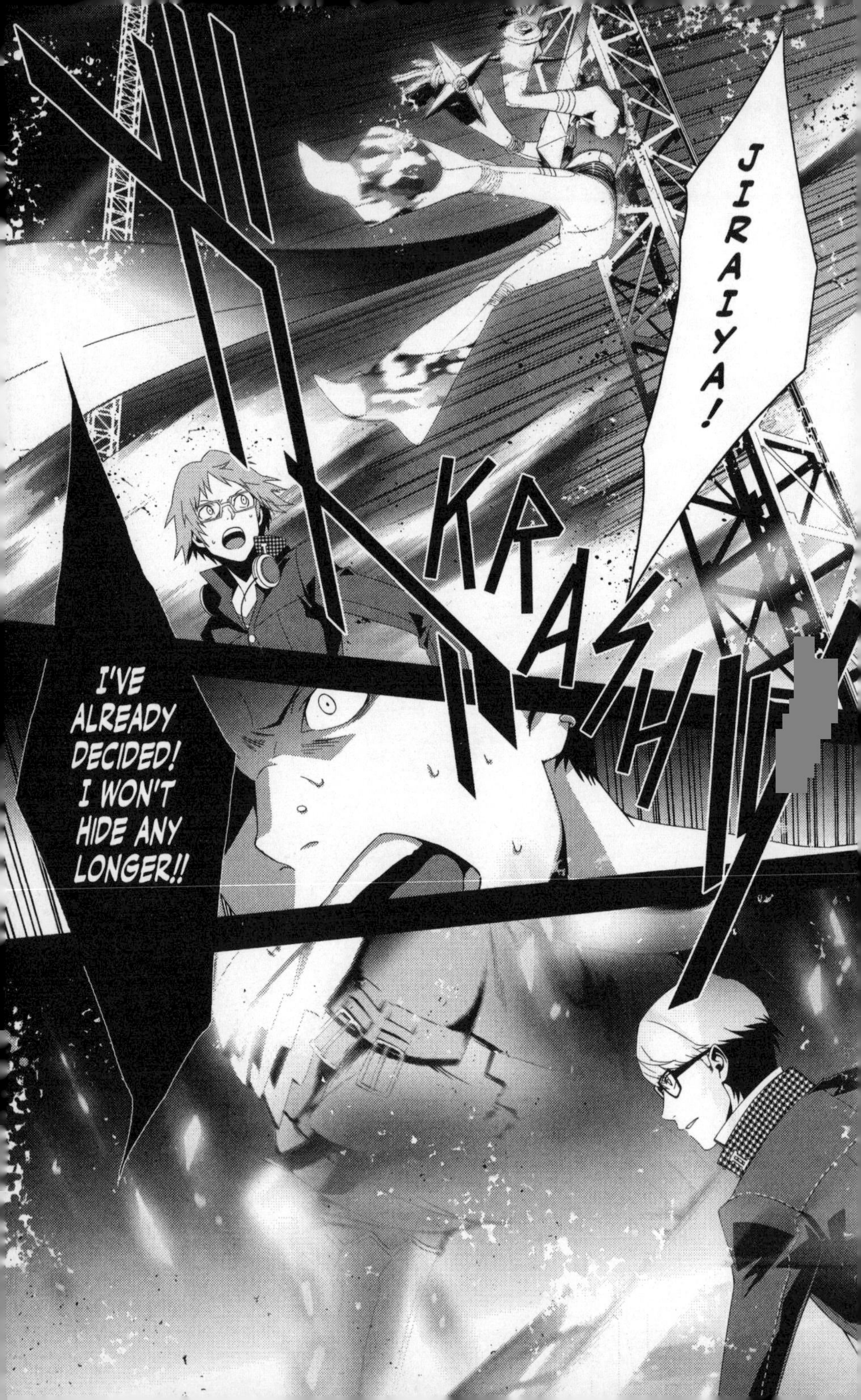
JIRAIYA!
KRASH
I'VE ALREADY DECIDED! I WON'T HIDE ANY LONGER!!

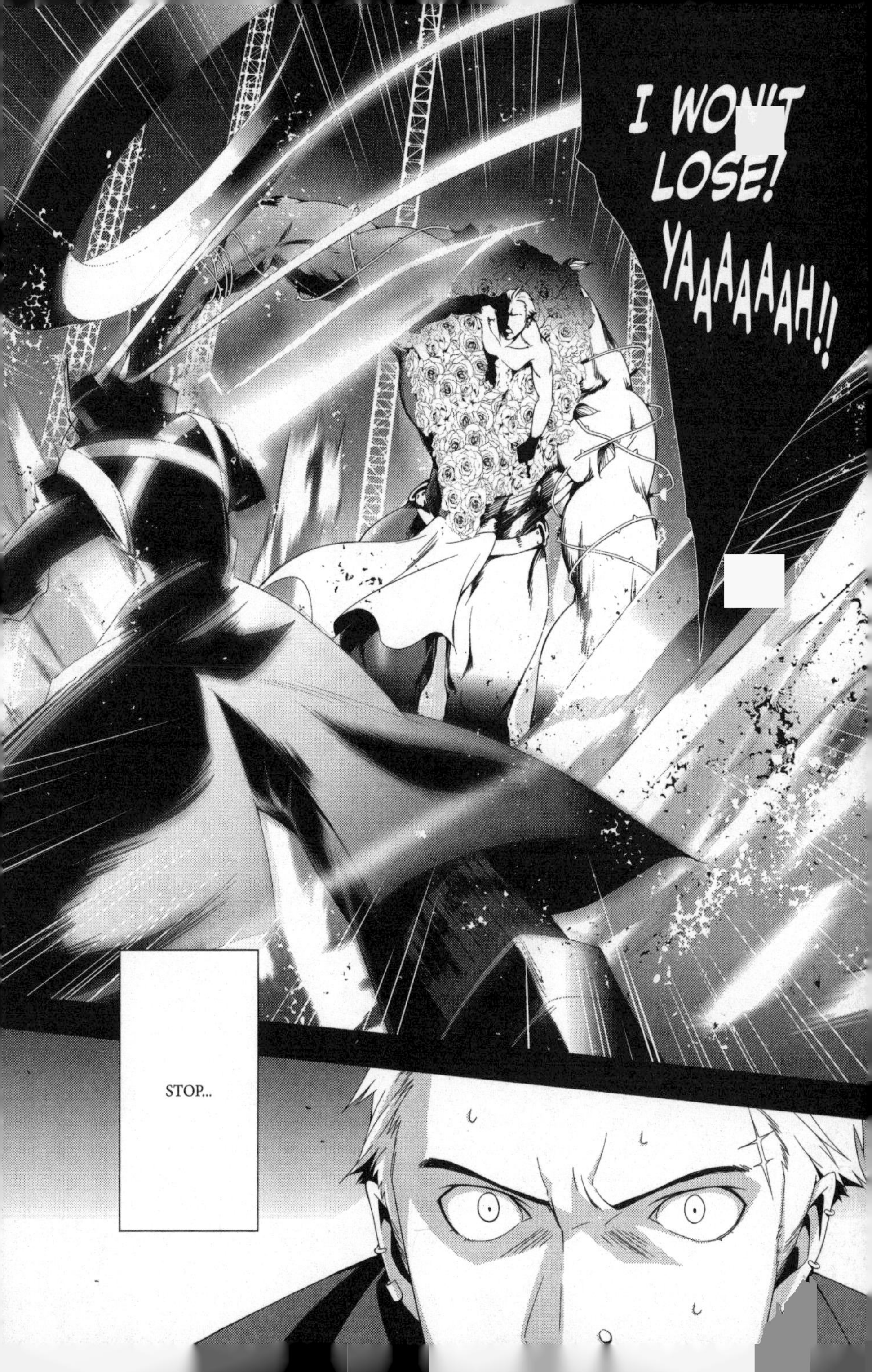
I WON'T LOSE! YAAAAAH!!
STOP...

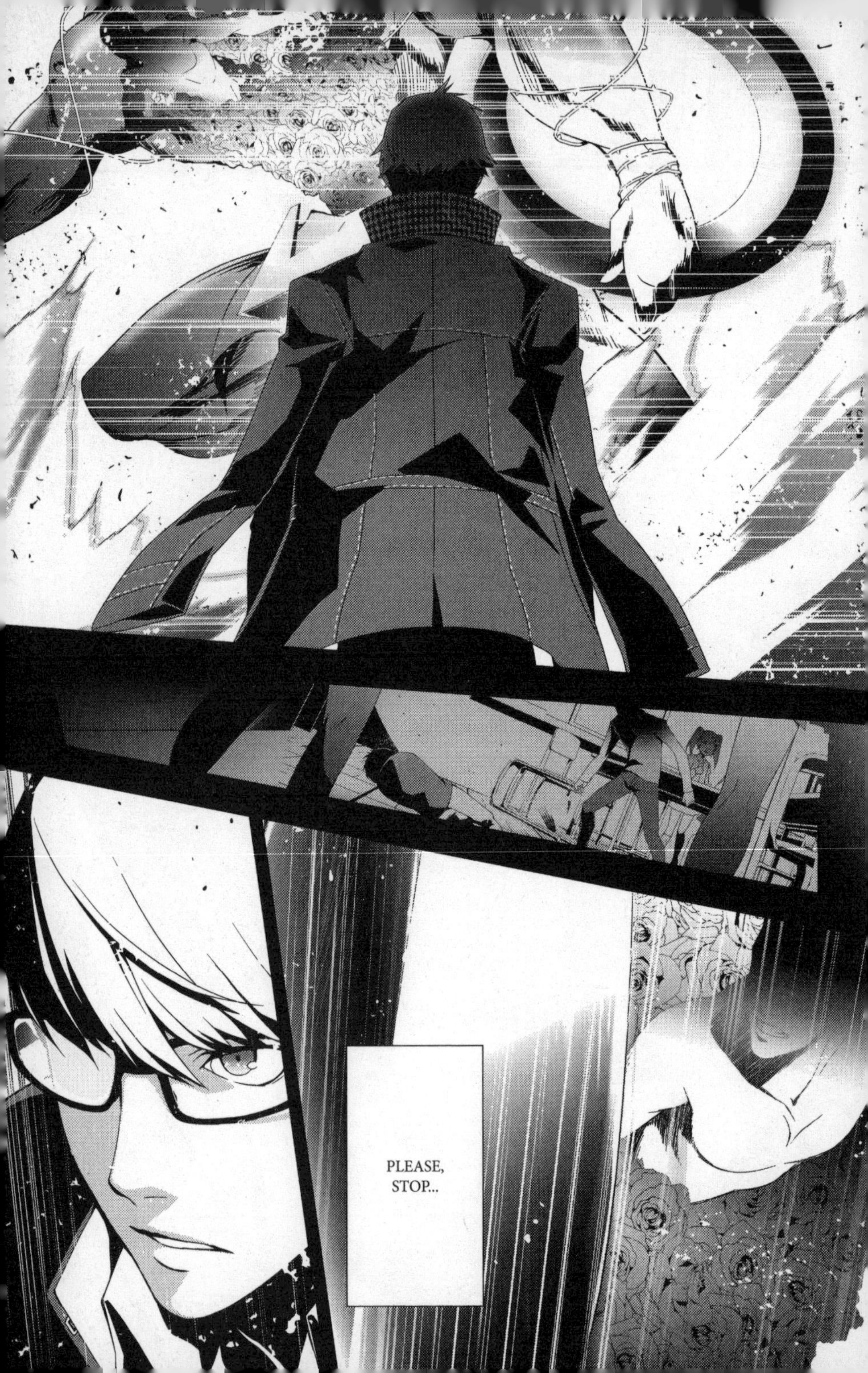
PLEASE,
STOP...

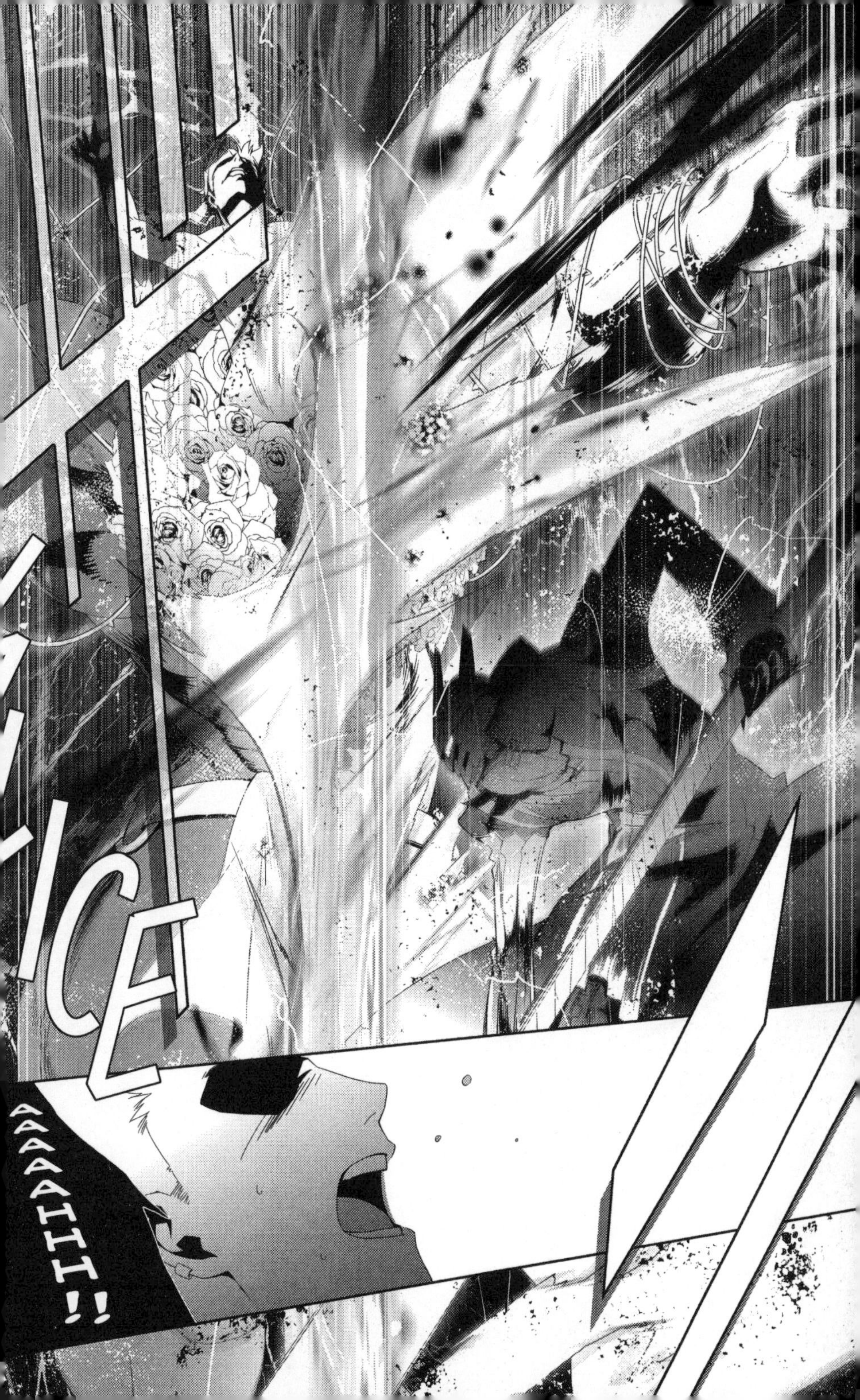
ICE
AAAAAHHH!!

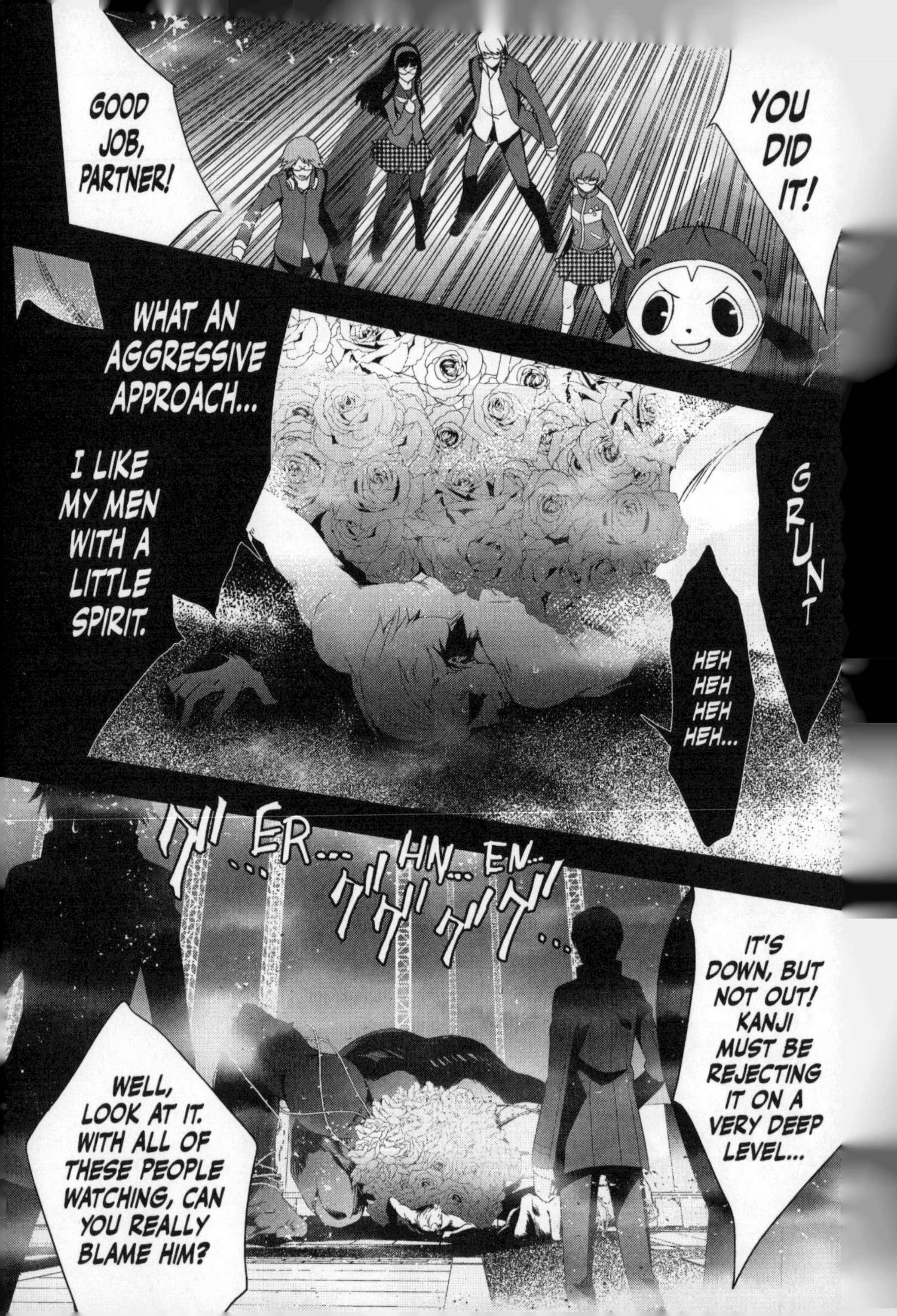
YOU DID IT!
GOOD JOB, PARTNER!
GRUNT
WHAT AN AGGRESSIVE APPROACH...
I LIKE MY MEN WITH A LITTLE SPIRIT.
HEH HEH HEH HEH...
ER... HN... EN...
IT'S DOWN, BUT NOT OUT! KANJI MUST BE REJECTING IT ON A VERY DEEP LEVEL...
WELL, LOOK AT IT. WITH ALL OF THESE PEOPLE WATCHING, CAN YOU REALLY BLAME HIM?

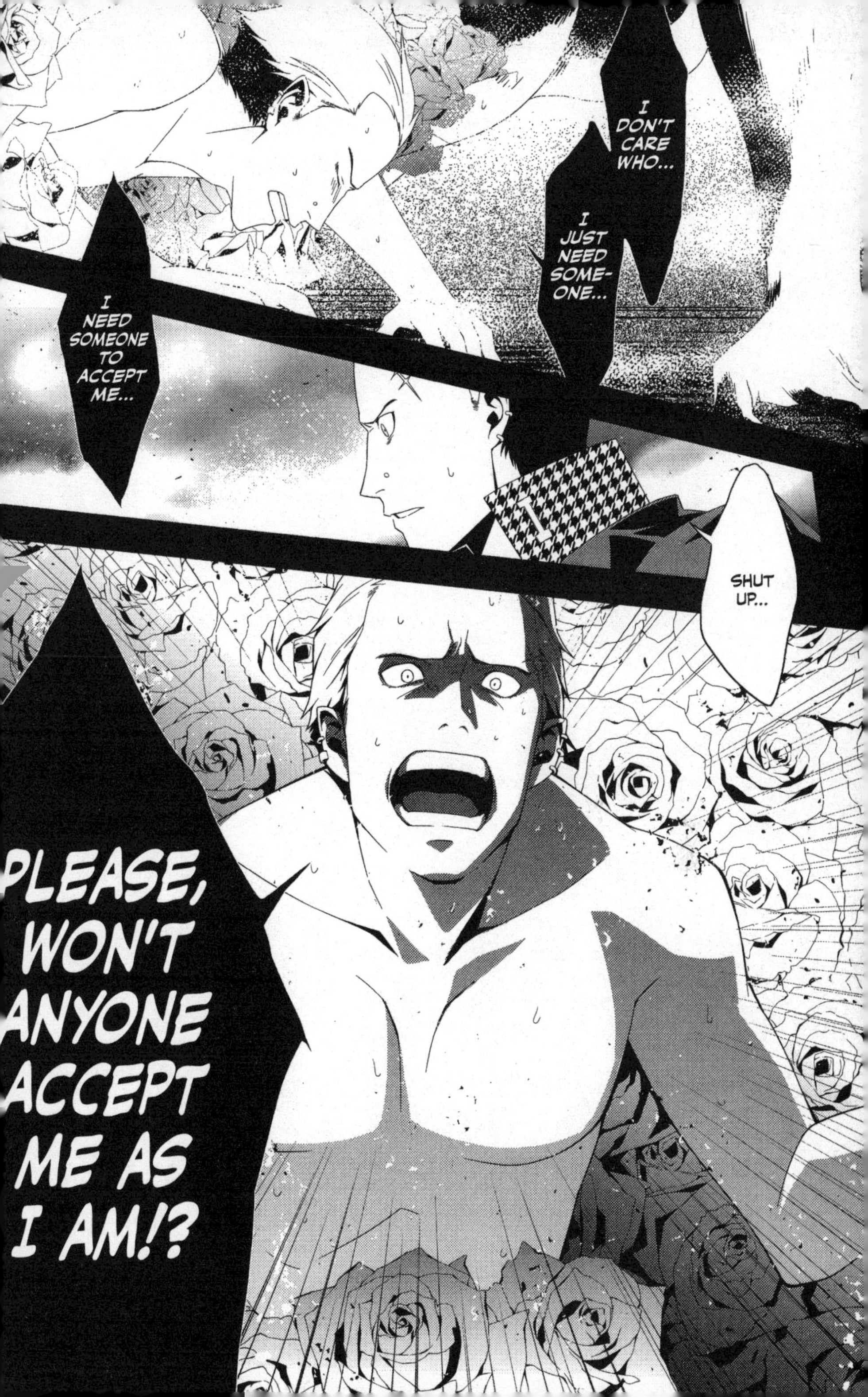
I DON'T CARE WHO...
I JUST NEED SOME-ONE...
I NEED SOMEONE TO ACCEPT ME...
SHUT UP...
PLEASE, WON'T ANYONE ACCEPT ME AS I AM!?

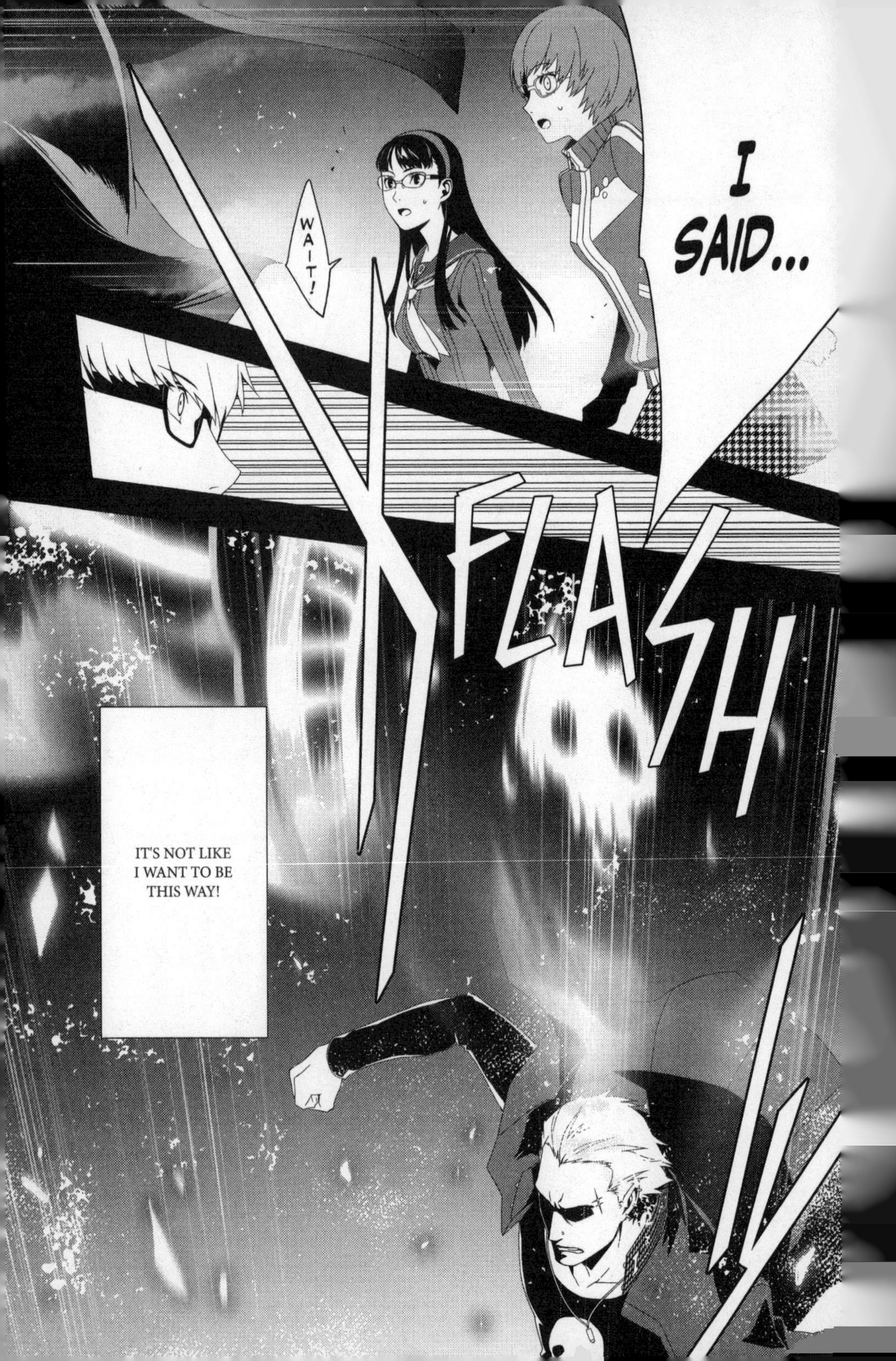
I SAID...
WAIT!
FLASH
IT'S NOT LIKE I WANT TO BE THIS WAY!

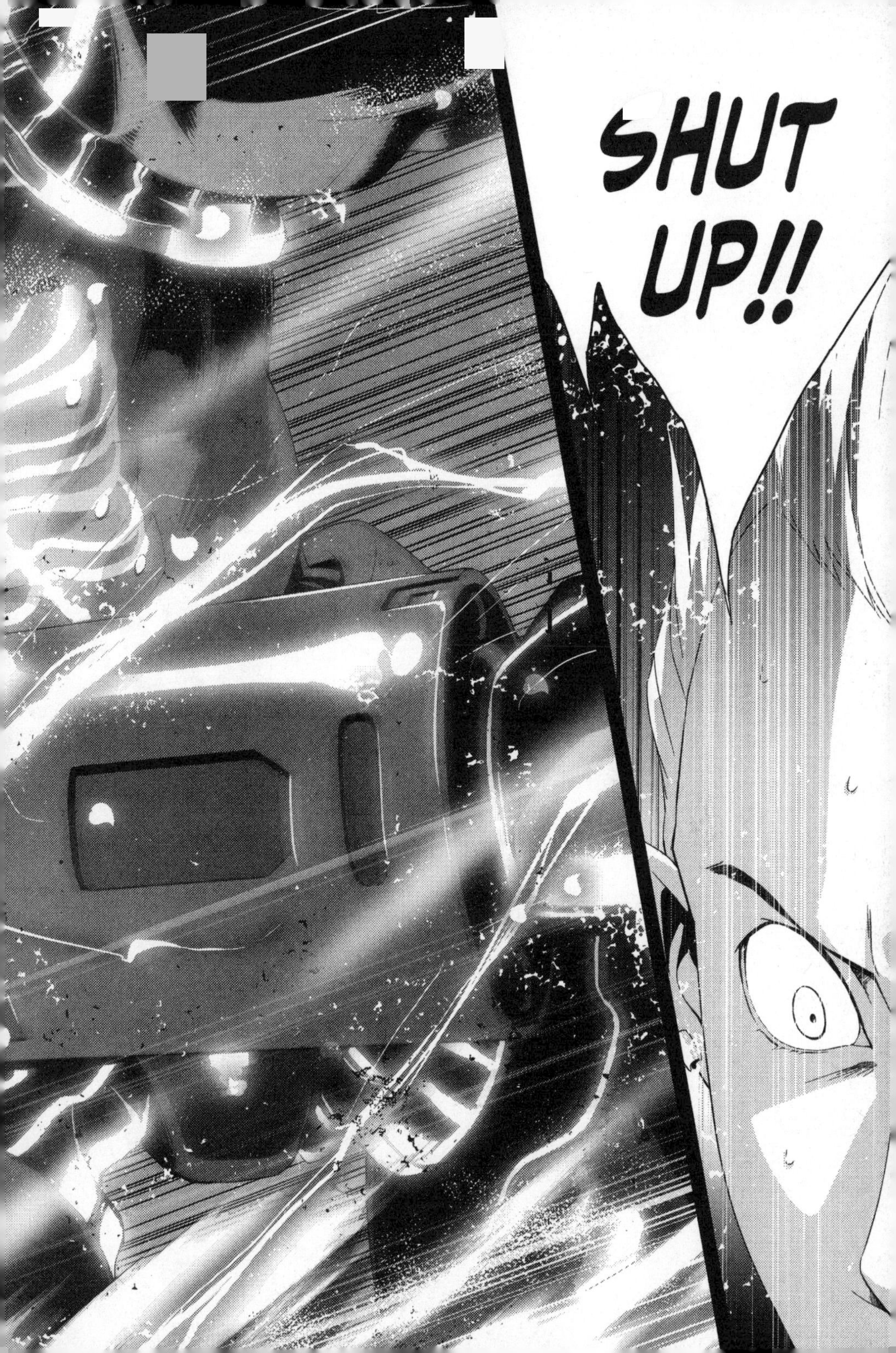
SHUT UP!!

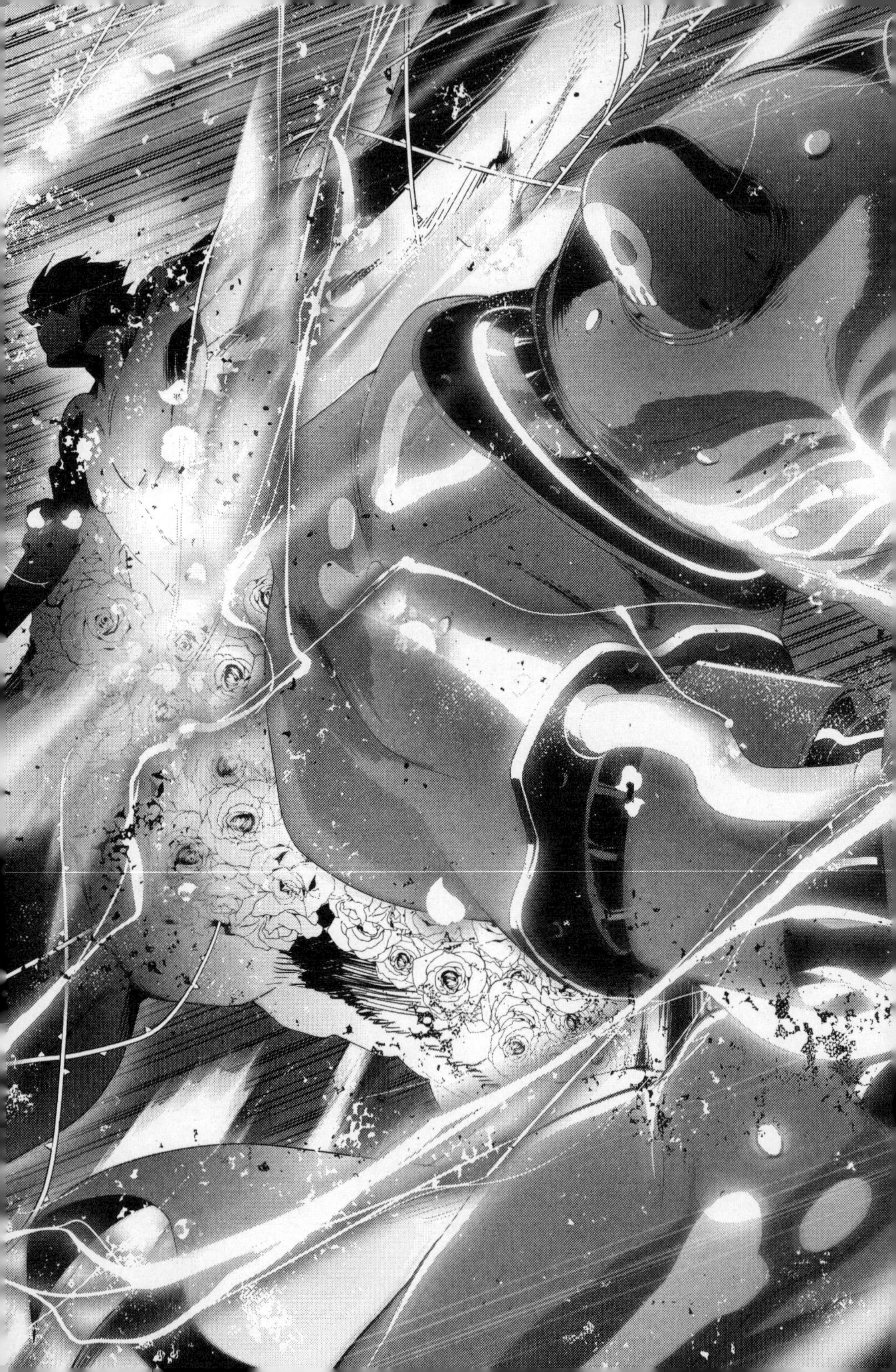

巽完二
Kanji Tatsumi

Kanji is very strong on the outside, but quite gentle on the inside. All of the "shows" on the Midnight Channel were quite shocking. I felt like each Persona was pretty realistic in terms of representing aspects of a character's personality, and similarly, the sheer chaos of the Midnight Channel seemed to reflect the turbulent emotions of youths quite accurately. It's all quite risqué, even for a modern game. Just wait until you see the next character!

Anyway, I digress. Back to Kanji. Throughout the "Persona" series, we've always had some great delinquent-type characters in the cast. "Persona 4" is no exception, as Kanji sports a multilayered and complex personality. His chaotic nature seems so unlikely when coupled with his humble roots as the son of a textile shop owner. He is also younger than the other main characters. I suppose these perceived gaps in his character are what make him so appealing.

Who knows how Kanji's character will develop in this manga? All of the other characters so far already have quite a few questionable traits, and Kanji is just another great addition to the team!

I look forward to tearing it up with Kanji some more... tastefully, of course.

PERSONA 4 CHARACTER NOTE

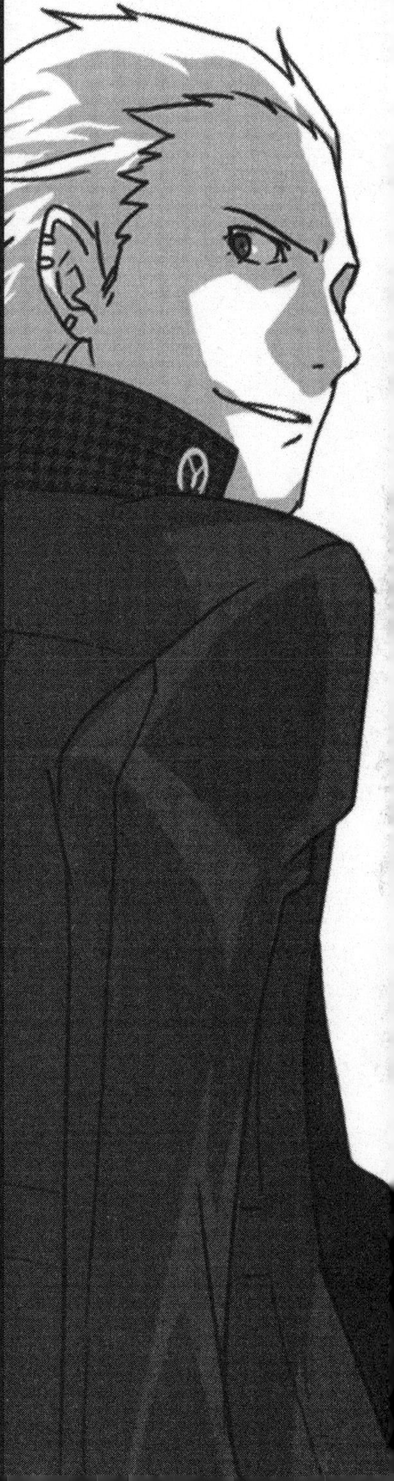

高

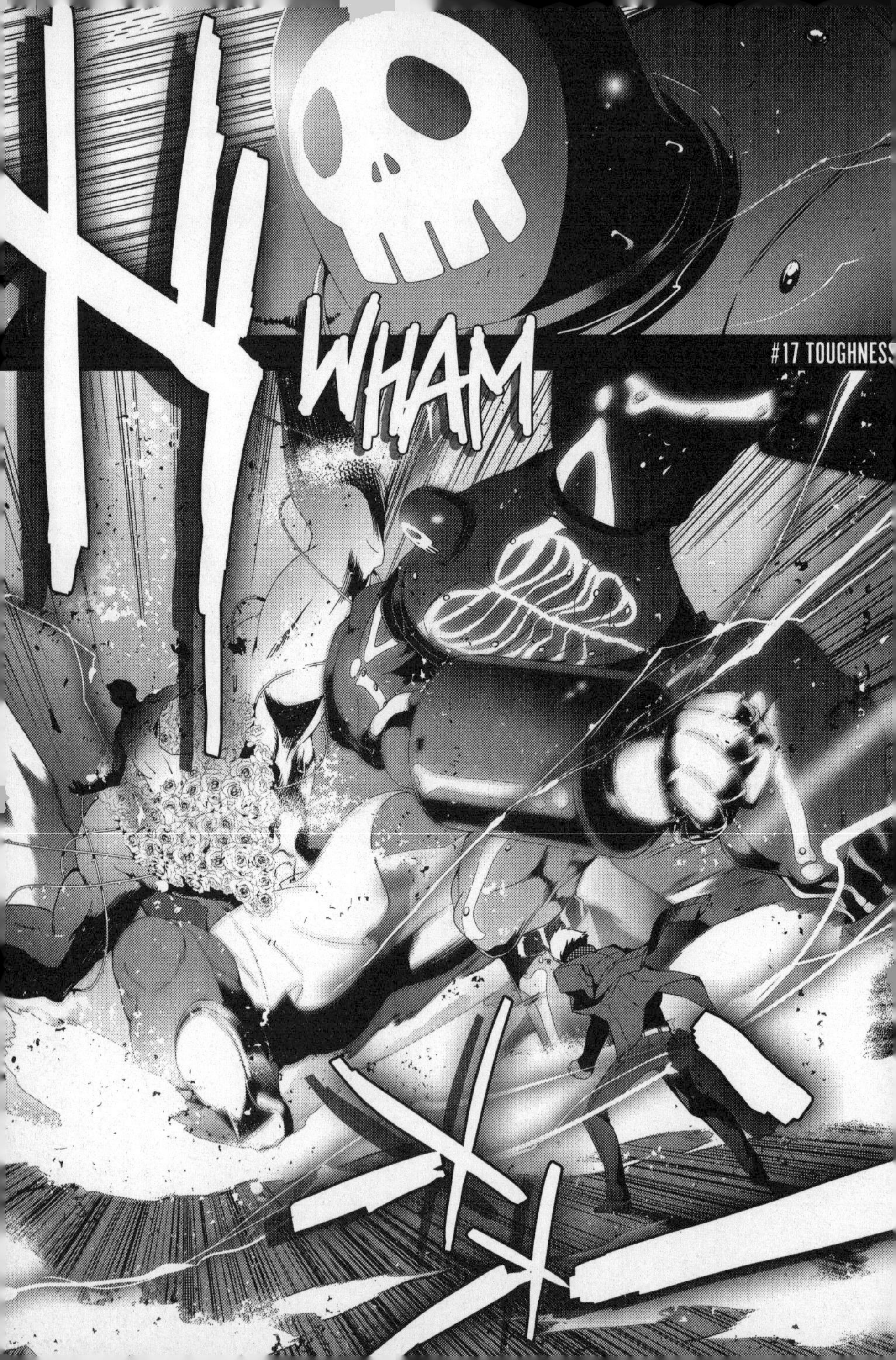
WHAM
#17 TOUGHNESS

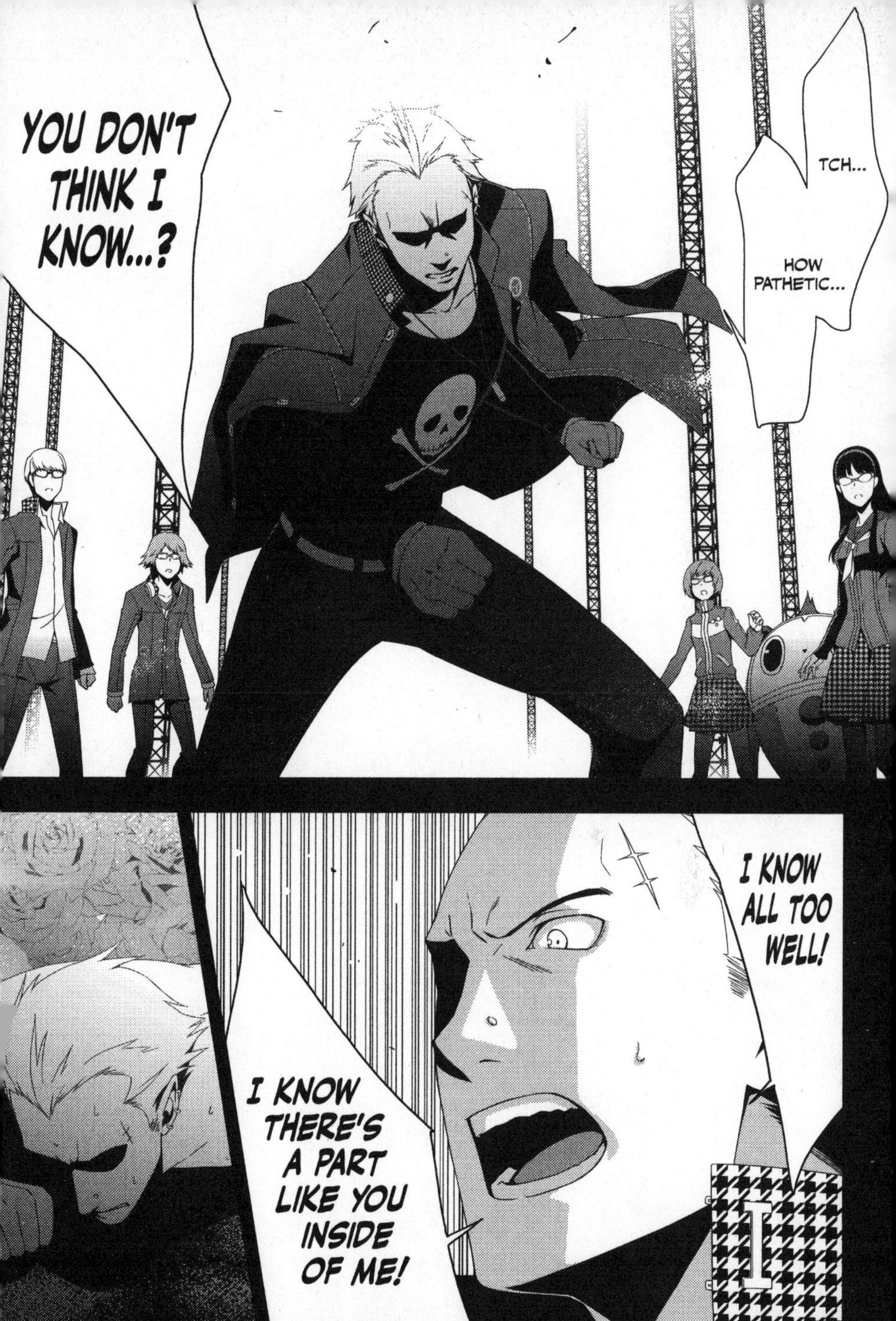
TCH...
HOW PATHETIC...
YOU DON'T THINK I KNOW...?
I KNOW ALL TOO WELL!
I KNOW THERE'S A PART LIKE YOU INSIDE OF ME!

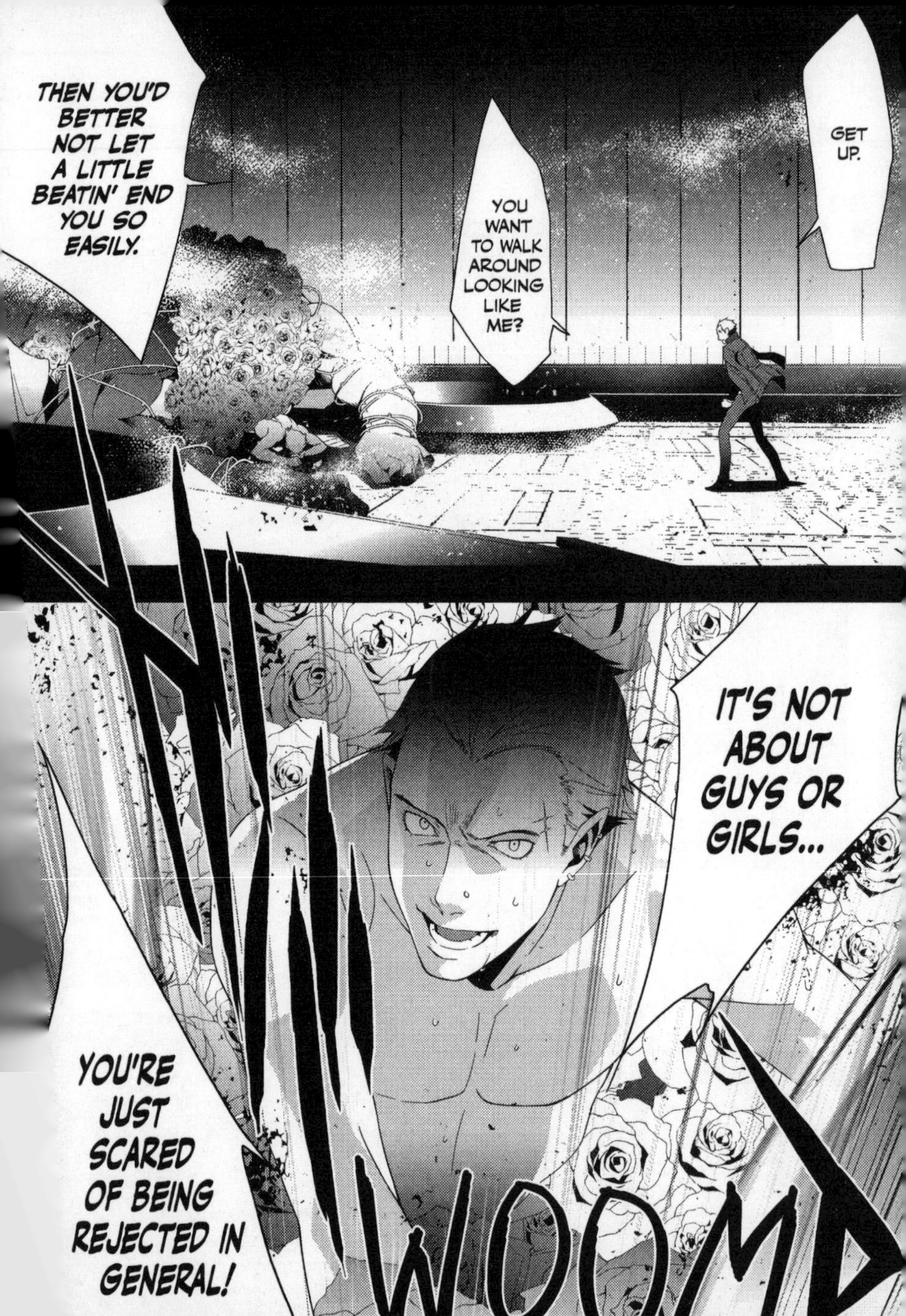
GET UP.
YOU WANT TO WALK AROUND LOOKING LIKE ME?
THEN YOU'D BETTER NOT LET A LITTLE BEATIN' END YOU SO EASILY.
IT'S NOT ABOUT GUYS OR GIRLS...
YOU'RE JUST SCARED OF BEING REJECTED IN GENERAL!
WOOMP

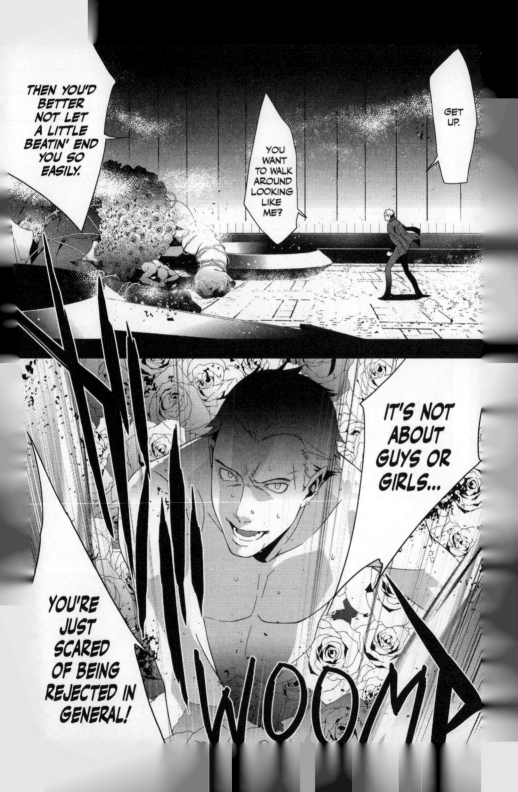

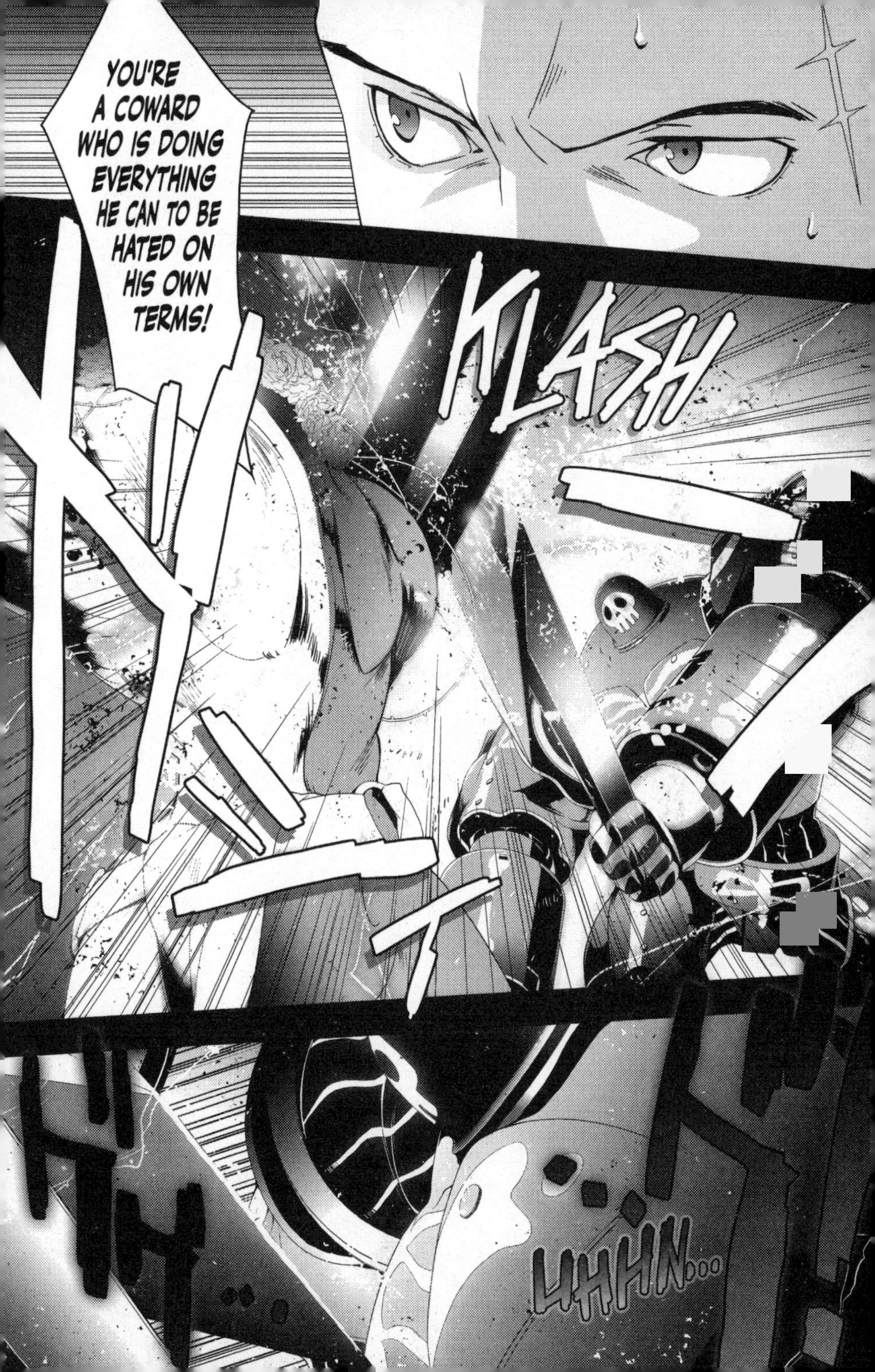
YOU'RE A COWARD WHO IS DOING EVERYTHING HE CAN TO BE HATED ON HIS OWN TERMS!
KLASH
UHHN...

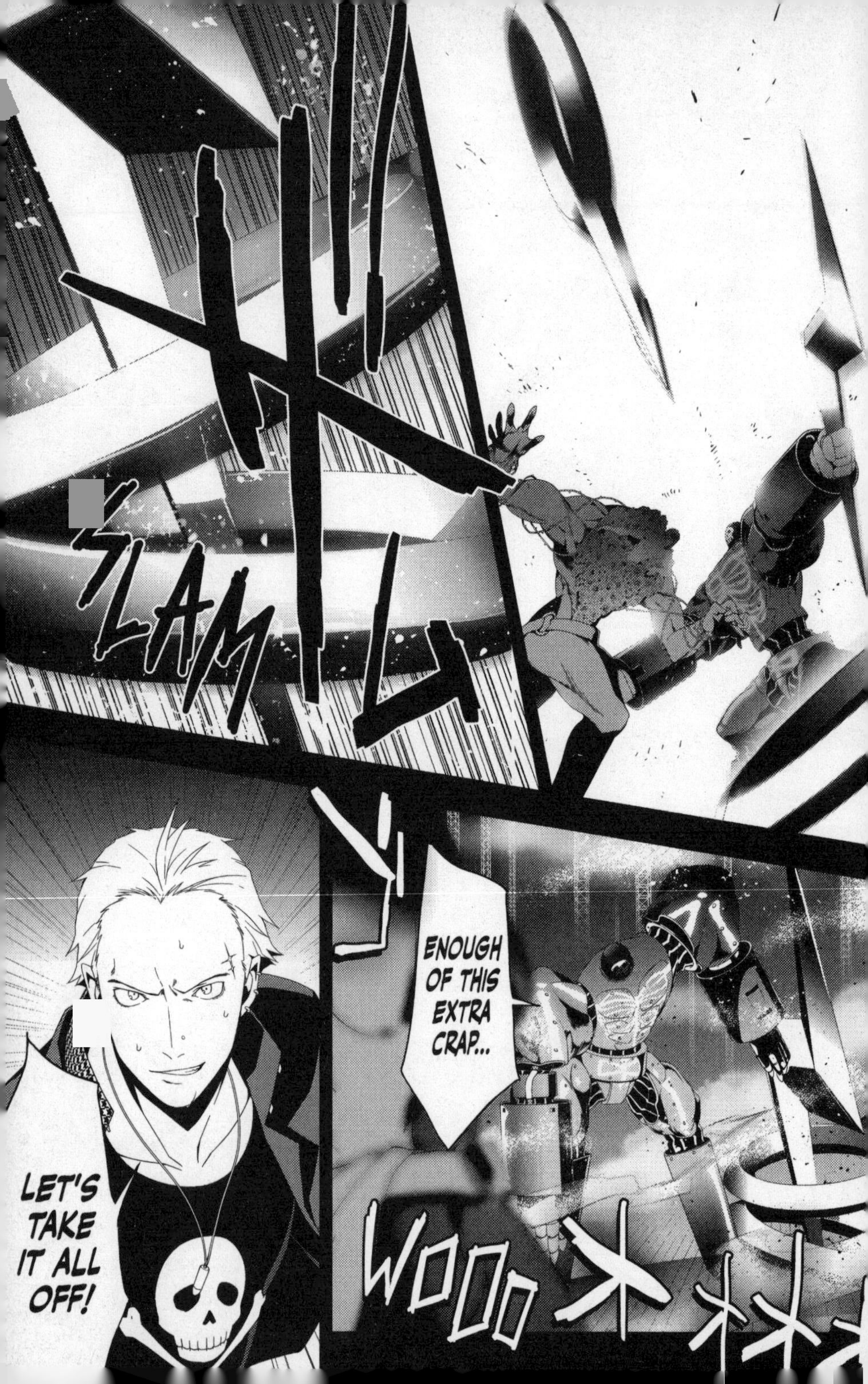
SLAM
ENOUGH OF THIS EXTRA CRAP...
WOOO
LET'S TAKE IT ALL OFF!

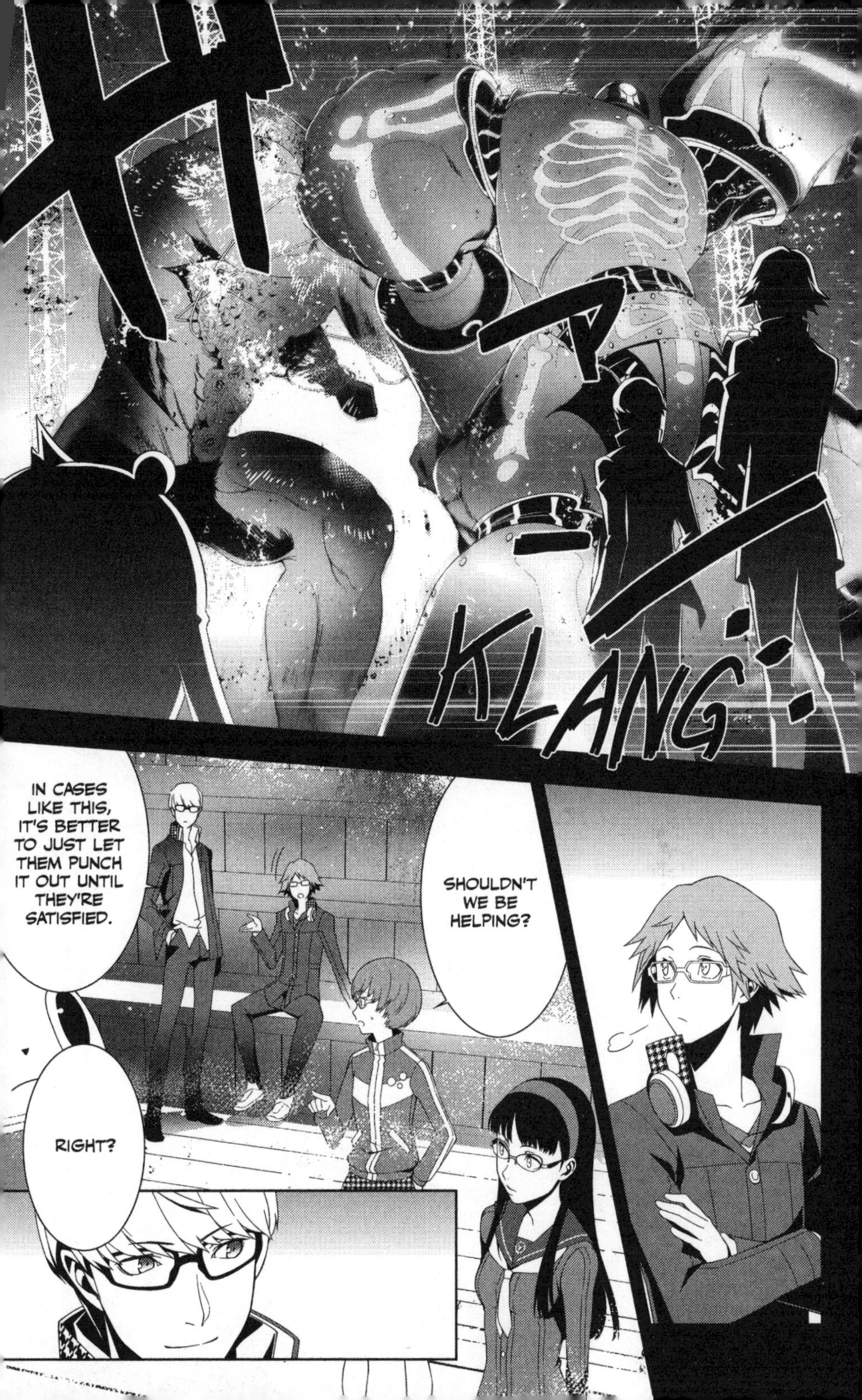
KLANG
SHOULDN'T WE BE HELPING?
IN CASES LIKE THIS, IT'S BETTER TO JUST LET THEM PUNCH IT OUT UNTIL THEY'RE SATISFIED.
RIGHT?

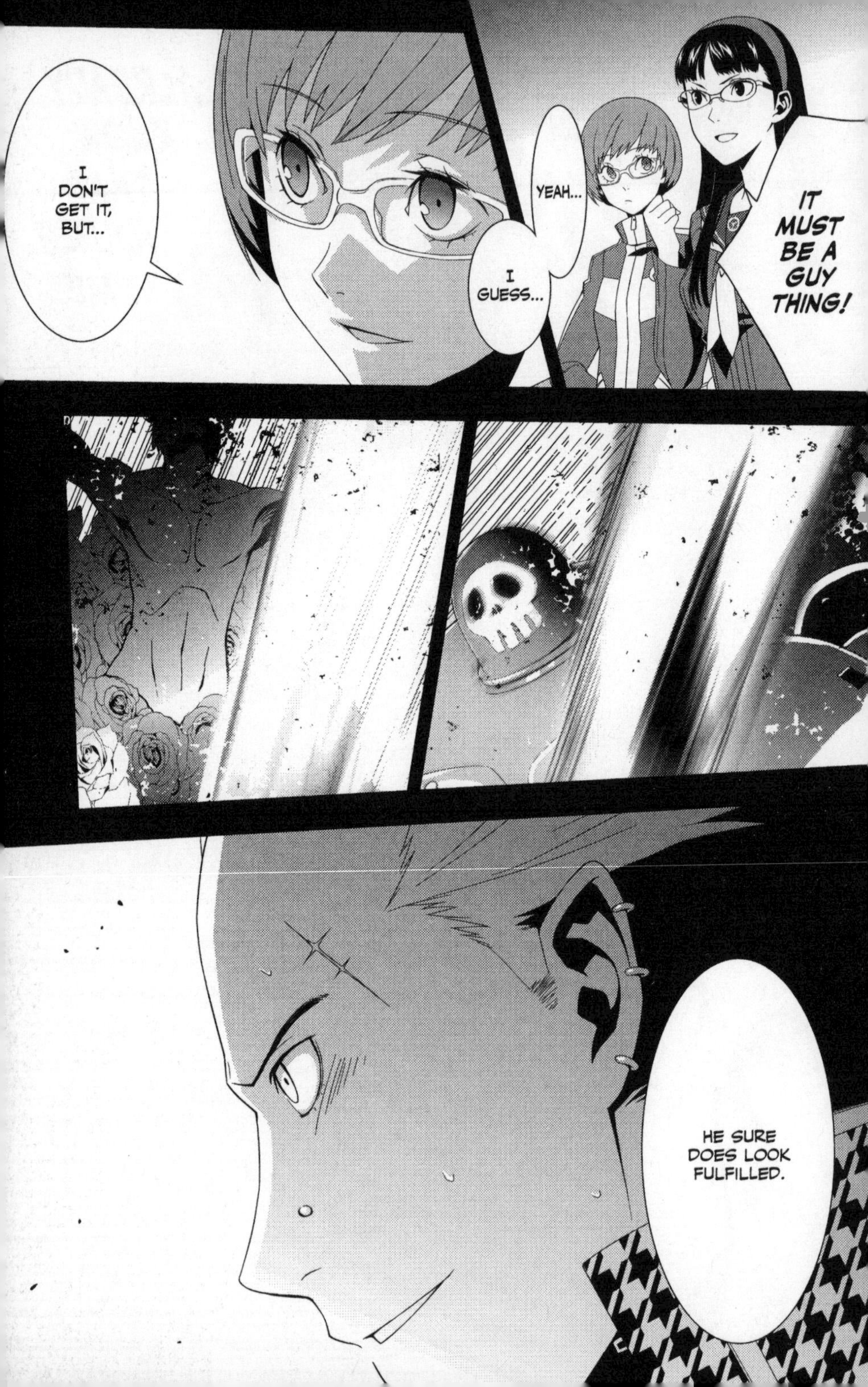
IT MUST BE A GUY THING!
YEAH...
I GUESS...
I DON'T GET IT, BUT...
HE SURE DOES LOOK FULFILLED.

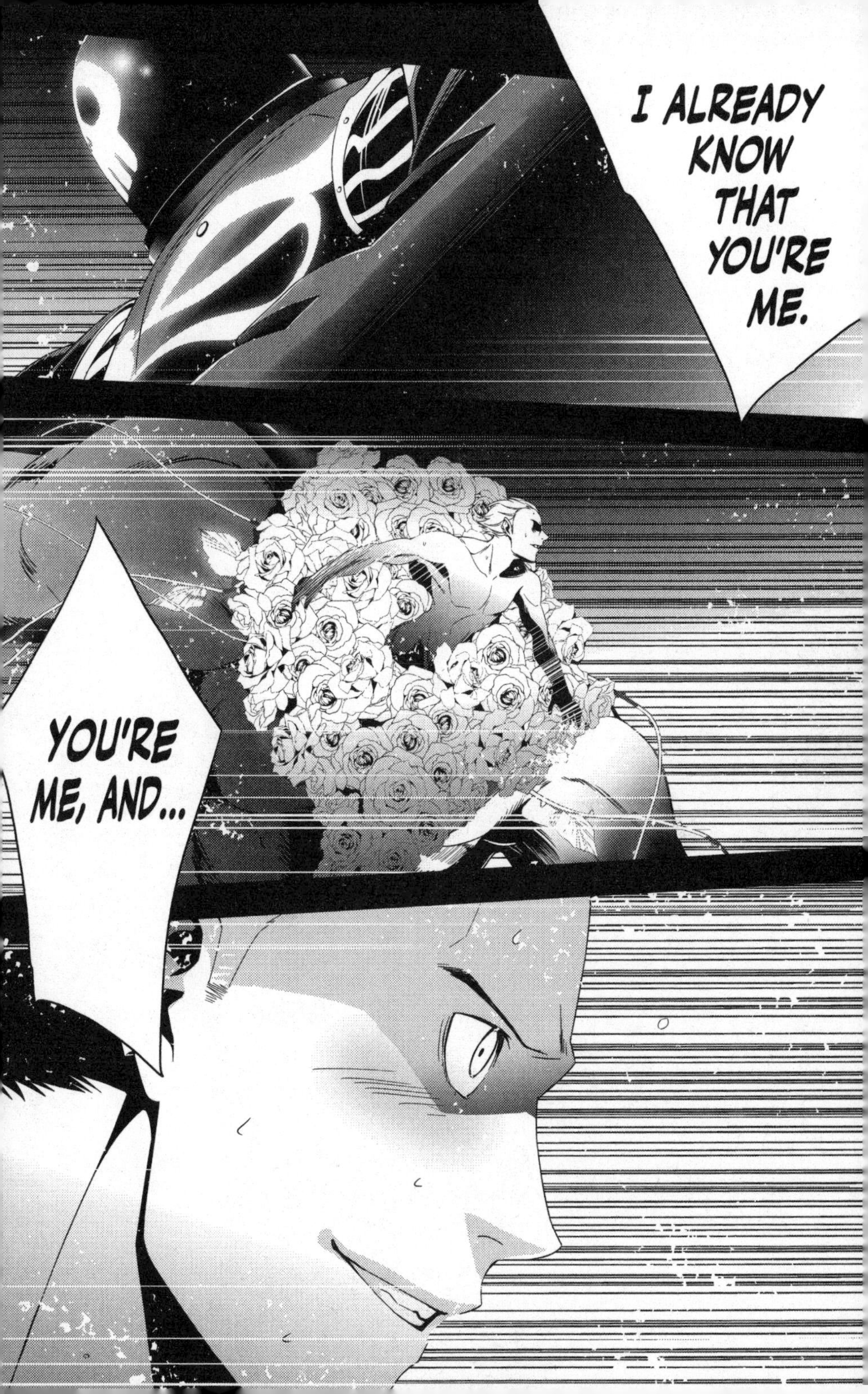
I ALREADY KNOW THAT YOU'RE ME.
YOU'RE ME, AND...

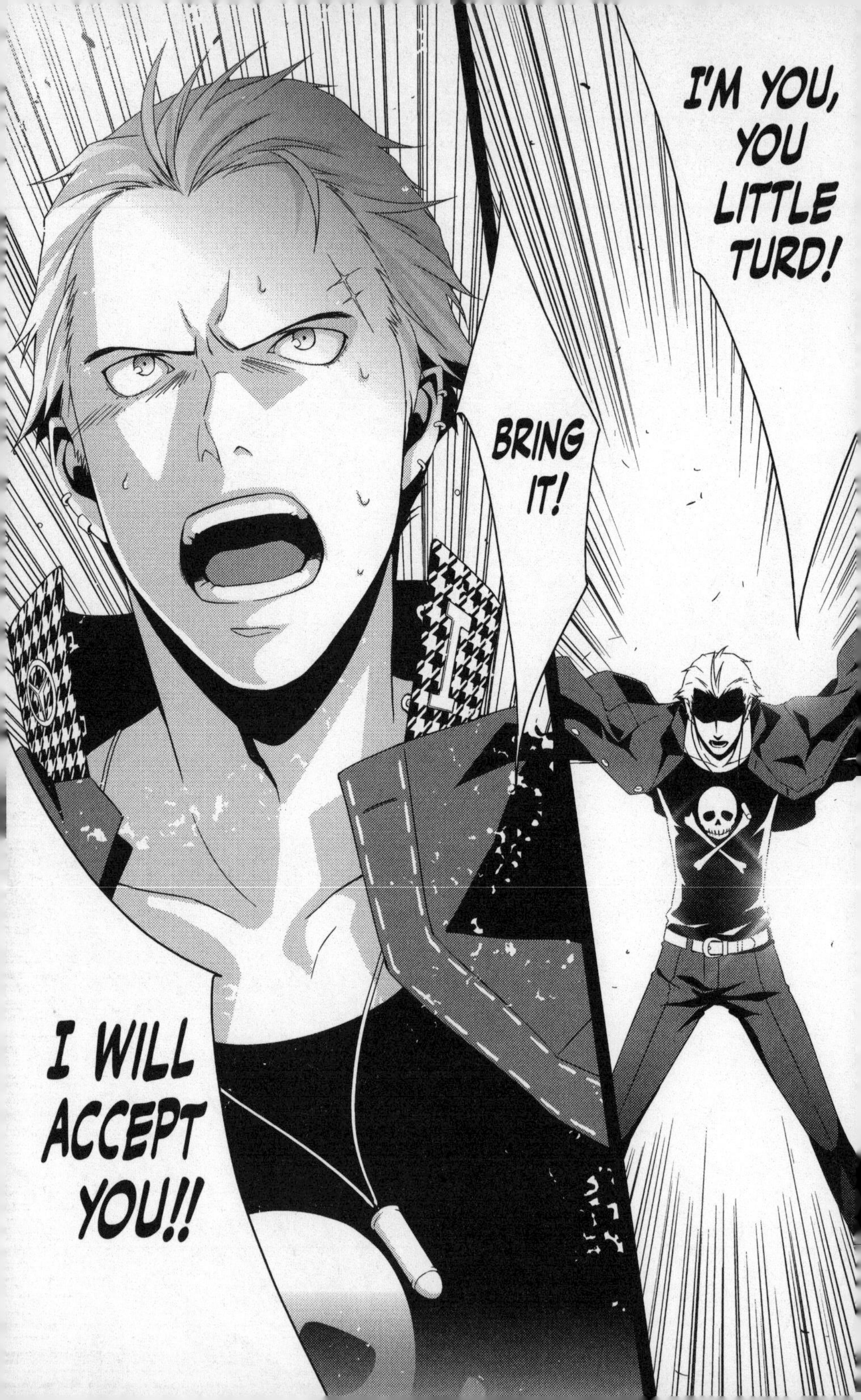
I'M YOU, YOU LITTLE TURD!
BRING IT!
I WILL ACCEPT YOU!!

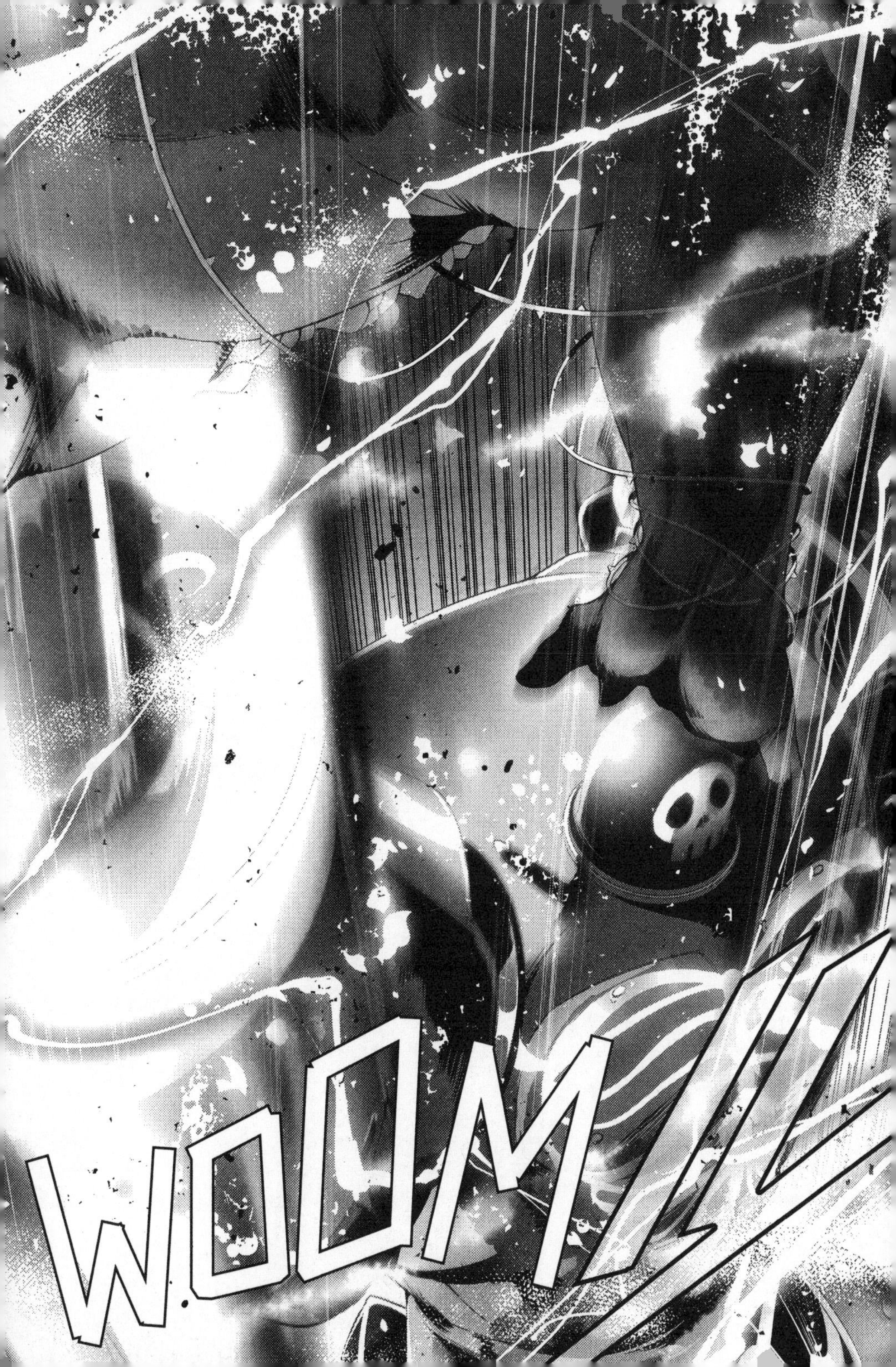
WOOM!!

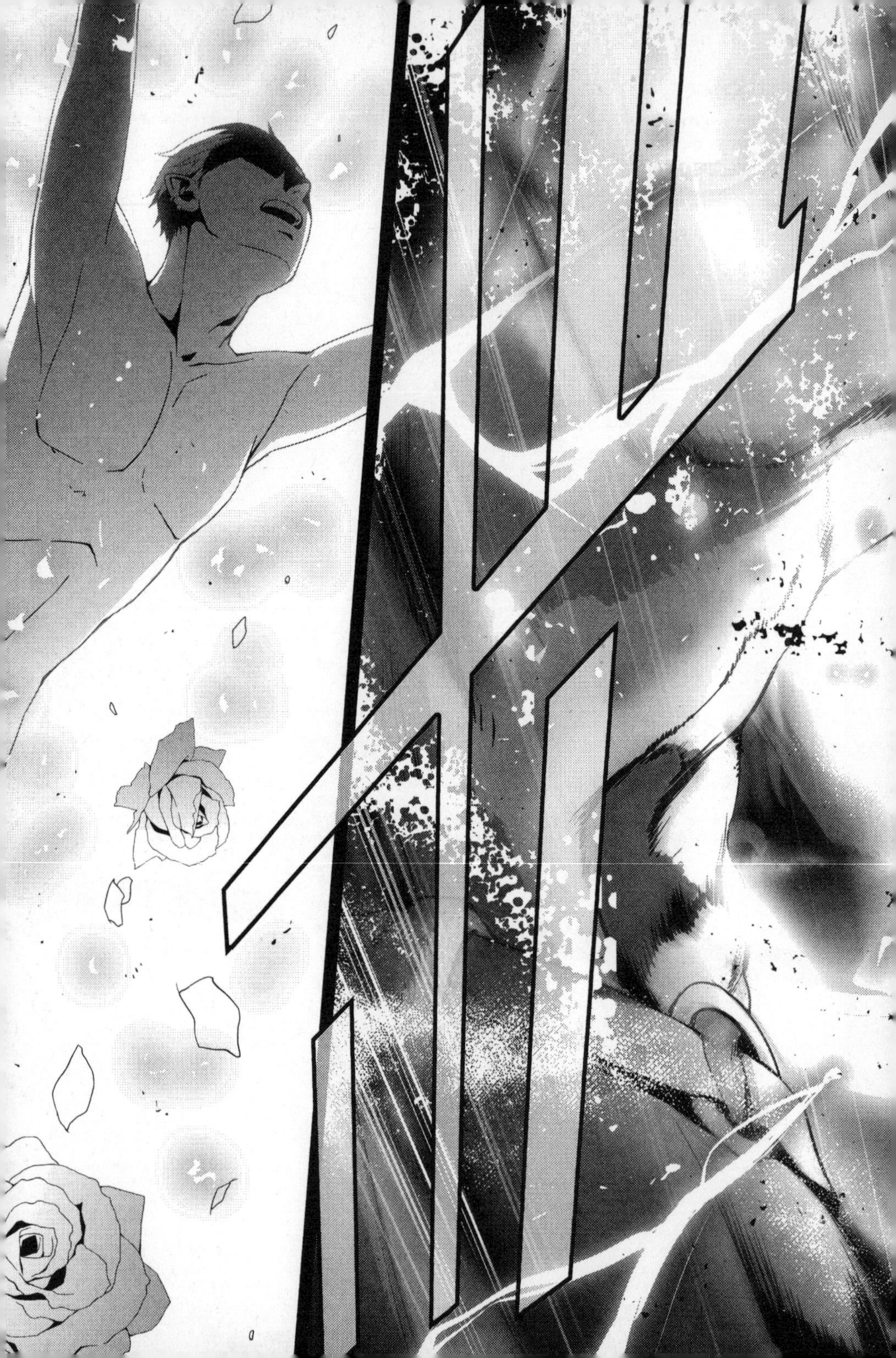

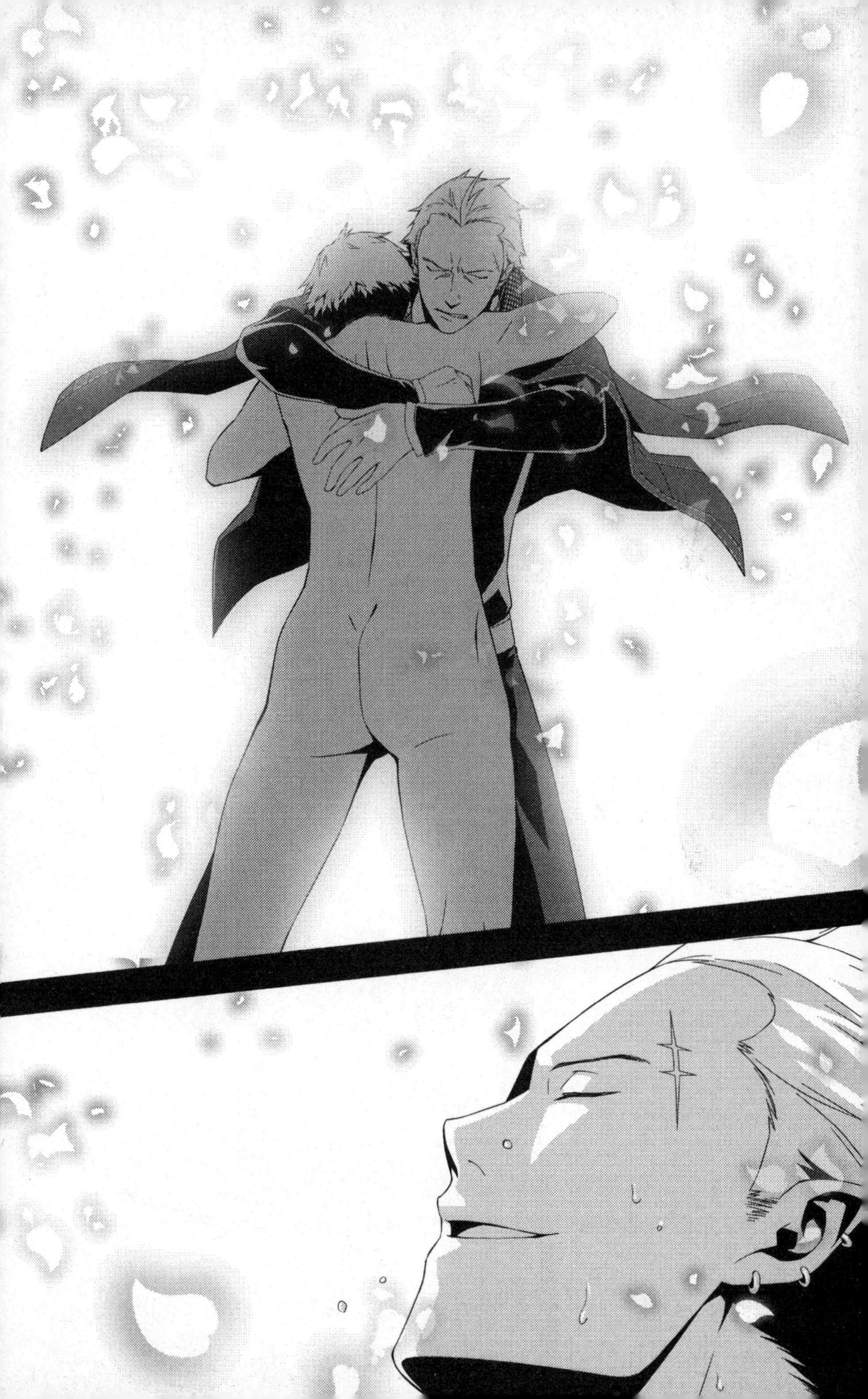

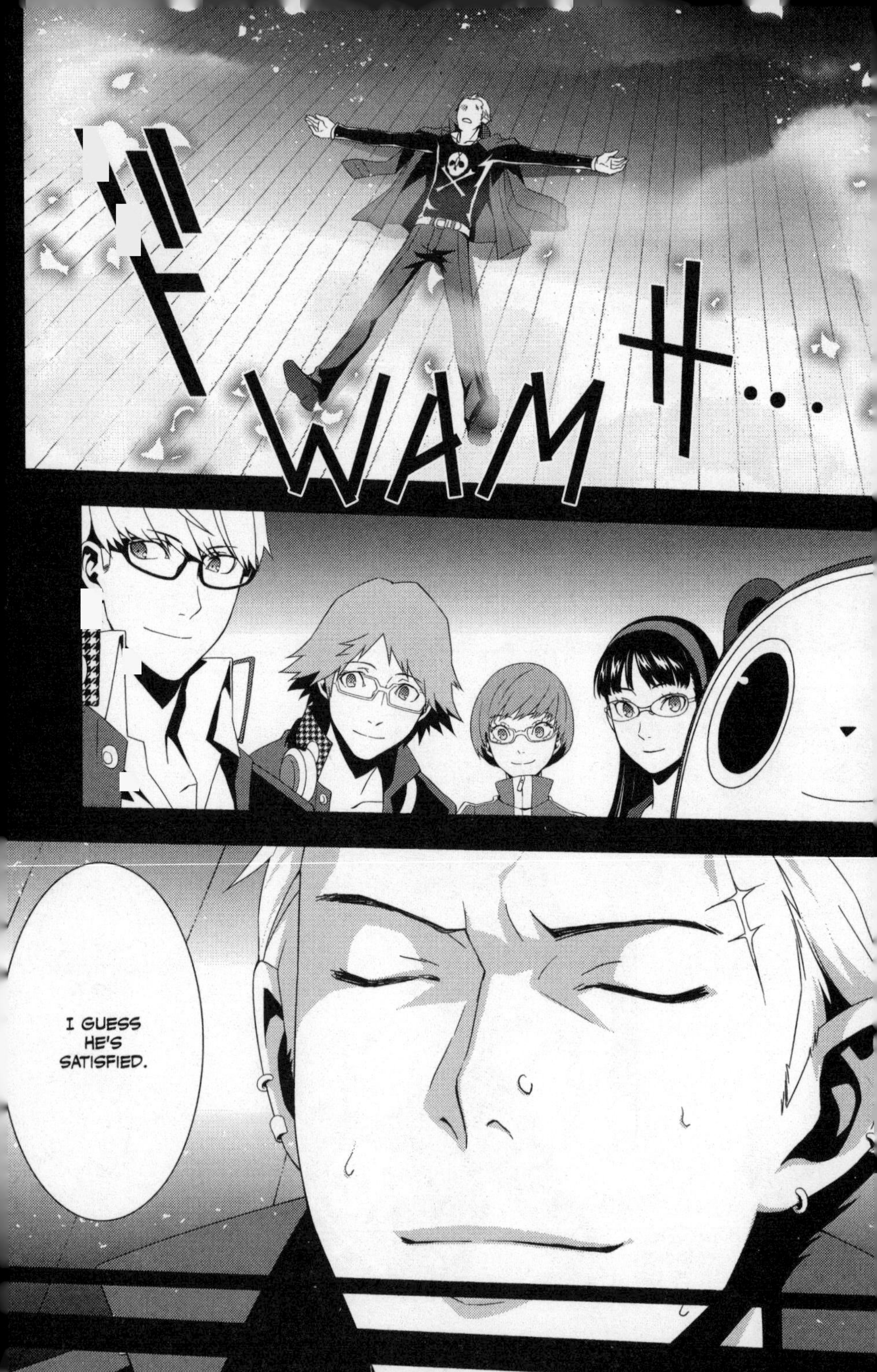
WAMM...
I GUESS HE'S SATISFIED.

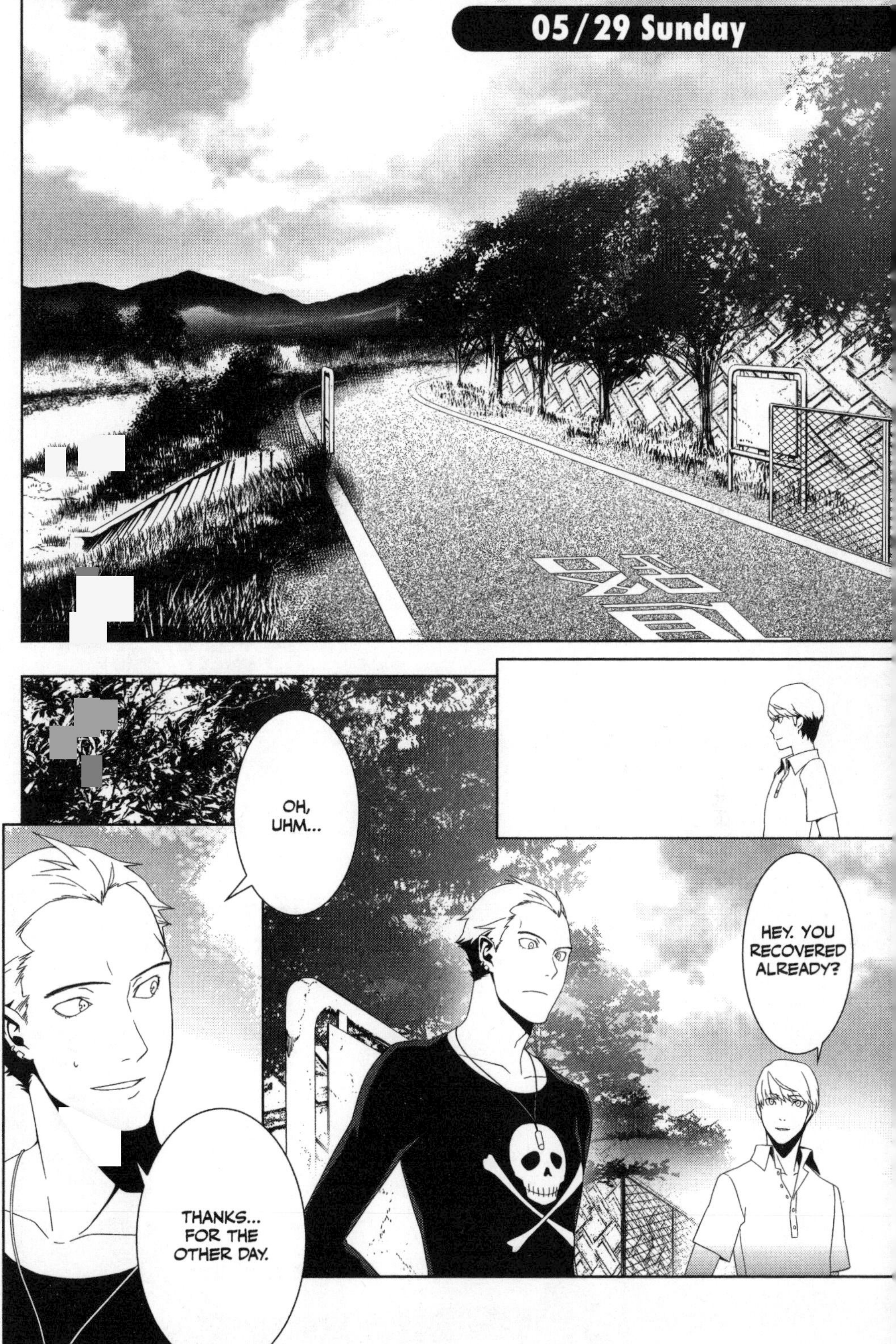
05/29 Sunday
HEY. YOU RECOVERED ALREADY?
OH, UHM...
THANKS... FOR THE OTHER DAY.

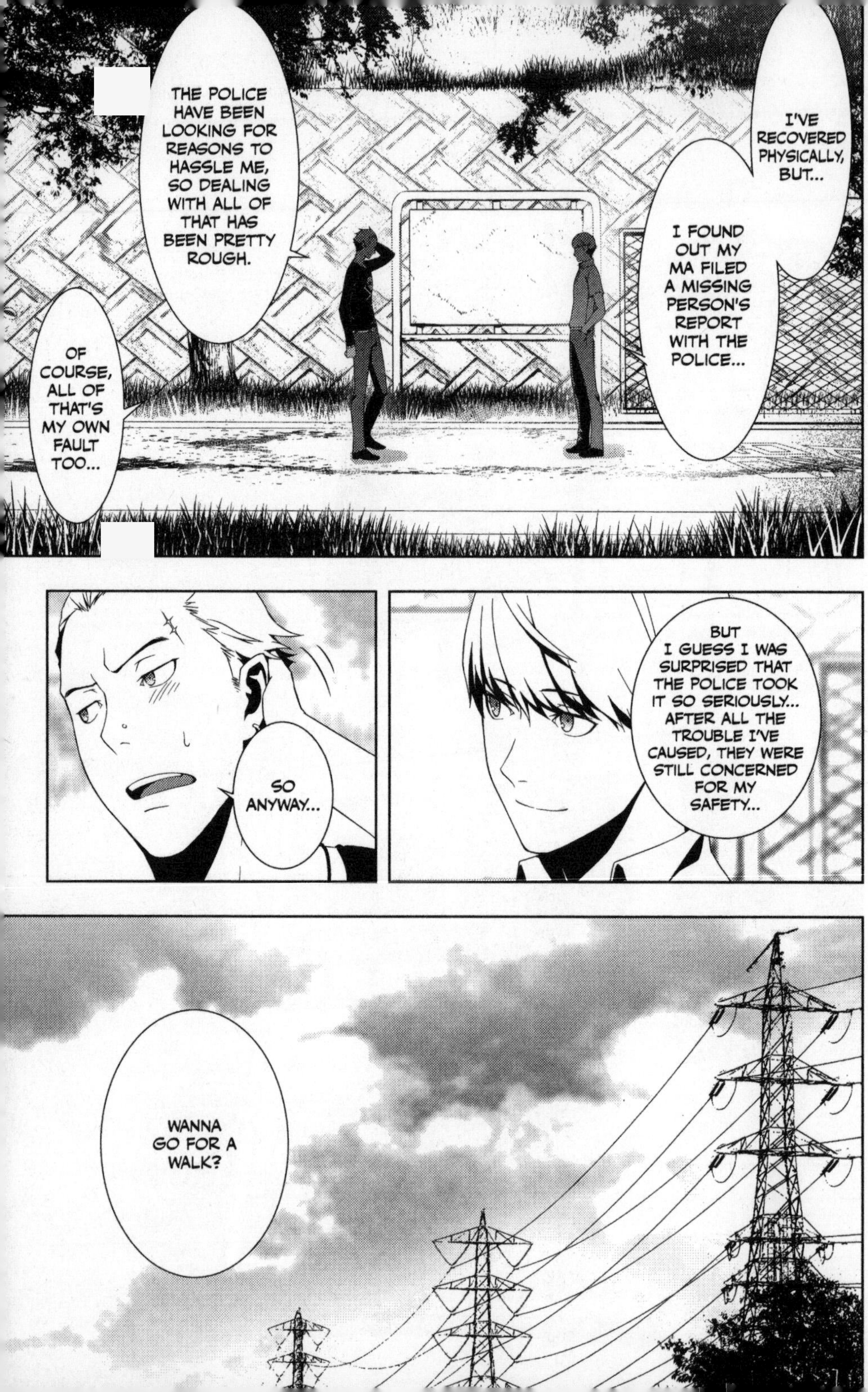
I'VE RECOVERED PHYSICALLY, BUT...
I FOUND OUT MY MA FILED A MISSING PERSON'S REPORT WITH THE POLICE...
THE POLICE HAVE BEEN LOOKING FOR REASONS TO HASSLE ME, SO DEALING WITH ALL OF THAT HAS BEEN PRETTY ROUGH.
OF COURSE, ALL OF THAT'S MY OWN FAULT TOO...
BUT I GUESS I WAS SURPRISED THAT THE POLICE TOOK IT SO SERIOUSLY... AFTER ALL THE TROUBLE I'VE CAUSED, THEY WERE STILL CONCERNED FOR MY SAFETY...
SO ANYWAY...
WANNA GO FOR A WALK?

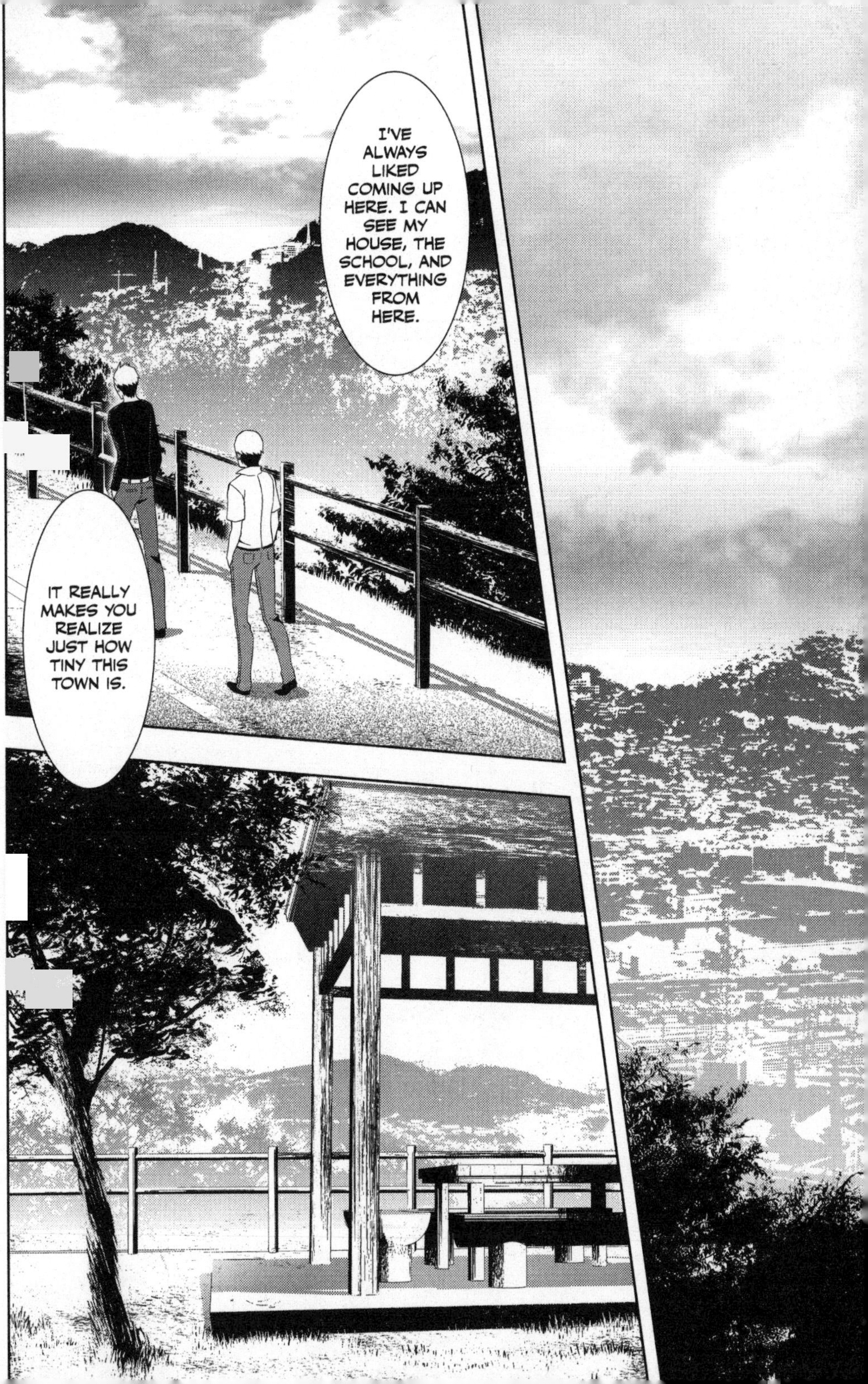
I'VE ALWAYS LIKED COMING UP HERE. I CAN SEE MY HOUSE, THE SCHOOL, AND EVERYTHING FROM HERE.
IT REALLY MAKES YOU REALIZE JUST HOW TINY THIS TOWN IS.

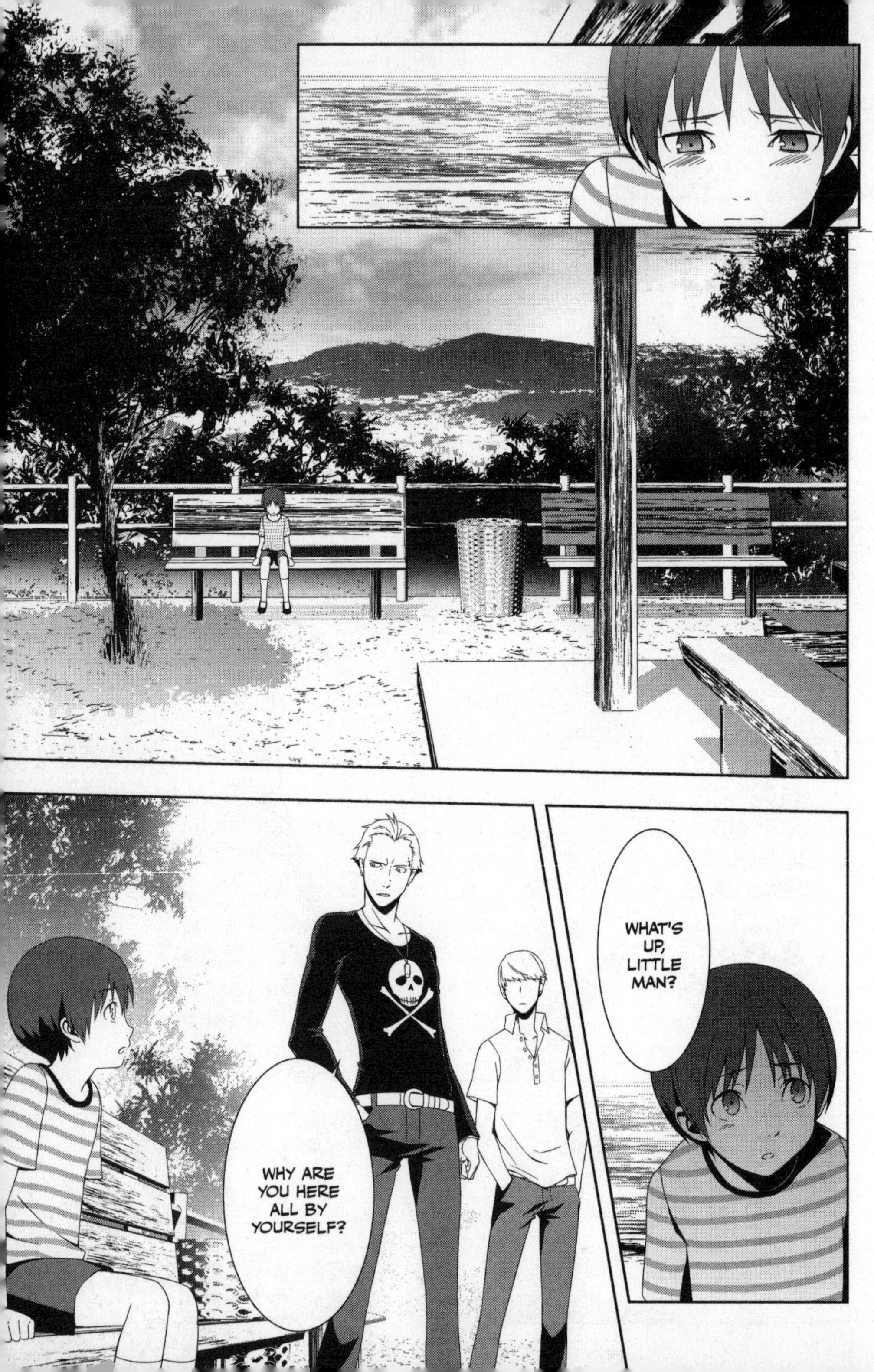
WHAT'S UP, LITTLE MAN?
WHY ARE YOU HERE ALL BY YOURSELF?

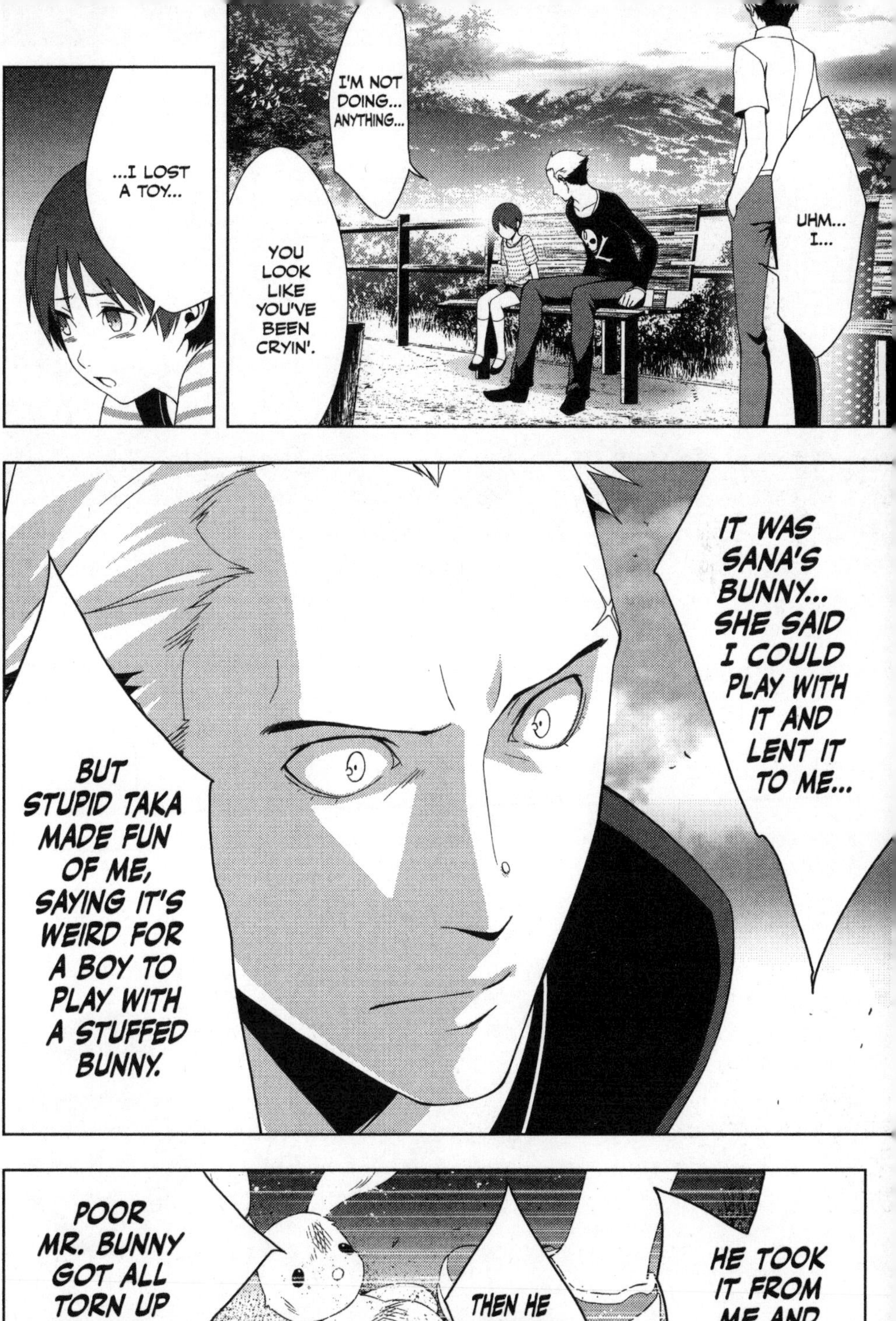
UHM... I...
I'M NOT DOING... ANYTHING...
YOU LOOK LIKE YOU'VE BEEN CRYIN'.
...I LOST A TOY...
IT WAS SANA'S BUNNY... SHE SAID I COULD PLAY WITH IT AND LENT IT TO ME...
BUT STUPID TAKA MADE FUN OF ME, SAYING IT'S WEIRD FOR A BOY TO PLAY WITH A STUFFED BUNNY.
HE TOOK IT FROM ME AND THREW IT...
THEN HE STOMPED ON IT...
POOR MR. BUNNY GOT ALL TORN UP AND DIRTY.

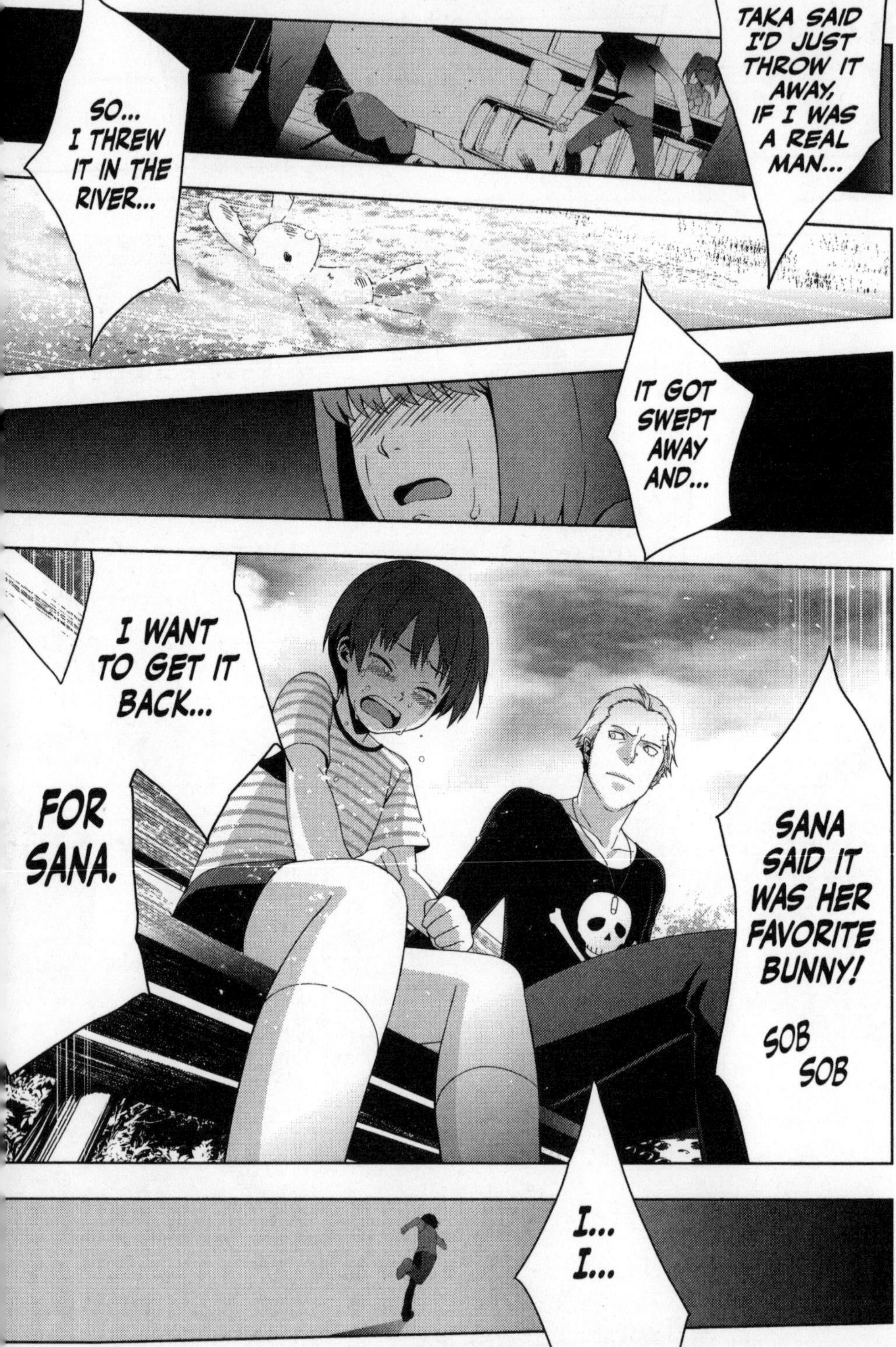
TAKA SAID I'D JUST THROW IT AWAY, IF I WAS A REAL MAN...
SO... I THREW IT IN THE RIVER...
IT GOT SWEPT AWAY AND...
SANA SAID IT WAS HER FAVORITE BUNNY!
SOB SOB
I WANT TO GET IT BACK...
FOR SANA.
I... I...

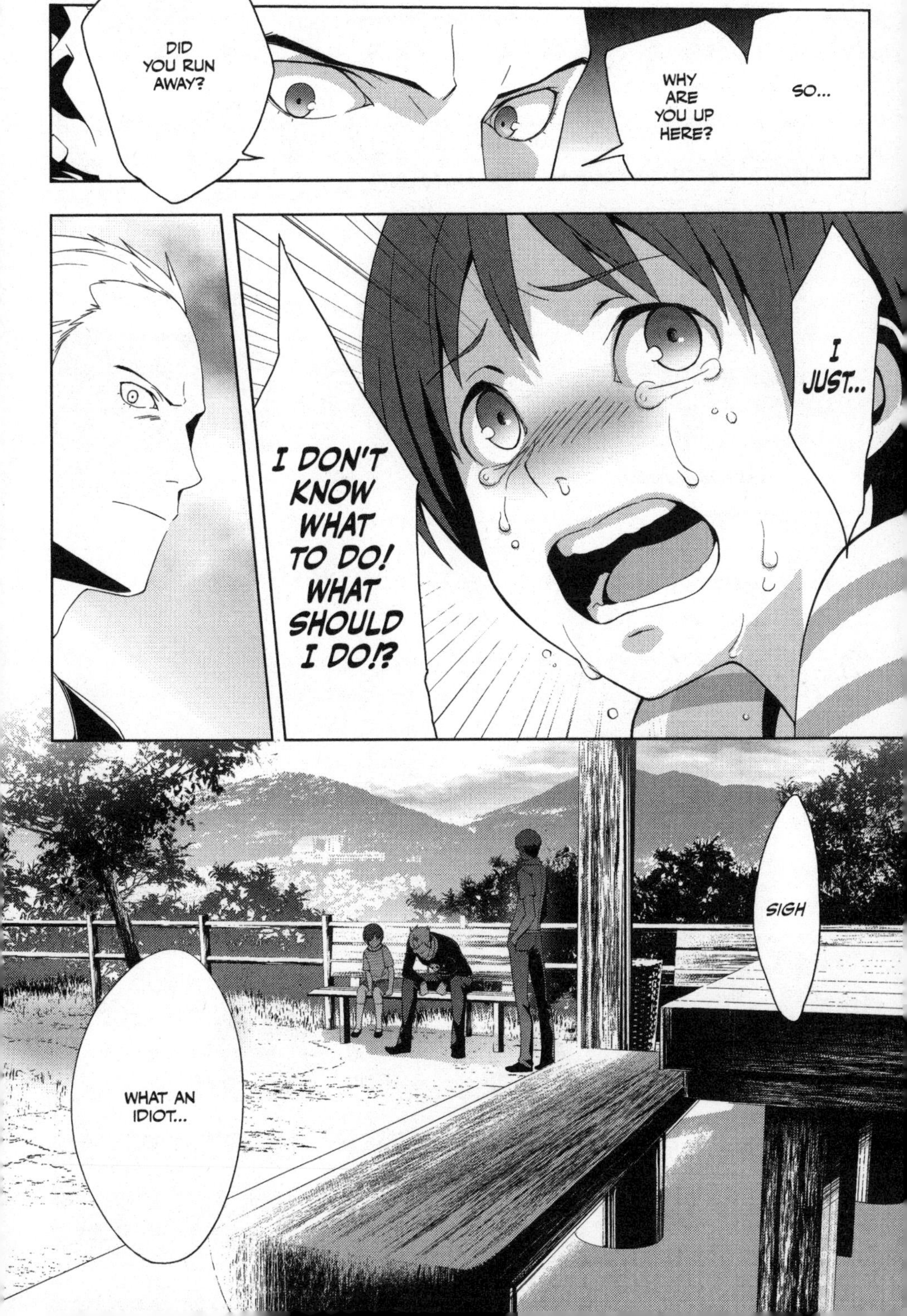
SO...
WHY ARE YOU UP HERE?
DID YOU RUN AWAY?
I JUST...
I DON'T KNOW WHAT TO DO! WHAT SHOULD I DO!?
SIGH
WHAT AN IDIOT...

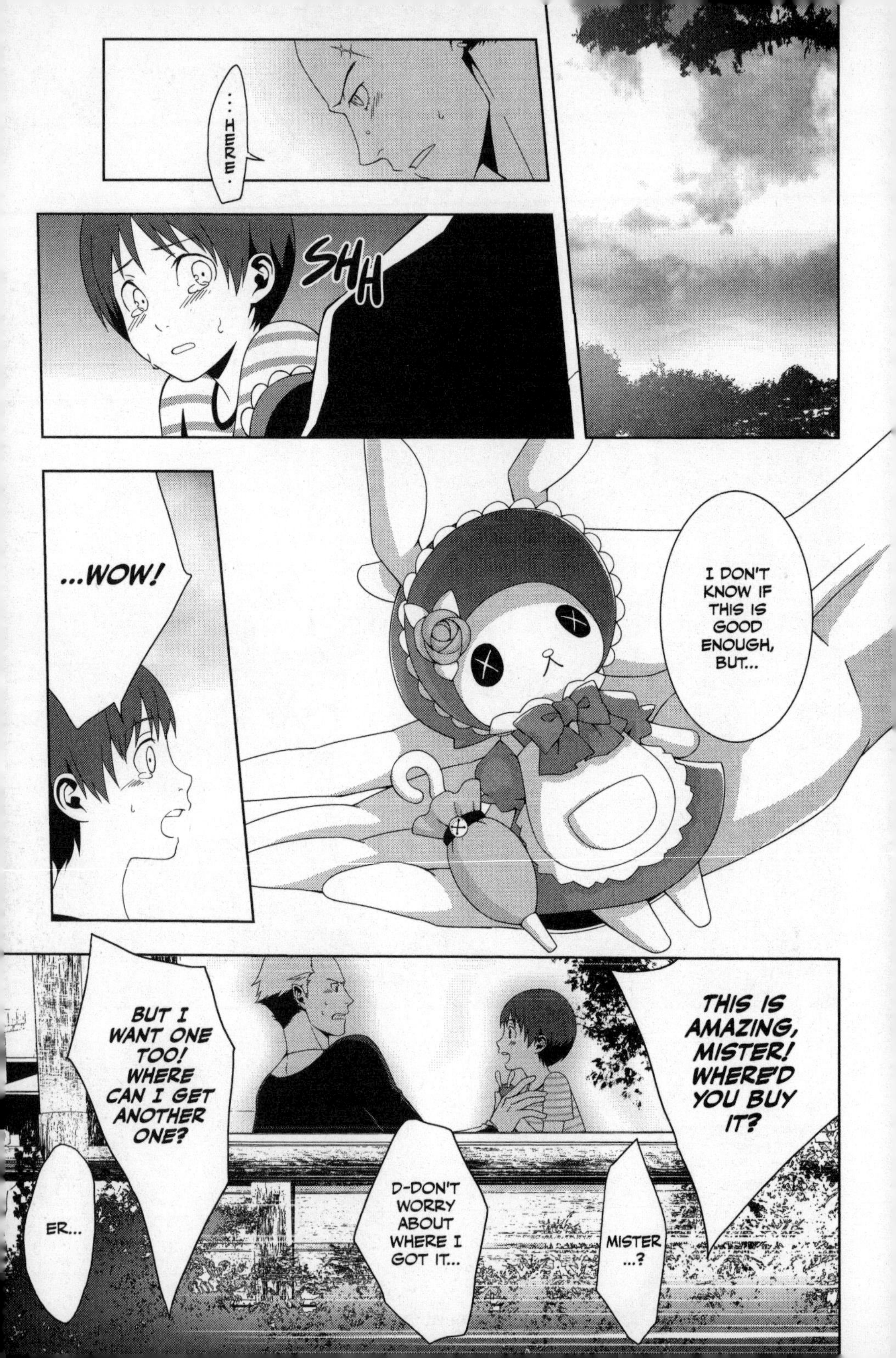
...HERE.
SHH
I DON'T KNOW IF THIS IS GOOD ENOUGH, BUT...
...WOW!
THIS IS AMAZING, MISTER! WHERE'D YOU BUY IT?
BUT I WANT ONE TOO! WHERE CAN I GET ANOTHER ONE?
MISTER ...?
D-DON'T WORRY ABOUT WHERE I GOT IT...
ER...

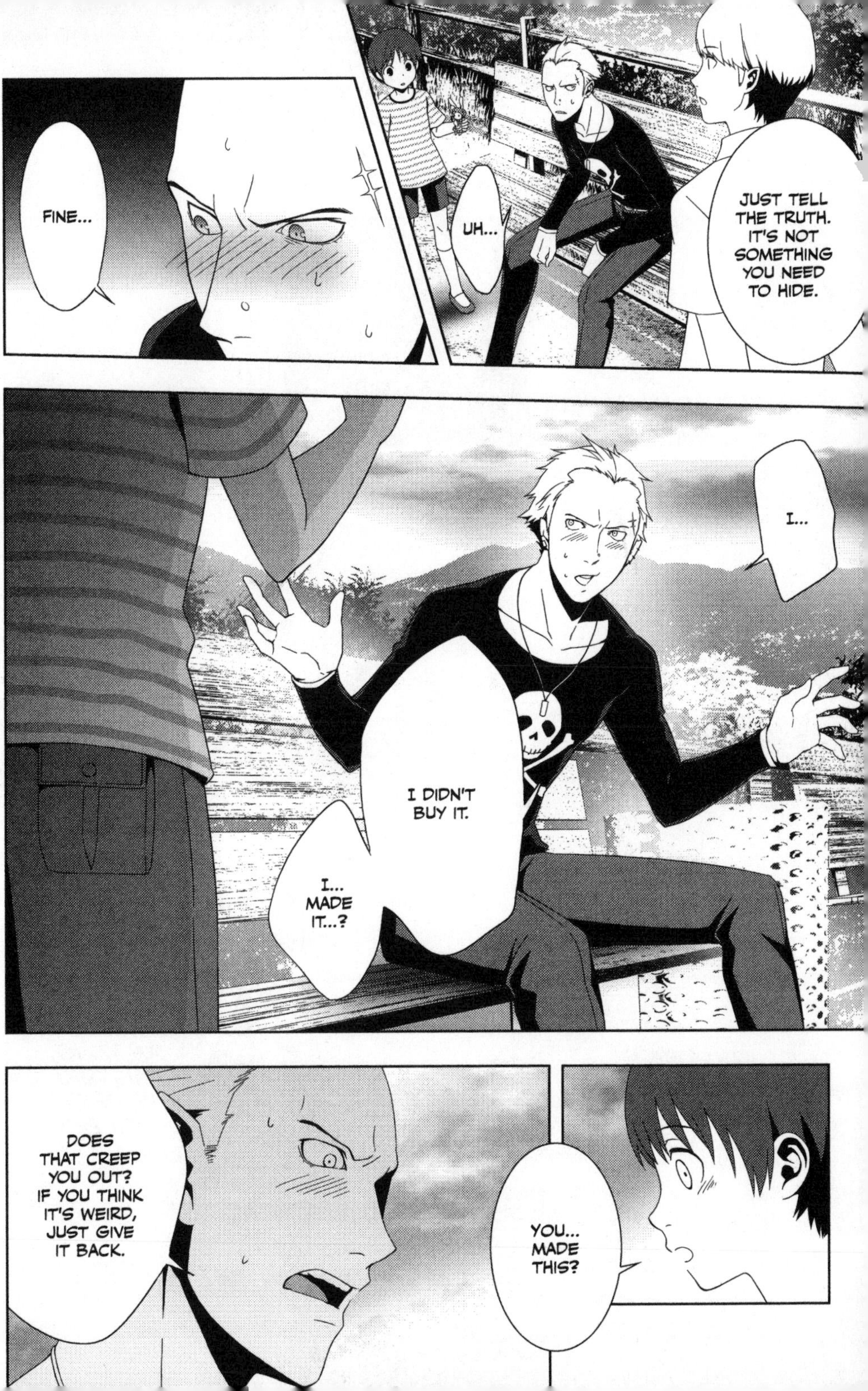
JUST TELL THE TRUTH. IT'S NOT SOMETHING YOU NEED TO HIDE.
UH...
FINE...
I...
I DIDN'T BUY IT.
I... MADE IT...?
YOU... MADE THIS?
DOES THAT CREEP YOU OUT? IF YOU THINK IT'S WEIRD, JUST GIVE IT BACK.

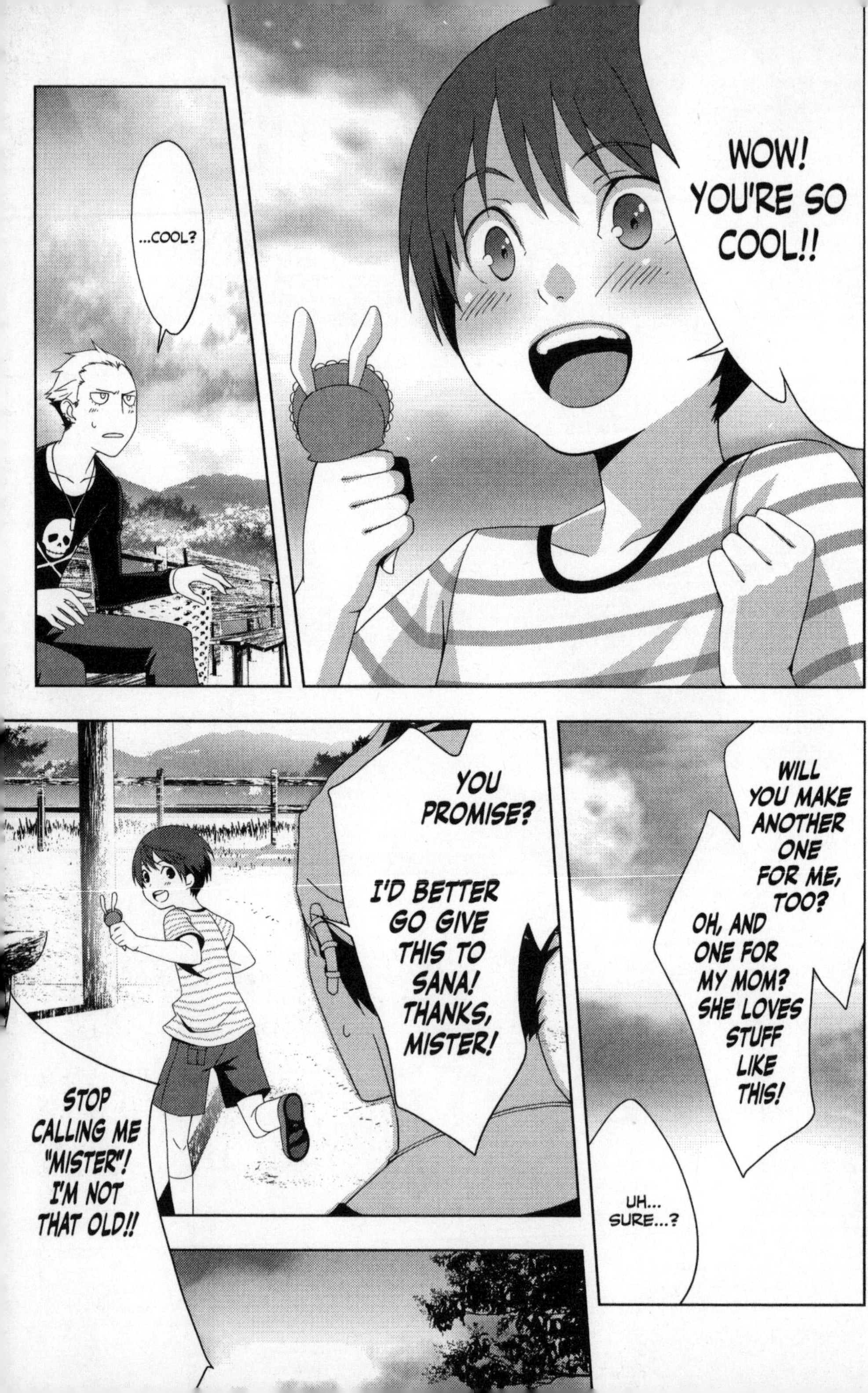
WOW! YOU'RE SO COOL!!
...COOL?
WILL YOU MAKE ANOTHER ONE FOR ME, TOO?
OH, AND ONE FOR MY MOM? SHE LOVES STUFF LIKE THIS!
UH... SURE...?
YOU PROMISE?
I'D BETTER GO GIVE THIS TO SANA! THANKS, MISTER!
STOP CALLING ME "MISTER"! I'M NOT THAT OLD!!

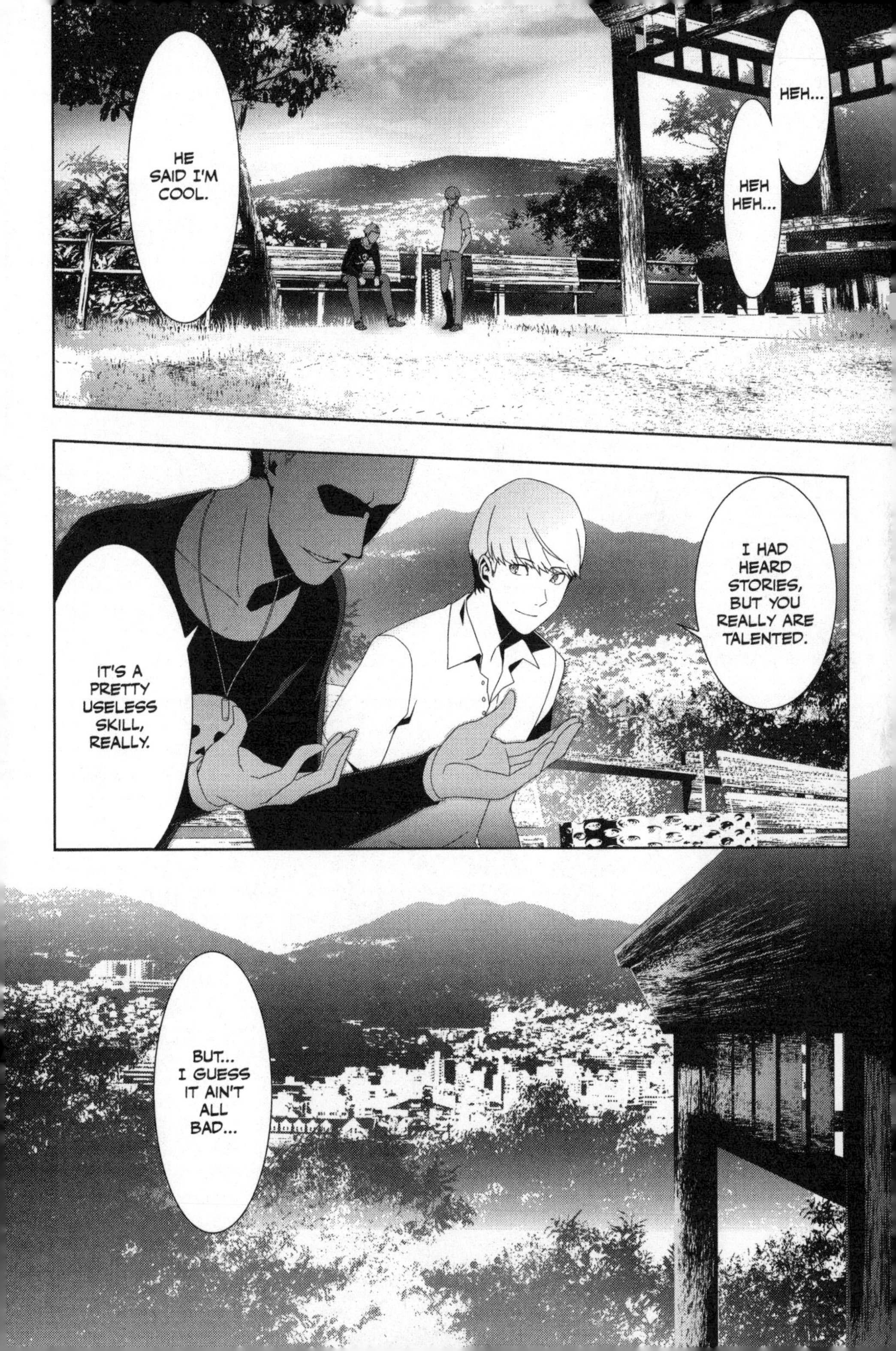
HEH...
HEH HEH...
HE SAID I'M COOL.
I HAD HEARD STORIES, BUT YOU REALLY ARE TALENTED.
IT'S A PRETTY USELESS SKILL, REALLY.
BUT... I GUESS IT AIN'T ALL BAD...

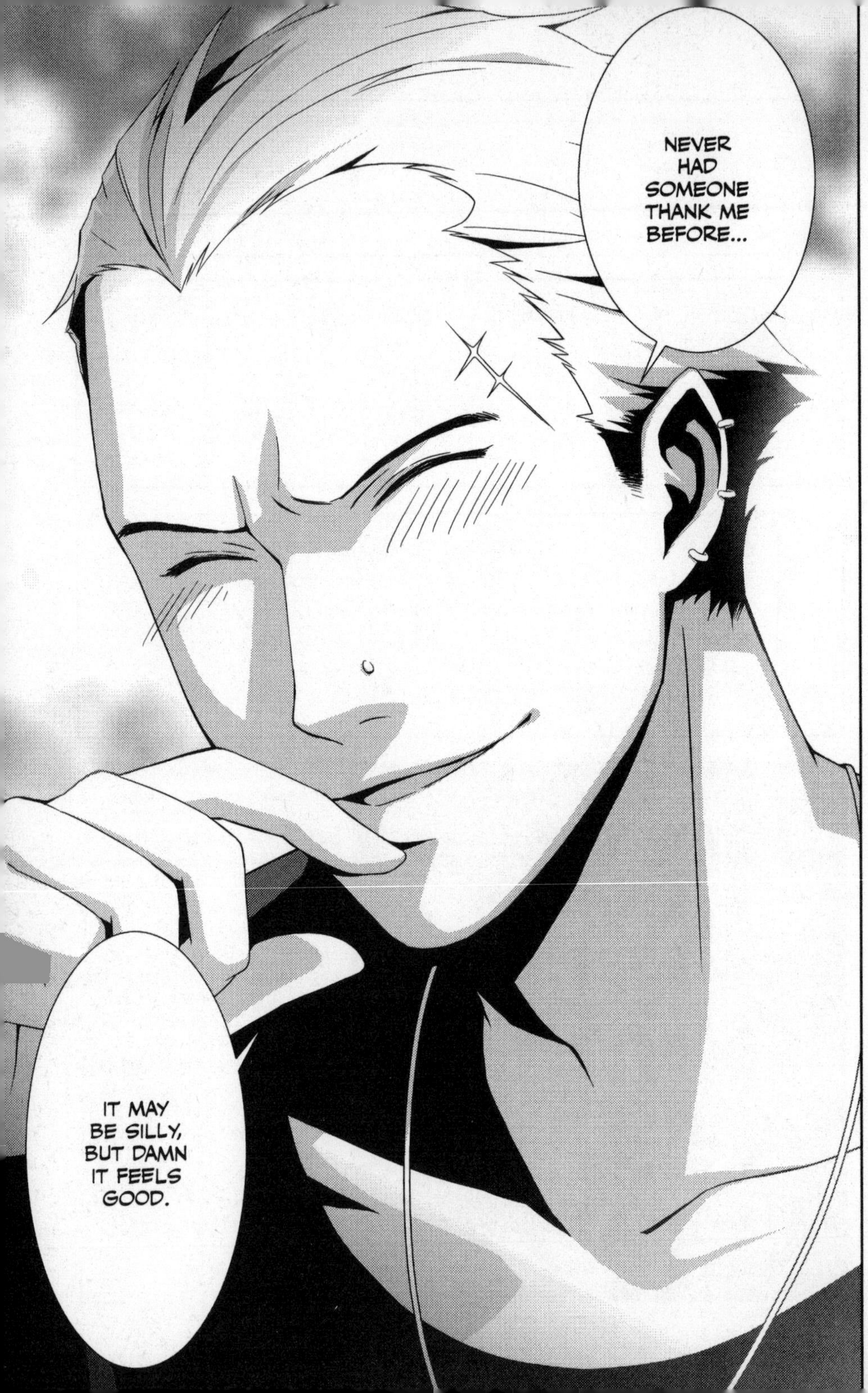
NEVER HAD SOMEONE THANK ME BEFORE...
IT MAY BE SILLY, BUT DAMN IT FEELS GOOD.

Sogabenoweight

SOGABE now viii

I've Been keeping Busy Doing all kinds of stuff, as usual. By the time this Book hits shelves, I imagine my P4 illustrations will Be out in the moon magazine. I think, anyway.

thank you for purchasing volume 3 of my persona 4 manga.

I mentioned in the "sogabe now" of volume 2 that I make a hobby of Daydreaming about the places I'D like to visit. well, for the first time in about a Decade, I Decided to visit my hometown of Sapporo and paid my respects at some family graves. my family is Shinto and not BuDDhist, so it's not exactly like visiting graves the way most people would think... But it's all the same idea.

oBviously, it wouldn't Be very appropriate to share photos of gravestones, so instead I offer this little snapshot of a tv tower at night. we live in such wonderful times that I can take such stunning photos with my little cell phone. I've Been living in tokyo for about 10 years now, But I think I'D Be more comfortable living in Sapporo. might Be nice to Be known as the local manga artist... I often imagine it would Be hard to live in a place like inaBa without a car... yeah, a car! getting my license would solve so many problems! anyway, the P4 manga still continues. I hope you'll keep reading!

-fin-

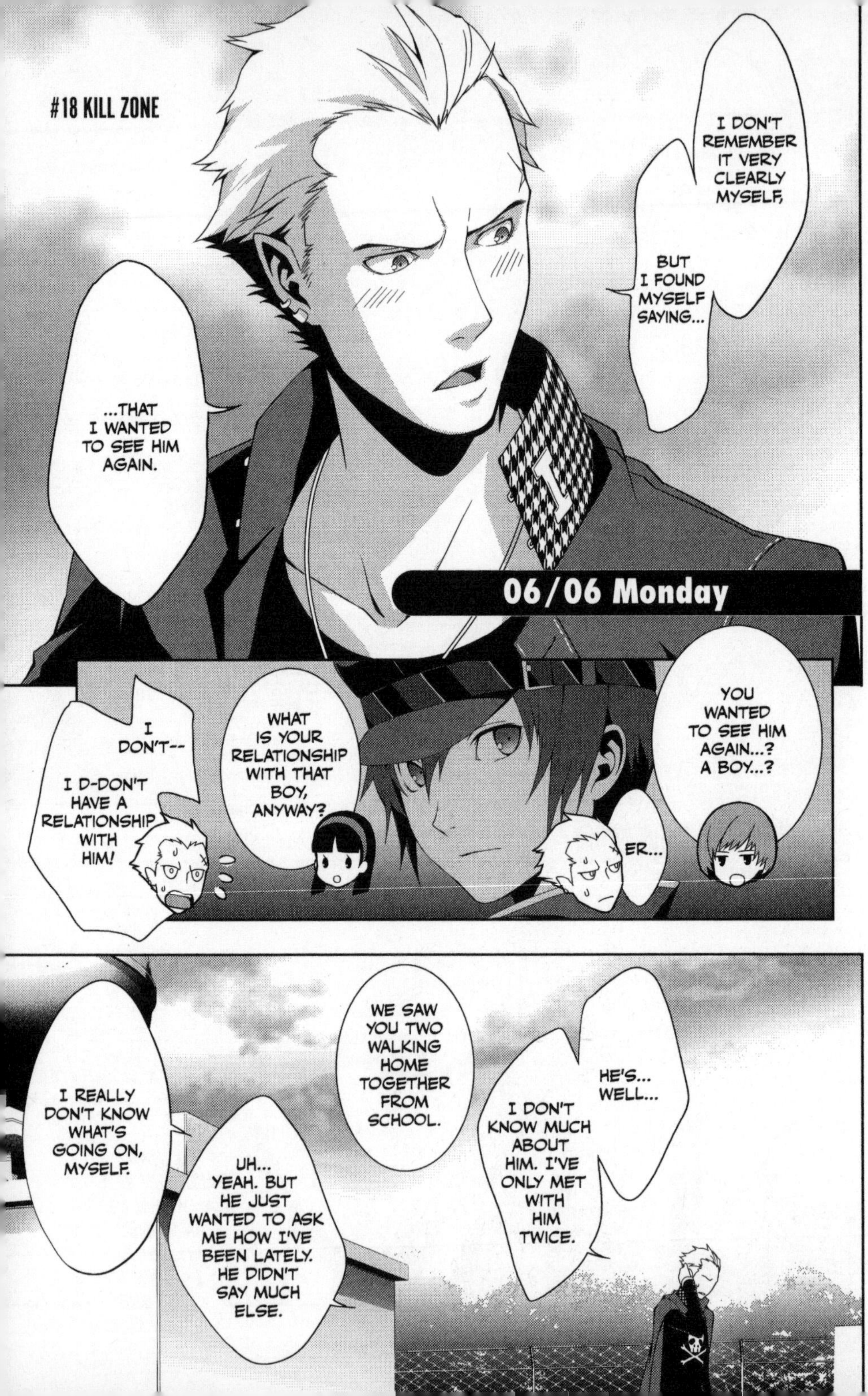
#18 KILL ZONE
I DON'T REMEMBER IT VERY CLEARLY MYSELF,
BUT I FOUND MYSELF SAYING...
...THAT I WANTED TO SEE HIM AGAIN.
06/06 Monday
YOU WANTED TO SEE HIM AGAIN...? A BOY...?
ER...
WHAT IS YOUR RELATIONSHIP WITH THAT BOY, ANYWAY?
I DON'T--
I D-DON'T HAVE A RELATIONSHIP WITH HIM!
HE'S... WELL...
I DON'T KNOW MUCH ABOUT HIM. I'VE ONLY MET WITH HIM TWICE.
WE SAW YOU TWO WALKING HOME TOGETHER FROM SCHOOL.
UH... YEAH. BUT HE JUST WANTED TO ASK ME HOW I'VE BEEN LATELY. HE DIDN'T SAY MUCH ELSE.
I REALLY DON'T KNOW WHAT'S GOING ON, MYSELF.

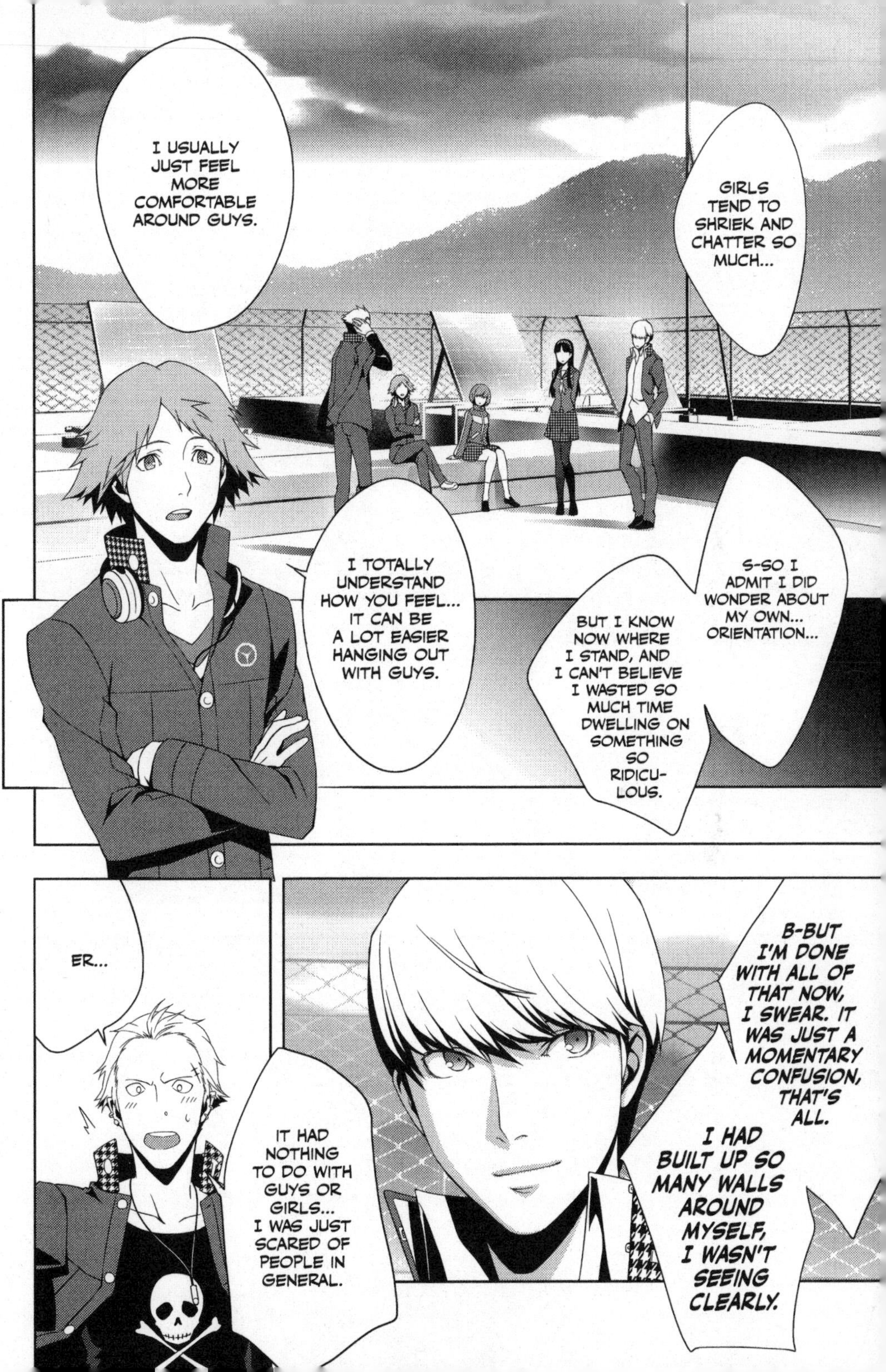
GIRLS TEND TO SHRIEK AND CHATTER SO MUCH...
I USUALLY JUST FEEL MORE COMFORTABLE AROUND GUYS.
S-SO I ADMIT I DID WONDER ABOUT MY OWN... ORIENTATION...
BUT I KNOW NOW WHERE I STAND, AND I CAN'T BELIEVE I WASTED SO MUCH TIME DWELLING ON SOMETHING SO RIDICU-LOUS.
I TOTALLY UNDERSTAND HOW YOU FEEL... IT CAN BE A LOT EASIER HANGING OUT WITH GUYS.
B-BUT I'M DONE WITH ALL OF THAT NOW, I SWEAR. IT WAS JUST A MOMENTARY CONFUSION, THAT'S ALL.
I HAD BUILT UP SO MANY WALLS AROUND MYSELF, I WASN'T SEEING CLEARLY.
ER...
IT HAD NOTHING TO DO WITH GUYS OR GIRLS... I WAS JUST SCARED OF PEOPLE IN GENERAL.

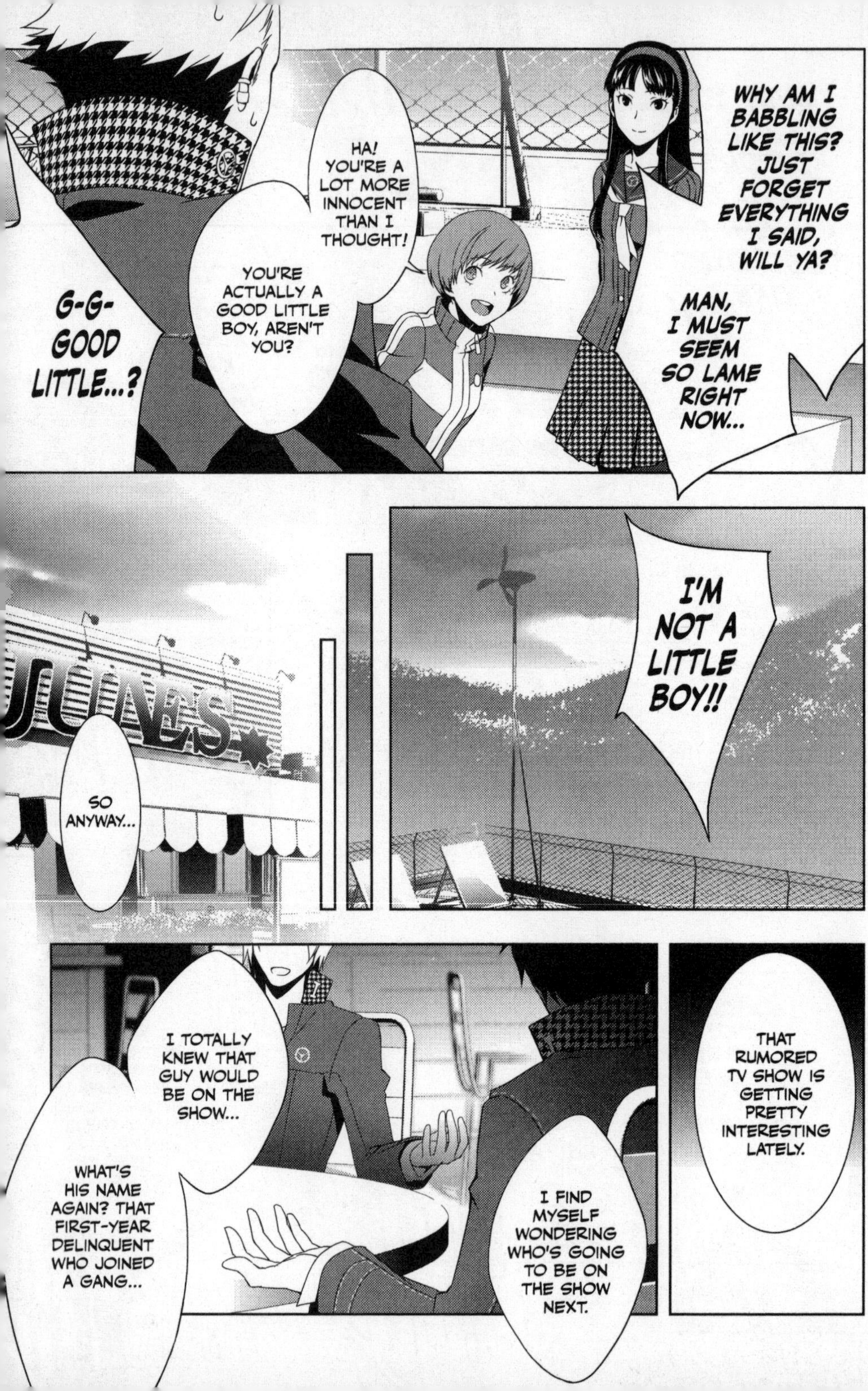
WHY AM I BABBLING LIKE THIS? JUST FORGET EVERYTHING I SAID, WILL YA?
MAN, I MUST SEEM SO LAME RIGHT NOW...
HA! YOU'RE A LOT MORE INNOCENT THAN I THOUGHT!
YOU'RE ACTUALLY A GOOD LITTLE BOY, AREN'T YOU?
G-G-GOOD LITTLE...?
I'M NOT A LITTLE BOY!!
SO ANYWAY...
THAT RUMORED TV SHOW IS GETTING PRETTY INTERESTING LATELY.
I FIND MYSELF WONDERING WHO'S GOING TO BE ON THE SHOW NEXT.
I TOTALLY KNEW THAT GUY WOULD BE ON THE SHOW...
WHAT'S HIS NAME AGAIN? THAT FIRST-YEAR DELINQUENT WHO JOINED A GANG...

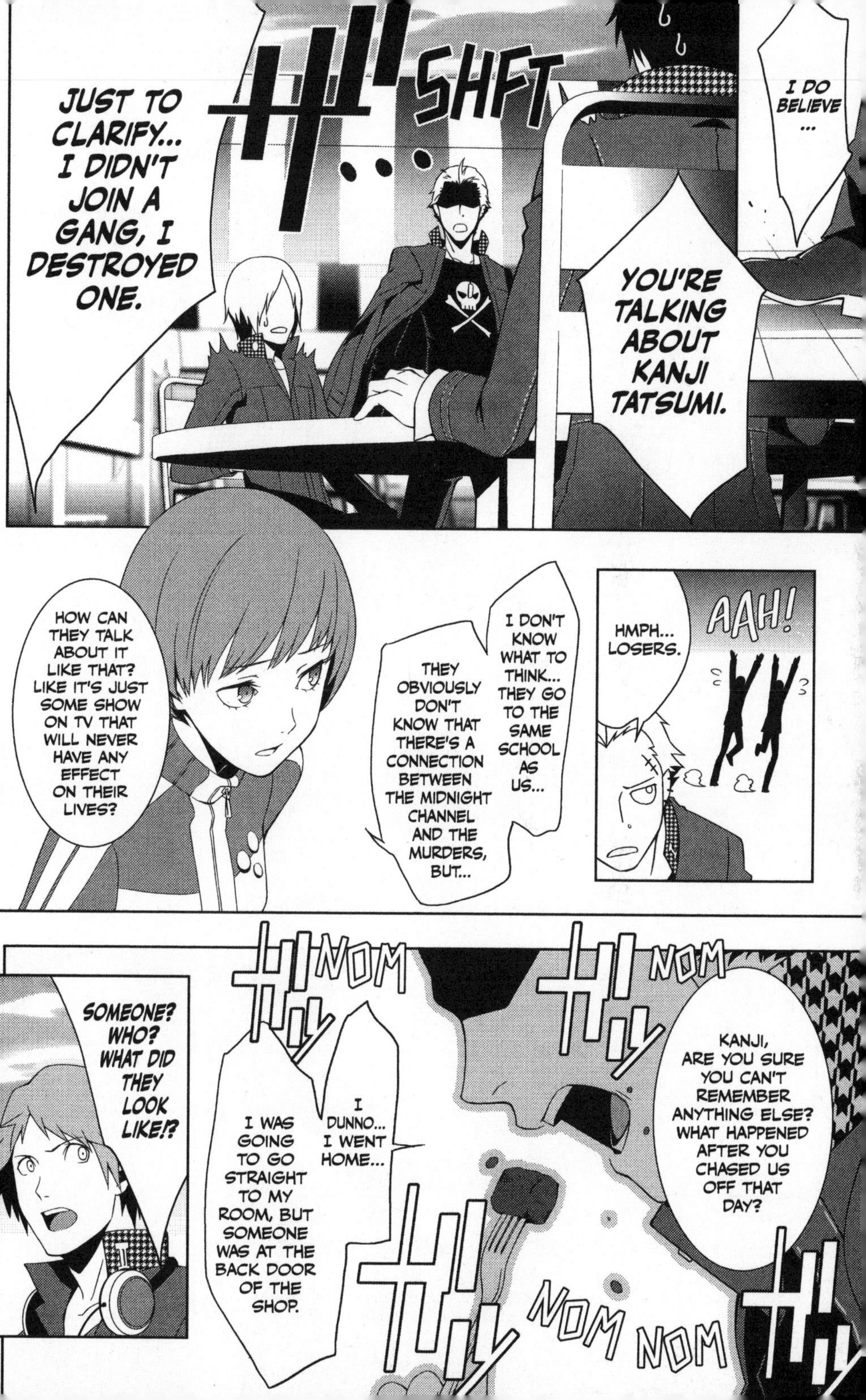
I DO BELIEVE ...
YOU'RE TALKING ABOUT KANJI TATSUMI.
SHFT
...
JUST TO CLARIFY... I DIDN'T JOIN A GANG, I DESTROYED ONE.
AAH!
HMPH... LOSERS.
I DON'T KNOW WHAT TO THINK... THEY GO TO THE SAME SCHOOL AS US...
THEY OBVIOUSLY DON'T KNOW THAT THERE'S A CONNECTION BETWEEN THE MIDNIGHT CHANNEL AND THE MURDERS, BUT...
HOW CAN THEY TALK ABOUT IT LIKE THAT? LIKE IT'S JUST SOME SHOW ON TV THAT WILL NEVER HAVE ANY EFFECT ON THEIR LIVES?
KANJI, ARE YOU SURE YOU CAN'T REMEMBER ANYTHING ELSE? WHAT HAPPENED AFTER YOU CHASED US OFF THAT DAY?
NOM
NOM
I DUNNO... I WENT HOME...
I WAS GOING TO GO STRAIGHT TO MY ROOM, BUT SOMEONE WAS AT THE BACK DOOR OF THE SHOP.
NOM NOM
SOMEONE? WHO? WHAT DID THEY LOOK LIKE!?

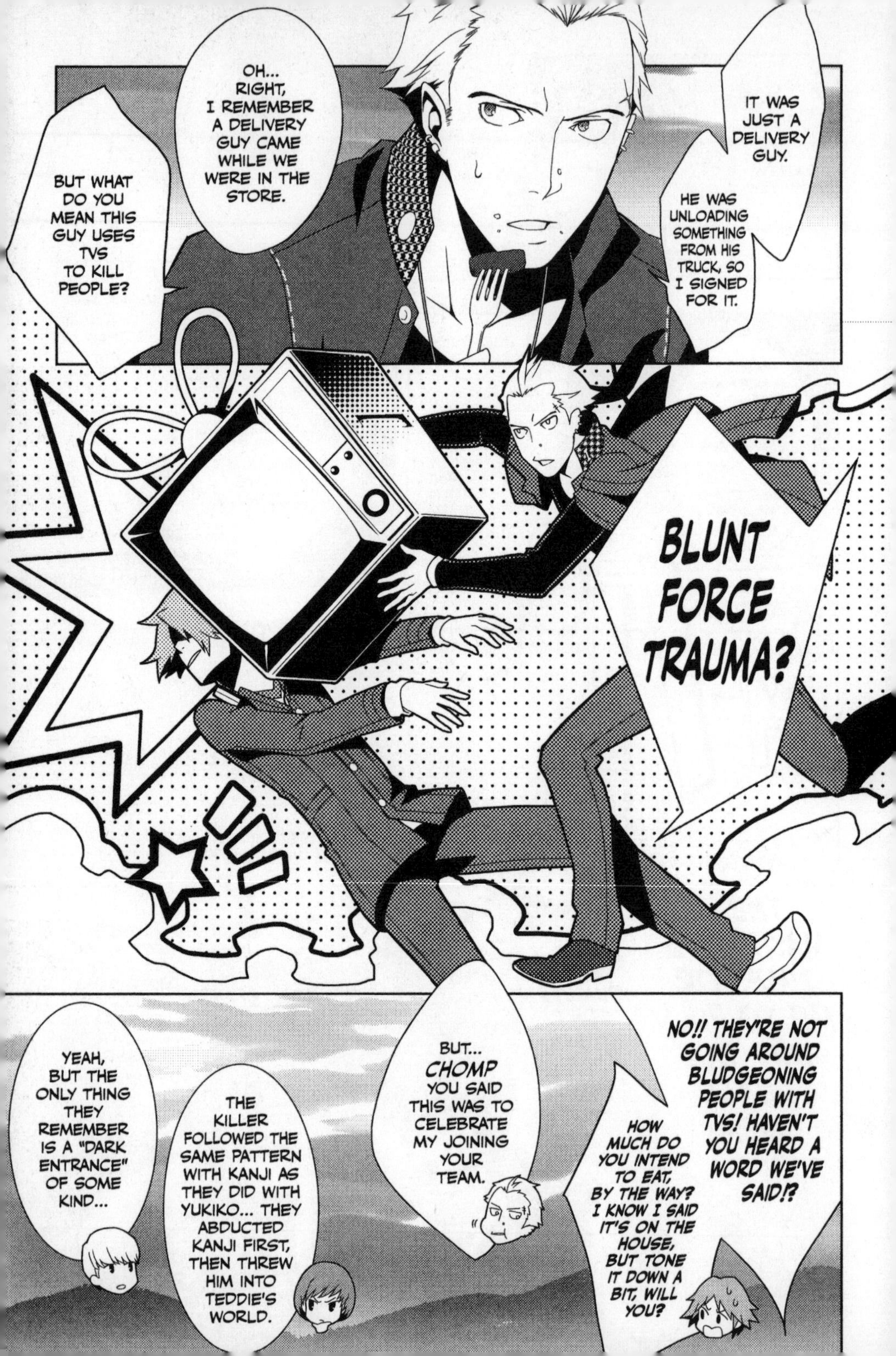
IT WAS JUST A DELIVERY GUY.
HE WAS UNLOADING SOMETHING FROM HIS TRUCK, SO I SIGNED FOR IT.
OH... RIGHT, I REMEMBER A DELIVERY GUY CAME WHILE WE WERE IN THE STORE.
BUT WHAT DO YOU MEAN THIS GUY USES TVS TO KILL PEOPLE?
BLUNT FORCE TRAUMA?
NO!! THEY'RE NOT GOING AROUND BLUDGEONING PEOPLE WITH TVS! HAVEN'T YOU HEARD A WORD WE'VE SAID!?
HOW MUCH DO YOU INTEND TO EAT, BY THE WAY? I KNOW I SAID IT'S ON THE HOUSE, BUT TONE IT DOWN A BIT, WILL YOU?
BUT... CHOMP YOU SAID THIS WAS TO CELEBRATE MY JOINING YOUR TEAM.
THE KILLER FOLLOWED THE SAME PATTERN WITH KANJI AS THEY DID WITH YUKIKO... THEY ABDUCTED KANJI FIRST, THEN THREW HIM INTO TEDDIE'S WORLD.
YEAH, BUT THE ONLY THING THEY REMEMBER IS A "DARK ENTRANCE" OF SOME KIND...

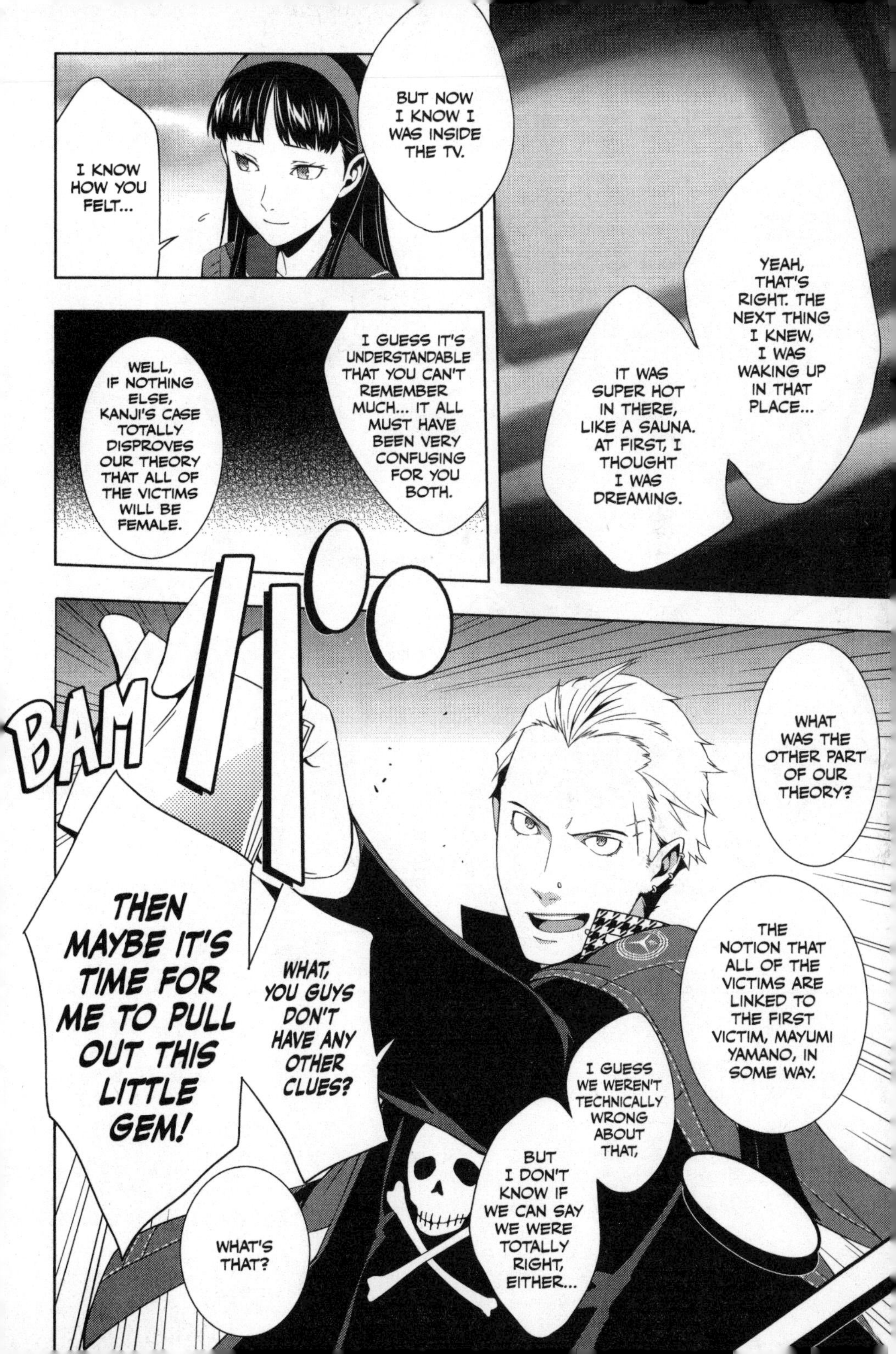
YEAH, THAT'S RIGHT. THE NEXT THING I KNEW, I WAS WAKING UP IN THAT PLACE...
IT WAS SUPER HOT IN THERE, LIKE A SAUNA. AT FIRST, I THOUGHT I WAS DREAMING.
BUT NOW I KNOW I WAS INSIDE THE TV.
I KNOW HOW YOU FELT...
I GUESS IT'S UNDERSTANDABLE THAT YOU CAN'T REMEMBER MUCH... IT ALL MUST HAVE BEEN VERY CONFUSING FOR YOU BOTH.
WELL, IF NOTHING ELSE, KANJI'S CASE TOTALLY DISPROVES OUR THEORY THAT ALL OF THE VICTIMS WILL BE FEMALE.
WHAT WAS THE OTHER PART OF OUR THEORY?
THE NOTION THAT ALL OF THE VICTIMS ARE LINKED TO THE FIRST VICTIM, MAYUMI YAMANO, IN SOME WAY.
I GUESS WE WEREN'T TECHNICALLY WRONG ABOUT THAT,
BUT I DON'T KNOW IF WE CAN SAY WE WERE TOTALLY RIGHT, EITHER...
WHAT, YOU GUYS DON'T HAVE ANY OTHER CLUES?
THEN MAYBE IT'S TIME FOR ME TO PULL OUT THIS LITTLE GEM!
BAM
WHAT'S THAT?

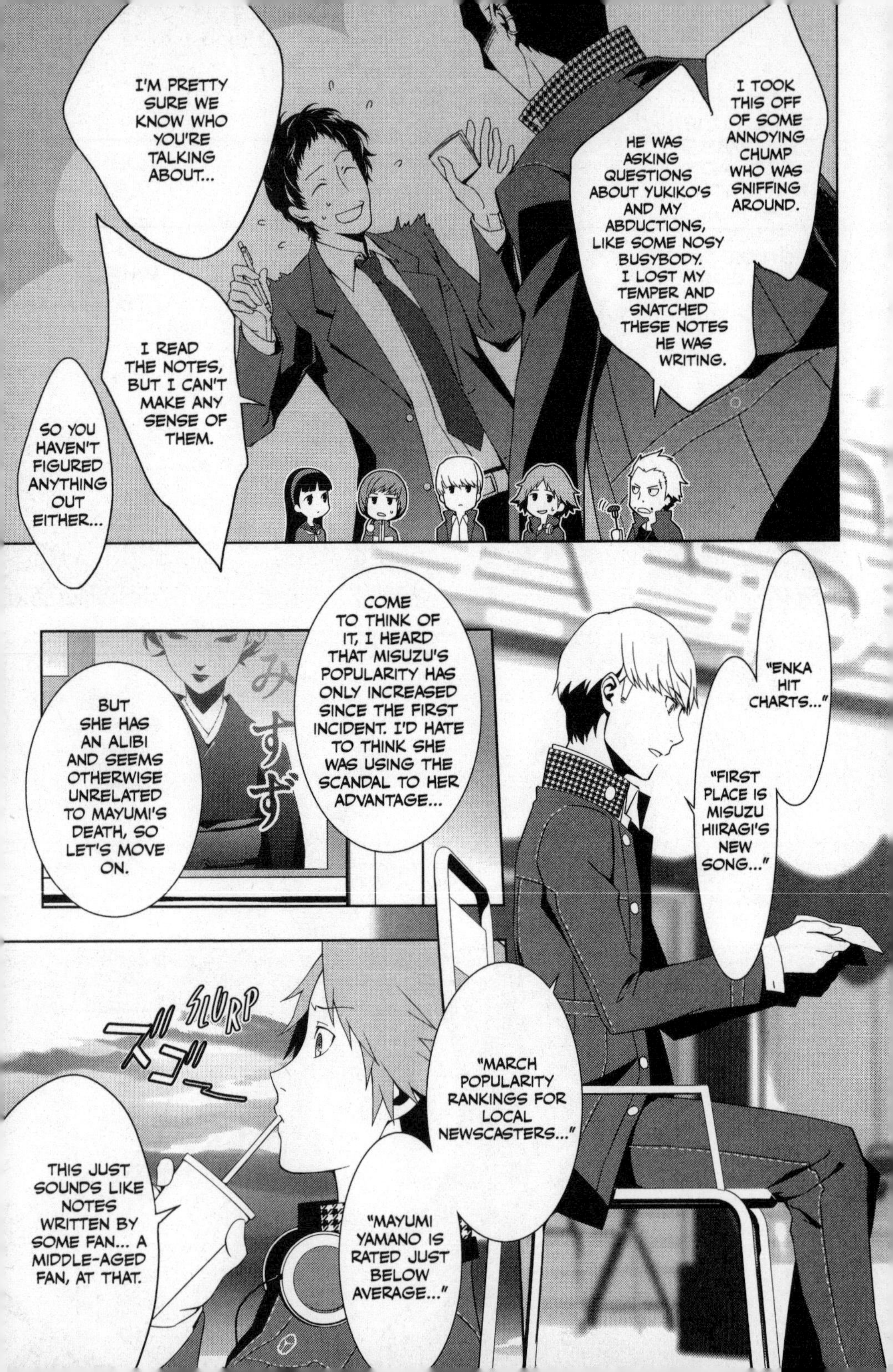
I TOOK THIS OFF OF SOME ANNOYING CHUMP WHO WAS SNIFFING AROUND.
HE WAS ASKING QUESTIONS ABOUT YUKIKO'S AND MY ABDUCTIONS, LIKE SOME NOSY BUSYBODY. I LOST MY TEMPER AND SNATCHED THESE NOTES HE WAS WRITING.
I'M PRETTY SURE WE KNOW WHO YOU'RE TALKING ABOUT...
I READ THE NOTES, BUT I CAN'T MAKE ANY SENSE OF THEM.
SO YOU HAVEN'T FIGURED ANYTHING OUT EITHER...
"ENKA HIT CHARTS..."
"FIRST PLACE IS MISUZU HIIRAGI'S NEW SONG..."
COME TO THINK OF IT, I HEARD THAT MISUZU'S POPULARITY HAS ONLY INCREASED SINCE THE FIRST INCIDENT. I'D HATE TO THINK SHE WAS USING THE SCANDAL TO HER ADVANTAGE...
BUT SHE HAS AN ALIBI AND SEEMS OTHERWISE UNRELATED TO MAYUMI'S DEATH, SO LET'S MOVE ON.
"MARCH POPULARITY RANKINGS FOR LOCAL NEWSCASTERS..."
"MAYUMI YAMANO IS RATED JUST BELOW AVERAGE..."
SLURP
THIS JUST SOUNDS LIKE NOTES WRITTEN BY SOME FAN... A MIDDLE-AGED FAN, AT THAT.

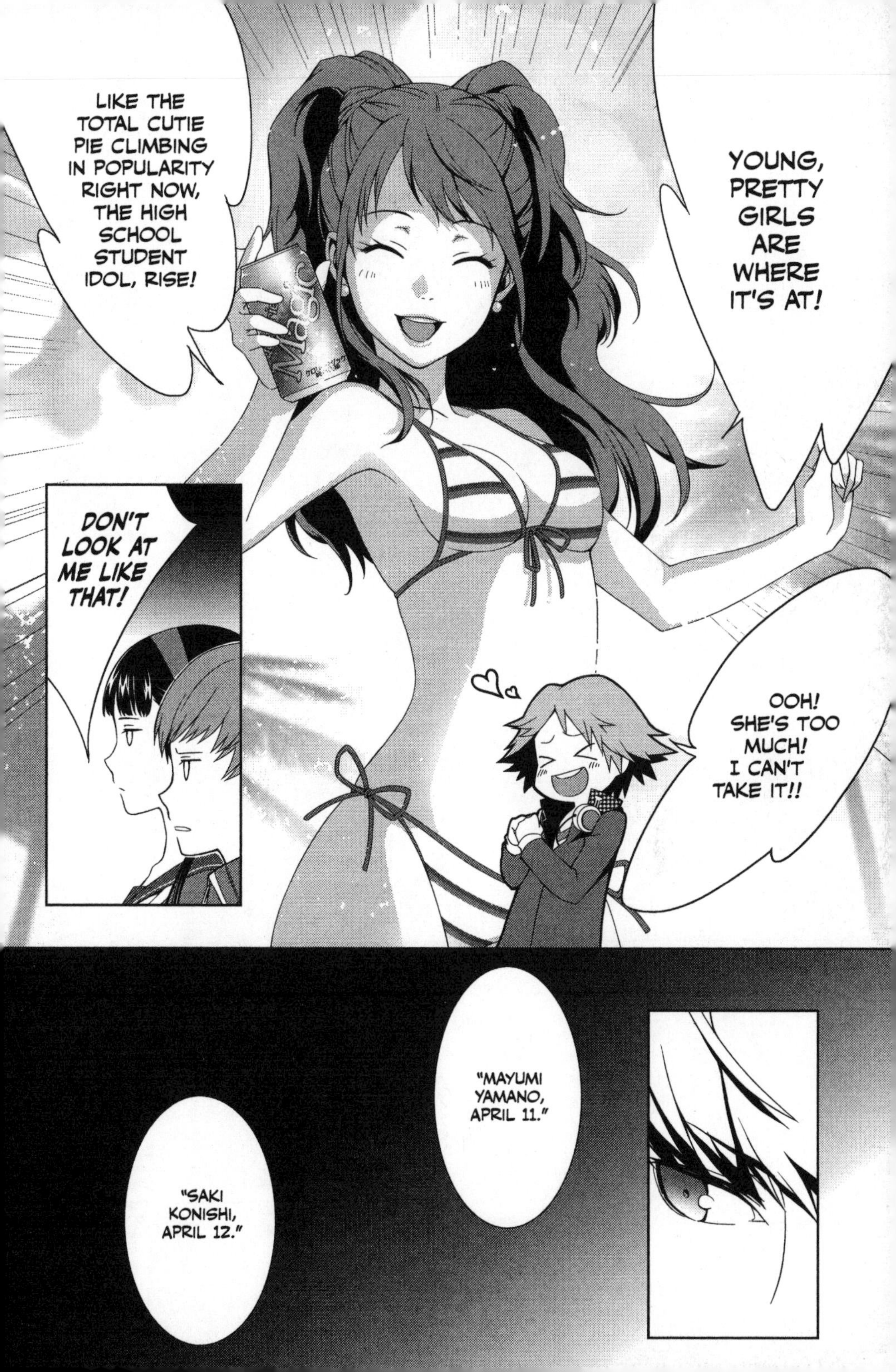
YOUNG, PRETTY GIRLS ARE WHERE IT'S AT!
LIKE THE TOTAL CUTIE PIE CLIMBING IN POPULARITY RIGHT NOW, THE HIGH SCHOOL STUDENT IDOL, RISE!
OOH! SHE'S TOO MUCH! I CAN'T TAKE IT!!
DON'T LOOK AT ME LIKE THAT!
"MAYUMI YAMANO, APRIL 11."
"SAKI KONISHI, APRIL 12."

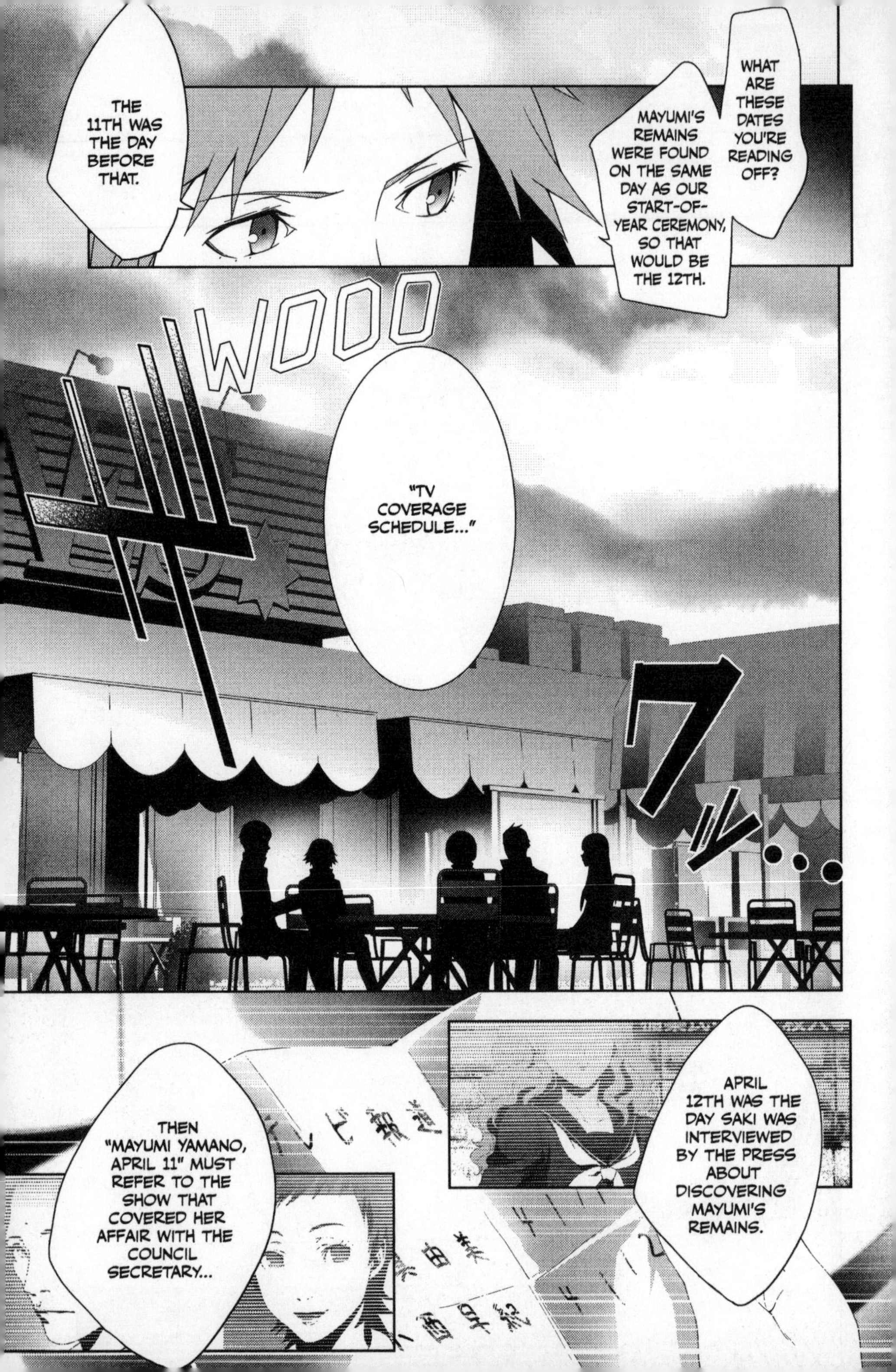
WHAT ARE THESE DATES YOU'RE READING OFF?
MAYUMI'S REMAINS WERE FOUND ON THE SAME DAY AS OUR START-OF-YEAR CEREMONY, SO THAT WOULD BE THE 12TH.
THE 11TH WAS THE DAY BEFORE THAT.
WOOO
"TV COVERAGE SCHEDULE..."
ワッ…
APRIL 12TH WAS THE DAY SAKI WAS INTERVIEWED BY THE PRESS ABOUT DISCOVERING MAYUMI'S REMAINS.
THEN "MAYUMI YAMANO, APRIL 11" MUST REFER TO THE SHOW THAT COVERED HER AFFAIR WITH THE COUNCIL SECRETARY...

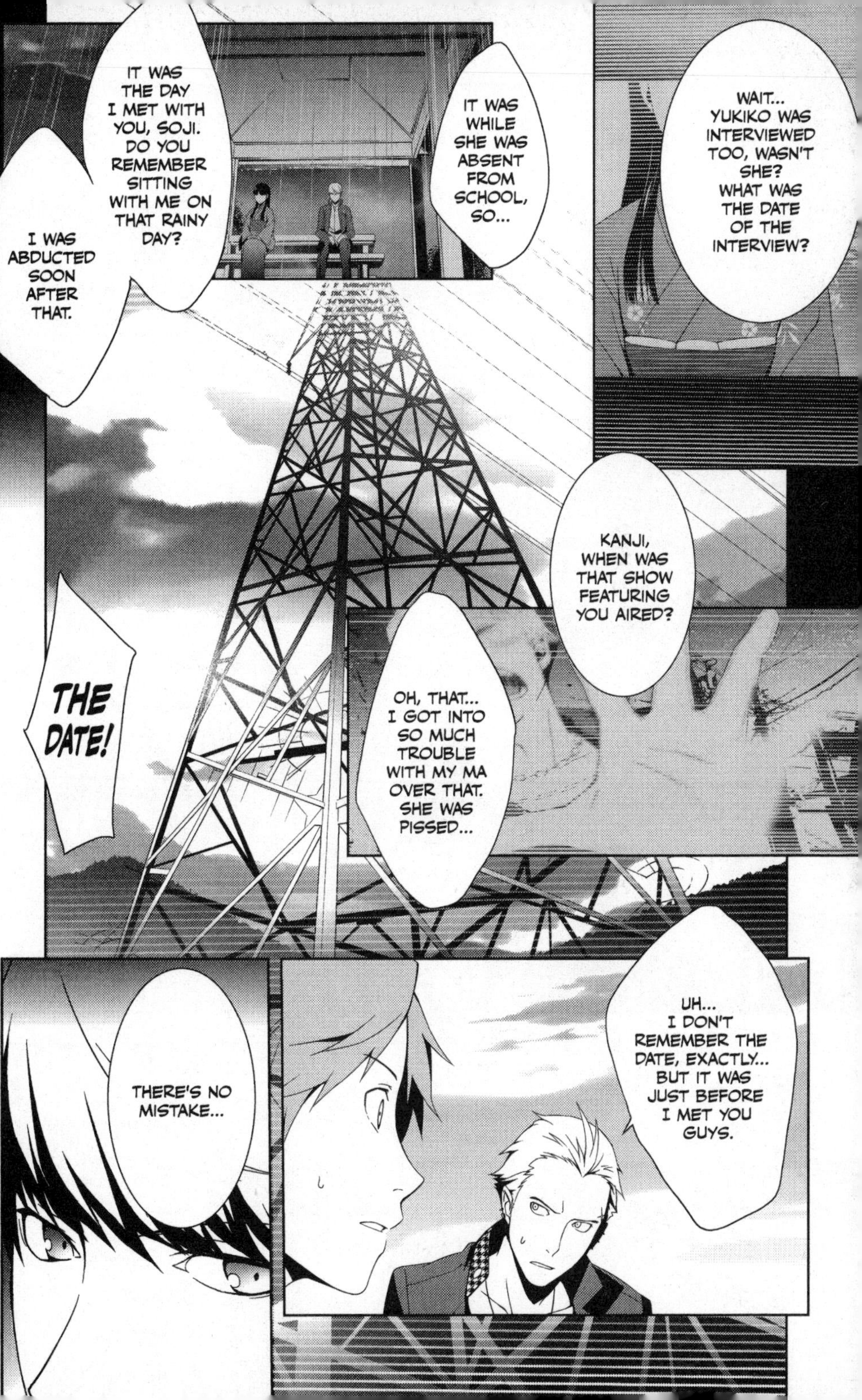
WAIT... YUKIKO WAS INTERVIEWED TOO, WASN'T SHE? WHAT WAS THE DATE OF THE INTERVIEW?
IT WAS WHILE SHE WAS ABSENT FROM SCHOOL, SO...
IT WAS THE DAY I MET WITH YOU, SOJI. DO YOU REMEMBER SITTING WITH ME ON THAT RAINY DAY?
I WAS ABDUCTED SOON AFTER THAT.
KANJI, WHEN WAS THAT SHOW FEATURING YOU AIRED?
OH, THAT... I GOT INTO SO MUCH TROUBLE WITH MY MA OVER THAT. SHE WAS PISSED...
THE DATE!
UH... I DON'T REMEMBER THE DATE, EXACTLY... BUT IT WAS JUST BEFORE I MET YOU GUYS.
THERE'S NO MISTAKE...

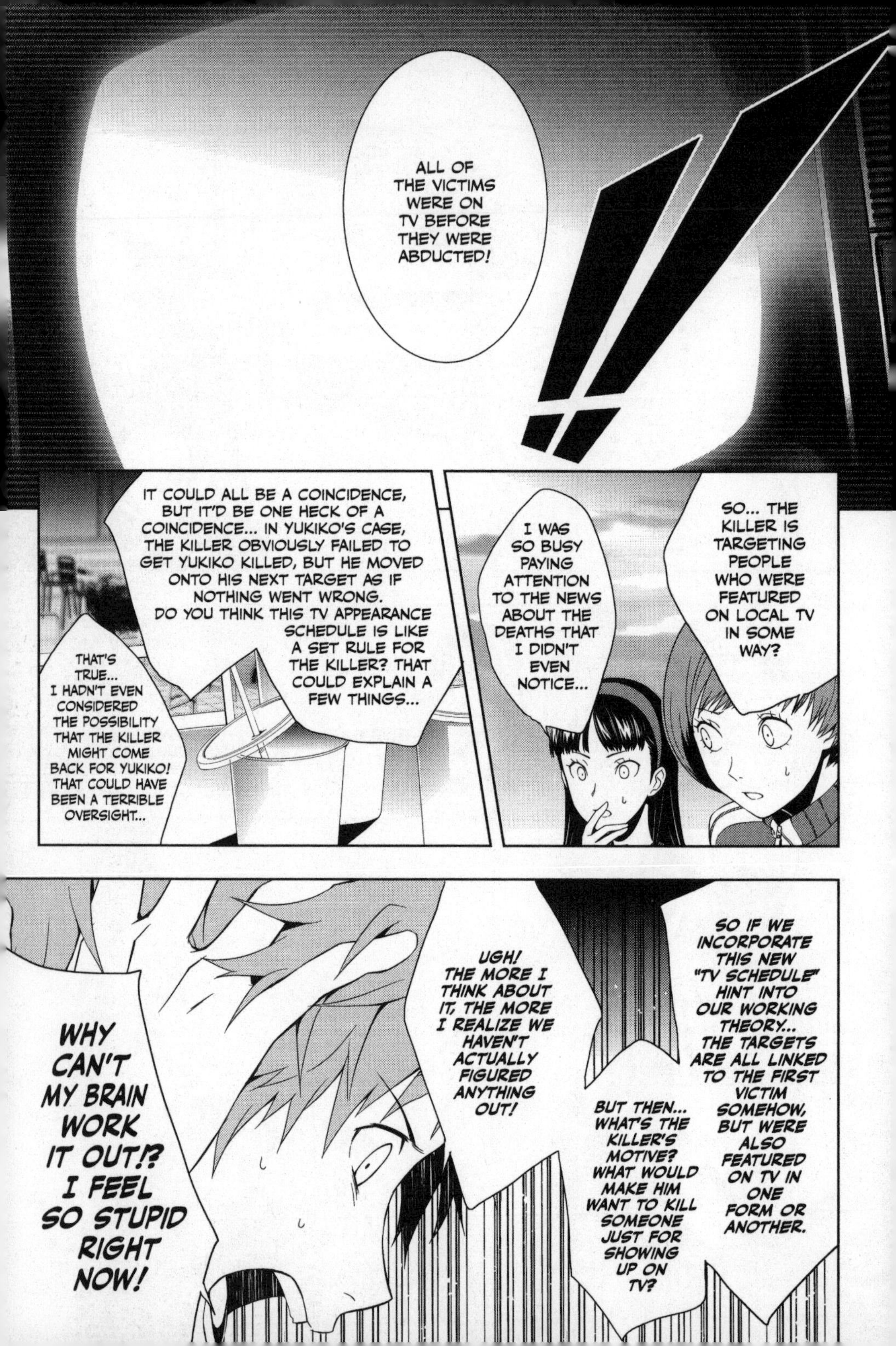
ALL OF THE VICTIMS WERE ON TV BEFORE THEY WERE ABDUCTED!
SO... THE KILLER IS TARGETING PEOPLE WHO WERE FEATURED ON LOCAL TV IN SOME WAY?
I WAS SO BUSY PAYING ATTENTION TO THE NEWS ABOUT THE DEATHS THAT I DIDN'T EVEN NOTICE...
IT COULD ALL BE A COINCIDENCE, BUT IT'D BE ONE HECK OF A COINCIDENCE... IN YUKIKO'S CASE, THE KILLER OBVIOUSLY FAILED TO GET YUKIKO KILLED, BUT HE MOVED ONTO HIS NEXT TARGET AS IF NOTHING WENT WRONG. DO YOU THINK THIS TV APPEARANCE SCHEDULE IS LIKE A SET RULE FOR THE KILLER? THAT COULD EXPLAIN A FEW THINGS...
THAT'S TRUE... I HADN'T EVEN CONSIDERED THE POSSIBILITY THAT THE KILLER MIGHT COME BACK FOR YUKIKO! THAT COULD HAVE BEEN A TERRIBLE OVERSIGHT...
SO IF WE INCORPORATE THIS NEW "TV SCHEDULE" HINT INTO OUR WORKING THEORY... THE TARGETS ARE ALL LINKED TO THE FIRST VICTIM SOMEHOW, BUT WERE ALSO FEATURED ON TV IN ONE FORM OR ANOTHER.
UGH! THE MORE I THINK ABOUT IT, THE MORE I REALIZE WE HAVEN'T ACTUALLY FIGURED ANYTHING OUT!
BUT THEN... WHAT'S THE KILLER'S MOTIVE? WHAT WOULD MAKE HIM WANT TO KILL SOMEONE JUST FOR SHOWING UP ON TV?
WHY CAN'T MY BRAIN WORK IT OUT!? I FEEL SO STUPID RIGHT NOW!

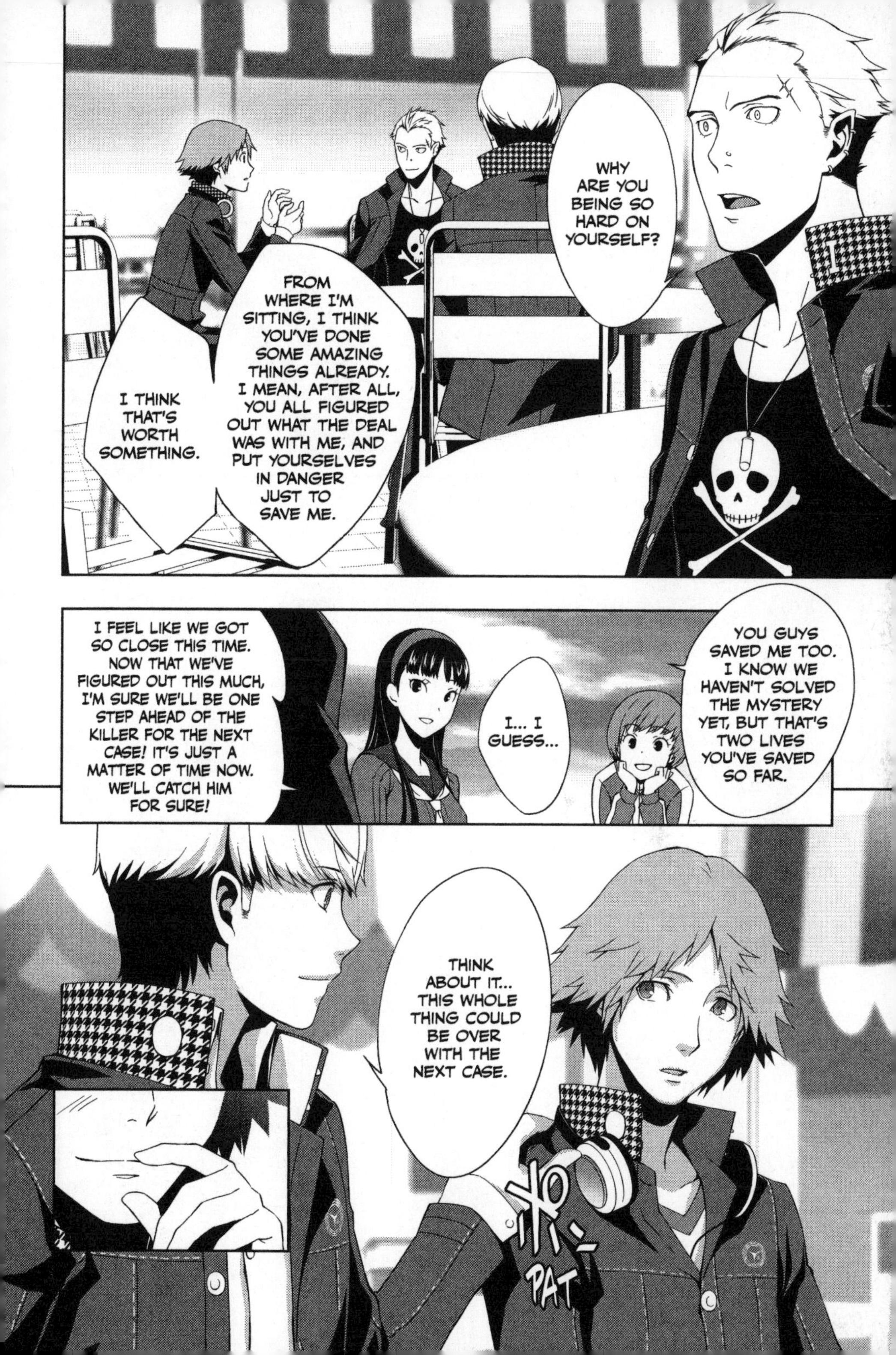
WHY ARE YOU BEING SO HARD ON YOURSELF?
FROM WHERE I'M SITTING, I THINK YOU'VE DONE SOME AMAZING THINGS ALREADY. I MEAN, AFTER ALL, YOU ALL FIGURED OUT WHAT THE DEAL WAS WITH ME, AND PUT YOURSELVES IN DANGER JUST TO SAVE ME.
I THINK THAT'S WORTH SOMETHING.
YOU GUYS SAVED ME TOO. I KNOW WE HAVEN'T SOLVED THE MYSTERY YET, BUT THAT'S TWO LIVES YOU'VE SAVED SO FAR.
I... I GUESS...
I FEEL LIKE WE GOT SO CLOSE THIS TIME. NOW THAT WE'VE FIGURED OUT THIS MUCH, I'M SURE WE'LL BE ONE STEP AHEAD OF THE KILLER FOR THE NEXT CASE! IT'S JUST A MATTER OF TIME NOW. WE'LL CATCH HIM FOR SURE!
THINK ABOUT IT... THIS WHOLE THING COULD BE OVER WITH THE NEXT CASE.
PAT

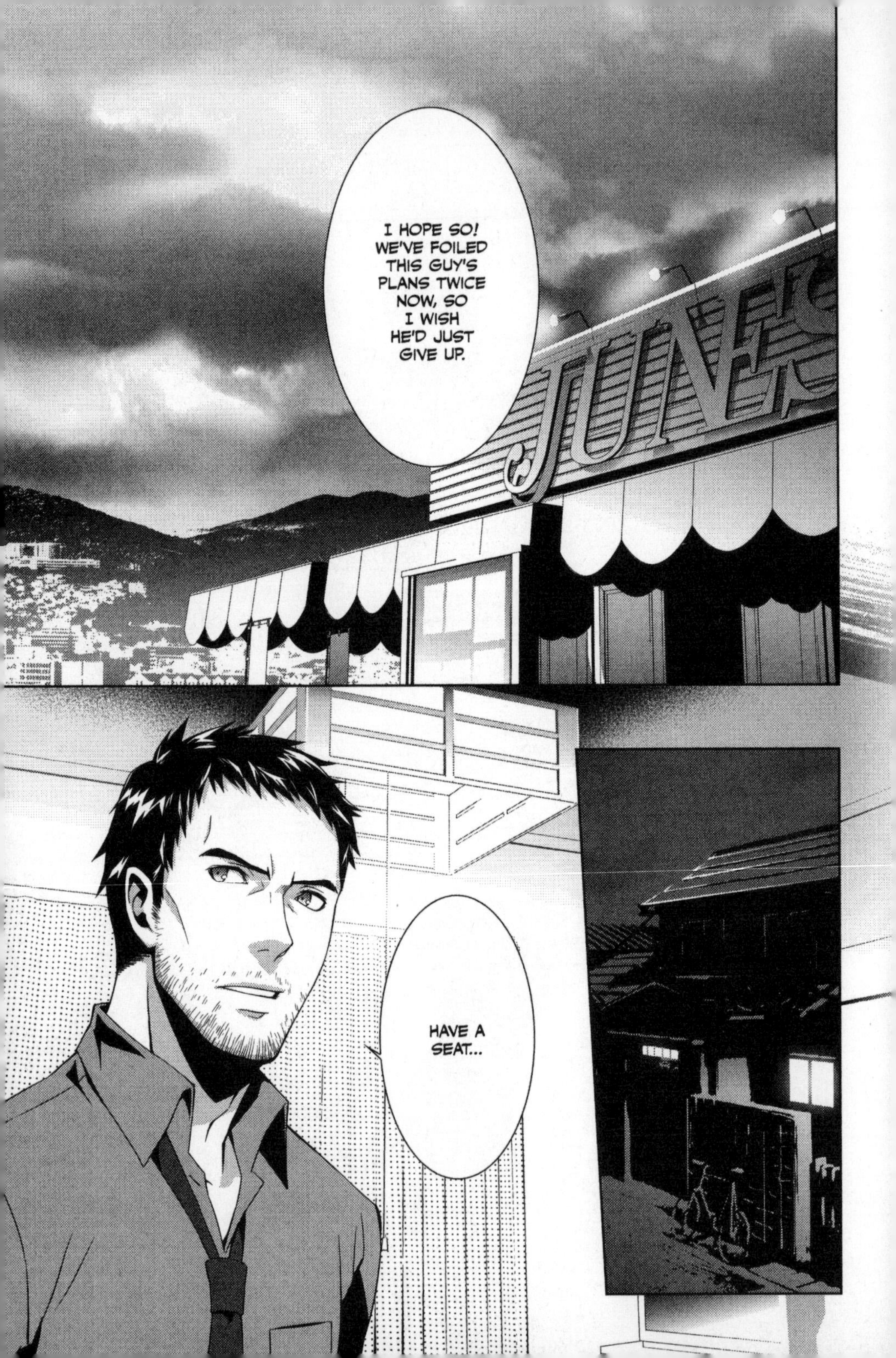
I HOPE SO! WE'VE FOILED THIS GUY'S PLANS TWICE NOW, SO I WISH HE'D JUST GIVE UP.
HAVE A SEAT...

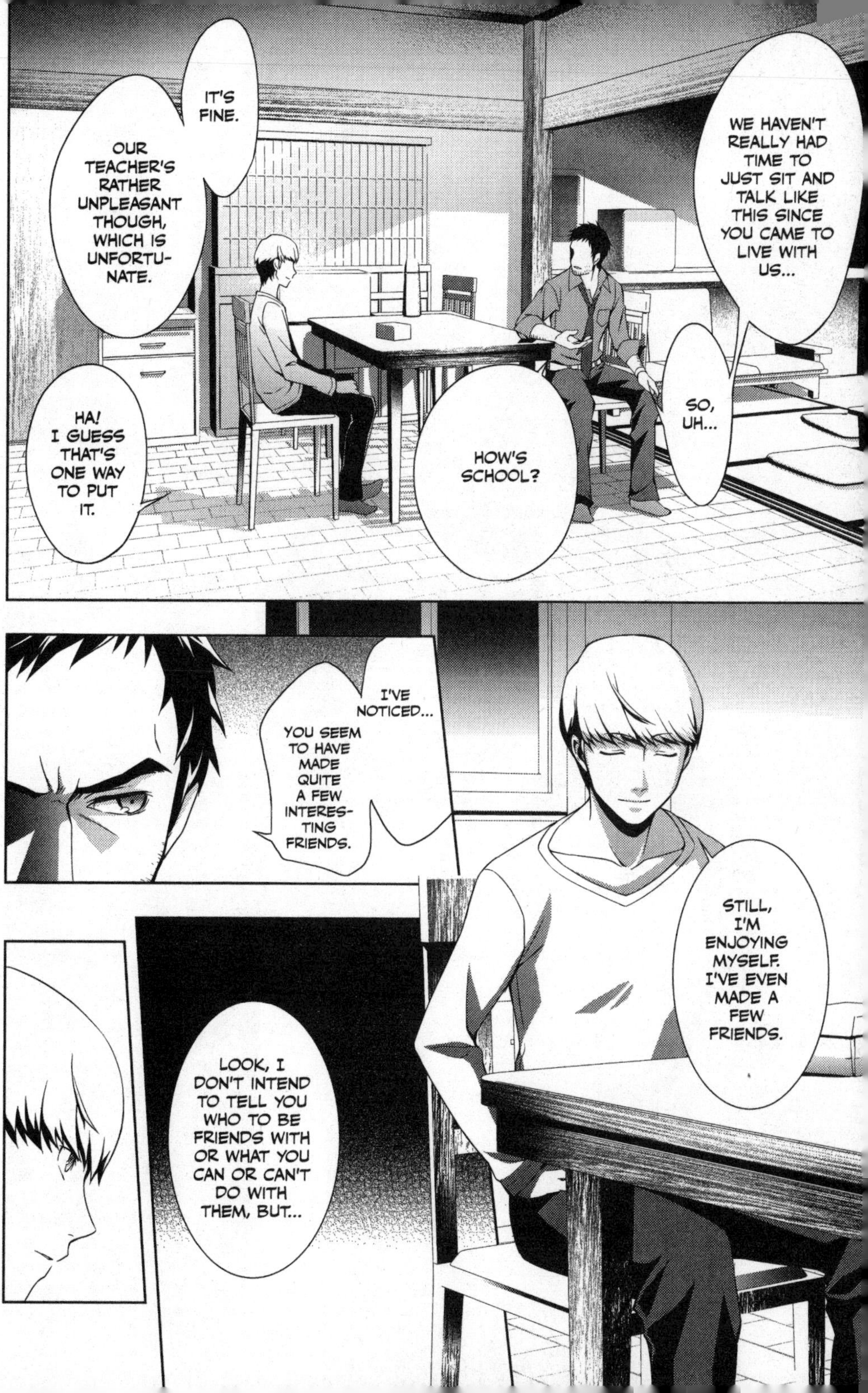
WE HAVEN'T REALLY HAD TIME TO JUST SIT AND TALK LIKE THIS SINCE YOU CAME TO LIVE WITH US...
SO, UH...
HOW'S SCHOOL?
IT'S FINE.
OUR TEACHER'S RATHER UNPLEASANT THOUGH, WHICH IS UNFORTU-NATE.
HA! I GUESS THAT'S ONE WAY TO PUT IT.
STILL, I'M ENJOYING MYSELF. I'VE EVEN MADE A FEW FRIENDS.
I'VE NOTICED...
YOU SEEM TO HAVE MADE QUITE A FEW INTERES-TING FRIENDS.
LOOK, I DON'T INTEND TO TELL YOU WHO TO BE FRIENDS WITH OR WHAT YOU CAN OR CAN'T DO WITH THEM, BUT...

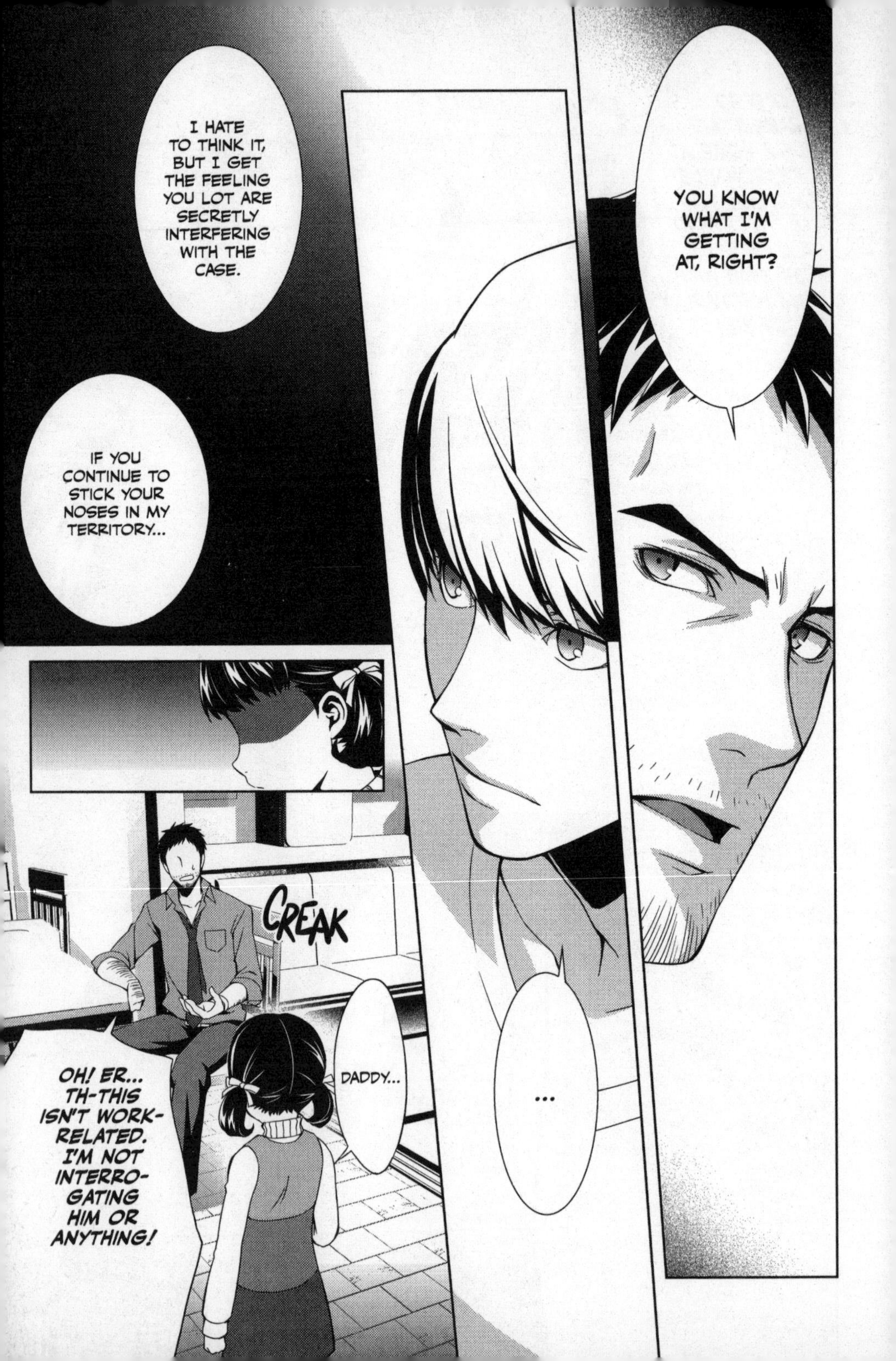
I HATE TO THINK IT, BUT I GET THE FEELING YOU LOT ARE SECRETLY INTERFERING WITH THE CASE.
IF YOU CONTINUE TO STICK YOUR NOSES IN MY TERRITORY...
YOU KNOW WHAT I'M GETTING AT, RIGHT?
...
CREAK
DADDY...
OH! ER... TH-THIS ISN'T WORK-RELATED. I'M NOT INTERRO-GATING HIM OR ANYTHING!

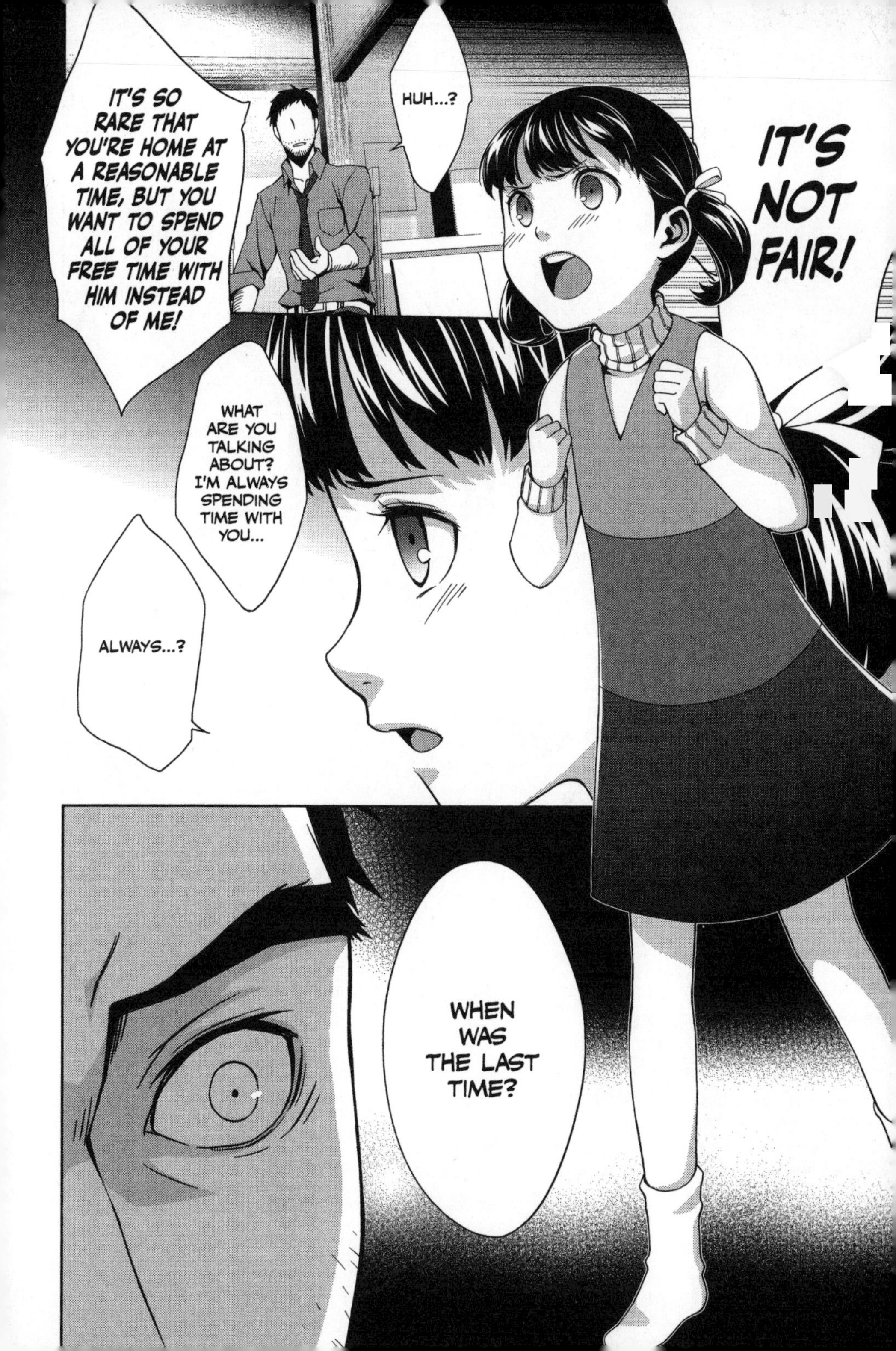
IT'S NOT FAIR!
HUH...?
IT'S SO RARE THAT YOU'RE HOME AT A REASONABLE TIME, BUT YOU WANT TO SPEND ALL OF YOUR FREE TIME WITH HIM INSTEAD OF ME!
WHAT ARE YOU TALKING ABOUT? I'M ALWAYS SPENDING TIME WITH YOU...
ALWAYS...?
WHEN WAS THE LAST TIME?

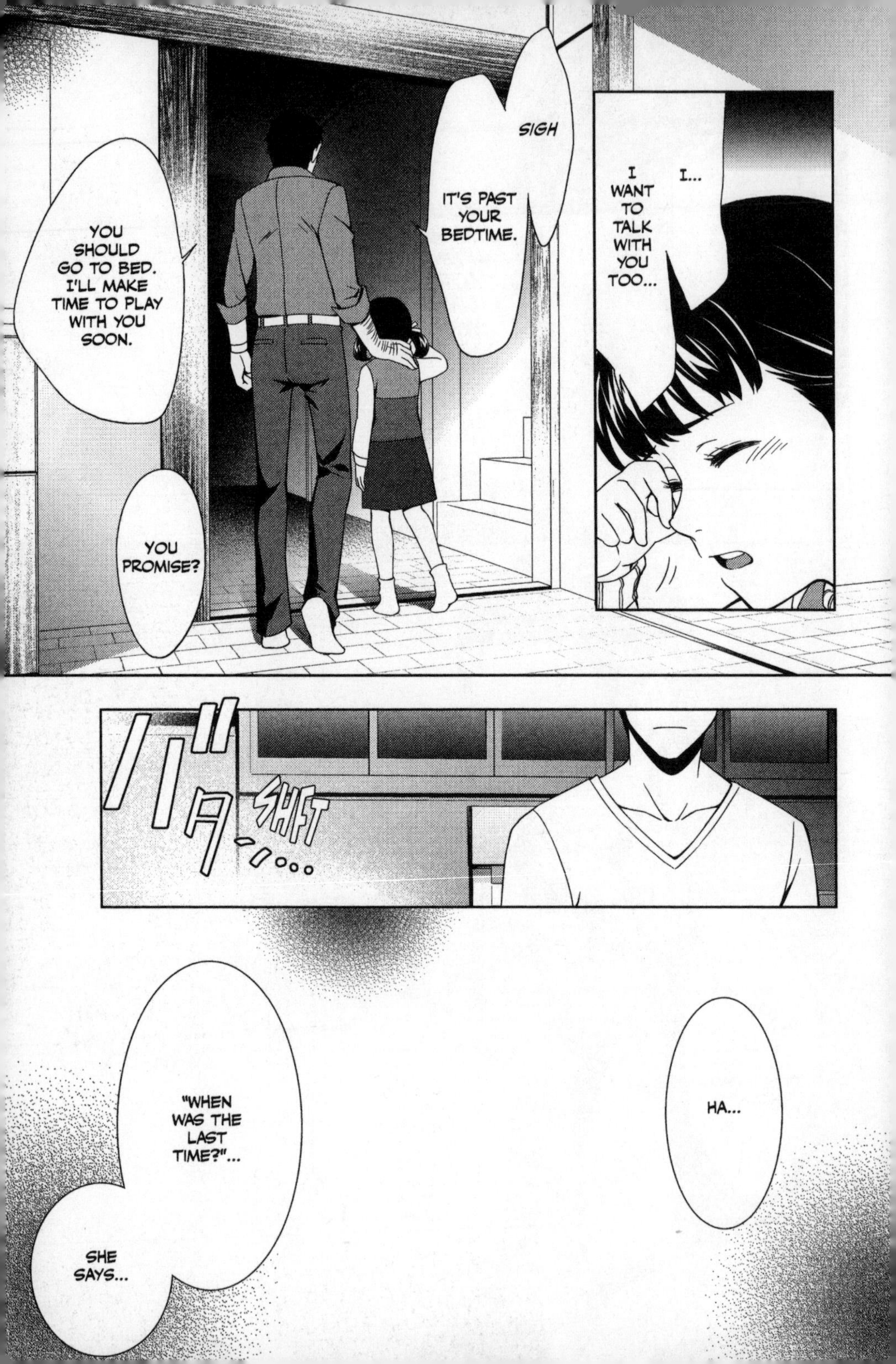
I...
I WANT TO TALK WITH YOU TOO...
SIGH
IT'S PAST YOUR BEDTIME.
YOU SHOULD GO TO BED. I'LL MAKE TIME TO PLAY WITH YOU SOON.
YOU PROMISE?
SHIFT
HA...
"WHEN WAS THE LAST TIME?"...
SHE SAYS...

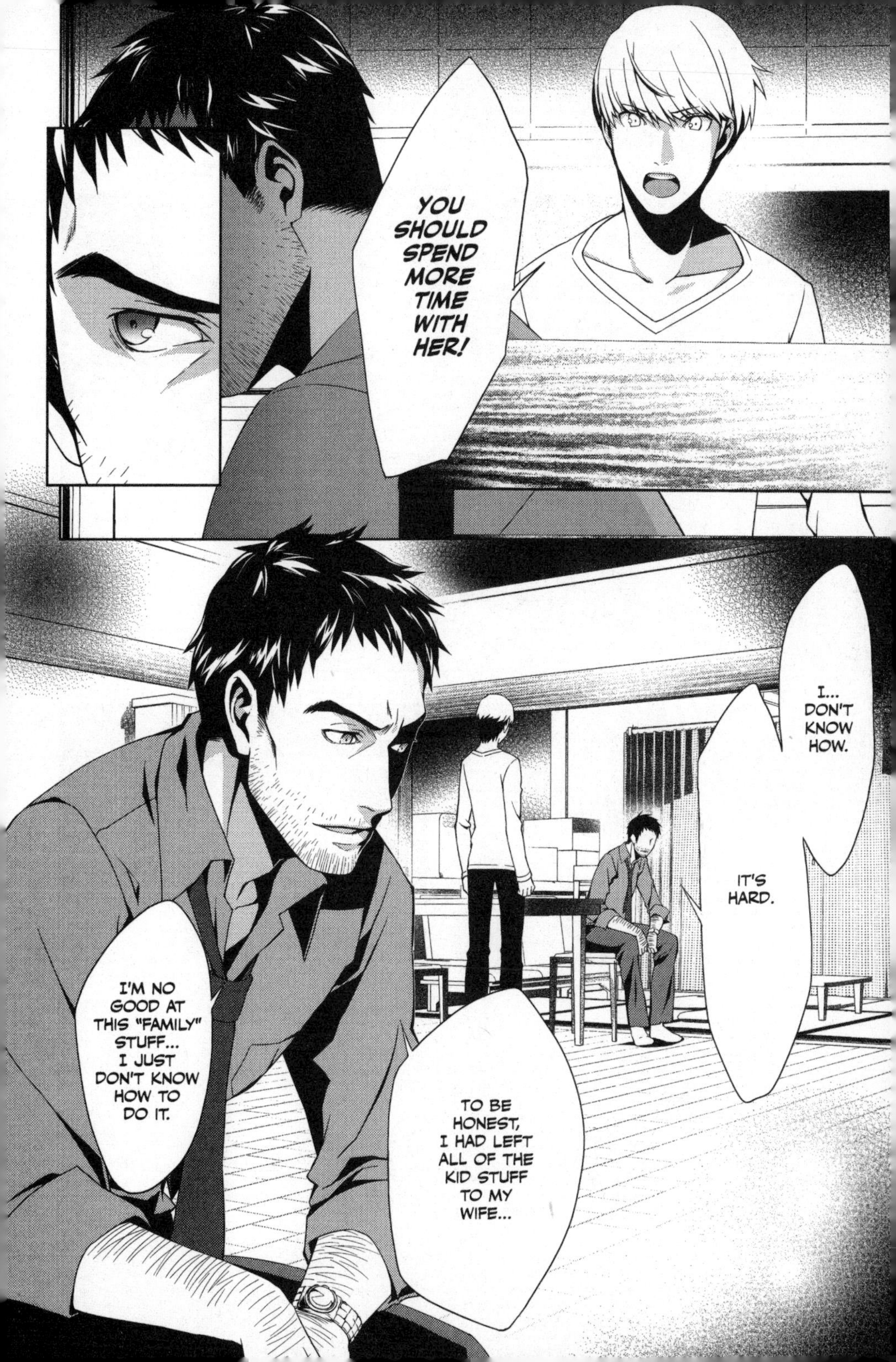
YOU SHOULD SPEND MORE TIME WITH HER!
I... DON'T KNOW HOW.
IT'S HARD.
TO BE HONEST, I HAD LEFT ALL OF THE KID STUFF TO MY WIFE...
I'M NO GOOD AT THIS "FAMILY" STUFF... I JUST DON'T KNOW HOW TO DO IT.

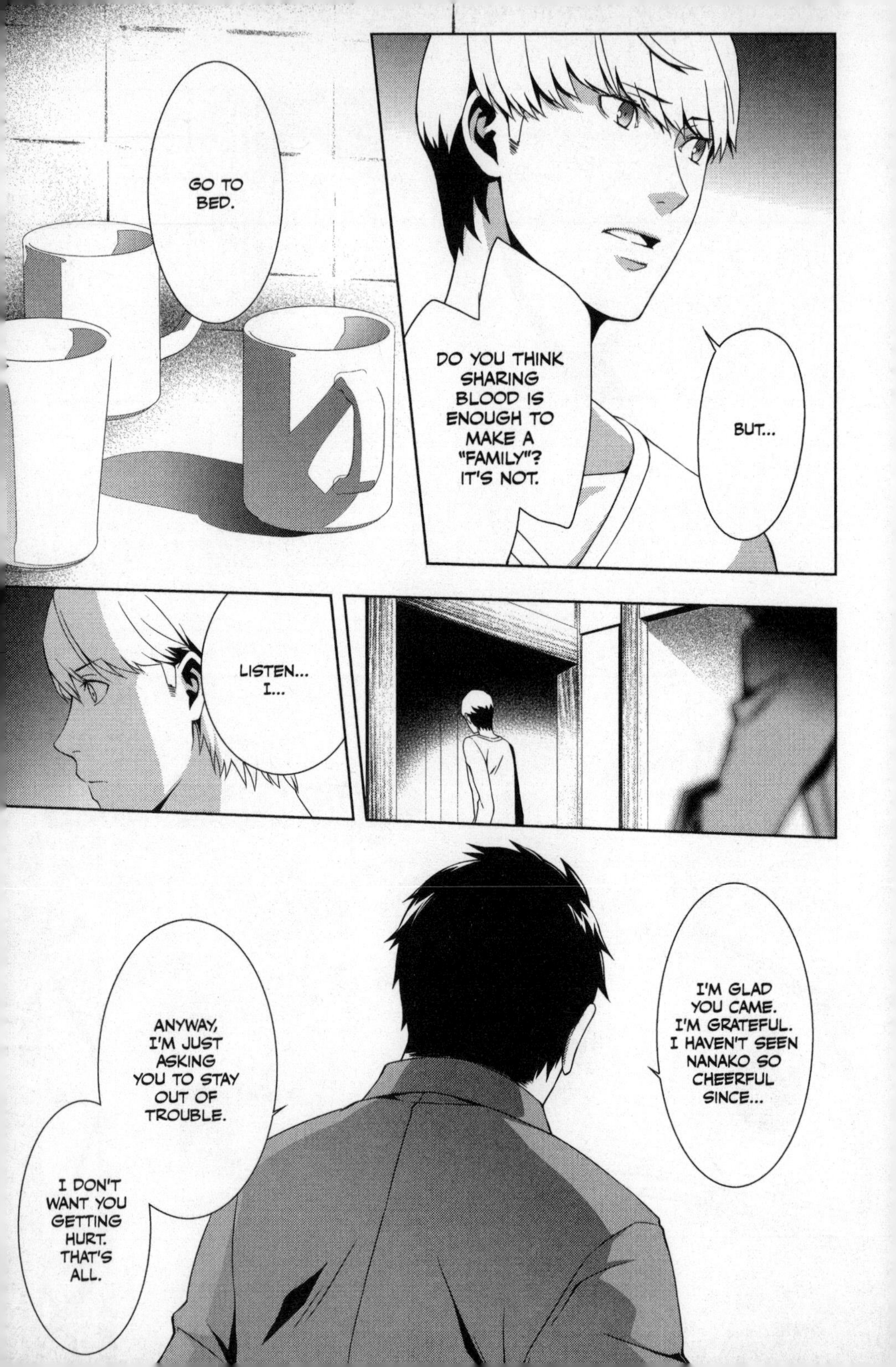
BUT...
DO YOU THINK SHARING BLOOD IS ENOUGH TO MAKE A "FAMILY"? IT'S NOT.
GO TO BED.
LISTEN... I...
I'M GLAD YOU CAME. I'M GRATEFUL. I HAVEN'T SEEN NANAKO SO CHEERFUL SINCE...
ANYWAY, I'M JUST ASKING YOU TO STAY OUT OF TROUBLE.
I DON'T WANT YOU GETTING HURT. THAT'S ALL.

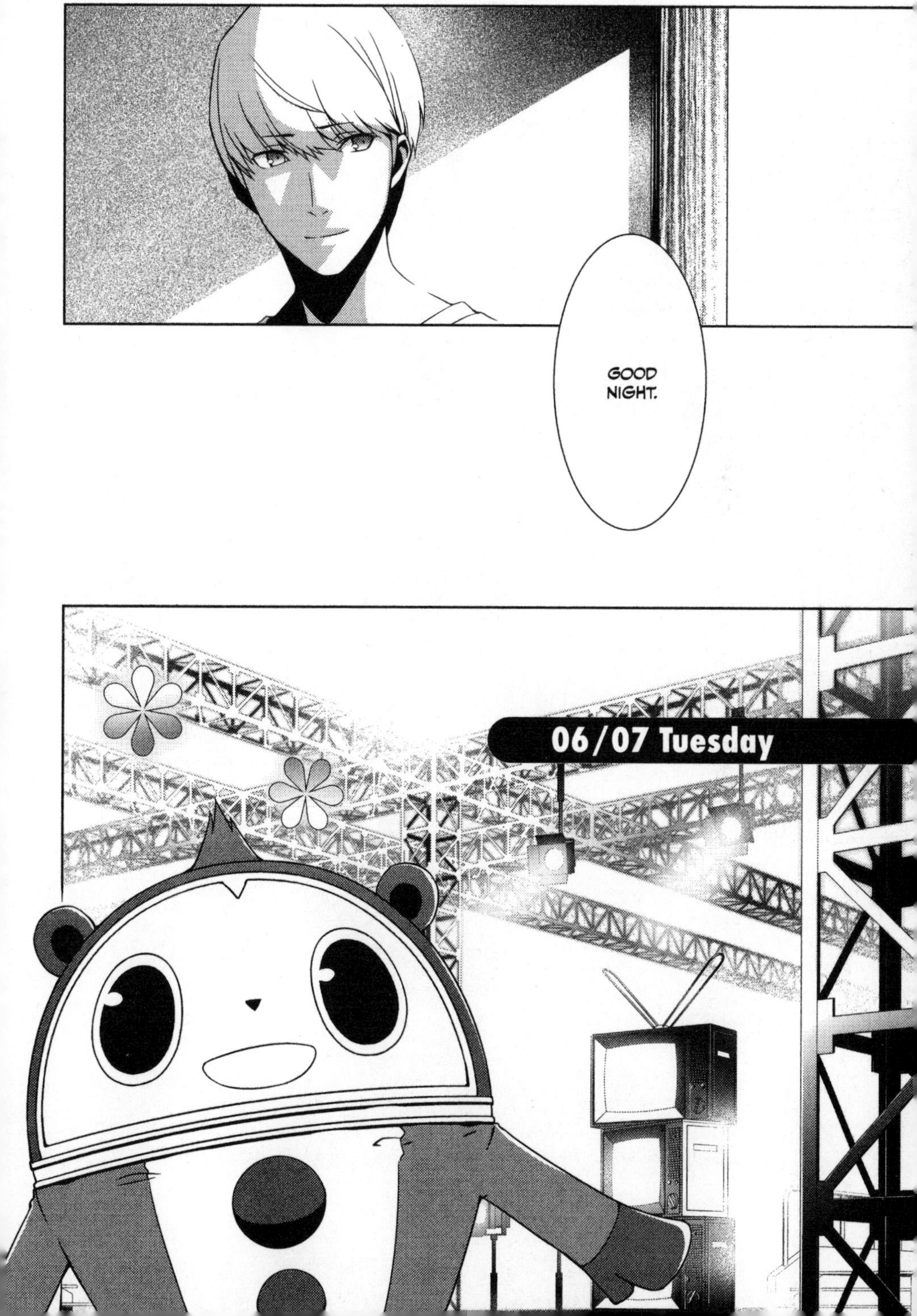
GOOD NIGHT.
06/07 Tuesday

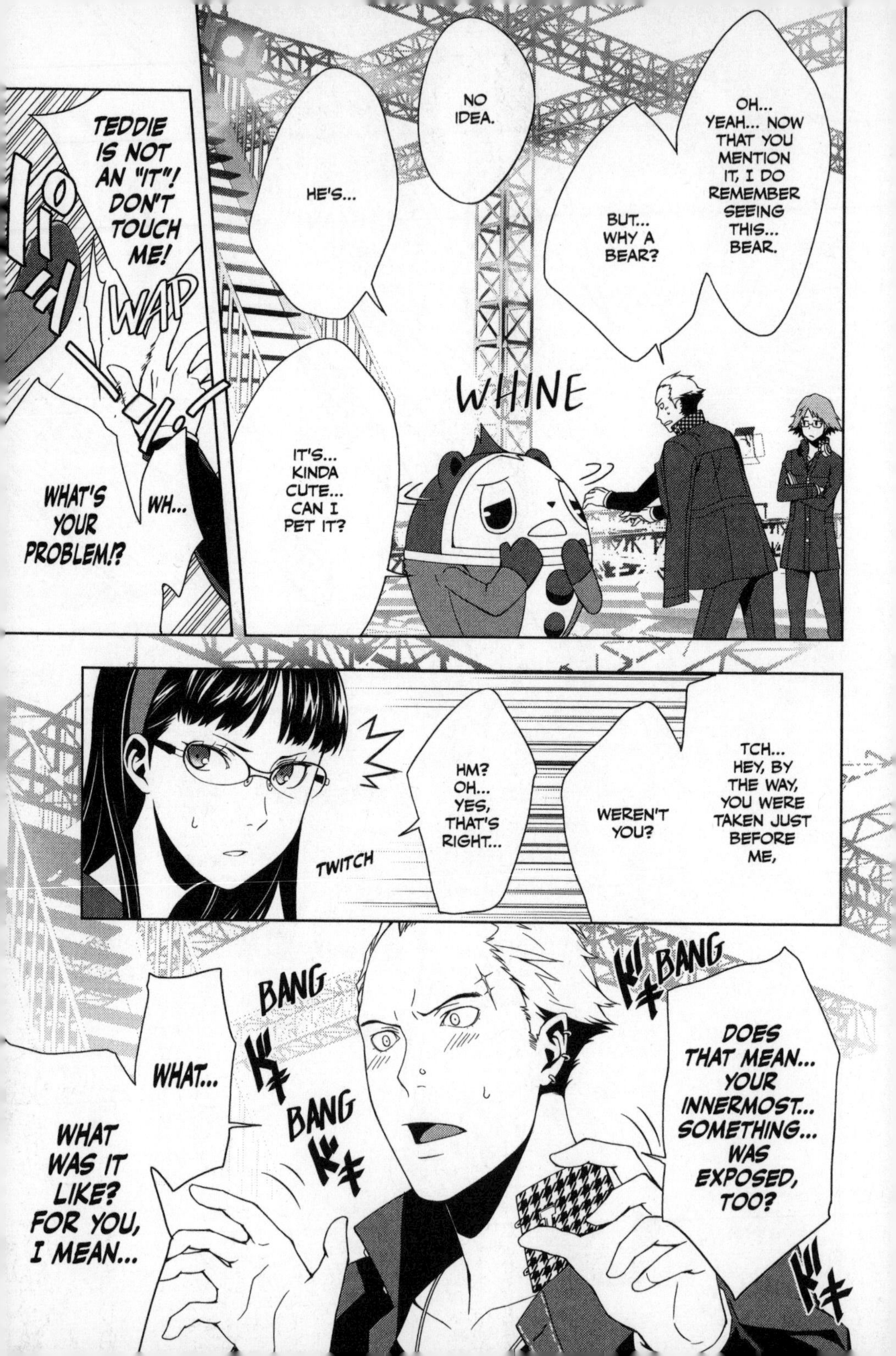
OH... YEAH... NOW THAT YOU MENTION IT, I DO REMEMBER SEEING THIS... BEAR.
BUT... WHY A BEAR?
NO IDEA.
HE'S...
WHINE
IT'S... KINDA CUTE... CAN I PET IT?
TEDDIE IS NOT AN "IT"! DON'T TOUCH ME!
WAP
WH...
WHAT'S YOUR PROBLEM!?
TCH... HEY, BY THE WAY, YOU WERE TAKEN JUST BEFORE ME,
WEREN'T YOU?
HM? OH... YES, THAT'S RIGHT...
TWITCH
ドキ BANG
DOES THAT MEAN... YOUR INNERMOST... SOMETHING... WAS EXPOSED, TOO?
ドキ
BANG
ドキ
BANG
ドキ
WHAT...
WHAT WAS IT LIKE? FOR YOU, I MEAN...

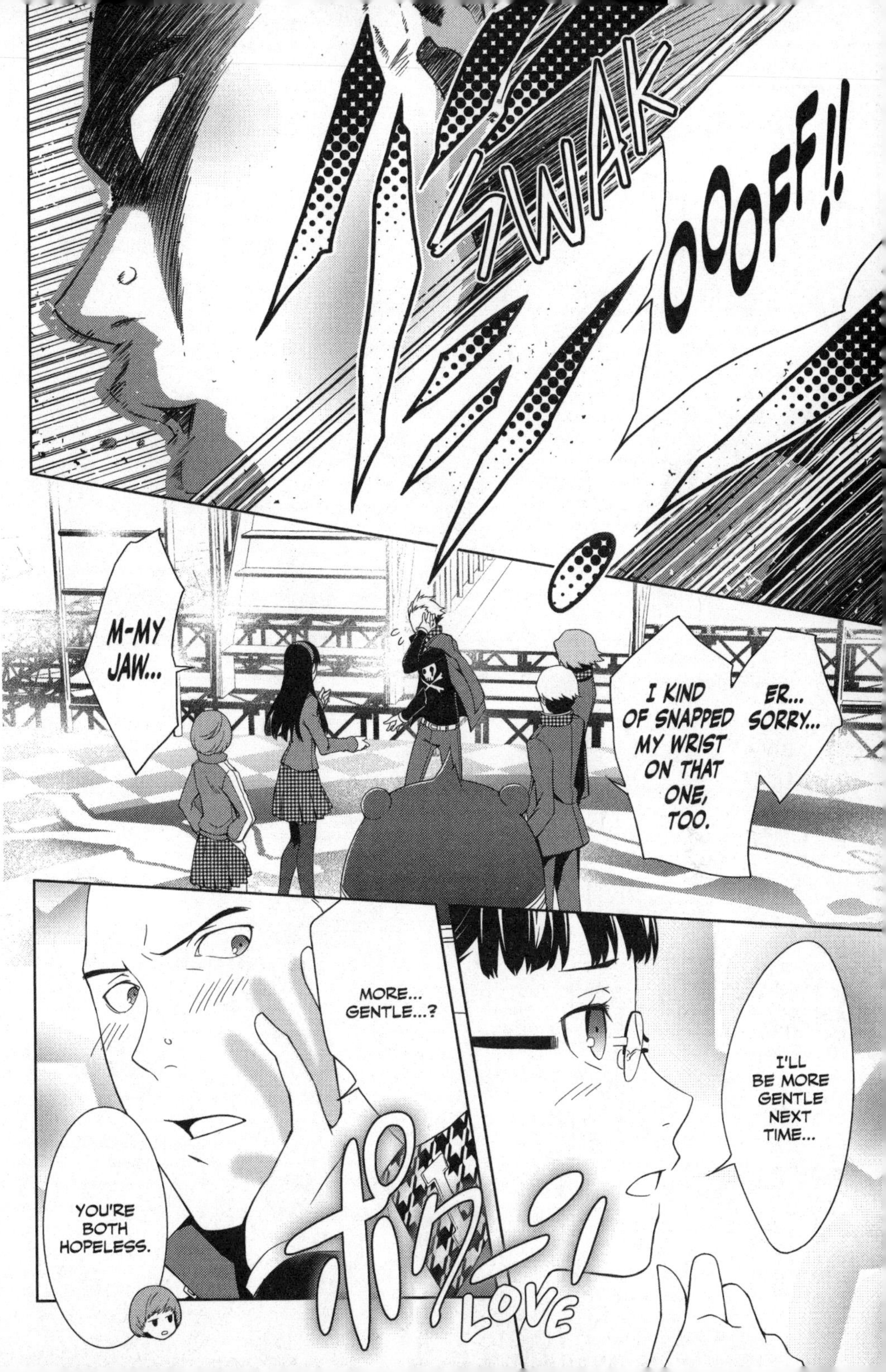
OOOFF!!
SWAK
ER... SORRY...
I KIND OF SNAPPED MY WRIST ON THAT ONE, TOO.
M-MY JAW...
I'LL BE MORE GENTLE NEXT TIME...
LOVE
MORE... GENTLE...?
YOU'RE BOTH HOPELESS.

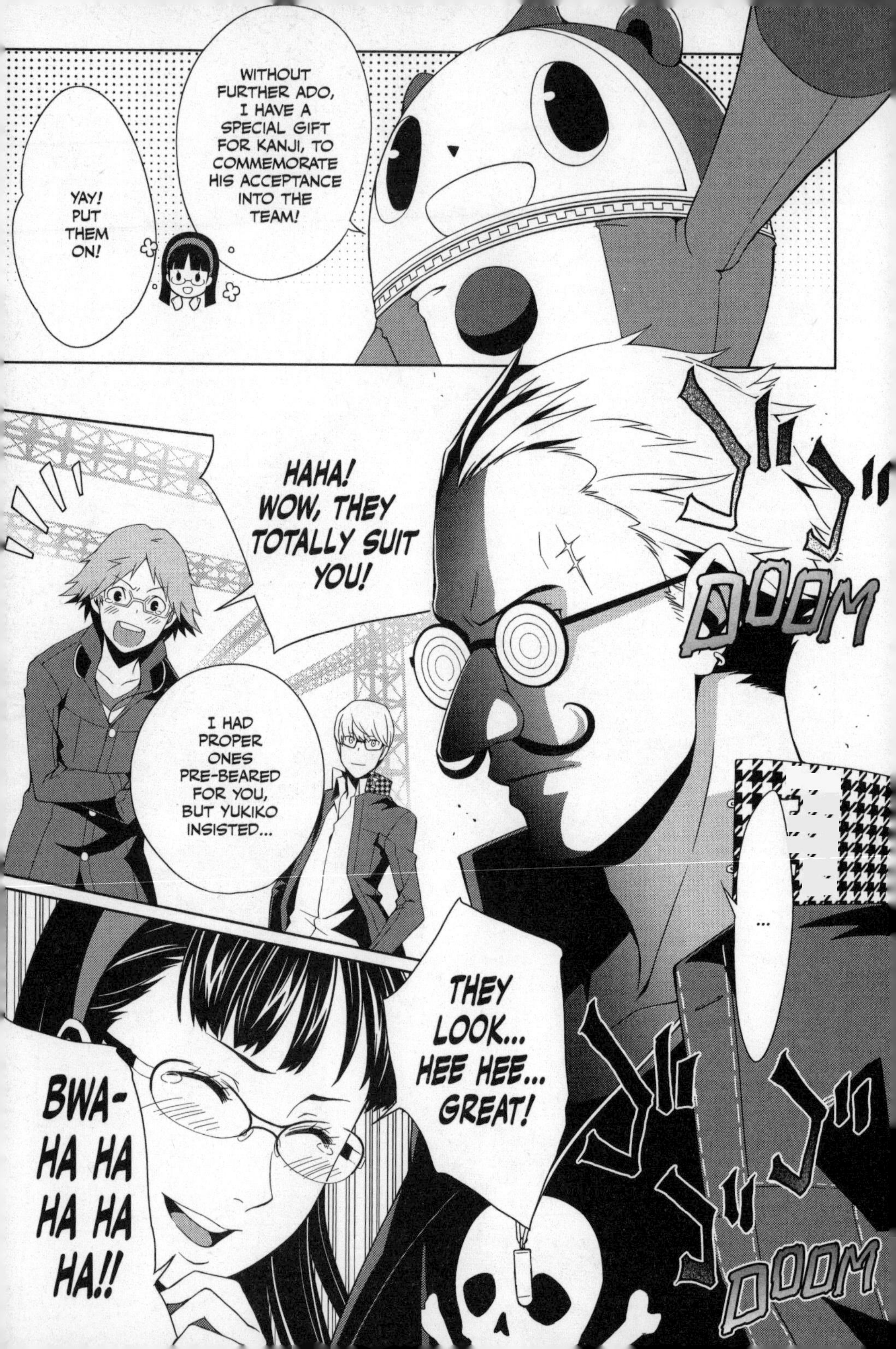

WITHOUT FURTHER ADO, I HAVE A SPECIAL GIFT FOR KANJI, TO COMMEMORATE HIS ACCEPTANCE INTO THE TEAM!
YAY! PUT THEM ON!
DOOM
...
DOOM
HAHA! WOW, THEY TOTALLY SUIT YOU!
I HAD PROPER ONES PRE-BEARED FOR YOU, BUT YUKIKO INSISTED...
THEY LOOK... HEE HEE... GREAT!
BWA-HA HA HA HA HA!!

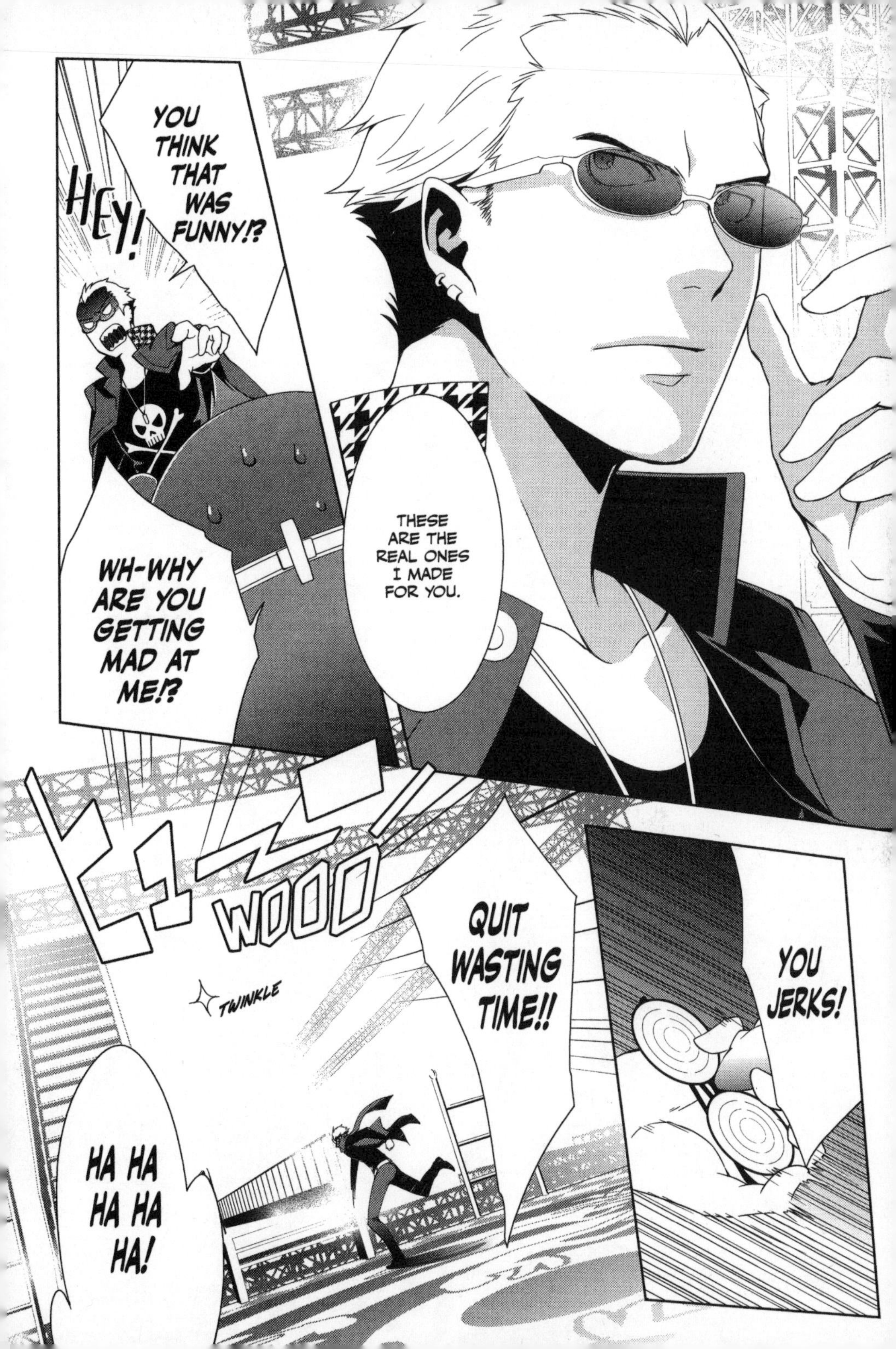
THESE ARE THE REAL ONES I MADE FOR YOU.
HEY!
YOU THINK THAT WAS FUNNY!?
WH-WHY ARE YOU GETTING MAD AT ME!?
YOU JERKS!
WOOO
QUIT WASTING TIME!!
TWINKLE
HA HA HA HA HA!

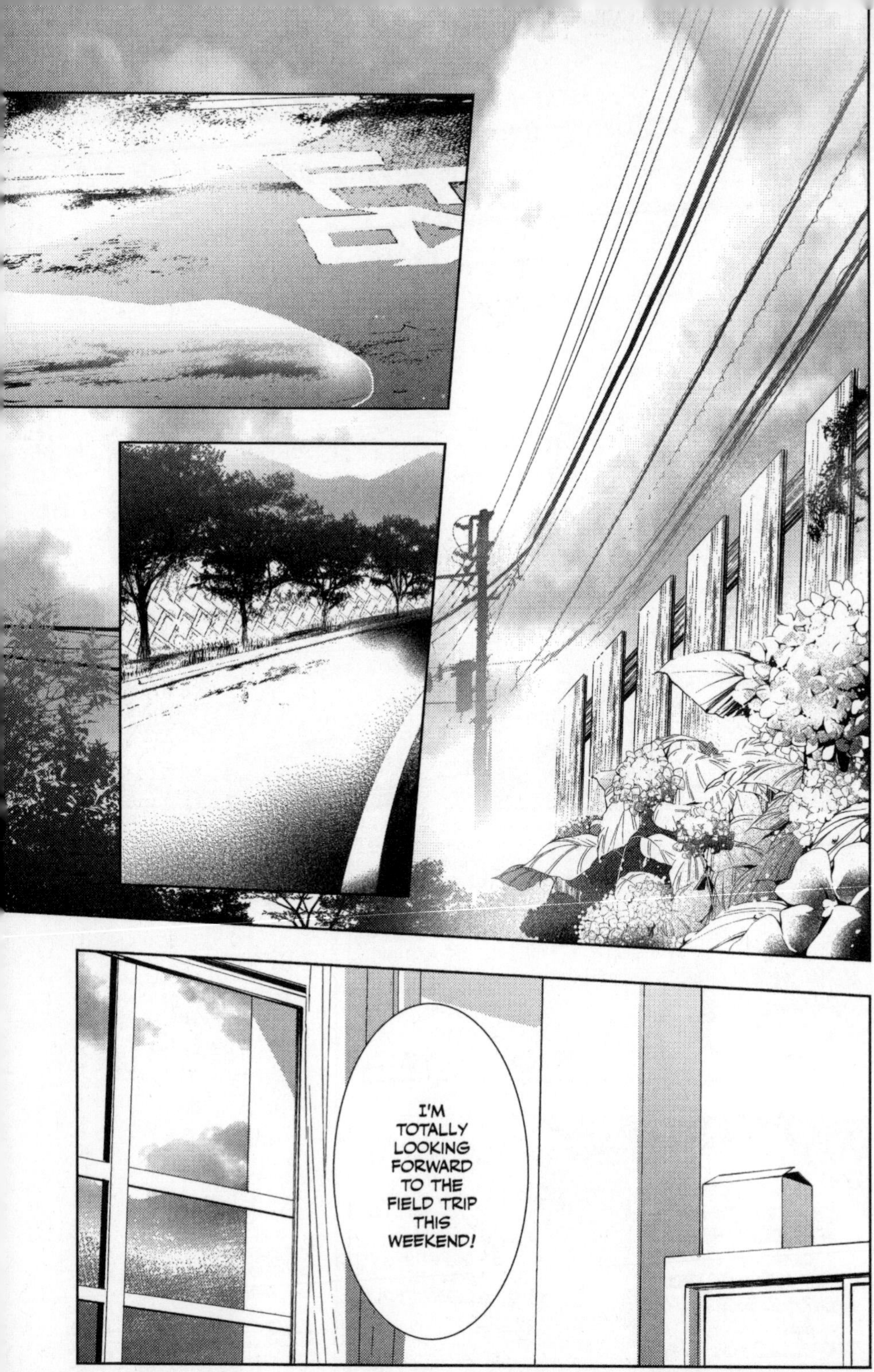
I'M TOTALLY LOOKING FORWARD TO THE FIELD TRIP THIS WEEKEND!

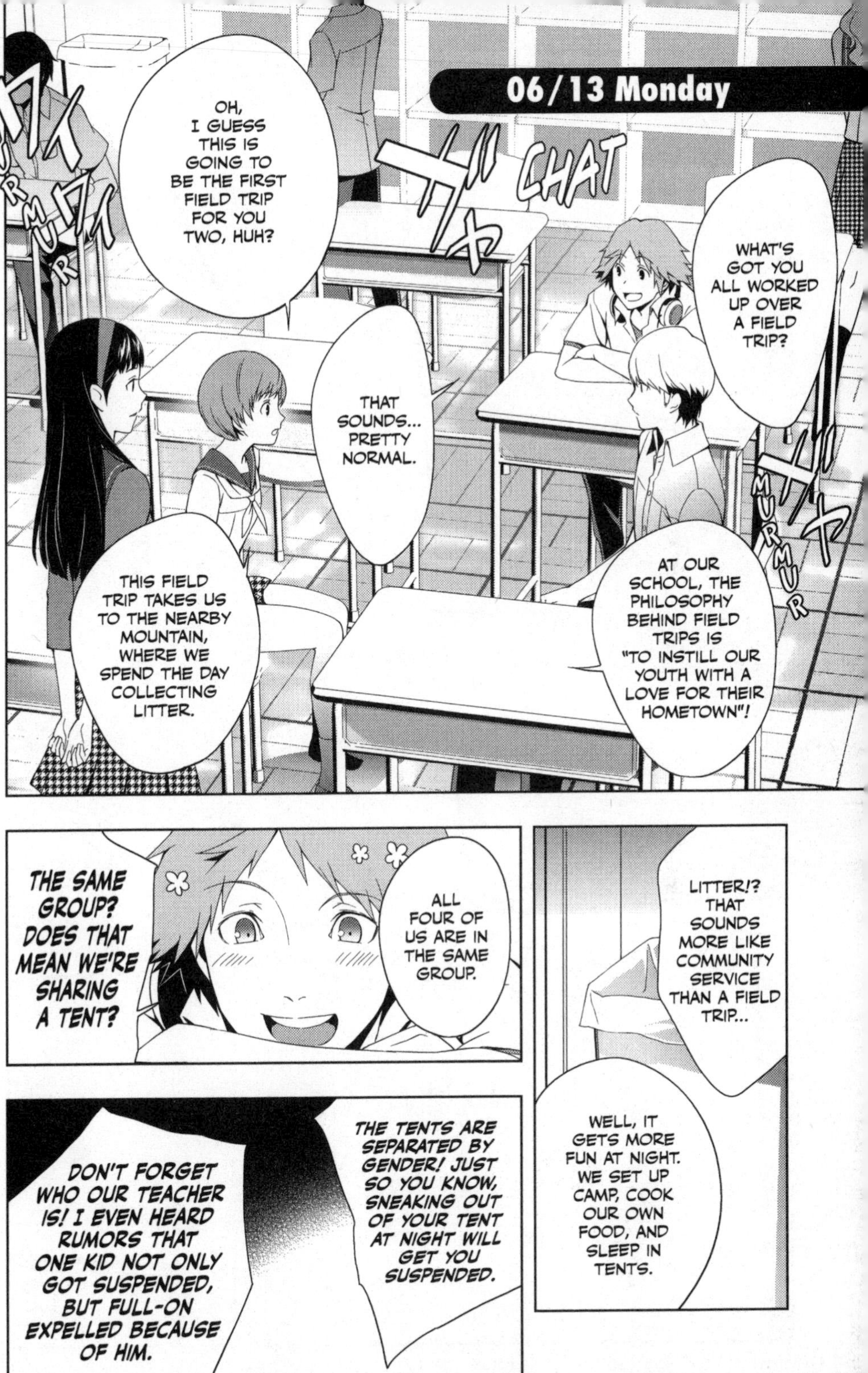
06/13 Monday
MURMUR
CHAT
MURMUR
WHAT'S GOT YOU ALL WORKED UP OVER A FIELD TRIP?
OH, I GUESS THIS IS GOING TO BE THE FIRST FIELD TRIP FOR YOU TWO, HUH?
AT OUR SCHOOL, THE PHILOSOPHY BEHIND FIELD TRIPS IS "TO INSTILL OUR YOUTH WITH A LOVE FOR THEIR HOMETOWN"!
THAT SOUNDS... PRETTY NORMAL.
THIS FIELD TRIP TAKES US TO THE NEARBY MOUNTAIN, WHERE WE SPEND THE DAY COLLECTING LITTER.
LITTER!? THAT SOUNDS MORE LIKE COMMUNITY SERVICE THAN A FIELD TRIP...
WELL, IT GETS MORE FUN AT NIGHT. WE SET UP CAMP, COOK OUR OWN FOOD, AND SLEEP IN TENTS.
ALL FOUR OF US ARE IN THE SAME GROUP.
THE SAME GROUP? DOES THAT MEAN WE'RE SHARING A TENT?
THE TENTS ARE SEPARATED BY GENDER! JUST SO YOU KNOW, SNEAKING OUT OF YOUR TENT AT NIGHT WILL GET YOU SUSPENDED.
DON'T FORGET WHO OUR TEACHER IS! I EVEN HEARD RUMORS THAT ONE KID NOT ONLY GOT SUSPENDED, BUT FULL-ON EXPELLED BECAUSE OF HIM.

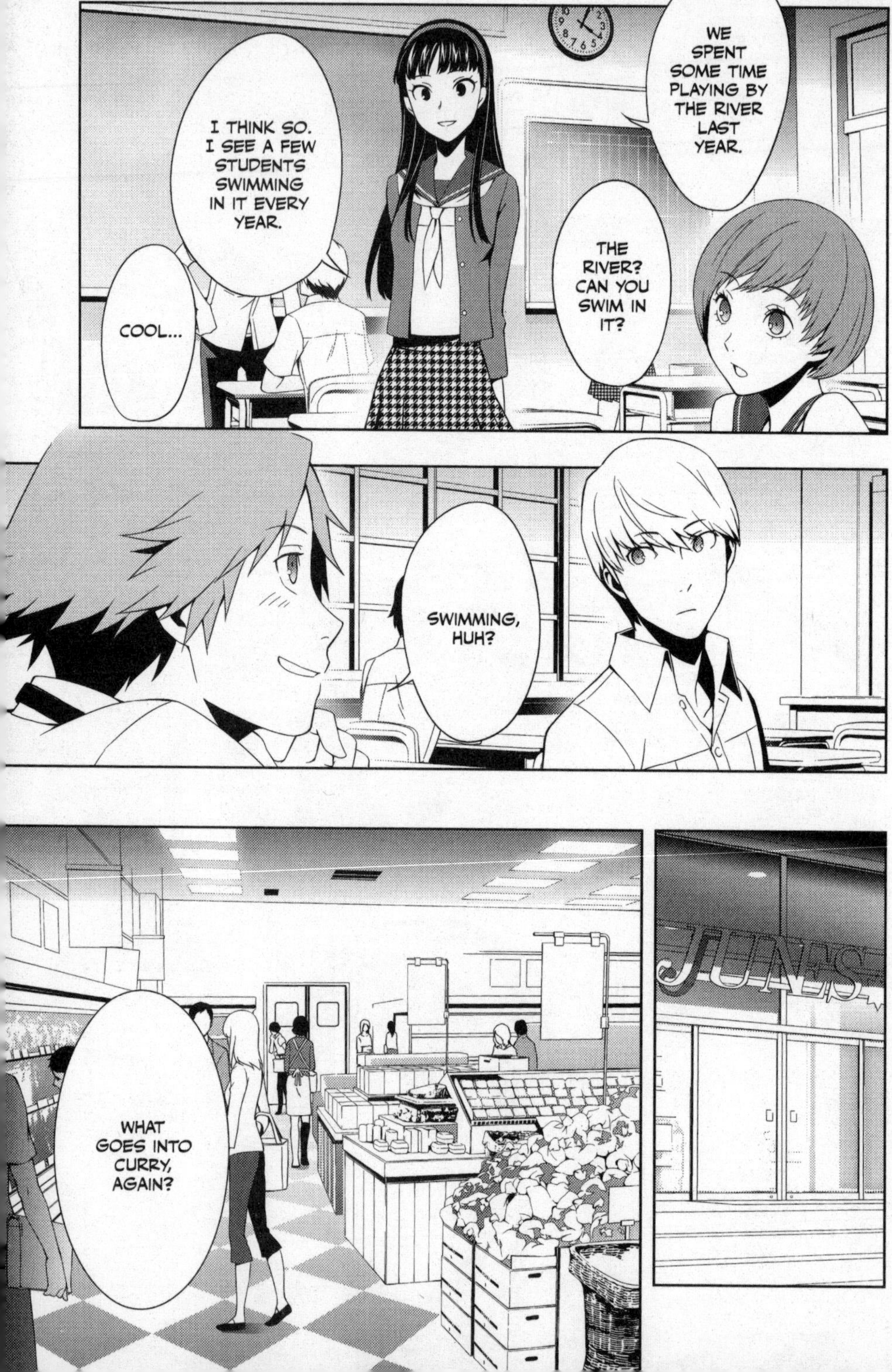
WE SPENT SOME TIME PLAYING BY THE RIVER LAST YEAR.
THE RIVER? CAN YOU SWIM IN IT?
I THINK SO. I SEE A FEW STUDENTS SWIMMING IN IT EVERY YEAR.
COOL...
SWIMMING, HUH?
WHAT GOES INTO CURRY, AGAIN?

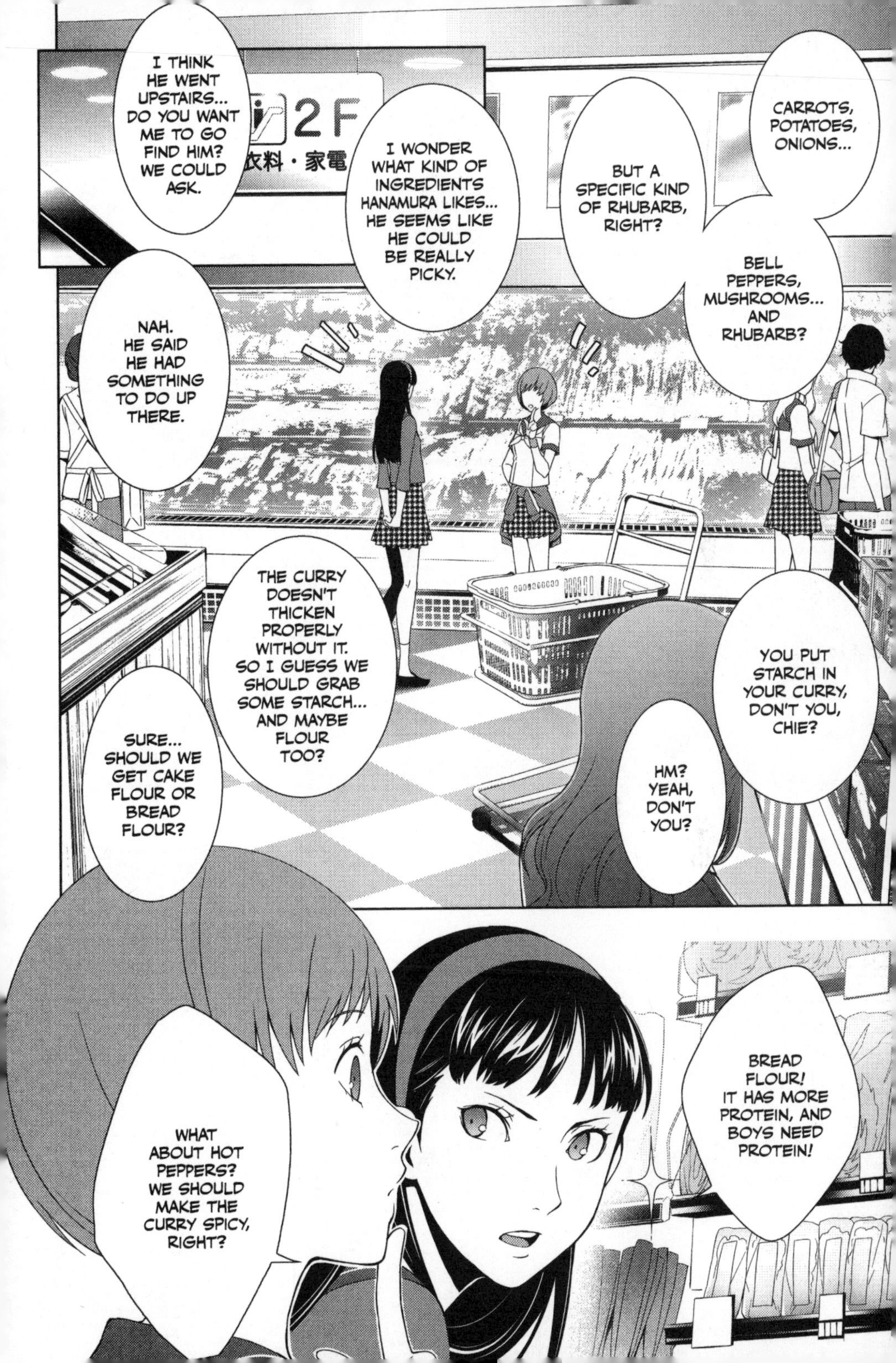

2F
衣料・家電
CARROTS, POTATOES, ONIONS...
BELL PEPPERS, MUSHROOMS... AND RHUBARB?
BUT A SPECIFIC KIND OF RHUBARB, RIGHT?
I WONDER WHAT KIND OF INGREDIENTS HANAMURA LIKES... HE SEEMS LIKE HE COULD BE REALLY PICKY.
I THINK HE WENT UPSTAIRS... DO YOU WANT ME TO GO FIND HIM? WE COULD ASK.
NAH. HE SAID HE HAD SOMETHING TO DO UP THERE.
YOU PUT STARCH IN YOUR CURRY, DON'T YOU, CHIE?
HM? YEAH, DON'T YOU?
THE CURRY DOESN'T THICKEN PROPERLY WITHOUT IT. SO I GUESS WE SHOULD GRAB SOME STARCH... AND MAYBE FLOUR TOO?
SURE... SHOULD WE GET CAKE FLOUR OR BREAD FLOUR?
BREAD FLOUR! IT HAS MORE PROTEIN, AND BOYS NEED PROTEIN!
WHAT ABOUT HOT PEPPERS? WE SHOULD MAKE THE CURRY SPICY, RIGHT?

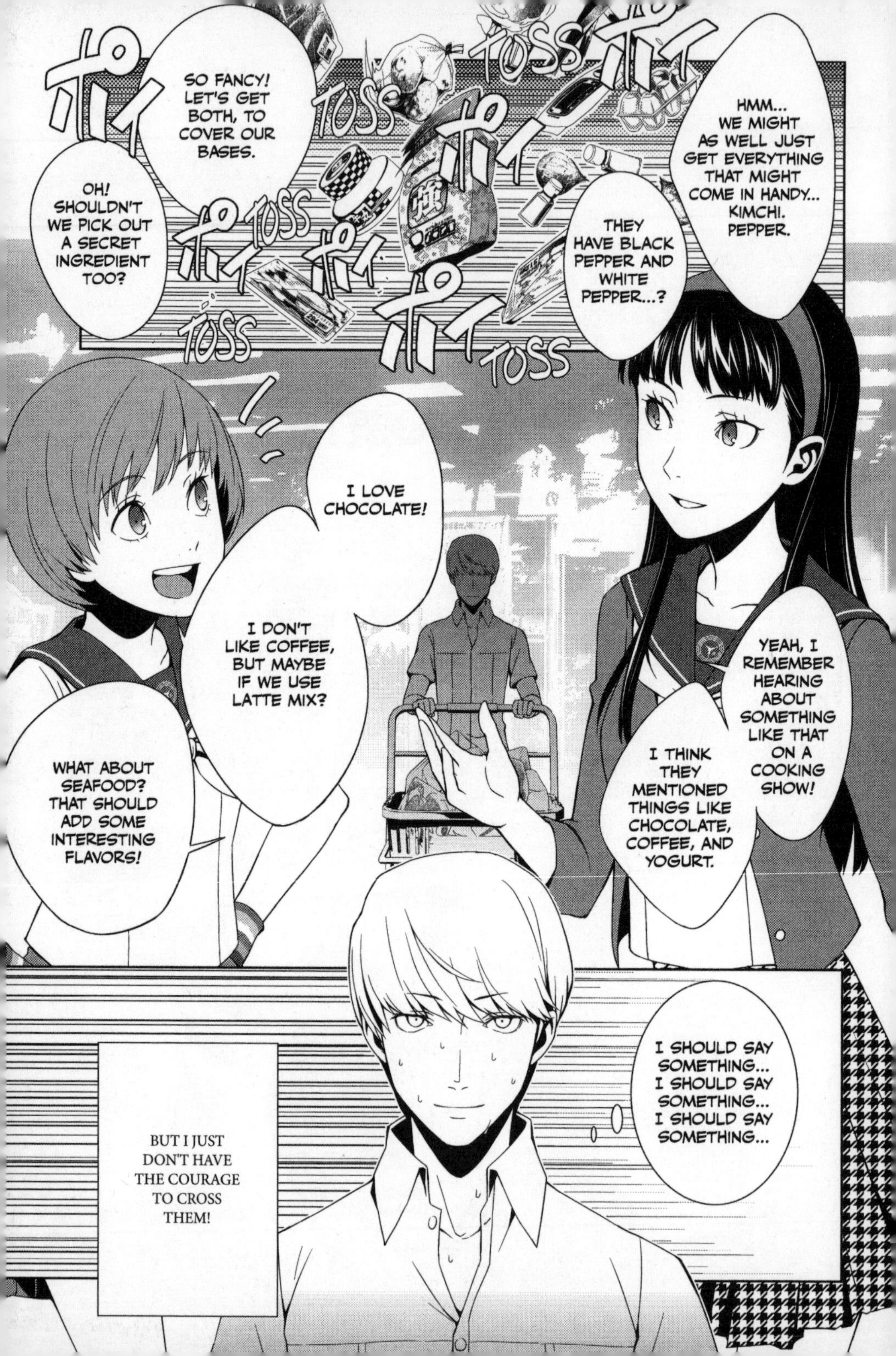
HMM... WE MIGHT AS WELL JUST GET EVERYTHING THAT MIGHT COME IN HANDY... KIMCHI. PEPPER.
THEY HAVE BLACK PEPPER AND WHITE PEPPER...?
SO FANCY! LET'S GET BOTH, TO COVER OUR BASES.
OH! SHOULDN'T WE PICK OUT A SECRET INGREDIENT TOO?
ポイ TOSS
ポイ TOSS
ポイ TOSS
ポイ TOSS
ポイ TOSS
ポイ TOSS
YEAH, I REMEMBER HEARING ABOUT SOMETHING LIKE THAT ON A COOKING SHOW!
I THINK THEY MENTIONED THINGS LIKE CHOCOLATE, COFFEE, AND YOGURT.
I LOVE CHOCOLATE!
I DON'T LIKE COFFEE, BUT MAYBE IF WE USE LATTE MIX?
WHAT ABOUT SEAFOOD? THAT SHOULD ADD SOME INTERESTING FLAVORS!
I SHOULD SAY SOMETHING... I SHOULD SAY SOMETHING... I SHOULD SAY SOMETHING...
BUT I JUST DON'T HAVE THE COURAGE TO CROSS THEM!

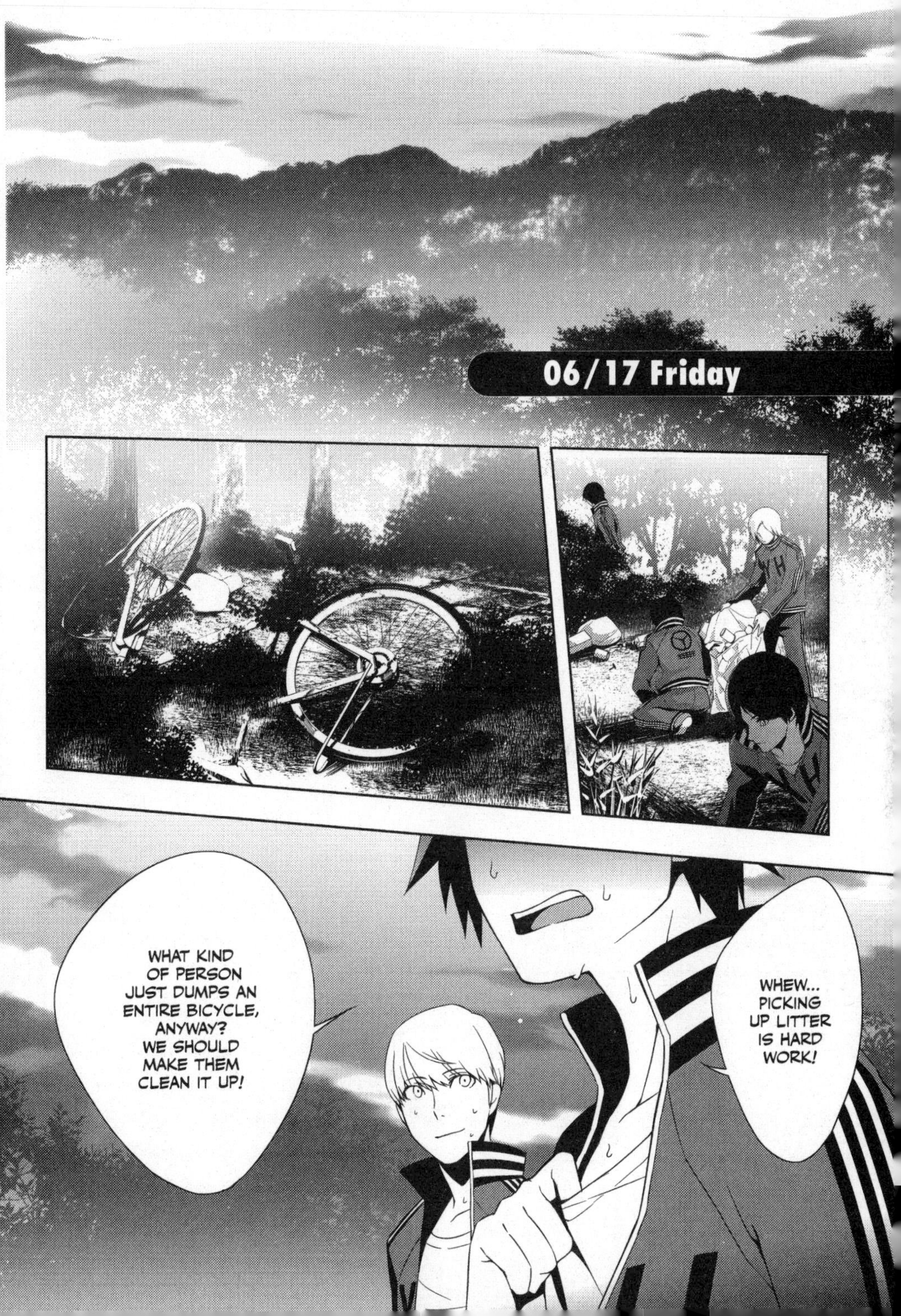
06/17 Friday
WHEW... PICKING UP LITTER IS HARD WORK!
WHAT KIND OF PERSON JUST DUMPS AN ENTIRE BICYCLE, ANYWAY? WE SHOULD MAKE THEM CLEAN IT UP!

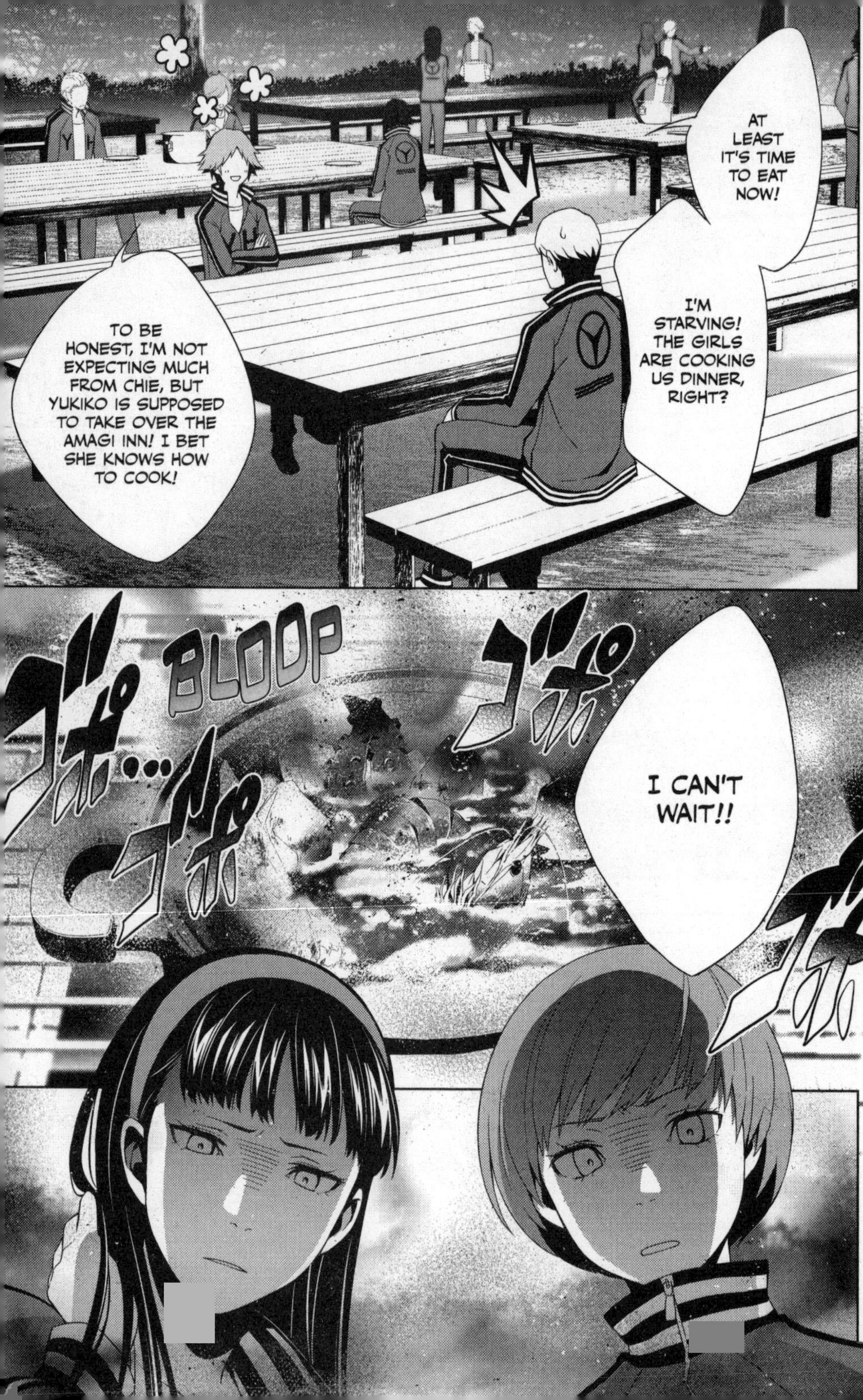
AT LEAST IT'S TIME TO EAT NOW!
I'M STARVING! THE GIRLS ARE COOKING US DINNER, RIGHT?
TO BE HONEST, I'M NOT EXPECTING MUCH FROM CHIE, BUT YUKIKO IS SUPPOSED TO TAKE OVER THE AMAGI INN! I BET SHE KNOWS HOW TO COOK!
I CAN'T WAIT!!
ゴポ
BLOOP
ゴポ…
ゴポ

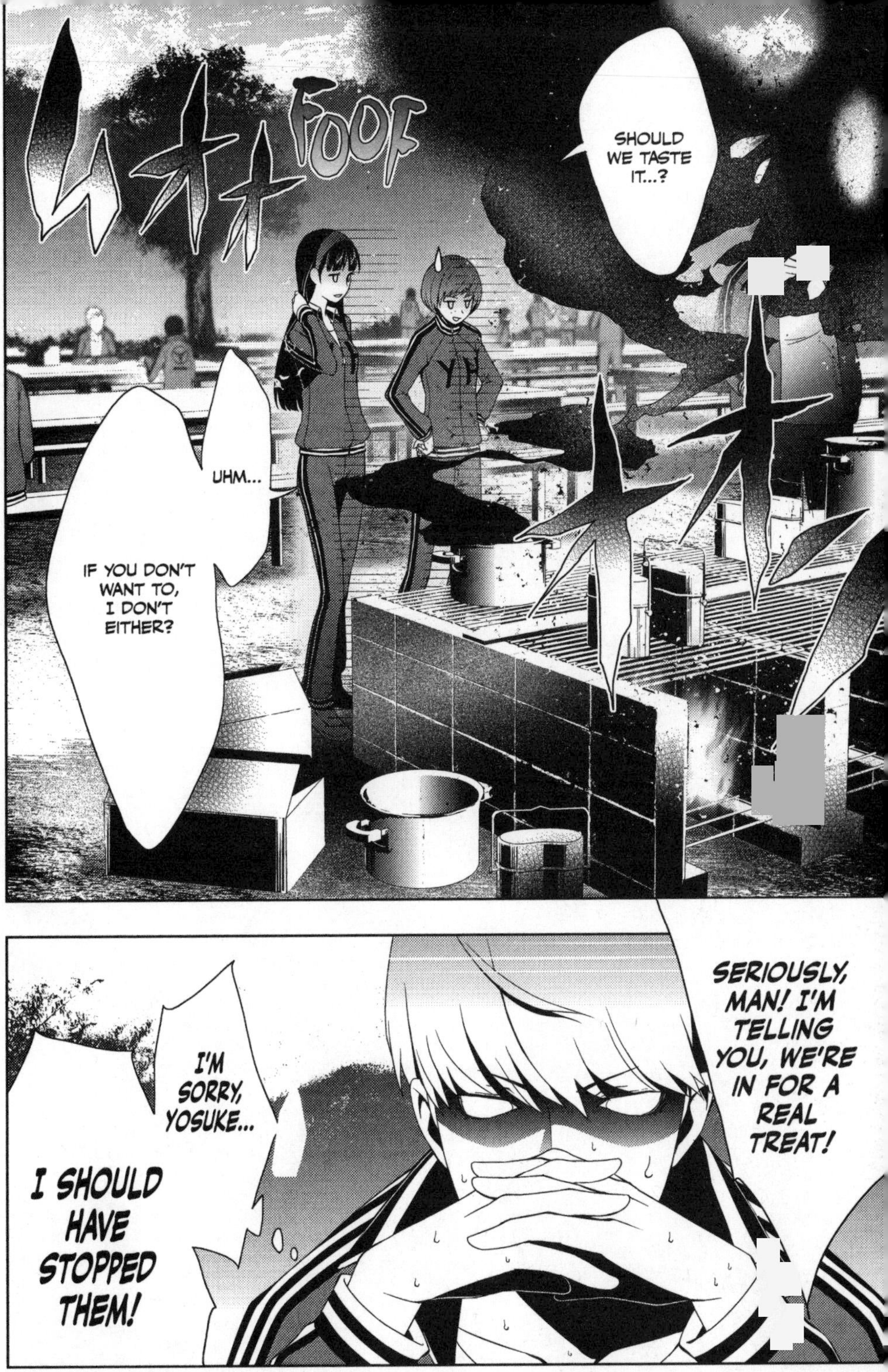
ムオォ
FOOF
SHOULD WE TASTE IT...?
UHM...
IF YOU DON'T WANT TO, I DON'T EITHER?
SERIOUSLY, MAN! I'M TELLING YOU, WE'RE IN FOR A REAL TREAT!
I'M SORRY, YOSUKE...
I SHOULD HAVE STOPPED THEM!

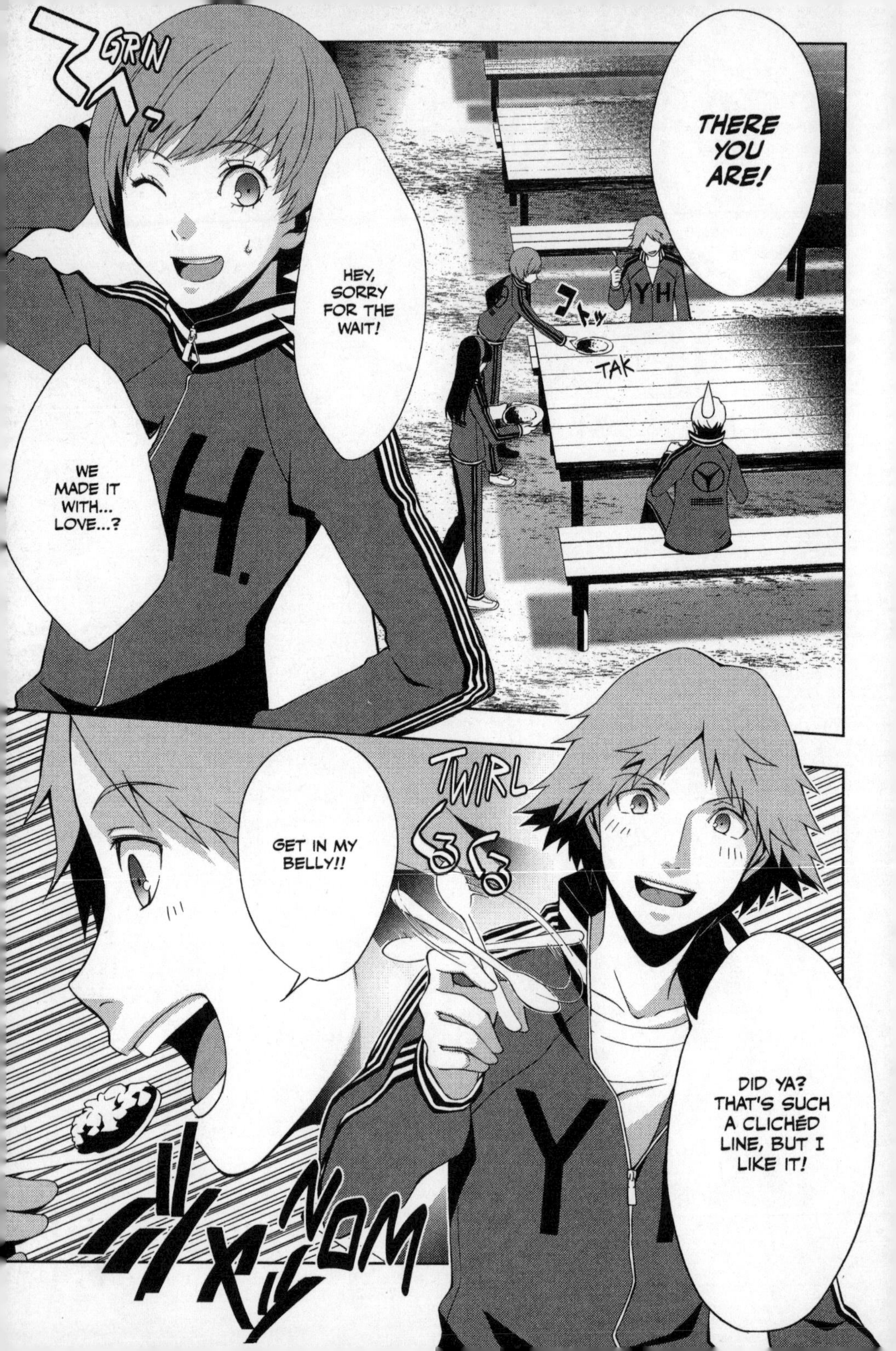
THERE YOU ARE!
TAK
HEY, SORRY FOR THE WAIT!
WE MADE IT WITH... LOVE...?
GRIN
DID YA? THAT'S SUCH A CLICHÉD LINE, BUT I LIKE IT!
TWIRL
GET IN MY BELLY!!
NOM

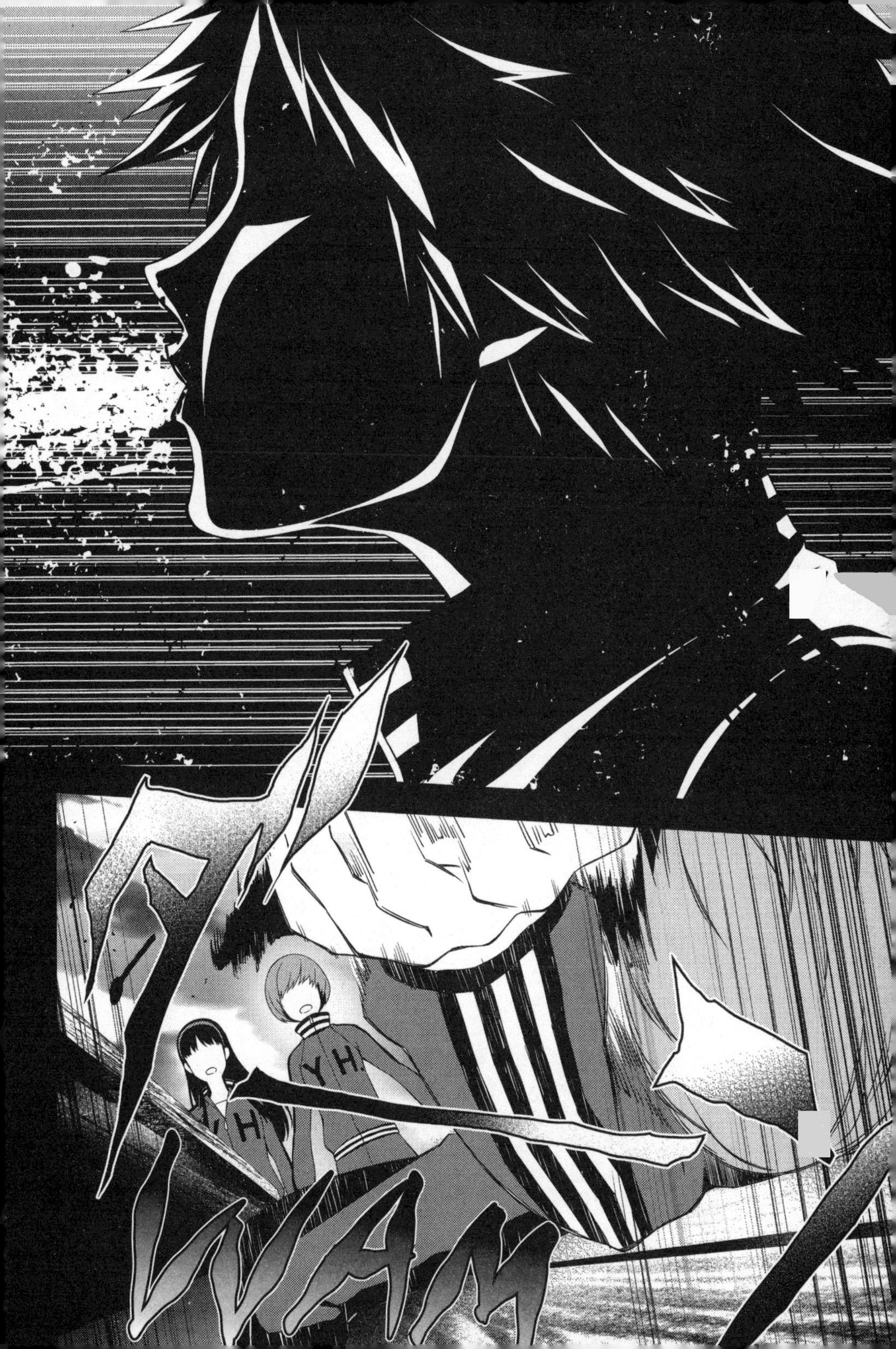
WHAM

-SILENT-
SHIVER
ER...
HUH...?

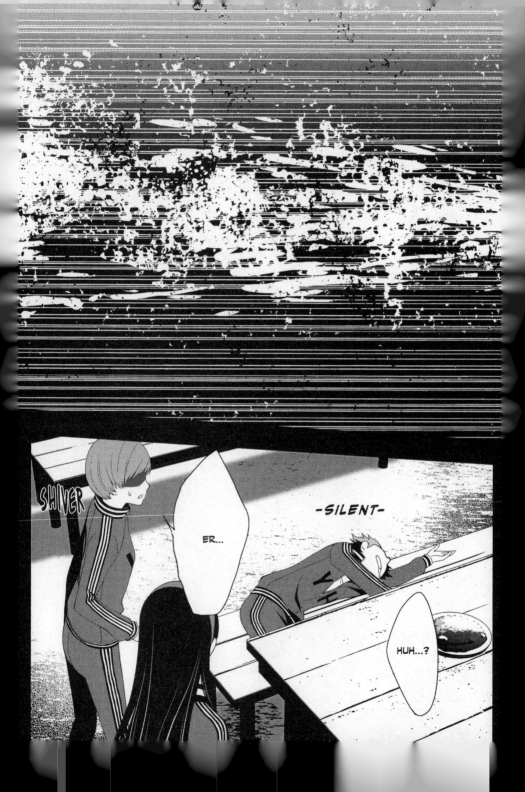

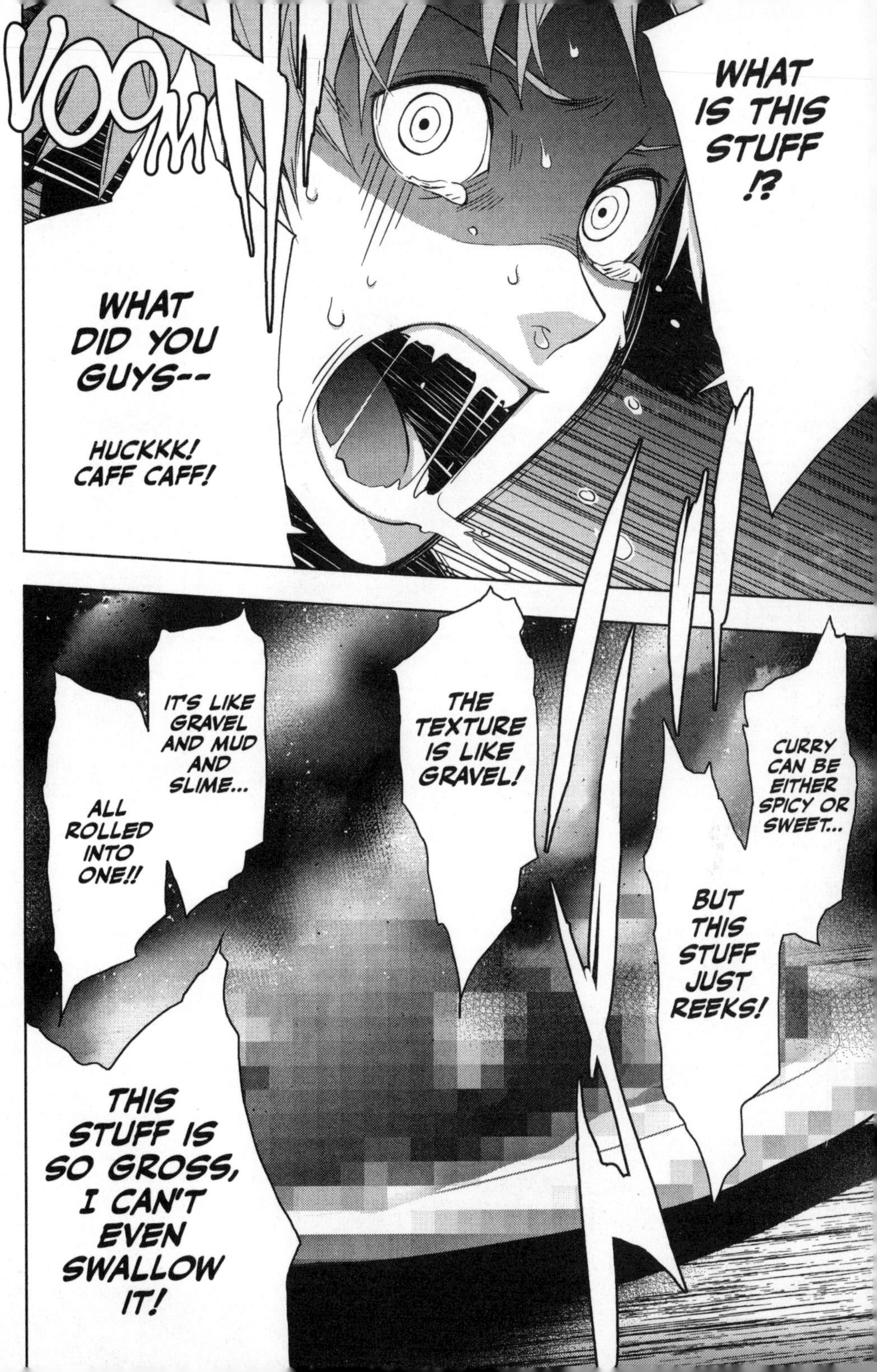

WHAT IS THIS STUFF!?
VOOM
WHAT DID YOU GUYS--
HUCKKK! CAFF CAFF!
CURRY CAN BE EITHER SPICY OR SWEET...
BUT THIS STUFF JUST REEKS!
THE TEXTURE IS LIKE GRAVEL!
IT'S LIKE GRAVEL AND MUD AND SLIME...
ALL ROLLED INTO ONE!!
THIS STUFF IS SO GROSS, I CAN'T EVEN SWALLOW IT!

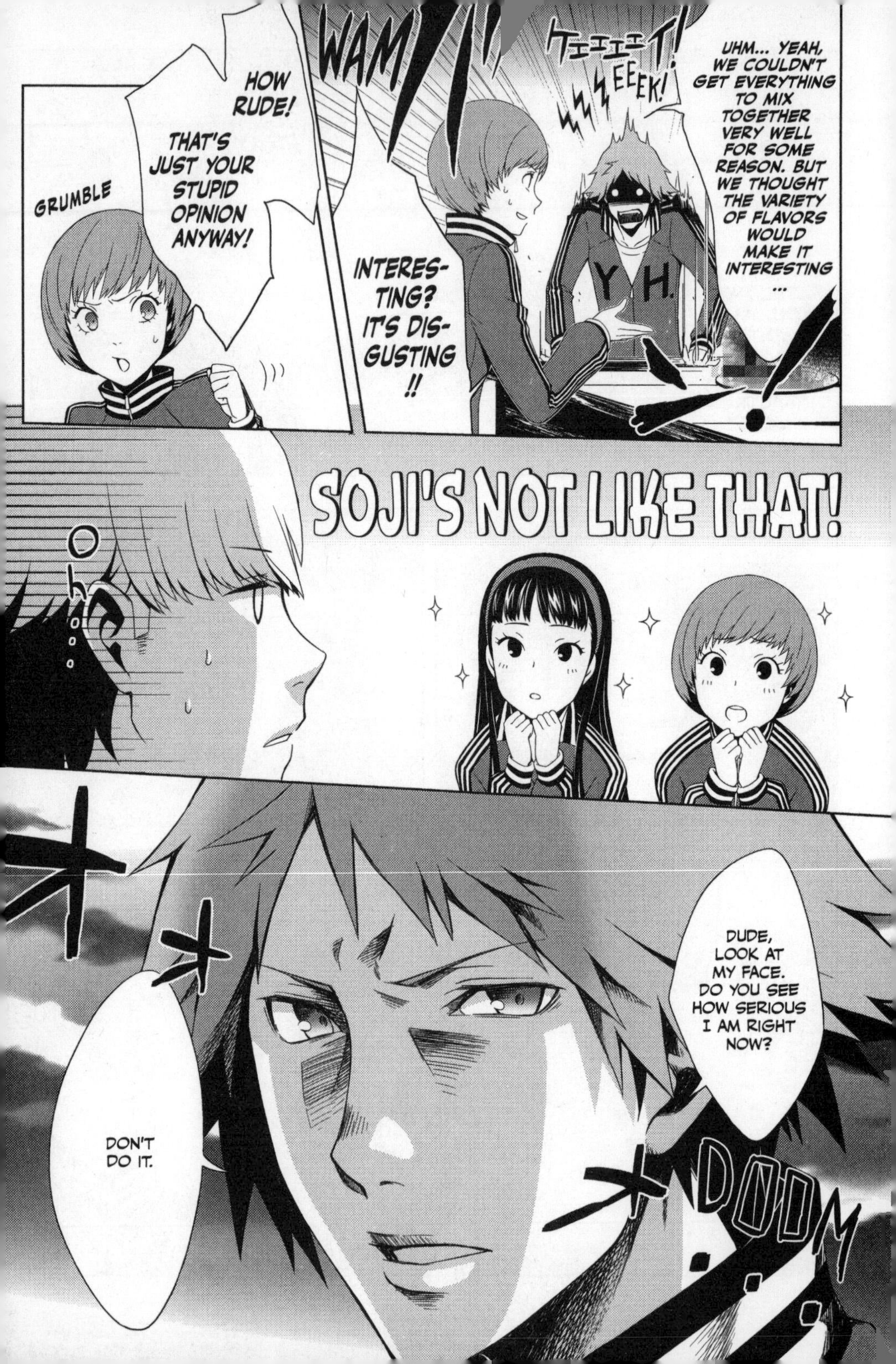
UHM... YEAH, WE COULDN'T GET EVERYTHING TO MIX TOGETHER VERY WELL FOR SOME REASON. BUT WE THOUGHT THE VARIETY OF FLAVORS WOULD MAKE IT INTERESTING ...
EEEK!
WAM
INTERES-TING? IT'S DIS-GUSTING!!
HOW RUDE!
THAT'S JUST YOUR STUPID OPINION ANYWAY!
GRUMBLE
SOJI'S NOT LIKE THAT!
DUDE, LOOK AT MY FACE. DO YOU SEE HOW SERIOUS I AM RIGHT NOW?
DOOM
DON'T DO IT.

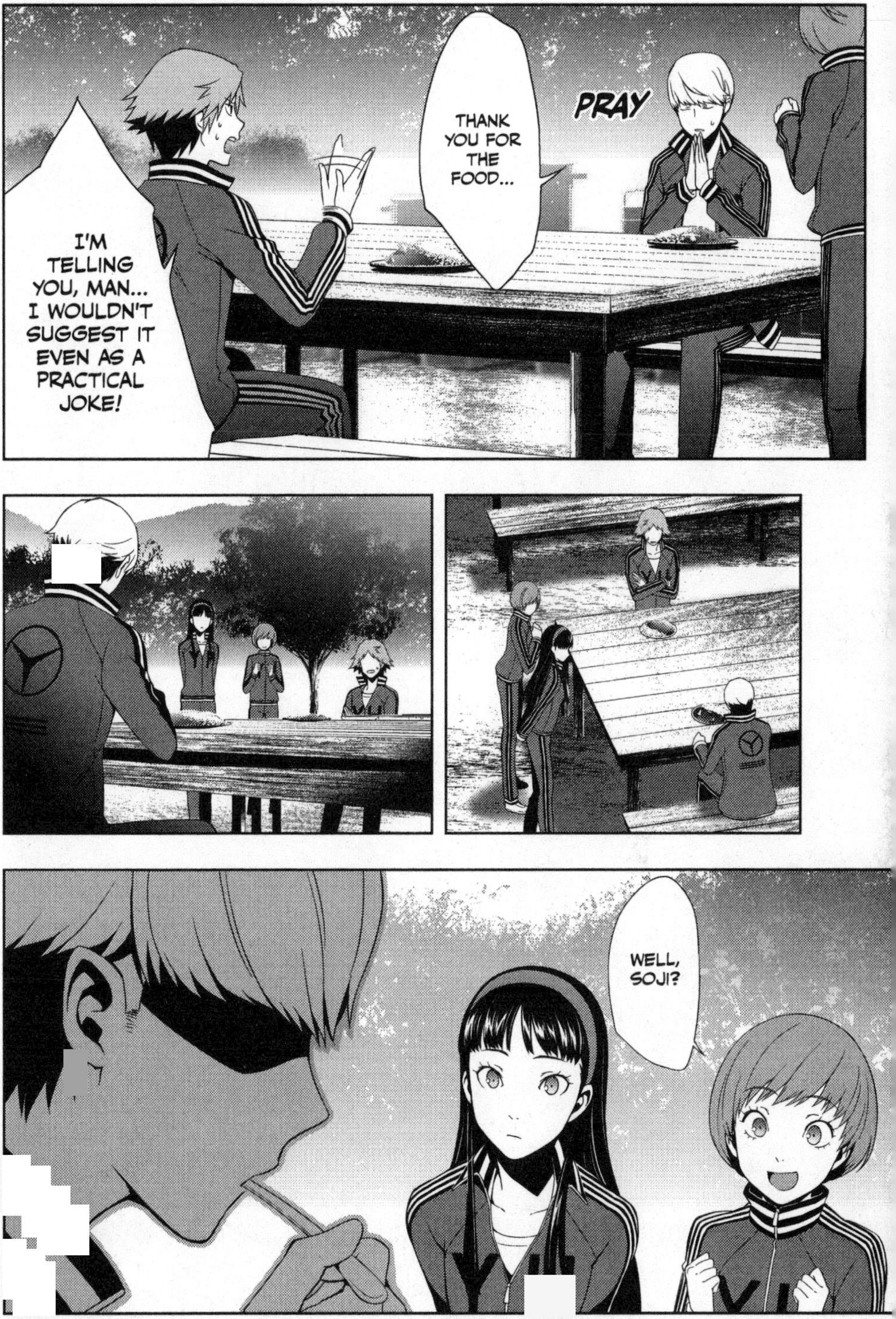
PRAY
THANK YOU FOR THE FOOD...
I'M TELLING YOU, MAN... I WOULDN'T SUGGEST IT EVEN AS A PRACTICAL JOKE!
WELL, SOJI?

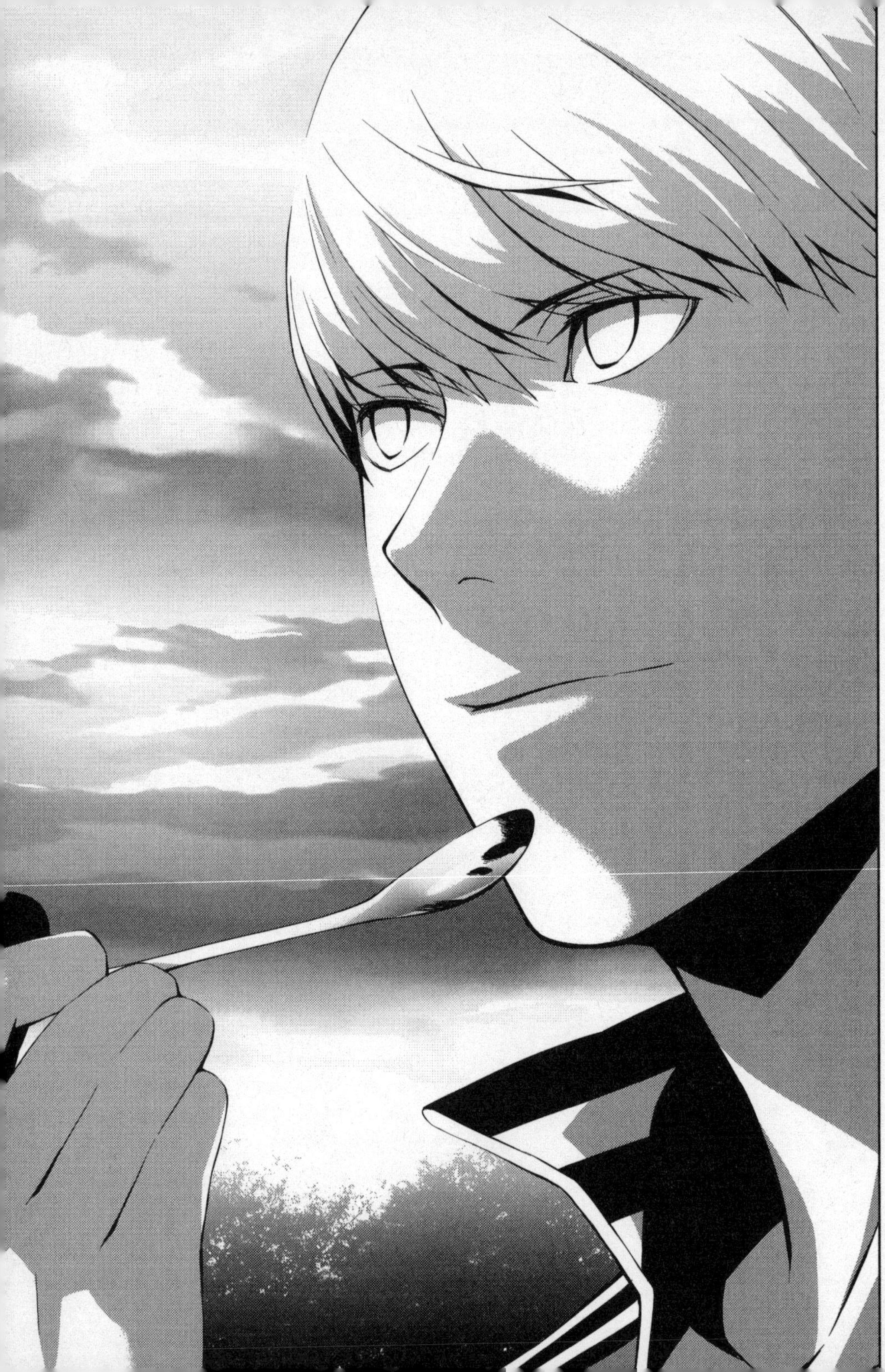

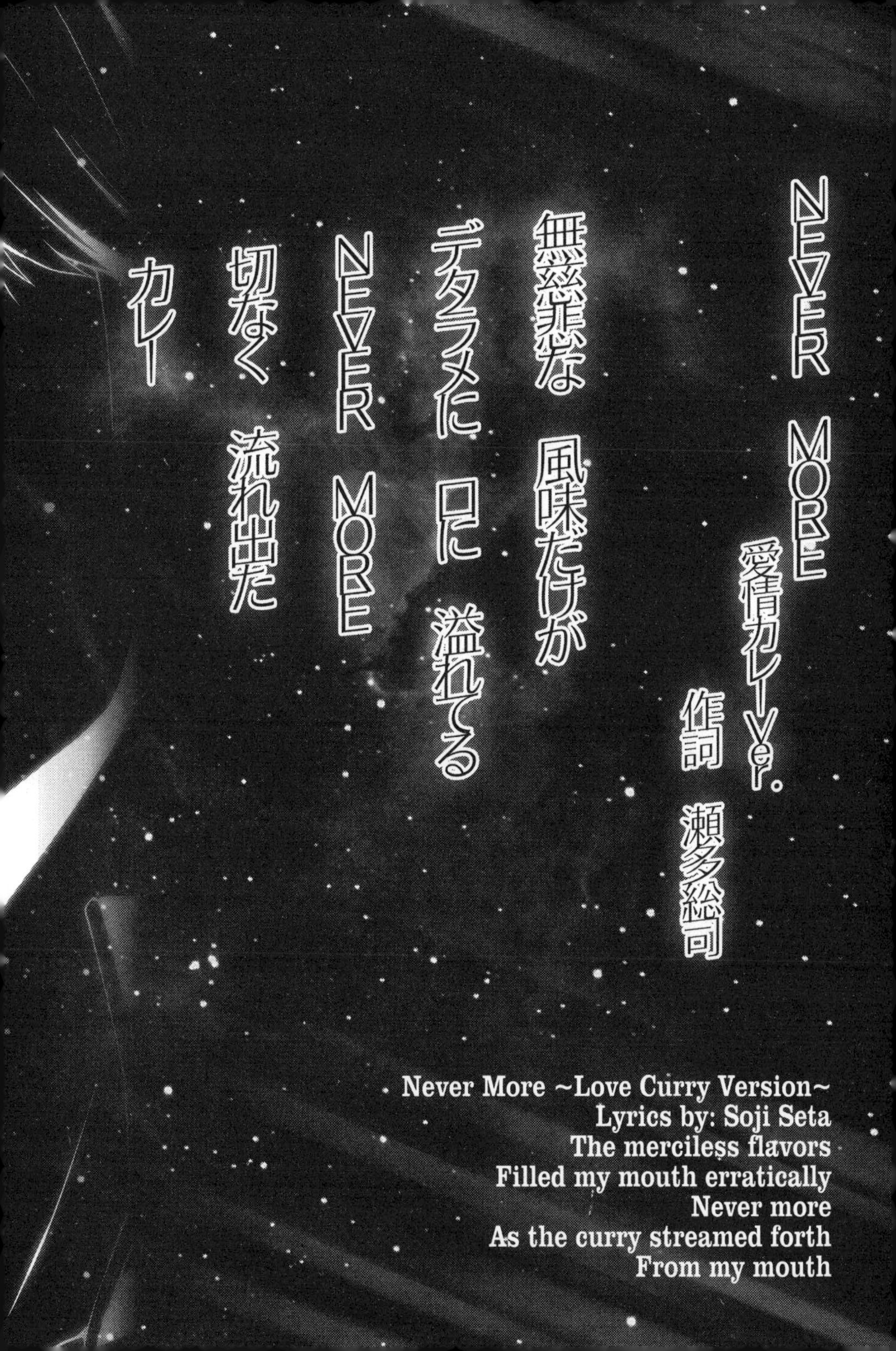
NEVER MORE 愛情カレーver。
作詞 瀬多総司
無慈悲な 風味だけが
デタラメに 口に 溢れてる
NEVER MORE
切なく 流れ出た
カレー
Never More ~Love Curry Version~
Lyrics by: Soji Seta
The merciless flavors
Filled my mouth erratically
Never more
As the curry streamed forth
From my mouth

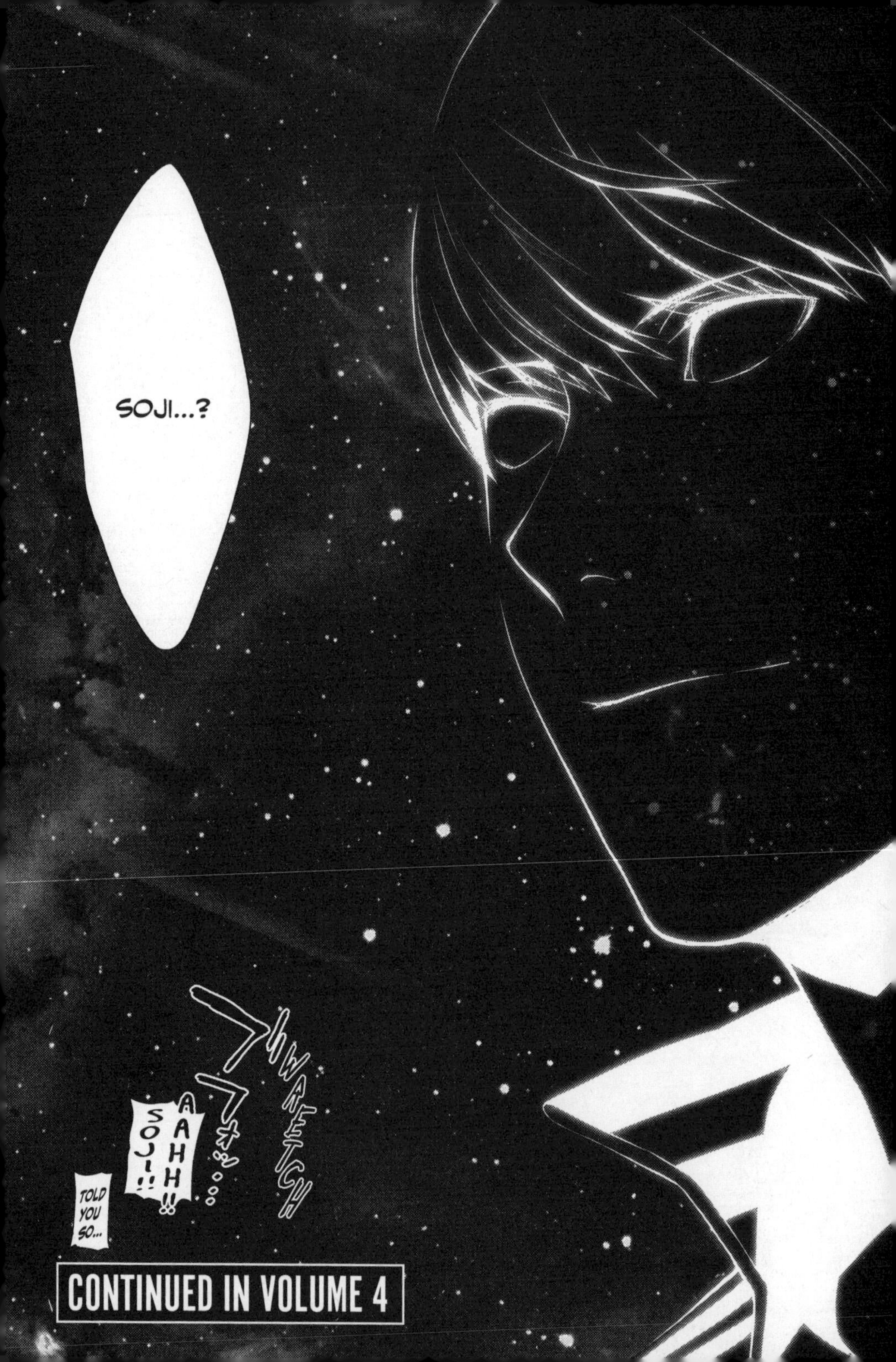
SOJI...?
SWAETCH
AAHH!!
SOJI!!
TOLD YOU SO...
CONTINUED IN VOLUME 4

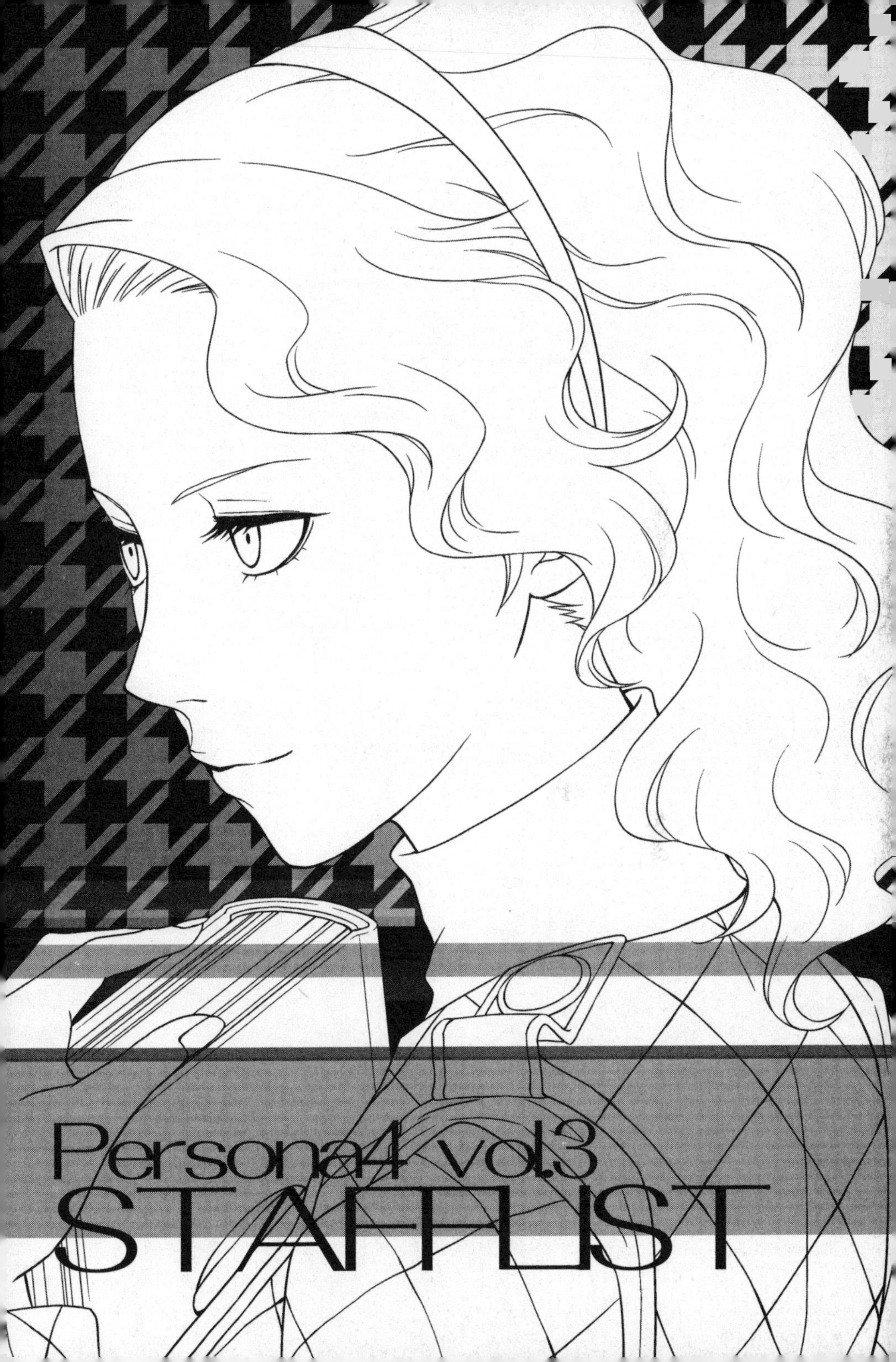
Persona4 vol.3
STAFFLIST

Original Work
ATLUS

Original Art Director
Shigenori SOEJIMA (ATLUS)

Manga / Story
Shuji SOGABE

Production / 3D Modeling & Layout / Art
Ryota HONMA (studioss)

Lead Artist
Haruna AOKI (studioss)

Art Team
Asami SAKUMA (studioss)

Design
Keiko SEKI (SELFISH GENE)
studioss

Editing
Naoki IIJIMA

Special Thanks
Junichi MORI (ATLUS)
Ikuya KOBAYASHI (ATLUS)

PERSONA 4 ORIGINAL STAFF

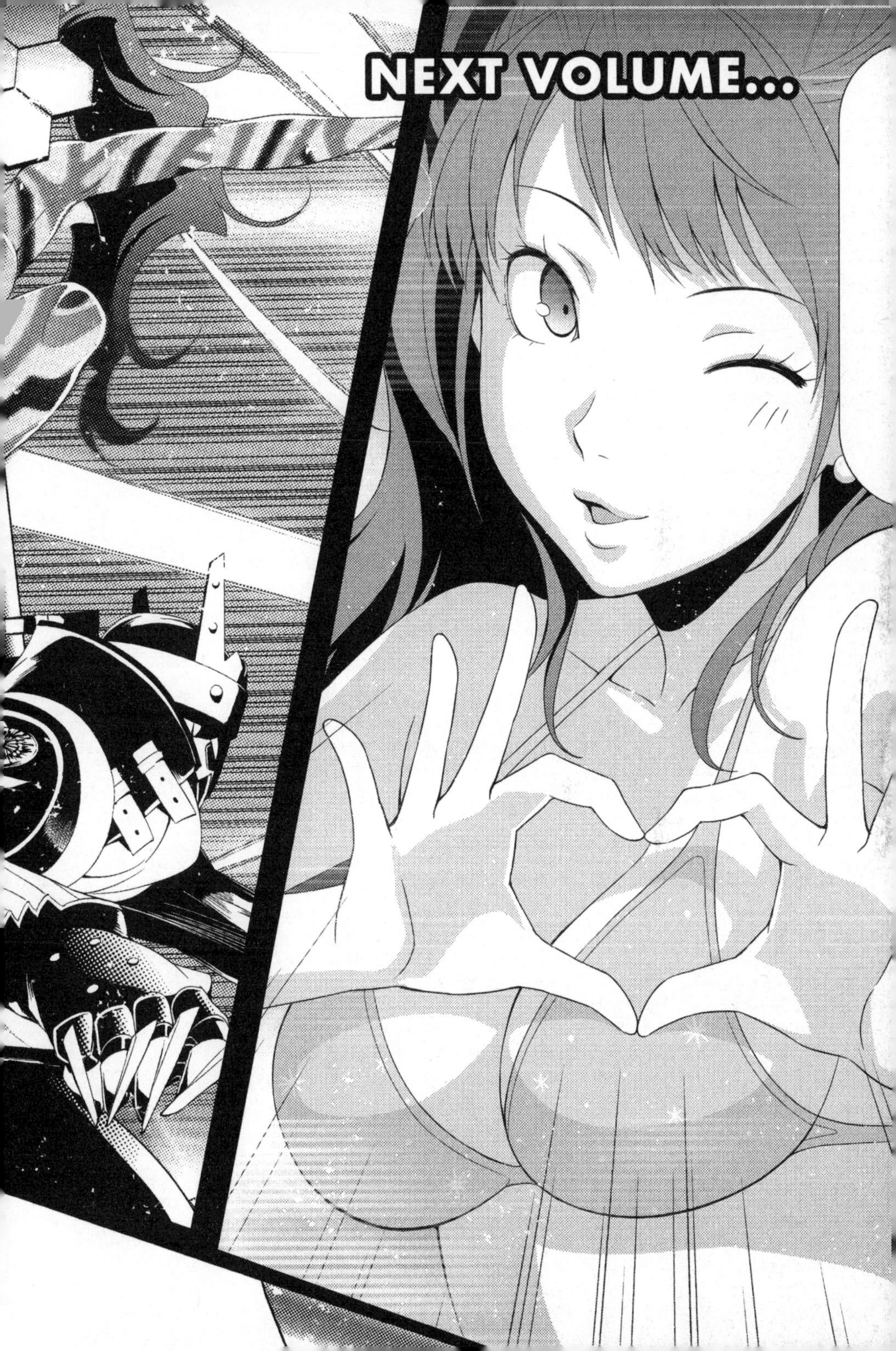
NEXT VOLUME...

PERSONA4

Persona4 Vol.4:
Shuji SOGABE/ATLUS

UDON

P.4 IV

PERSONA 4 VOL.4

SBN: 978-1-927925-81-2

Superstar teen idol Rise Kujikawa escapes o Inaba for a much-needed break from he limelight, and the usually sleepy town s caught in the grip of celebrity fever! But when Rise suddenly appears on the Midnight Channel and goes missing soon hereafter, it's up to Soji, Chie, and the est of the crew to rescue her from the TV World and figure out what – if anything – Rise shares in common with the previous kidnapping victims.

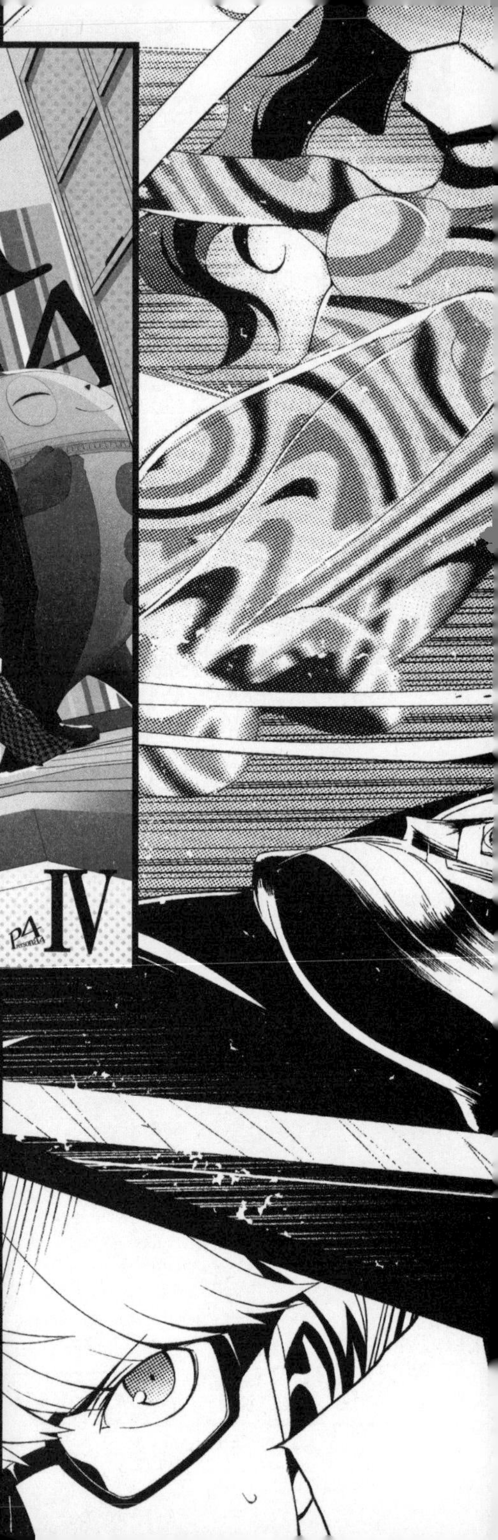

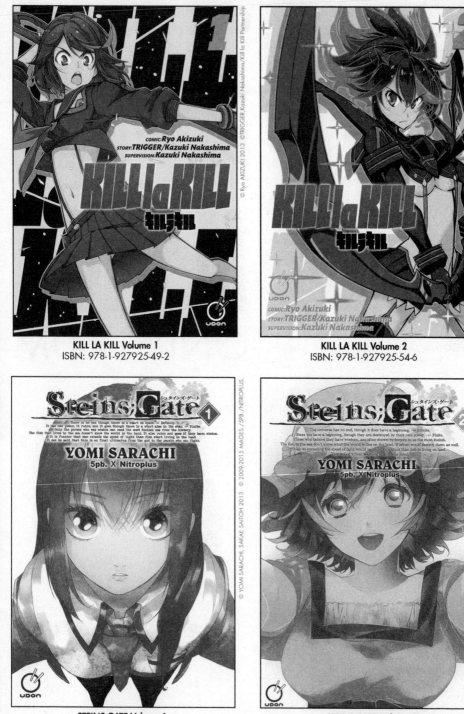

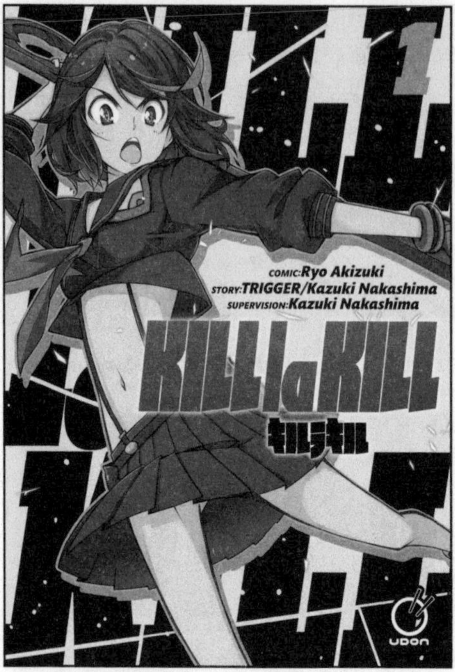
1
COMIC:Ryo Akizuki
STORY:TRIGGER/Kazuki Nakashima
SUPERVISION:Kazuki Nakashima
KILL la KILL
キルラキル
UDON

KILL LA KILL Volume 1
ISBN: 978-1-927925-49-2

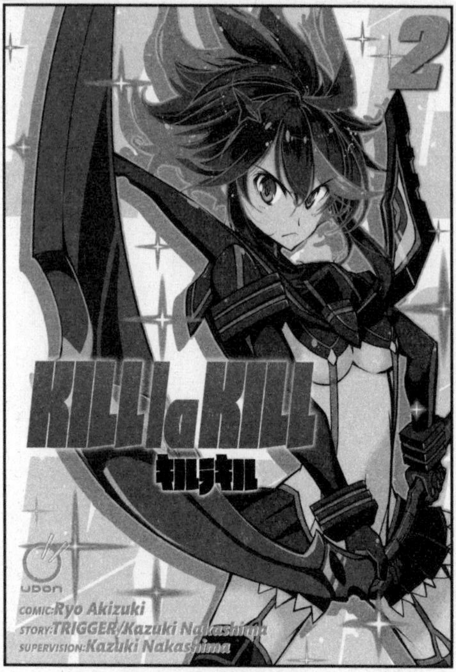
2
KILL la KILL
キルラキル
UDON
COMIC:Ryo Akizuki
STORY:TRIGGER/Kazuki Nakashima
SUPERVISION:Kazuki Nakashima

KILL LA KILL Volume 2
ISBN: 978-1-927925-54-6

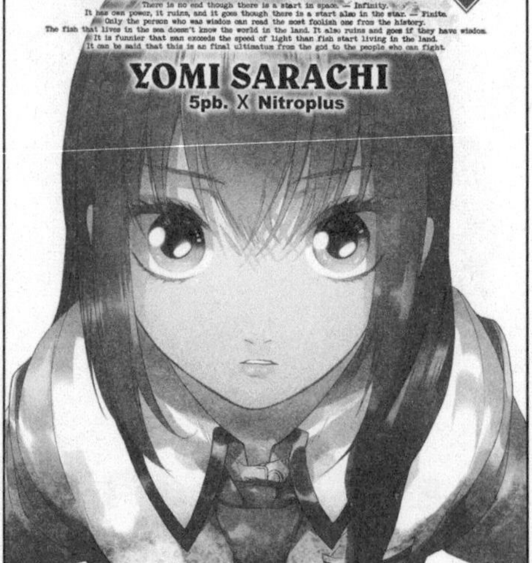
Steins;Gate
シュタインズ・ゲート
1
There is no end though there is a start in space. — Infinity.
It has own power, it ruins, and it goes though there is a start also in the star. — Finite.
Only the person who was wisdom can read the most foolish one from the history.
The fish that lives in the sea doesn't know the world in the land. It also ruins and goes if they have wisdom.
It is funnier that man exceeds the speed of light than fish start living in the land.
It can be said that this is an final ultimatum from the god to the people who can fight.
YOMI SARACHI
5pb. X Nitroplus
UDON

STEINS;GATE Volume 1
ISBN: 978-1-927925-50-8

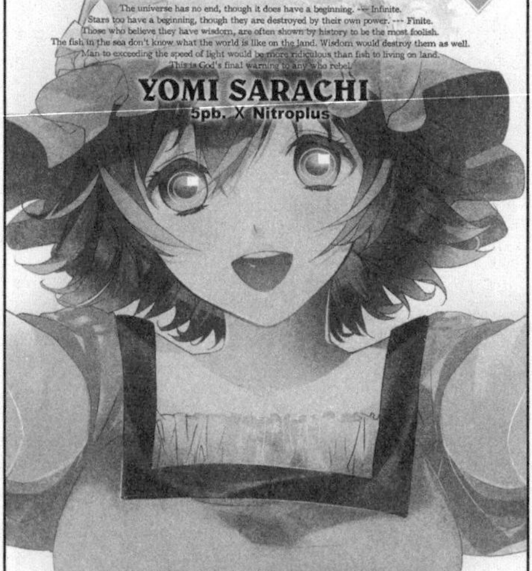
Steins;Gate
シュタインズ・ゲート
2
The universe has no end, though it does have a beginning. --- Infinite.
Stars too have a beginning, though they are destroyed by their own power. --- Finite.
Those who believe they have wisdom, are often shown by history to be the most foolish.
The fish in the sea don't know what the world is like on the land. Wisdom would destroy them as well.
Man to exceeding the speed of light would be more ridiculous than fish to living on land.
This is God's final warning to any who rebel.
YOMI SARACHI
5pb. X Nitroplus
UDON

STEINS;GATE Volume 2
ISBN: 978-1-927925-55-3

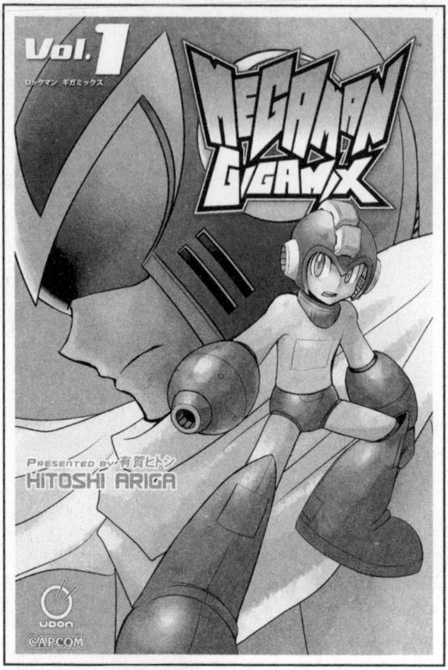
Vol. 1
ロックマン ギガミックス
MEGA MAN GIGAMIX
PRESENTED BY 有賀ヒトシ
HITOSHI ARIGA
UDON
CAPCOM

MEGA MAN GIGAMIX Volume 1
ISBN: 978-1-926778-23-5

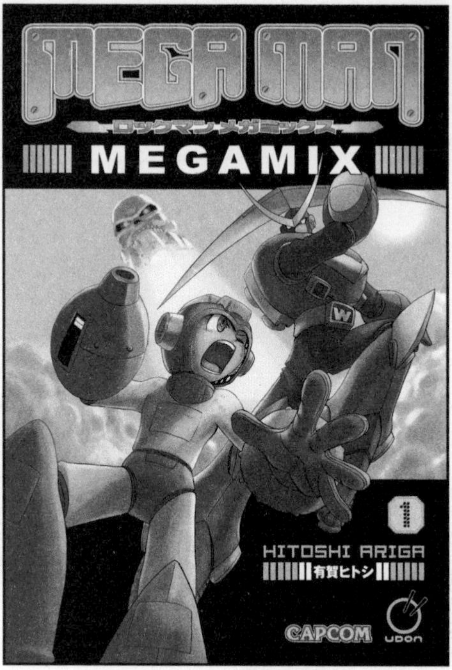
MEGA MAN
ロックマン メガミックス
MEGAMIX
1
HITOSHI ARIGA
有賀ヒトシ
CAPCOM
UDON

MEGA MAN MEGAMIX Volume 1
ISBN: 978-1-897376-16-4

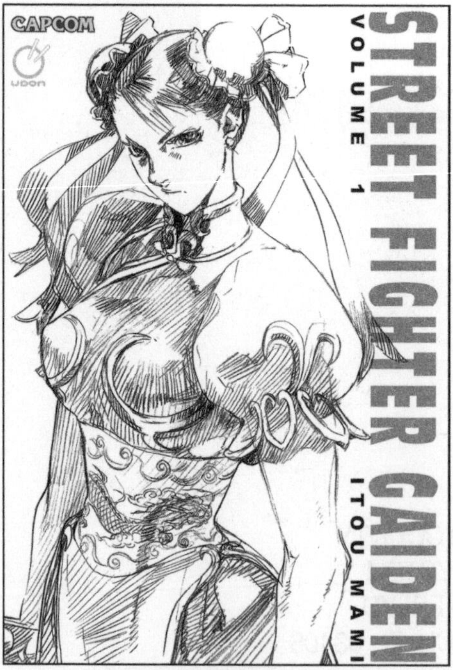
CAPCOM
UDON
STREET FIGHTER GAIDEN
VOLUME 1
ITOU MAMI

STREET FIGHTER GAIDEN Volume 1
ISBN: 978-1-926778-11-2

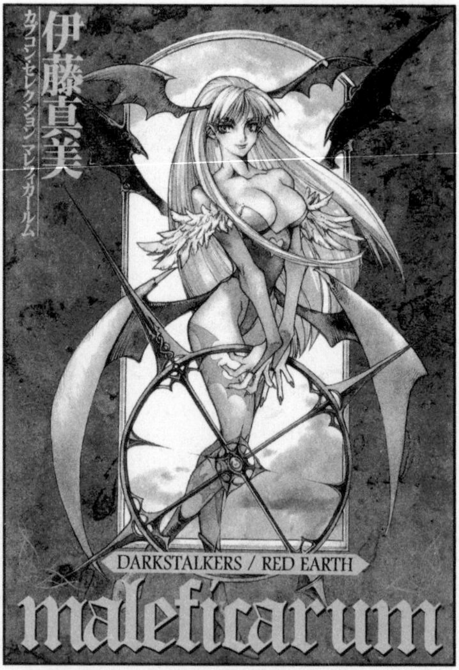
伊藤真美
カプコン・セレクション マレフィカールム
DARKSTALKERS / RED EARTH
maleficarum

DARKSTALKERS/RED EARTH: MALEFICARUM Volume 1
ISBN: 978-1-926778-08-2